SENSATION SEEKING
AND RISKY BEHAVIOR

SENSATION SEEKING AND RISKY BEHAVIOR

MARVIN ZUCKERMAN

American Psychological Association
Washington, DC

Published by
American Psychological Association
750 First Street, NE
Washington, DC 20002
www.apa.org

To order
APA Order Department
P.O. Box 92984
Washington, DC 20090-2984
Tel: (800) 374-2721
Direct: (202) 336-5510
Fax: (202) 336-5502
TDD/TTY: (202) 336-6123
Online: www.apa.org/books/
E-mail: order@apa.org

In the U.K., Europe, Africa, and the Middle East, copies may be ordered from
American Psychological Association
3 Henrietta Street
Covent Garden, London
WC2E 8LU England

Typeset in Goudy by World Composition Services, Inc., Sterling, VA

Printer: Maple–Vail Press, Binghamton, NY
Cover Designer: Minker Design, Bethesda, MD
Technical/Production Editor: Devon Bourexis

The opinions and statements published are the responsibility of the authors, and such opinions and statements do not necessarily represent the policies of the American Psychological Association.

Library of Congress Cataloging-in-Publication Data

Zuckerman, Marvin.
    Sensation seeking and risky behavior / by Marvin Zuckerman.
      p. cm.
    Includes bibliographical references and indexes.
    ISBN-13: 978-1-59147-738-9
    ISBN-10: 1-59147-738-7
    1. Sensation seeking. 2. Risk-taking (Psychology) I. Title.

BF698.35.S45Z835 2006
155.2'32—dc22   2006019296

British Library Cataloguing-in-Publication Data
A CIP record is available from the British Library.

Printed in the United States of America
First Edition

In Memoriam

Hans Eysenck and Jeffrey Gray

CONTENTS

LIST OF TABLES, FIGURES, AND EXHIBITS

TABLES

ix

FIGURES

EXHIBITS

PREFACE

This is the third book I have written on the topic of sensation seeking. The first described the theoretical origins of the construct, the research on sensory deprivation that grew from the theory, the development of scales used to measure it, the research in many areas using sensation seeking scales, and the beginning of the research on the biological basis of the trait (Zuckerman, 1979a). When the first sensation seeking scale was developed a little over 40 years ago (Zuckerman, Kolin, Price, & Zoob, 1964), I never dreamed the topic would become the major focus of my own research and would engage the interest of researchers in countries around the world. There has been a linear increase in citations to sensation seeking from 1964 to the present. Many constructs in personality theory rise and fall in interest over time. Sensation seeking not only has survived but has thrived. The reasons for this are the explanatory value of the construct to so many areas of research. The chapter headings of the second book (Zuckerman, 1994) illustrate the breadth of the construct: risk taking, sports, and vocations; social, sexual, and marital relationships; art, music, fantasy, and humor; smoking, drinking, drugs, and eating; and psychopathology. A second reason is the increasing evidence of a strong genetic and biological basis for this trait. The optimal level of arousal theory that evolved from the studies of sensory deprivation led me to explore the psychophysiological correlates of the trait in orienting and defensive reflexes and the cortical evoked potential (Zuckerman, 1990). Biochemical studies, beginning with gonadal hormones, but more recently leading to the enzymes and neurotransmitters in the brain, have led to the formulation of new biological models, "beyond the optimal level of arousal" (Zuckerman, 1995). The model has developed from comparative studies using other species, particularly cats and rats, as well as research on humans (Zuckerman, 1984b, 1996b). Genetic studies have indicated a relatively high heritability for the trait and even a specific gene associated with it (Ebstein et al., 1996).

The current book is focused on one of the phenomenal aspects: risky behavior. Risk taking was only one chapter in the 1994 volume, although it was involved in many other areas, like drugs and sex. Chapter 1 is an up-to-date account of the theory and research on sensation seeking. Chapter 2 focuses on the theories of risk. A frequent question attracting the interest of the media involves risk taking in extreme sports like skydiving: "Why do they do it?" is the question asked, particularly by low sensation seekers. Part of the answer is in the biological makeup of the high sensation seekers. But there is a cognitive dimension in how people process risk and persist in dangerous or unhealthy activities despite full knowledge of the risks involved. Knowledge about the health risks involved in smoking has been around for 40 years, and smoking has been reduced in the general population. Why do the makers of cigarettes and other drugs recruit new users from the young, in spite of the warnings on the packages and in the media? This is the type of question addressed in chapter 4, which focuses on substance use.

There have always been risks in sex, including pregnancy and sexually transmitted diseases. The advent of effective birth control methods like the contraceptive pill and the efficacy of penicillin in the treatment of the major venereal diseases led to a reduction in risk perception and a significant increase in premarital sexuality in men and women. But the appearance of AIDS in the 1980s, quickly spreading to pandemic proportions, has raised the stakes. How is sensation seeking involved in the willingness to take risks in pursuit of intense hedonic rewards? This question is addressed in chapter 5, which focuses on sex.

Crime is a major problem in any society but is a particular problem in one with a high percentage of unemployed and bored youth. One can understand the attraction of crime for those in poverty, in spite of the risks involved, but most people find the "thrill" of sadistic crimes baffling because of the lack of a monetary motive. Those with an antisocial personality disorder are often motivated by boredom and the need for excitement beyond the normal optimal level of arousal. Although most high sensation seekers find less harmful outlets for their need, psychopaths are unrestrained by normal bounds of social and moral constraint and can indulge in forms of sensation seeking that are harmful to others and risky for themselves. Understanding the role of sensation seeking in criminal behavior is essential to separate those primarily influenced by their social environment and those with motives that go beyond profit and influence. Chapter 6 provides a discussion of these topics regarding crime.

Once the role of sensation seeking in risky behavior is understood, the final question arises: What can be done to prevent or influence cessation of unhealthy forms of sensation seeking? Basic personality traits are difficult if not impossible to change, but their forms of expression should be malleable. Chapter 7, the final chapter in this book, reviews the attempts to prevent unhealthy risk taking in the young before it develops and to discourage it if it is already ongoing. These attempts have had some effects, although they are far from being as effective as treatments for other kinds of disorders that do not involve the sensation seeking motive, like anxiety and mood disorders. Sensation seekers must be appealed to by special messages designed to attract their attention. The emphasis on risky consequences in most campaigns may reach the low sensation seeker but has little effect on the high ones. Alternative, less risky forms of the activities may be the answer. "Safe sex" appeals and training are more effective than advocating no sex, and nicotine replacement in addition to behavior therapy is more effective than training in abstinence alone. This book should be helpful to those who plan programs to prevent or reduce unhealthy forms of sensation seeking. Sensation seekers constitute the majority of those engaged in risk-taking behavior, and therefore their psychology should not be ignored in the development of such programs.

ACKNOWLEDGMENTS

I retired in 2002 and have been professor emeritus at the University of Delaware since then. The Department of Psychology and the department chair, Thomas Di Lorenzo, have generously provided office space from which I venture forth to my new laboratory, the university library, to gather the information needed for my writing. A position as a research professor at the Department of Psychiatry and Human Behavior at the medical college of Thomas Jefferson University in Philadelphia, chair Michael Vergare, provides access to the medical library also important in my research. I am grateful to both institutions and chairs for providing these facilities.

The work on sensation seeking has progressed with the invaluable help of researchers around the world. This has been a truly international effort, and I would like to thank investigators from each country. There are many others in addition to the ones I include here, but space would not allow inclusion of all.

In the United States, my two colleagues at the University of Delaware, Mike Kuhlman and Jerry Siegel, have made invaluable contributions to the work: Mike, in the development of the alternative five-factor model and the questionnaire derived from it (the Zuckerman–Kuhlman Personality Questionnaire [ZKPQ]); Jerry, in the extension of the cortical evoked potential (EP) augmenting–reducing paradigm from humans to cats and rats, which has served as a comparative bridge extending the genetic and biochemical theories across species.

In Germany, Paul Schmitz has replicated the structure of the ZKPQ and applied it to the study of minority acculturation. Alois Angleitner and his colleagues have also investigated ZKPQ structure and developed a German form of the test that they have used in studies of the genetic and environmental influences on its subscales. Petra Netter and Juergen Hennig at the

University of Giessen have investigated the biochemical bases of sensation seeking and other personality traits in hormones and neurotransmitters.

Burkhard Brocke in Germany and Vilfredo De Pascalis in Italy have each conducted studies of the augmenting–reducing of the cortical EP in relation to sensation seeking. Montserrat Goma-i-Freixanet in Spain studied sensation seeking in participants in risky sports as well as prosocial vocations and antisocial criminality. Britt af Klinteberg, Lars von Knorring, and Lars Oreland in Sweden have done extensive research on the psychobiology of sensation seeking and impulsivity, and Sybil Eysenck in England and Ernie Barrett in America developed constructs and test measurements of impulsivity. In Israel, Joseph Glicksohn studies the role of cognition in impulsivity, and Tova Rosenbloom works on the role of sensation seeking in risky behaviors.

Alan Pickering in England is probing more deeply into the neurochemical basis of impulsive sensation seeking and psychoticism (Eysenck's closely related dimension). Michael Bardo at the University of Kentucky and Francoise Dellu and her colleagues, Piazza, Mayo, Le Moal, and Simon at the University of Bordeaux in France, are using rat models of sensation or novelty-seeking to explore its biochemical bases.

Adrian Funham in England and Roger Ulrich in America have explored the role of sensation seeking in art preferences and recreational activities. Lew Donohew and Rick Zimmerman at the University of Kentucky studied the role of sensation seeking in adolescent risk taking in drugs and sex and developed strategies of communication to use in prevention of such risky activities. A former student of Mike Kuhlman, Jeffrey Joireman played a crucial role in the later studies of the alternative five-factor model in relation to other trait models of personality. He is now engaged in studying the role of sensation seeking in aggression, particularly aggression as recreation.

Jan Strelau and his colleagues in Poland have studied sensation seeking in relation to his temperament theories of personality. He organized many conferences in Poland and Eastern Europe at which we talked science and drank a lot of vodka. I think fondly of those days and the dear friends I made in Poland.

A special note of appreciation must be extended to Robert Stelmack in Canada. Bob and I have been friends and colleagues since our early associations in the Society for Psychophysiological Research. Together with Ernie Barrett, we sold Hans Eysenck on the idea of forming the International Society for the Study of Individual Differences. This society has thrived and, with its journal, plays a central role in research on the psychobiology of personality. Bob has done important psychophysiological studies of personality, including sensation seeking, but particularly extraversion. He recently edited a festschrift consisting of chapters by many of the above-mentioned scientists written in my honor (Stelmack, 2004).

I am in debt to all of these colleagues, friends, and comrades in the adventure of psychological science. My greatest intellectual influence is reflected in the dedication of this book. Hans Eysenck lured me away from purely social–familial explanations of behavior to look more closely at genetic and psychophysiological ones. Jeffrey Gray guided me more deeply into the neurology and psychopharmacology underlying personality. Sadly, both of them died in the past decade. Correct or incorrect, our ideas live on in their influences on young investigators whose names are now unfamiliar to us but who will be celebrated in years to come.

SENSATION SEEKING AND RISKY BEHAVIOR

1

SENSATION SEEKING

> Only such "true believers" as expect from science a substitute for the religion they have relinquished will take it amiss if the investigator develops his views further or even transforms them.
> —Sigmund Freud, *Beyond the Pleasure Principle*

The theory of sensation seeking has evolved and changed over time. As Freud said, it is in the nature of scientific theory to change as new findings bring old ideas into question and suggest new interpretations of old data. This is particularly true for personality constructs. Even taxonomic theories like the Big Five (Costa & McCrae, 1992a; Goldberg, 1990) begin with a theoretical assumption, that is, that all the basic dimensions of human personality are expressed in the language, or the lexicon, and factor analyses of the relationships between these words as used to describe self or others will reveal the basic structure. Different assumptions are used by temperament theories built on observations of infant's and children's behaviors. I belong to a group of theorists who believe that basic personality traits have their roots in genes and biological mechanisms and their persisting interactions with the environment. There is an evolutionary history to basic behavioral traits, and therefore comparative studies using animal models should complement studies of humans. The question of what can be predicted from animals to humans, a "bottom-up" approach, is reversed in a "top-down" approach. What can we predict in animal behavior using biological markers shared by both species to identify the correlates?

Top-down theories of adult personality are usually operationalized in a questionnaire measure and then modified in view of the findings used to define the construct. This "bootstrap" approach may result in changes in the theory underlying the test or the test itself.

3

CONSTRUCT VALIDITY

Construct validity represents a two-way process between research and theory (Cronbach & Meehl, 1955). This is the path taken in the development of the Sensation Seeking Scales (SSS) from a theory of sensation seeking (Zuckerman, 1994). In this chapter, I describe the evolution of the theory and alternative tests developed either as shorter versions of the SSS or as versions based on other theories of the construct. The results relating sensation seeking to risky behaviors are dealt with in the subsequent chapters. Only the results related to the definition of the basic construct and its biological bases are treated in this chapter. Broader accounts can be found in previous volumes on the topic (Zuckerman, 1979a, 1994) and a more personal, autobiographical version (Zuckerman, 2004).

ORIGINS IN SENSORY DEPRIVATION RESEARCH

The idea for sensation seeking literally began in the dark. That is to say it began in the dark and silence of a sensory deprivation (SD) isolation chamber. In the decade between 1958 and 1968, my colleagues and I studied the experimental and subject variables affecting reactions to SD (Zuckerman, 1969b). There are wide individual reactions to this experimental situation in which subjects volunteer to spend anywhere from 1 hour to 2 weeks in environments in which visual and auditory sensory input is either reduced to a minimum or made invariant (as in a ganzfeld). Reactions included anxiety, boredom, hallucinations, and cognitive inefficiency. Most standard personality tests did not do a good job at predicting responses to this situation, characterized as a "walk-in inkblot" (Goldberger, 1961). Actually, one of the few successful predictors was a measure of "tolerance for primary process thinking" derived from the Rorschach inkblot test.

Optimal-Level Theories

We decided to use the optimal level of stimulation (OLS) and optimal level of arousal (OLA) theories as the basis for a questionnaire measure of individual differences in these constructs (Zuckerman, Kolin, Price, & Zoob, 1964). The OLS theory can be traced back to Wilhelm Wundt (1893), the founder of experimental psychology. Wundt noted that along a continuum of intensity of stimulation and sensation, there was an optimal point at which the stimulus was regarded as most pleasurable, but below or beyond this point, it was judged as less pleasurable or even aversive. Wundt's investigations were primarily concerned with the bitter and sweet dimensions of taste, not surprising because his research was subsidized by beer manufacturers.

One of the first OLA theories was formulated by Freud (Breuer & Freud, 1895/1955). He called it the "constancy principle," suggesting that there is an optimal level of "intracerebral tonic excitement" for different individuals: "On this level of tonic excitement the brain is accessible to all external stimuli" (Breuer & Freud, 1895/1955, p. 143). Some people (e.g., torpid types) felt best at low levels of excitement, whereas others (e.g., the vivacious types) needed higher levels. This early biological theory was later replaced by a drive reduction theory suggesting that all persons seek a state of low excitement, even though this desire is periodically upset by the drives of the life instinct toward appetitive pleasures, primarily sexual ones. The death instinct opposed the life drive, leading to a search for the ultimate reduction of all sensation (Freud, 1920/1955).

In the 1950s, a neurological basis for the OLA was furnished by the discovery of the role of the reticular activating system (RAS) in the regulation of cortical arousal. External or internal stimulation was thought to activate this system. The ascending RAS running from the brain stem to the cortex produces a nonspecific arousal of the cortex. A descending system from the cortex to the RAS dampens arousal if the cortex is overloaded. The entire system functions as a homeostat to keep cortical arousal at some optimal level given task demands and point in the diurnal cycle. Hebb (1955) presented an OLA inverted-U-shaped curve to describe the relationship between the arousal function and cue function (see Figure 1.1). The latter refers to the organism's ability to use cues for discrimination, learning, and performance. Emotions are also affected, with unpleasant emotions like boredom at the low end below the OLA and anxiety at the high end beyond the OLA. Positive emotions are localized at or close to the OLA. Hebb did not discuss the possibility of individual differences in the OLA.

Sensory deprivation is an extreme situation far below the OLA of nearly all persons in a waking state but is further below the OLA for some individuals than for others. I hypothesized that high sensation seekers were persons with a high OLA and therefore should be more stressed by SD than low sensation seekers (Zuckerman, 1969a). Sensation seekers were thought to seek more novel and intense forms of sensation to reach a higher OLA, at which they felt and functioned better. Low sensation seekers were closer to their OLA in situations with less change in stimulation and therefore should be less stressed in SD. Although I tied sensation seeking to individual differences in the OLS and OLA (Zuckerman, 1969a, Postulate III, pp. 429–430), there was another possibility. Although high and low sensation seekers might not differ in their OLAs, they might differ in their normal levels of arousal in the nonstimulated state. High sensation seekers might be more chronically underaroused and therefore need more stimulation to

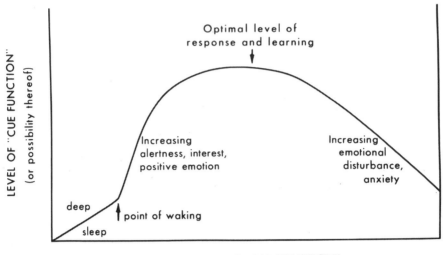

Figure 1.1. The relationship between arousal and cue function (response and learning). From "Drives and the CNS (Conceptual Nervous System)," by D. O. Hebb, 1955, *Psychological Review, 62*, p. 250. Copyright 1955 by the American Psychological Association.

reach their OLA. This is the hypothesis that H. J. Eysenck (1967) used to explain the biological basis for the difference between extraverts and introverts. H. J. Eysenck's hypothesis depended on stimulus intensity, not novelty, and looked primarily to EEG research to determine levels of arousal in introverts and extraverts with and without stimulation (Zuckerman, 1991).

In the early 1960s, we began writing items for a general SSS based on the OLS–OLA theory (Zuckerman et al., 1964). But translating theory into questionnaire items referring to behavioral preferences, intentions, and values is not an obvious task.

We approached it by thinking of prototypes among friends and figures in public life and how they thought and behaved. They drank heavily and were attracted to adventurous and risky activities (like Ernest Hemingway); used drugs that provided unusual sensations and experiences (like Timothy Leary); sought variety in sexual partners and activities (like Norman Mailer); liked to travel and experience new and exotic places and cultures; and were easily bored by conventional people, preferring the company of unconventional and nonconforming groups like artists, "hippies," and "gays." Some of our items were put in the form of intentions, for instance, "I would like to . . ." rather than actual experiences because many of the exotic sports, like mountain climbing and scuba diving, and psychedelic drug use were uncommon at that time. We reasoned that those who were already doing those things would respond positively, as would those who would like to or intended to do them at some time in the future. The items were put into a forced-choice rather than a true–false form because of the big furor over the role of social desirability as a determinant of item response in true–false forms. We tried to word the two choices for an item in forms that were equally socially desirable or undesirable. Although some critics feared that the forced-choice form would make the items unpalatable to test takers, some studies of test reactions showed that, with the exception of a few people with obsessive–compulsive disorder, most subjects were not put off by the need to make a choice between two statements, neither of which precisely expressed their preferences. The test instructions anticipated this problem by telling them to pick the closest choice even if not precisely the expression of their behavior or preferences.

Investigators who stop test development at this point, depending on *face validity* (which should be called *faith* validity) of the content and not concerning themselves with reliability and construct validity, may have a test suitable for popular magazines or newspapers, but not for scientific studies. Our first question was whether there was a general factor running through the diverse kinds of item content (Zuckerman et al., 1964). Item–total correlations and a subsequent factor analysis revealed that there was a general factor that included most of the items we had written. There were some indications of additional factors after rotation, but we did not have enough items to define these with any precision, so we constructed the first SSS Form II (SSS–II) on the basis of an unrotated general factor common to both men and women (Zuckerman et al., 1964).

The SSS–II was developed primarily with a narrow construct validity in mind, namely, prediction of responses to SD. But the theory seemed to suggest a wider applicability to behavior in many other situations. Almost immediately, we noticed something that posed a challenge to the theory, which suggested that the deprivation of stimulation in SD would be particularly threatening and stressful for high sensation seekers. The subjects for SD experiments were chosen by putting ads in the college newspapers in the Philadelphia vicinity offering money for participation in the experiment. The experimental conditions were fully described to them. We thought that offering money would attract a random sample of the college population. On the basis of appearance alone, we had the impression that we were attracting primarily high sensation seekers. Long hair on men (still unfashionable in the early 1960s), motorcycle helmets, and unusual styles of dress suggested a selective factor. When we scored the SSS–II later, we confirmed our hunch. The experiment was attracting more high than low sensation seekers, based on general college norms.

Why would high sensation seekers, presumably with a high OLS, be more attracted to a situation in which they would be isolated and deprived

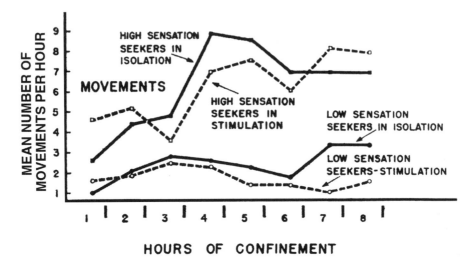

Figure 1.2. Restless movements by high and low sensation seekers in conditions of sensory deprivation and confinement in social isolation with some stimulation. From "Comparison of Stress Effects of Perceptual and Social Isolation," by M. Zuckerman et al., 1966, *Archives of General Psychiatry, 14*, p. 362. Copyright 1966 by the American Medical Association. Reprinted with permission.

of stimulation? We began to question them after the experiment. There had been some sensationalism of the SD experiments in the media and even in a movie in which one got the impression that deprivation of stimulation could produce a kind of temporary insanity with hallucinations and delusions. The high sensation seekers actually anticipated some kind of interesting and exciting "trip" without drugs. Most were disappointed because complex hallucinations are not common in the durations of experiments we were doing. The low sensation seekers anticipated a stressful experience but needed the money. We realized that sensation seeking involved more than simple intensity of stimulation. The desire for novel experiences was more important for the high sensation seekers, outweighing the risk portrayed in the media.

Restlessness is one expression of boredom. The subjects were confined to a bed in the dark, sound-proof room except when they had to use the toilet or eat sandwiches provided for lunch (Zuckerman et al., 1966). The bed had an inflated air mattress attached to a pressure transducer so that any movements while on the bed were recorded. Figure 1.2 shows the movements of high and low sensation seekers in two conditions. One was the complete SD condition. In the other, called a stimulation condition, the lights in the room remained on and some minimal stimulation was provided with music played into the room. In retrospect, this latter condition was not a very stimulating one if *stimulation* is defined in terms of stimulus change. Most subjects found it as boring as the complete SD situation, although somewhat less anxiety provoking.

The movements for the first 3 hours of confinement in both conditions were not very different in high and low sensation seekers. However, after that, the restless movements increased steadily over the remaining hours in the high sensation seekers but remained fairly low and stable in the low sensation seekers. The two groups did not differ in anxiety increase over time in the experiment. We subsequently discovered that anxiety in SD is related to measures of neuroticism or trait anxiety, particularly when there has been no prior experience in the SD room under stimulation conditions (Zuckerman, Persky, Link, & Basu, 1968). In other words, the novelty of the experience interacted with the trait of neuroticism to produce anxiety. Some of these subjects panicked and asked to be let out after only a few minutes in the dark room. Many correlation and factor analytic studies have shown that there is no relationship between neuroticism or trait anxiety and sensation seeking (Zuckerman, 1979a, 1994).

Boredom and anxiety are aversive states and are one result of SD. Another prediction from an OLS theory is that given the option of responding to produce stimulation, the high sensation seekers will respond more for the reward of stimulation and the reduction of stimulus deprivation. A. Jones (1964, 1969), in a series of SD studies that allowed such response, found that subjects responded particularly for series of stimuli, which provided maximum information (random, unpredictable sequences). Lambert and Levy (1972) allowed subjects to press a bar that rewarded them with visual stimulation (slides) and found that high sensation seekers responded more over time than low sensation seekers.

Both intense and novel stimuli produced more arousal than weak or familiar stimuli, so we had written items based on the need for both intensity and novelty of stimuli, but the items reflecting a desire for novel and changing experiences were more related to the broad general factor than those reflecting intensity of experience (Zuckerman et al., 1964). One expression of a need for novelty is in design preferences. In an early study using the SSS–II, we used the Barron–Welsh Preference for Designs (Barron & Welsh, 1952) test to compare the preferences of high and low sensation seekers (Zuckerman, Bone, Neary, Mangelsdorf, & Brustman, 1972). Figure 1.3 shows designs liked more by high sensation seekers, and Figure 1.4 shows designs liked more by low sensation seekers.

There are clear differences in design preferences. Low sensation seekers like designs that are simple, symmetrical, and familiar, whereas high sensation seekers like those that are asymmetrical, novel, and complex. High sensation seekers scored high on Barron's (1953) design scale, Preference for Complexity.

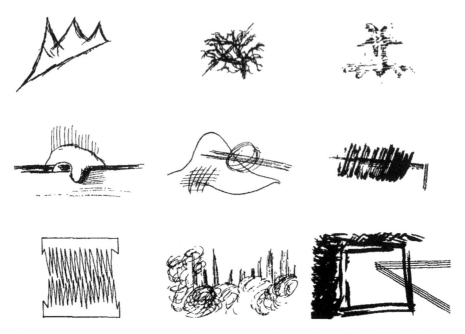

Figure 1.3. Designs liked more by high sensation seekers. From "What Is the Sensation Seeker? Personality Trait and Experience Correlates of the Sensation Seeking Scales," by M. Zuckerman, R. N. Bone, R. Neary, R. Mangelsdorf, and B. Brustman, 1972, *Journal of Consulting and Clinical Psychology, 39,* p. 317. Copyright 1972 by the American Psychological Association.

Interest and attention are expressed in behavioral and physiological responses called *orienting reflexes* (ORs). Animals or humans cease their ongoing activity and turn their head and sensory organs in the direction of the stimulus and show a phasic increase in physiological arousal, such as an increase in skin conductance (SC) or a deceleration of heart rate (HR). If the stimulus is very intense or threatening, a defensive reflex (DR) may be seen. If the stimulus is unexpected and intense, a startle reflex (SR) may occur. The OR may be differentiated from the DR in HR changes: The OR is a deceleratory HR over the first few seconds after stimulus presentation, whereas the DR is an acceleratory response (Graham, 1979). The OR maximizes information intake. In fact, Pavlov called it the "What is it?" reflex. It habituates quickly when the stimulus is repeated and information is fully extracted. The DR is an emergency response preparing for action (fight or flight). The SR is a fast protective reflex involving contraction of flexor muscles (flinching).

Neary and Zuckerman (1976) used the SSS–II to investigate the SC response (SCR) to a simple visual stimulus, followed by a more complex one (see Figure 1.5). The high sensation seekers showed a stronger response

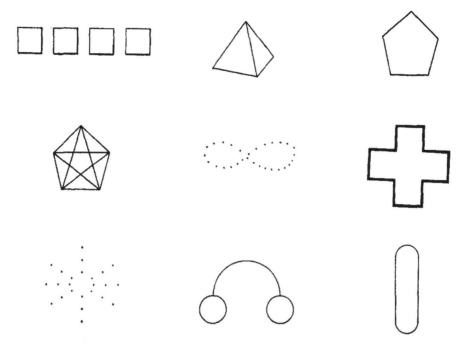

Figure 1.4. Designs liked more by low sensation seekers. From "What Is the Sensation Seeker? Personality Trait and Experience Correlates of the Sensation Seeking Scales," by M. Zuckerman, R. N. Bone, R. Neary, R. Mangelsdor, and B. Brustman, 1972, *Journal of Consulting and Clinical Psychology, 39,* p. 318. Copyright 1972 by the American Psychological Association.

than the low sensation seekers to the first trial presentation of the simple stimulus when it was novel. But on the second trial, the high sensation seekers dropped to the habituated level of the low sensation seekers and continued to habituate over the next 8 trials at the level of the lows. When a new stimulus was presented, the stronger OR in the high sensation seekers was again seen. There were no differences in basal levels of arousal prior to stimulus presentation. The OR responses of the high sensation seekers differed from those of the low sensation seekers only in response to a novel stimulus.

Early replication attempts yielded mixed results. However, B. D. Smith, Perlstein, Davidson, and Michael (1986) had success using visual and auditory stimuli with content of interest to high sensation seekers. B. D. Smith, Davidson, Smith, Goldstein, and Perlstein (1989) also investigated the influence of emotional intensity by using words graded in intensity of meanings. High sensation seekers showed stronger SCRs than low sensation seekers to loaded stimuli and to high-intensity words, particularly on the first trial presentations of the stimuli, when they were novel. There were no differences in response to neutral stimuli.

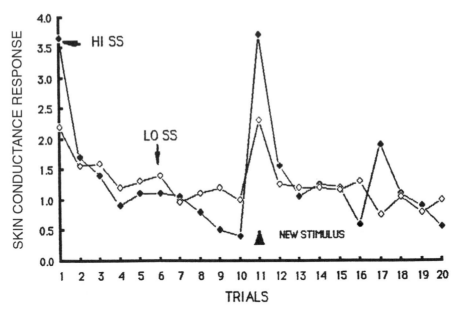

Figure 1.5. Skin conductance responses to a simple (Trials 1–10) and a complex (Trials 11–20) visual stimulus. Hi = high; lo = low; SS = sensation seekers. From "Sensation Seeking, Trait and State Anxiety, and the Electrodermal Orienting Reflex," by R. S. Neary and M. Zuckerman, 1976, *Psychophysiology,"* *13,* p. 207. Copyright 1976 by Blackwell. Reprinted with permission.

The SSS General Scale was also related to sexual experience, drinking, and drug use of college students, but these studies will be discussed in the subsequent chapters on risk taking (Zuckerman, Bone, Neary, Mangelsdorf, & Brustman, 1972).

Development of Sensation Seeking Scale Forms IV and V

As mentioned previously, the SSS–II General Scale showed some evidence of subfactors among the item content (Farley, 1967). To investigate this possibility, additional items that might represent these factors were added. Originally it was thought that the factors might be grouped by sensory modalities (i.e., visual, auditory, olfactory, somesthetic, kinesthetic). However, the factors resulting from the analyses were quite different from what was expected (Zuckerman, 1971). Four factors emerged, which have proven quite robust across nations and translations of the SSS (Zuckerman, 1994). These four factors are described in the list that follows in terms of their item content. Subsequent work with the SSS has shown the greater relevance of some of the subscales than others in predicting specific behavioral phenomena and biological correlates.

1. *Thrill and Adventure Seeking (TAS).* The items in this subscale indicate the desire to engage in physical activities that provide unusual sensations and experiences, such as mountain climbing, skydiving, or scuba diving. Most of these activities are perceived as moderately risky, which is what deters lower sensation seekers from engaging in them. It is the sensation rewards that attract the high sensation seekers, not the risk.

2. *Experience Seeking (ES).* This subscale describes seeking sensation and new experiences through the mind and the senses (music, art, travel) and through a nonconforming general lifestyle with like-minded friends. In the 1970s, we informally called it the "hippie factor," and even used the term *hippie* in one of the items. In the 1980s, we discovered that the term *hippie* no longer had relevance to the younger generations, so we substituted the term *punk.* One should really anticipate anachronisms when devising a test that may have continued use through more than 1 decade and one generation.

3. *Disinhibition (Dis).* Dis items refer to seeking sensation through other people, a hedonistic lifestyle, "wild" parties, sexual variety, and drinking to disinhibit. It is an ancient form of sensation seeking, finding social acceptance in bacchanals and carnivals; shows few if any relationships to education, race, or class; and is the subscale most highly related to certain of the biological correlates of sensation seeking such as the HR OR, gonadal hormones, and augmenting of the cortical evoked potential (EP). It is also the subscale that best differentiates psychopathic personalities from nonpsychopathic criminals and normals. However, taken alone, a high score on Dis is normal. It becomes more likely to be a sign of psychopathy when combined with an aggression scale (not included in the SSS Form V [SSS–V]).

4. *Boredom Susceptibility (BS).* This subscale represents the fourth factor, the weakest one to emerge from factor analyses. It is less internally reliable than the other three subscales. The items represent an aversion to any kind of monotonous conditions and restlessness when confined to such conditions. There is a dislike of people who are not exciting or interesting, even if they are reliable. It is most highly related to the Dis subscale and like Dis is high in psychopathic personalities.

SSS Form IV (SSS–IV; Zuckerman, 1971), included 72 items, unevenly distributed among the four subfactor scales and including the SSS–II General Scale. The correlations among the subscales were moderate

(*Mdn r*s = .30–.58). The SSS–V (Zuckerman, Eysenck, & Eysenck, 1978) represented an attempt to shorten the test by selecting items with the highest loadings on one of the subscales relative to the other three subscales. Ten best items were selected for each of the four subscales. Instead of a separate SSS General Scale, the SSS Total score for all 40 items was used as an overall measure of sensation seeking. The mode of selecting items guaranteed that the correlations between subscales would be lower than in the SSS–IV, although nearly all were still significant (*Mdn r*s = .14–.41). Some have questioned the existence of a broad general factor because of the low correlations among some of the subscales in SSS–V, but it should be recognized that this was the result of a deliberate attempt to sharpen the discriminant validity of the subscales going from SSS–IV to SSS–V.

Demographic Studies

The two most significant demographic factors affecting the SSS are gender and age (Zuckerman, 1979a, 1994; Zuckerman & Neeb, 1980). Men score higher than women on all subscales except ES, and this is generally the finding in many different cultures. The largest gender differences are on TAS and Dis. SS scores increase with age in children's scales (Russo et al., 1993) but in adult populations they peak in late adolescence and steadily decline with age thereafter (L. Ball, Farnill, & Wangeman, 1983; Zuckerman et al., 1978). Similar findings on the Venturesomeness scale were reported by S. B. G. Eysenck, Pearson, Easting, and Allsopp (1985). By age 60, the total score on SSS–V is about half of that obtained from subjects in their late adolescence. The age decline is most marked on TAS and Dis but is less in ES, and BS shows no age change. It is tragic that whereas the forms of sensation seeking expressed in TAS, Dis, and ES decline with age, the capacity to be bored (BS) does not.

Socioeconomic factors have a weaker effect on the SSS and are largely confined to women on the ES scale (Zuckerman & Neeb, 1980). Blacks score lower on the subscales except on Dis, in which there is no race difference (Zuckerman, 1994). TAS and ES scales represent activities and interests, such as extreme sports and art preferences, which may be of less interest in the larger African American culture. In contrast, Dis and BS represent more universal and cross-cultural modes of sensation seeking.

Construct Validity Research Using the Sensation Seeking Scale Forms IV and V

The use of subscales enabled researchers to show which scales were most highly related to specific phenomena and physiological and hormonal functions. As might be expected, art and design preferences are most highly related to the ES subscale, and engagement in extreme sports, to the TAS subscale. However, in most cases there are also significant correlations with the Total score and at least one other of the subscales. In musical preferences, all of the subscales were related to a preference for rock music, but ES was also related to preferences for folk and jazz, reflecting the greater openness to experience of experience seekers and their greater exposure to other kinds of music (Litle & Zuckerman, 1986).

PSYCHOPHYSIOLOGICAL STUDIES

Orienting and Defensive Reflexes

By the time HR was used as a measure of OR, the new forms (SSS–IV and SSS–V) had been developed. HR, unlike SCR, had the advantage of being able to detect DRs and SRs as well as ORs. Low to moderate intensities of stimuli tend to elicit ORs, whereas more intense stimuli tend to produce DRs, or SRs if unexpected. Orlebeke and Feij (1979) did the first study of sensation seeking using HR. In response to a moderate tone of 80 dB, high and low scorers on the Dis subscale demonstrated striking differences between their responses. Those high on Dis typically showed an OR (HR deceleration), whereas those low on Dis usually had a DR (HR acceleration).

Ridgeway and Hare (1981) found similar results, which were stronger for the Dis subscale than for the Total score. Zuckerman, Simons, and Como (1988) found similar differences with the Dis subscale, but in this study the OR and DR differences were found using different stimulus intensities. A less intense stimulus (60 dB) produced greater HR deceleration in high Dis than in low Dis subjects, whereas an intense stimulus (100 dB) elicited more HR acceleration in the low Dis than in the high Dis subjects.

This research confirms the importance of intensity as well as novelty of stimulation in the construct of sensation seeking. The differences in HR response of high and low sensation seekers described previously occurred only on the first presentations of the stimuli in a series of trials and therefore represent a combination of the influences of novelty and intensity. ORs and DRs may be viewed as opposite modes of reacting to the intensity dimension of stimuli. High Dis subjects are more accessible or attentive to such stimuli, whereas low Dis types show more of a defensive emotional reaction. The next topic concerns a more direct measure of cortical reactivity and one simply related to the intensity dimension of stimulation rather than an interaction of intensity and novelty.

The Cortical Evoked Potential

Buchsbaum and Silverman (1968) developed a method for analyzing the cortical response to intensity of stimulation using the cortical EP method. The EP represents responses of different parts of the brain, subcortical and cortical, to a brief stimulus like a flash of light, a tone, or a somesthetic electrical stimulus. For visual stimulation, they used the P1–N1 component of the EP occurring at about 100 to 140 milliseconds after the stimulus. This component usually represents the first impact of stimulus intensity on the cortex. Earlier components represent subcortical reactions, and later components represent more processed information such as stimulus familiarity or novelty.

Measuring the response to increasing intensities of stimulation, Buchsbaum and Silverman (1968) found wide individual differences in the slopes of the stimulus-intensity/EP correlation. Some individuals showed what might be expected in all subjects if this were a simple psychophysiological reaction, namely, a positive slope indicating a cortical response in proportion to the intensity of the stimulus. Many subjects did show this type of reaction to varying degrees, but others showed little increase of EP amplitude over intensity or even a significant decrease at the highest intensities. They called the first type of reactors "augmenters" and the latter type "reducers," although they used a continuous distribution of slopes to make these distinctions.

The use of the augmenting–reducing terms was, in retrospect, an unfortunate one. Petrie (1967) used these terms to describe a kinesthetic–somaethetic sensory discrimination response involving estimates of the width of a block of wood before and after stimulating the fingers by rubbing another larger block of wood. Those who increased their estimates were called "augmenters," and those who decreased them were called "reducers." This was said to be a measure of brain function, although its claim to be so is questionable (Zuckerman, 1986a). The Kinesthetic Aftereffect (KAE) has no retest reliability as one should demand for a physiological trait. The behavioral and personality characteristics associated with EP augmenting tend to be associated with KAE reducing (Davis, Cowles, & Kohn, 1983). No direct correlation is generally found between the methods. The choice is between an actual measure of brain reactivity, the EP, and one based on a peripheral psychophysical measure. Another problem is that the KAE uses kinesthetic stimulation, whereas the EP method, which is most related to personality, uses visual or auditory stimulation. I use the terms *augmenting* and *reducing* strictly in relation to the EP method.

Buchsbaum (1971) suggested that there might be a relationship between augmenting–reducing and sensation seeking. Zuckerman, Murtaugh, and Siegel (1974) put this to the test using a range of intensities of visual

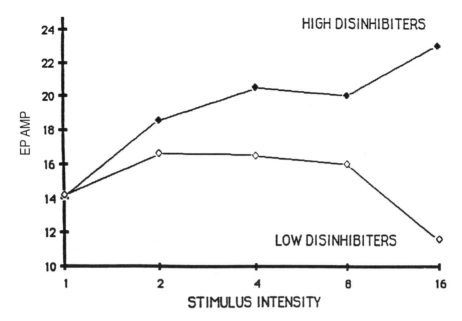

Figure 1.6. Visual evoked potentials (EPs) of high and low scorers on the Disinhibition subscale of the Sensation Seeking Scale as a function of stimulus intensity. AMP = amplitude. From "Sensation Seeking and Cortical Augmenting–Reducing," by M. Zuckerman, T. T. Murtaugh, and J. Siegel, 1974, *Psychophysiology, 11*, p. 539. Copyright 1974 by Blackwell. Reprinted with permission.

stimulation (flashes) on subjects who had taken the SSS. They found a significant relationship only with the Dis subscale. Figure 1.6 shows the relationship, plotting the mean EPs for subjects above and below the median on Dis. High Dis subjects showed an augmenting pattern of response, whereas low Dis subjects showed a reducing pattern, with a significant decrease in cortical responses to the brightest light flashes. These were not a function of artifacts like blinking and therefore represented some kind of cortical inhibition in response to intense stimulation. The actual correlation between Dis and the EP slope was .59.

Zuckerman, Simons, and Como (1988) demonstrated the same relationship for the auditory EP, again with the Dis subscale only. Their results are shown in Figure 1.7. Zuckerman (1990) summarized the results for both visual and auditory EP studies done subsequent to the 1974 study. Replication of the results, particularly in relation to Dis, have been good, especially for the auditory EP (8 of 10 studies), and additional replications have appeared since 1990 (e.g., Brocke, Beauducel, John, Debener, & Heileman, 2000).

I have advocated a comparative approach to sensation seeking (Zuckerman, 1984b). Sensation seeking is not a uniquely human trait. Most species of mammals demonstrate individual differences, which might be called

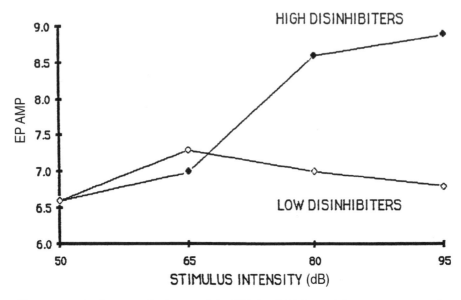

Figure 1.7. Auditory evoked potentials (EPs) of high and low scorers on the Disinhibition subscale of the Sensation Seeking Scale as a function of stimulus intensity for the short interstimulus interval condition (2 seconds). AMP = amplitude. From "Sensation Seeking and Stimulus Intensity as Modulators of Cortical, Cardiovascular, and Electrodermal Response: A Cross-Modality Study," by M. Zuckerman, R. F. Simons, and P. G. Como, 1988, *Personality and Individual Differences, 9*, p. 368. Copyright 1988 by Elsevier Science. Reprinted with permission.

"boldness," "approach behavior," or "explorativeness," in unfamiliar environments or in response to novel stimuli. In many nonhuman species, particularly primates, boldness is also related to dominance and aggressiveness.

My colleague Jerome Siegel used the augmenting–reducing paradigm, in a top-down approach, to identify similar EP differences in cats and rats and to relate these to behavioral trait differences in these species. Cats were classified as augmenters or reducers using the visual cortical EP. Their contrasts in behavior from studies by Lukas and Siegel (1977) and P. M. Saxton, Siegel, and Lukas (1987) are shown in Table 1.1.

In behavioral reactions to novel stimuli, augmenter cats were more active, exploratory, and aggressive, whereas reducer cats were more fearful and tended to withdraw rather than approach the object. In an experimental situation in which the cats were put into an unfamiliar box with a lever that produced food reinforcement on a fixed interval schedule, the augmenter cats were quick to habituate to the strange environment and learn the lever press that produced positive reinforcement. The reducer cats took longer to adjust to the unfamiliar environment (neophobia) and to learn the response, and they responded at a lower rate. However, when the cats were exposed to a different schedule, differential reinforcement for a low rate of

TABLE 1.1
Correlates of Augmenting–Reducing in Cats

Conditions	Reducers	Augmenters
Reactions to novel stimuli	Withdrawal Fearful	Approach Aggressive
Fixed interval reward schedule	Longer to habituate and learn the response	Quicker to habituate to experimental situation, learn response, make more responses
DRL reward schedule	Learned more quickly Made fewer errors	Learned more slowly Made more errors

Note. Based on data from studies by Lukas and Siegel (1977) and Saxton, Siegel, and Lukas (1987). DRL = differential reinforcement for a low rate of response.

response and loss of reinforcement if they exceeded that rate, the reducer rats were superior in performance. The augmenter cats were poor on this schedule because of their lack of restraint or inhibitory control in modulating their rate of response. This cat model is consistent with the latest trait version of sensation seeking, which combines impulsivity with sensation seeking ("Impulsive Sensation Seeking"; Zuckerman, 1996b).

Siegel, Sisson, and Driscoll (1993) used another species to study augmenting–reducing in two strains bred for behavioral characteristics. Both strains were selectively bred from the parent Wistar strain. The Roman high-avoidance (RHA) strain was bred for superior performance in learning an active avoidance response in a shock shuttle-box. The Roman low-avoidance (RLA) strain performed poorly because they tended to freeze and were slow to learn how to avoid the shock. The augmenting–reducing characteristics of the strains using a visual EP are shown in Figure 1.8.

Nearly all of the RHAs were EP augmenters, and almost all of the RLAs were reducers. The RHAs (augmenters) are more active and exploratory in the open-field test, are more aggressive in response to shock, are more ready to drink alcohol, have a high tolerance for barbiturates, and responded more for electrical brain stimulation reward in the lateral hypothalamus at high intensities. The female RHAs who had pups tended to be neglectful of them, spending less time on the nest. The RLAs are less exploratory and aggressive, less likely to drink alcohol, and have a low tolerance for barbiturates. The female RLAs are "good mothers," spending more time in the nest with the pups. They were more sensitive than the RHAs to low intensities of brain stimulation, but when the intensities were high they used an escape response to terminate the stimulation. The difference between RHAs and RLAs in behavioral response to brain stimulation is analogous to their reflexive defensive responses to high-intensity external stimulation.

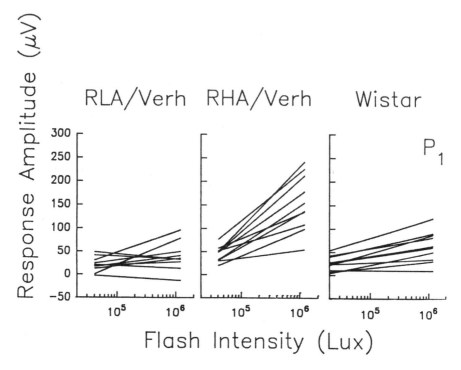

Figure 1.8. Visual evoked potentials as a function of stimulus intensity in Roman high-avoidance (RHA) rats and Roman low-avoidance (RLA) rats and the parental Wistar stock rats. P1 = first positive peak in evoked potential after the stimulus, Verh = first negative peak after the stimulus. From "Augmenting and Reducing of Visual Evoked Potentials in Roman High- and Low-Avoidance Rats," by J. Siegel, D. F. Sisson, and P. Driscoll, 1993, *Physiology and Behavior, 54*, p. 709. Copyright 1993 by Elsevier Science. Reprinted with permission.

When an animal model is used for a human trait in either a top-down or a bottom-up approach, the model assumes some equivalence of behavior in the two species. The assumptions may not be entirely correct. A rat's behavior in the empty open-field test, for instance, is said to be a measure of fearfulness or explorativeness, depending on whether the animal freezes or quickly moves to the center of the arena. Inhibited behavior is accompanied by defecation, a sign of emotionality in the rat. The behavior may be like the first time human sensation seekers try a new risky activity, like skydiving. Their anticipatory reactions are a mixture of pleasure in anticipating a new kind of experience and an inborn fear of falling from heights. If the fear is much greater, the adventurer will not jump. However, many sensation seeking situations do not involve any significant degree of fear, and fearfulness, or trait anxiety, is not related to sensation seeking. The rat model therefore involves two different traits that are independent in humans but not in rats. The use of a common biological marker, like the EP paradigm here described, goes beyond mere analogy in behavior to confirm the model.

Thus far I have been largely speaking of psychophysiological methods for testing the sensation seeking construct. The RHAs and RLAs also differ on a number of biochemical measures, as I describe later in this chapter. First, let me discuss the biochemical findings on sensation seeking and the new theoretical models emerging from these.

BIOCHEMICAL STUDIES

Sex Hormones

The sex hormone testosterone is associated with aggression, sexuality, and explorativeness in other species. Castration reduces these activities in male animals. Such radical methods of reducing testosterone levels are clearly not ethical in humans, so that most of the data is correlational. However, a study of hypogonadal men with low testosterone levels found that they had low levels of sensation seeking (O'Carroll, 1984). Men with functional impotence but normal testosterone levels had normal levels of sensation seeking. Subsequent administration of testosterone to both groups increased their sex drive and interest, but it did not change their scores on the SSS. Sensation seeking is a trait that might have its origins in earlier prenatal testosterone levels, which affect the developing brain. However, testosterone does vary with gender and age, being markedly higher in men than in women and dropping with age after late adolescence. Sensation seeking shows the same gender and age differences so that it might reflect the influence of gradually changing levels of the hormonal substrate.

Daitzman, Zuckerman, Sammelwitz, and Ganjam (1978) found that androgens and estrogens in males were positively associated with the Dis subscale of the SSS. Daitzman and Zuckerman (1980), using more hormone-specific plasma measures, confirmed that male subjects scoring high on Dis were higher in testosterone and estradiol than subjects low on Dis. Estrogens in men are largely produced by conversion from testosterone and therefore have a different significance than the ovary-produced estrogen in women. In fact, the aromatization hypothesis suggests that androgens in males have their major motivational effects after conversion to estrogenic metabolites (Brain, 1983). The low Dis subjects were not low on testosterone compared with normal men of their age, but the high Dis subjects had unusually high testosterone levels. These findings were confirmed by Aluja and Torrubia (2004) and by Gerra et al. (1999), who found correlations between sensation seeking measures and plasma testosterone.

Monoamine Oxidase

Monoamine oxidase (MAO) is an enzyme that catabolizes monoamines after they are taken up in the presynaptic neuron, thereby regulating the level of the neurotransmitter. Type-A MAO (MAO-A) seems to be primarily involved in the regulation of serotonin and norepinephrine (NE), whereas dopamine (DA) in humans is oxidized by Type B (MAO-B; Glover, Sandler, Owen, & Riley, 1977). Mice with MAO-A gene knockout have elevated levels of serotonin, NE, and DA and are hyperaggressive, whereas mice with MAO-B gene knockout have elevated levels of phenylethylamine and the MAO-B inhibitor deprenyl and do not show increased aggressiveness (Shih, Chen, & Ridd, 1999). MAO-B is positively correlated with serotonergic activity in particular brain areas (Adolfsson, Gottfries, Oreland, Roos, & Winblad, 1978). These investigators have suggested that MAO-B and serotonin regulators are governed by the same set of genes. MAO-inhibiters have been used in the treatment of depression, and MAO-B inhibition potentiates the activity of DA (Deutch & Roth, 1999). MAO is negatively correlated with testosterone in men and estradiol in women (Briggs & Briggs, 1972)

MAO-B obtained from blood platelets was first related inversely to sensation seeking in studies by Murphy et al. (1977) and by Schooler, Zahn, Murphy, and Buchsbaum (1978). Since those early findings, many studies have been done attempting to replicate this interesting relationship. Significant negative correlations between MAO-B and the SSS General or Total score were found in 10 of the 15 groups in the studies. The median correlation was only .25. Significant or not, in 13 of the 15 groups, the relationship was in the negative direction. If the relationship was due to chance, half of the correlations would be negative and half would be positive. There were no significant correlations in the groups consisting entirely of females, possibly because estrogen influences MAO levels, and it is difficult to control for the phase of the estrus cycle in individual subjects. A reliable but weak relationship is not surprising because MAO-B only influences behavior through its effect on the monoamine it regulates, primarily DA.

In humans, MAO-B is also related to a number of disorders, as shown in Table 1.2. All of these disorders, with the possible exception of anorexia and paranoid schizophrenia, are characterized by high sensation seeking and impulsivity. The fact that low levels of MAO are found in the relatives, usually sons, of alcoholics and patients with bipolar disorder is evidence that the low levels are part of a genetic vulnerability to these disorders. Bipolar disorders in the manic phase are an expression of impulsive sensation seeking totally out of control. The Dis subscale comes closest to measuring their actual behavior in pursuit of parties, sex, drinking, drugs, and gambling. However, even when those with bipolar disorder are in a remitted or depressed phase, they still score high on the SSS describing their typical (trait)

TABLE 1.2
Psychopathology and Monoamine Oxidase (MAO)

Disorder or description of subjects with low MAO-B	Researcher(s)
Attention-deficit/hyperactivity disorder	Shekim et al. (1986)
Antisocial personality disorder	Lidberg et al. (1985); Sher et al. (1994)
Borderline personality disorder	Reist et al. (1990)
Criminality	Coursey et al. (1979); Garpenstrand et al. (2002); af Klinteberg (1996); Stalenheim (2004)
Alcoholism	Coccini et al. (2002); Hallman et al. (2001); La Grange et al. (1995); Major & Murphy (1978)
Well relatives of alcoholics	Schukit (1994); Sher (1993)
Drug abuse	L. von Knorring et al. (1987); Sher et al. (1994)
Pathological gambling	Blanco et al. (1996)
Bipolar mood disorder	Murphy & Weiss (1972)
Well relatives of people with bipolar mood disorders	Leckman et al. (1977)
Paranoid schizophrenia[a]	Zureik & Meltzer (1988)
Anorexia	Díaz-Marsá et al. (2000)

Note. MAO-B = Type-B MAO. [a]People with other types of schizophrenia have higher levels of MAO.

attitudes and behaviors (Cronin & Zuckerman, 1992). Even in unscreened college populations, low MAO is found in those who smoke, use drugs, and have a record of felonious criminal behavior (Coursey, Buchsbaum, & Murphy, 1979).

Descending to a lower level in the phylogenetic tree, monkeys with low MAO-B are more dominant, aggressive, sexually active, and sociable and spend more time in play than high MAO monkeys (Redmond, Murphy, & Baulu, 1979).

Because MAO is not a neutransmitter itself, it must exert its effect through the monoamine(s) it regulates. Some hint of the relationships that might exist between the monoamines and sensation seeking in studies of humans is derived from studies of biochemical correlates of EP augmenting–reducing.

MAO is low in EP augmenters and it is high in EP reducers (L. von Knorring & Perris, 1981). Augmenters among patients tend to have low levels of cerebrospinal fluid (CSF) serotonin, DA metabolites, and endorphins, and reducers have higher levels. This last finding on endorphins makes sense because these naturally produced morphine-like compounds have sedative effects on behavior and could be the source of the cortical inhibition seen in reducers. A rare kind of experimental study on humans showed that administration of zimeldine, a selective inhibiter of serotonin uptake, causes a reduction in the amplitude–intensity slope of the EP, suggesting a direct effect of serotonin on the sensorimotor centers in the brain (L. von Knorring & Johansson, 1980). Serotonin has generally inhibitory effects, in opposition to NE, which produces arousal in the cortex, and DA, which has activating effects on reward seeking behavior.

I previously discussed the behavioral characteristics of the RHA rats (EP augmenters) and the RLA rats (EP reducers). These strains are linked to human sensation seeking by the EP marker so that the RHAs are models for impulsive sensation seekers and the RLAs, for inhibited low sensation seekers. The RHAs show strong dopaminergic increases in the prefrontal cortex, whereas the RLAs show little response of this monoamine. In contrast, the RLAs show a strong serotonergic response and an increase in corticotrophin releasing factor (CRF) in the hypothalamus. CRF releases adrenocorticotropic hormone from the pituitary gland, which would cause the release of cortisol from the adrenal cortex. At the human level, cortisol was found to be inversely related to sensation seeking (high in low sensation seekers). The rat model suggests that stress activates the dopaminergic system in high sensation seekers and the serotonergic system in low sensation seekers. As a consequence, the hypothalamic–pituitary–adrenocortical may be activated in the low sensation seeker, resulting in passive avoidance and inhibitory behavior in the presence of stress or threat. These differences could explain the greater readiness of high sensation seekers to engage in risky behaviors because risk would engender more anxiety and inhibition in the low sensation seekers.

Theoretical Modifications (1984)

By 1979 I had already suggested that the optimal level of cortical activity and the sensitivity of the RAS was not a cogent basis for the trait, which is why that book was subtitled *Beyond the Optimal Level of Arousal* (Zuckerman, 1979a). After reviewing the animal and human findings on the monoamines (Zuckerman, 1984b), I formulated a model based on an optimal level of catecholamine system activity (CSA). CSA includes DA and NE. This model is shown in Figure 1.9.

It was suggested that in an unstimulated state and a low basal level of CSA, both DA and NE are low in high sensation seekers and are far below their optimal levels of CSA, producing an aversive state of boredom. This is why the sensation seeker has high boredom susceptibility and a need for sensation seeking through activities (as in TAS), people (as in Dis), or novel experiences (as in ES). The low sensation seeker at the same low

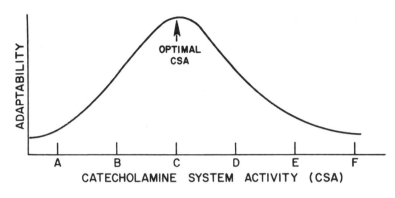

MOOD	1. Depression 2. Anxiety	Boredom, Apathy	Positive Feelings	Euphoria	1. Anxiety 2. Depression	Panic
ACTIVITY	Minimal	Limited	Active	Hyperactive	Aimless Limited	Stereotyped
SOCIAL INTERACTION	Withdrawn or Hostile	Introverted (state)	Sociable	Hypersociable	Unsociable	Aggressive-Hostile Interactive
CLINICAL CONDITION	Major Depression	Normal	Normal	Cyclothymic Hypomanic	Anxiety Disorder	Paranoid Disorder

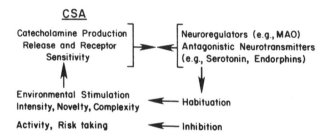

Figure 1.9. A model for the relationships of mood, activity, social interaction, and clinical conditions to catecholamine system activity. MAO = monoamine oxidase. From "Sensation Seeking: A Comparative Approach to a Human Trait," by M. Zuckerman, 1984, *Behavioral and Brain Sciences, 7*, p. 431. Copyright 1984 by Cambridge University Press. Reprinted with permission.

level of CSA is more content and happy. Increases in CSA through activities or drugs may move high sensation seekers closer to their optimal levels for mood but may push low sensation seekers beyond their optimal levels, and positive feelings may shift to negative ones. At an even higher level, the high sensation seeker may become euphoric and manic, whereas the low will become anxious and stressed.

The theory notes the inhibitory effect of serotonin and neuroregulators like MAO on CSA and their role in habituation, which dampens the arousing effect of stimuli by repetition and postulates that it is responsible for inhibition of arousal and sensation seeking activity. It was assumed, therefore, that low sensation seekers are characterized by higher levels of serotonergic activity as well as MAO and endorphins.

The two catecholamines were assumed to work in the same direction. The only differentiation is that both were said to be involved in the pursuit of novel sensation, with high NE providing the energetic component of the drive and DA, the reward seeking component. Stimulant drugs like cocaine and amphetamine release both DA and NE and therefore are rewarding to high sensation seekers but are likely to make low sensation seekers anxious. However, there was one curious finding that confounded the theory. High sensation seekers should prefer stimulant drugs to drugs that have a sedative effect. But research showed that there is no clear preference for stimulant drugs among high sensation seekers (Zuckerman, 1983a, 1994). Young heroin users are as high in sensation seeking as are cocaine users (Craig, 1982; Platt & Labate, 1976). What distinguishes high from low sensation seekers among drug abusers is that the highs had tried a greater variety of drugs than the lows. Given blind testing of amphetamine, diazepam (a tranquilizer), and placebo, both high and low sensation seekers rated their reactions as more positive to amphetamine (Carrol, Zuckerman, & Vogel, 1982). These findings raised questions for any kind of optimal level theories.

Further Theoretical Modifications (1995)

During the later 1980s, I was influenced by the theories of Gray (1982, 1987). Gray was a bottom-up type of theorist, drawing his basic models from neuropsychological research with rats. What was interesting to me and other theorists was his use of behavioral systems as the connecting constructs between the underlying neurological, neurochemical systems and the overlying personality traits. The three basic behavioral systems are the behavioral approach system (BAS), underlying impulsivity, the behavioral inhibition system (BIS), underlying anxiety, and the fight–flight system, underlying aggression (or H. J. Eysenck's, 1967, Psychoticism [P] dimension). Whereas Gray (1987) regarded impulsivity, the trait expression of the BAS, as a combination of H. J. Eysenck's Extraversion (E), Neuroticism (N), and P, I regard impulsivity as closely linked with sensation seeking (related to E and P in H. J. Eysenck's system but not to N). In my five-factor theory, one of the major factors is described as Impulsive Sensation Seeking (Zuckerman, Kuhlman, & Camac, 1988). Gray regarded the dopaminergic pathway in the mesolimbic system as the neurological site of the BAS. NE and serotonin were thought to be the basis of the BIS. The dorsal ascending NE system is an arousal system activated by novel stimuli or stimuli associated with threat or punishment, but the data from human subjects would suggest that it is low, rather than high, levels of serotonin that are associated with

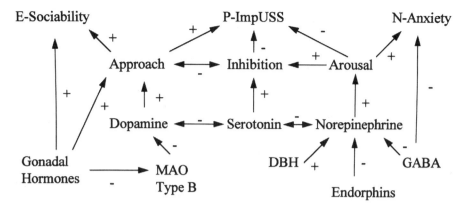

Figure 1.10. A biobehavioral model for sensation seeking. E = Extraversion; P = Psychoticism; ImpUSS = Impulsive Unsocialized Sensation Seeking; N = Neuroticism; MAO = monoamine oxidase; DBH = dopamine beta-hydroxylase. From "Good and Bad Humors: Biochemical Bases of Personality and Its Disorders," by M. Zuckerman, 1995, *Psychological Science, 6*, p. 331. Copyright 1995 by Blackwell. Reprinted with permission.

anxiety and depression. The serotonin reuptake inhibitors, which keep the system activated, are the drug of choice in the treatment of depression and are also effective in the treatment of panic disorder. Because serotonin mediates behavioral inhibition, it was natural for Gray to assume it functioned in the inhibition associated with anxiety. But it also may be involved in the type of behavioral inhibition associated with low sensation seeking. The low sensation seeker is cautious and avoids risky situations but is not necessarily fearful.

My last (for now) version of a biosocial–biochemical model of sensation seeking (Zuckerman, 1995) is shown in Figure 1.10. The figure shows only three of the five traits in the Zuckerman–Kuhlman alternative-five model. There are biological bases postulated for the other two (Zuckerman, 2003, 2006a), but their inclusion would make the figure impossibly complex and the focus here is on the Impulsive Sensation Seeking factor.

Three behavioral mechanisms are assumed to underlie sensation seeking. High sensation seeking is a function of a strong approach and weak inhibition and arousal systems. These are interactive, as are the neurotransmitters underlying them. DA is positively associated with approach, serotonin with inhibition, and NE with arousal. Sensation seeking, therefore, is associated with a strong dopaminergic reactivity, and weak serotonergic and noradrenergic reactivities. Note that I am not talking about basal levels of these neurotransmitters but reactivity to stimuli, whether novel, positive, or negative. Reactivity depends on sensitivity of receptor cells, not the absolute levels of neurotransmitters stored in the presynaptic neurons.

TABLE 1.3
Animal Models for Sensation Seeking (and Related Traits)
and Monoamines

Behavioral trait	Biochemical trait
RHA vs. RLA Rats	
General Behavior: RHA VEP augmenters vs. RLA reducers are more exploratory, impulsive, aggressive, nonnurturing to pups, responsive to high-intensity brain stimulation, drink alcohol (Siegel & Driscoll, 1996). *Shock stress:* RHA VEP augmenters exhibit active avoidance; RLA reducers are passive, hyperemotional (Siegel & Driscoll, 1996).	*Basal state:* RHA > RLA in density of D1 receptors in NA. *Stress:* RHA increase DA in prefrontal cortex (D'Angio et al., 1988), decrease 5-HT in hypothalamus; RLA increase 5-HIAA in hypothalamus (Driscoll et al., 1983), increase in CRF and plasma corticosterone (Driscoll & Bättig, 1982).
HR vs. LR Rats (Dellu et al., 1996)	
General Behavior: HR more exploratory, respond more for amphetamine and food reward, more preference for novelty.	*Basal state:* HR higher DA activity in NA lower DA in cortex. DA in NA correlates pos., DA in cortex correlates neg. with activity in novel situations. *Stress:* HR more increase in DA in NA.
Dominant vs. Submissive Monkeys (Kaplan et al., 2002)	
General Behavior: dominance and submission.	*Basal state:* Dominants have higher levels of HVA and MHPG in CSF. HVA and MHPG correlate pos. with social rank. No diff. on 5-HIAA.

Note. RHA = Roman high avoidance; RLA = Roman low avoidance; D1 = dopamine 1 (receptors); DA = dopamine; VEP = visual evoked potentials (cortical); 5-HT = 5-hydroxytryptamine (serotonin); 5-HIAA = 5-hydroxyindoleacetic acid (serotonin metabolite); CRF = corticotropin releasing factor; CSF = cerebrospinal fluid; HR = high reactive (to novelty), LR = low reactive; NA = nucleus accumbens; pos. = positively; neg. = negatively; HVA = homovanillic acid; MHPG = 3-methoxy-4 hydroxyphenylglyco; diff. = difference.

Enzymes like MAO and dopamine beta-hydroxylase (DBH) may also affect reactivity. Interactions among the three monoamines are also a factor, as shown by double-headed arrows in the figure. Hormones like testosterone and the endorphins may affect the trait through their own activation or suppression effects or through their effects on neurotransmitters.

Monoamine Research With Animals

To what extent is the latest model supported by research? Table 1.3 summarizes some of the animal studies. I have already discussed the studies contrasting RHA and RLA rats. Dellu, Piazza, Mayo, LeMoal, and Simon (1996) constructed another rat model, using reactions to novel environments to select high and low reactives (HRs and LRs), with *reactivity* defined in terms of explorativeness. The HRs had higher levels of the DA metabolite dihydroxyphenylacetic acid (DOPAC) in the nucleus accumbens and lower levels in the prefrontal lobes. A measure of explorativeness correlated positively with DOPAC in the nucleus accumbens and negatively with DOPAC in the prefrontal cortex. Other investigators have suggested reciprocal effects between DA in the prefrontal lobes and in the nucleus accumbens. The RHA rats did show higher levels of DA reactivity to stress in the prefrontal lobes, but this could be due to enhanced receptor sensitivity produced by low levels in the basal state. The results of these studies suggest that we may have to be more specific in pharmacological studies of personality. The nucleus accumbens is the major site for reward from electrical self-stimulation and stimulant drugs (amphetamine and cocaine; Bozarth, 1987). The nucleus accumbens is part of the medial forebrain bundle hypothesized to be the major neurological locus for sensation seeking.

Dominance is a trait correlated with sensation seeking in humans and exploration in animals. Although it is not a direct analogue of sensation seeking, it would be difficult to find a submissive sensation seeker or a dominant low sensation seeker. A study of monkeys living in a natural colony assessed dominance and aggressiveness and took CSF samples for assay of DOPAC (Kaplan, Manuck, Fontenot, & Mann, 2002). They found higher levels of CSF homovanillic acid (HVA) in the more dominant and aggressive monkeys. CSF levels, of course, do not tell us the origins in the brain (or spinal cord) of the CSF metabolite. Human CSF studies of the monoamines are discussed in the next subsection.

Ellison (1977) did chemical lesioning of the serotonergic and noradrenergic systems in rats living in a specially constructed laboratory community with passageways, burrows, and a common arena in which rats could interact. Chemical lesioning of the serotonergic system produced increases in explorativeness, sociability, and aggression. Lesioning of the noradrenergic system produced less social interaction but more explorativeness. Lesioning of both systems increased the effects of the lesioning of the serotonergic system alone. These studies support the part of the theory claiming that low levels of serotonin (disinhibition) and low levels of NE (low arousal) are characteristic in high sensation seekers.

Monoamine Research With Humans

Table 1.4 summarizes monoamine research done with human subjects. The earliest approach was to examine levels of the neurotransmitters or their metabolites in CSF, plasma, or urine. The CSF measures obtained from lumbar spinal taps are closest to the brain itself, although some of their source may be in the spinal cord. Even the part originating in the

TABLE 1.4
Monoamines and Sensation Seeking: Human Studies

	Results related to sensation seeking
Behavioral expressions	Risk taking, drinking, drugs, smoking, gambling, sex, extreme sports, reckless fast driving, volunteering for dangerous or stressful jobs. Preferences for novel, intense, or complex stimuli.
Dopamine and metabolites basal levels in CSF	No significant correlations with DA metabolites in CSF (Ballenger et al., 1983; Limson et al., 1991).
Responses to challenges by DA agonists	*Apomorphine effect on growth hormone (GH):* Pos. correlation with SSS–BS (Wiesbeck et al., 1996) and NS (Wiesbeck et al., 1995). *Bromocryptine (BC) effect on GH:* GH pos. correlations with NS and neg. correlations with BC inhibition measured by PRL in addicts and controls (Gerra et al., 2000). No correlation of SSS–Dis and SSS–BS with PRL (Depue, 1995). *Lisuride effect on prolactin (PRL):* No correlation of PRL with SSS–ES and SSS–Dis (Netter et al., 1996).
Seratonin metabolite (5-HIAA) in CSF	No correlations with SSS (Ballenger et al., 1983; Limson et al., 1991).
Responses to challenges by serotonin agonists	*Fenfluramine effect on PRL:* PRL and SSS–Dis and SSS–BS (Depue, 1995). Neg. correlation with NS, addicts only (Gerra et al., 2000). Blunted serotonin response in high SSS–ES (Netter et al., 1996). Blunted serotonin responsivity to Pinodel correlates with SSS–Dis (Hennig et al. 1998).
NE and metabolite (MHPG) in CSF and plasma	CSF NE (but not MHPG) neg. correlation with SSS–Gen in normal controls (Ballenger et al., 1983). Plasma MHPG neg. correlation with Total SSS in normal controls (Arqué et al., 1988). Plasma NE pos. correlation with NS in normal males (Gerra et al., 1999).
Challenge to NE by clonidine	No correlation with NS in either addicts or controls, but a pos. correlation with harm avoidance in addicts (Gerra et al., 2000).

Note. DA = dopamine; CSF = cerebrospinal fluid; pos. = positive; neg. = negative; SSS = Sensation Seeking Scale; SSS–BS = Boredom Susceptibility subscale of SSS; SSS–Dis = Disinhibition subscale of SSS; SSS–Gen = SSS General Scale; PRL = prolactin; NE = norepinephrine; MHPG = 3-methoxy-4-hydroxyphenylglycol; NS = novelty seeking.

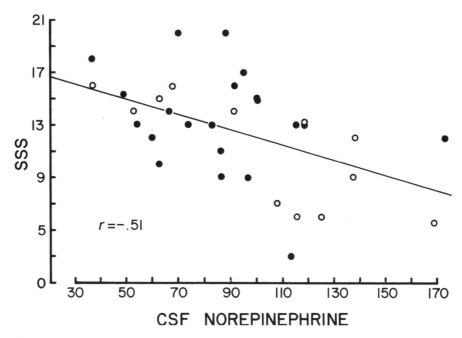

Figure 1.11. A scatterplot for the correlation of cerebrospinal fluid (CSF) norepinephrine and sensation seeking. Solid circles represent male data; open circles represent female data. SSS = Sensation Seeking Scale; CSF = Cerebrospinal fluid. From "Biochemical Correlates of Personality Traits in Normals: An Exploratory Study," by J. C. Ballenger et al., *Personality and Individual Differences, 4*, p. 621. Copyright 1983 by Elsevier Science. Reprinted with permission.

CSF-filled ventricles of the brain is indefinite in the part of the brain it comes from. Although the CSF is obtained in what is supposed to be a basal state, the drawing of a sample from a spinal puncture is not exactly a stress-free situation, either in anticipation or execution of the procedure.

The studies referred to in the table yielded null results in correlating CSF monoamines with personality, except for one notable exception: Ballenger et al. (1983) found a substantial ($r = -.51$) negative correlation between CSF NE and the SSS General Scale as shown in Figure 1.11. This result has not yet been replicated, although the strength of the association is promising. Perhaps the low level of NE is an indicator of the lack of fearful arousal in high sensation seekers, but plasma NE correlated positively with novelty seeking (NS) in one study (Gerra et al., 1999). The metabolites of NE, DA, and 5-HT (5-hydroxytryptamine [serotonin])—3-methoxy-4-hydroxyphenylglycol (MHPG), HVA, and 5-hydroxyindoleacetic (5-HIAA), respectively—in CSF, plasma, and urine were not related to sensation seeking, except for a negative correlation with plasma MHPG.

Better results on serotonin have been found in studies using neurotransmitter agonists and antagonists to measure the response of the systems as assessed by hormonal reactions. Several studies found that the prolactin response to a serotonin agonist correlated negatively with the SSS or NS scales (Depue, 1995; Gerra et al., 2000; Hennig et al., 1998; Netter, Hennig, & Roed, 1996) and also with impulsivity, aggression, and H. J. Eysenck's P scale (Depue, 1995). P is the best marker for the Impulsive Unsocialized Sensation Seeking factor. Dis was not related to DA reactivity, although the P scale was negatively related to response to a DA antagonist, suggesting higher DA reactivity in high P scorers. Netter et al. (1996) found insensitivity to a serotonin stimulant in high sensation seekers but no relationship to indicators of DA reactivity to an agonist.

Wiesbeck, Mauerer, Thome, Jakob, and Boening (1995) found a significant relationship between growth hormone (GH) release by a DA agonist (a putative measure of D2 receptor sensitivity) and Cloninger's (1987b) Novelty Seeking (NS) scale. The subjects were abstinent alcoholic individuals, but there was no relationship of the GH response and their alcohol history factors.

In another study using controls as well as alcoholic individuals, Wiesbeck et al. (1996) correlated the GH response to the SSS. Only the BS subscale of the SSS correlated significantly with GH response to the DA agonist in the controls and in the alcoholic individuals with a positive family history for alcoholism. Both alcoholic groups were significantly higher than the controls on BS.

The studies of humans confirm evidence of higher serotonergic reactivity in low sensation seekers found in animals, but there is mixed evidence of high dopaminergic reactivity in high sensation seekers, possibly because this is confined to the limbic system pathway and not evident in the indirect samples of activity measured in humans.

GENETICS

Twin Studies

Individual differences that have a strong biological determination would be expected to show high levels of heritability through the heritability of the biological traits on which they are based. Sensation seeking satisfies this criterion, as I show in this section.

Fulker, Eysenck, and Zuckerman (1980) did the first biometric study of sensation seeking using a sample of English twins (see Table 1.5). They found a heritability for the SSS–V Total score of .58. This is quite high for a personality trait, most of which have heritabilities falling between .30 and .50 (Bouchard, 1994; Loehlin, 1992). There was no evidence of a shared environmental factor (as with most personality traits), and the remainder

TABLE 1.5
Correlations and Heritabilities of Sensation Seeking: Twin Studies

Study	Sex	IT	FT	h^2
Fulker, Eysenck, & Zuckerman (1980):	M	.63	.21	.58
Twins raised together	F	.56	.21	—
Minnesota study: twins separated at or	M & F	.54	.32	—
near birth, raised separately	h^2	.54	.64	.59

Note. Values are from the Sensation Seeking Scale Form V Total score. IT = identical twins; FT = fraternal twins; h^2 = heritability; M = male; F = female.

of the variance is due to nonshared environment and error of measurement. The comparison of identical and fraternal twins raised in the same family environments has been questioned. The higher correlations between identical than between fraternal twins might be a function of the identicals being treated more alike than the fraternals, rather than their 100% genetic similarity, compared with the 50% common genes in the fraternals. Identical twins are treated more alike, but it is hard to tell how much this is a function of their physical similarity, their tendency to be more closely bonded, or the fact that they actually behave more similarly than fraternals. The question can be answered by studying twins who were separated soon after birth and raised in different families.

The Minnesota separated twin study has looked at sensation seeking (Hur & Bouchard, 1997). Lykken (personal communication, 1992) reported the data on separated twins shown in Table 1.5. The correlation between identical twins raised separately (r = .54) is also a direct measure of heritability because there is no shared environment. The correlation of separated fraternal twins must be doubled to obtain the heritability because they share only half of their genes. This yields a heritability of .64. If we average these two, we get a heritability of .59, which is nearly the same as the .58 obtained from Fulker et al.'s (1980) study of nonseparated twins. This seems to reinforce the conclusion that the shared environment contributes nothing to the twins' similarities on the trait. I discuss a caveat to this conclusion later in this chapter.

H. J. Eysenck (1983) analyzed the genetics of the subscales of the SSS using the data from the Fulker et al. (1980) study. He found evidence for a common genetic factor among all subscales and also some genetic factors specific to the individual subscales. Heritabilities of three of the subscales (ES, Dis, TAS) ranged from .42 to .56. BS was lower, probably because of its lower scale reliability. Hur and Bouchard (1997) analyzed the subscale data from the separated twin study, and Koopmans, Boomsma, Heath, and Lorenz (1995) did so for a Dutch sample of twins raised together. The heritabilities of the SSS subscales in all of these studies are shown in Table

TABLE 1.6
Heritabilities of the Sensation Seeking Scale (SSS) Subscales

SSS subscale	H. J. Eysenck (1983)		Koopmans et al. (1995)		Hur & Bouchard (1997)	
	M	F	M	F	M & F	*M* (all)
Dis	.51	.41	.62	.60	.46	.50
TAS	.45	.44	.62	.63	.54	.54
ES	.58	.57	.56	.58	.55	.57
BS	.41	.34	.48	.54	.40	.43

Note. Dis = Disinhibition; TAS = Thrill and Adventure Seeking; ES = Experience Seeking; BS = Boredom Susceptibility; M = males; F = females. From *Molecular Genetics and the Human Personality* (p. 198), edited by J. Benjamin, R. P. Ebstein, and R. H. Belmaker, 2002, Washington, DC: American Psychiatric Publishing. Copyright 2002 by American Psychiatric Publishing. Adapted with permission.

1.6. With the exception of the BS scale, the heritabilities for all of the other scales are relatively high (.50–.63) and not too different from one another.

Judging from the results comparing (a) identical and fraternal twins and (b) twins raised apart with twins raised together, sharing a common family environment, there is little or no effect of the shared environment. The environment itself is not assessed in these studies. Kraft and Zuckerman (1999) compared personality scores with college students' descriptions of their fathers' and mothers' affection, punishment and rejection, and control, using a parental description questionnaire. Children raised entirely by both biological parents and children from families with a stepfather were both used. Within the intact families, the Impulsive Sensation Seeking (ImpSS) subscale of the Zuckerman–Kuhlman Personality Questionnaire (ZKPQ; Zuckerman, 2002; Zuckerman, Kuhlman, Joireman, Teta, & Kraft, 1993) did not correlate with any of the dimensions of parental attitudes and behavior for either parent. If there had been some positive results, their interpretation would have been ambiguous because they could be expressions of genetic or environmental influences. But the absence of any significant results tends to support the idea of a lack of shared environmental influence on ImpSS.

Bratko and Butkovic (2003) gave parental attitude and behavior scales to the parents themselves and correlated parents' self-reports and those of their partners describing themselves and their spouses with their children's SSS scores. Only the father's control score correlated with the SSS Total and Dis scores. Fathers who were more permissive and less controlling in regard to their children's behaviors had children who were more disinhibited. Of course, this could be a genetic as well as an environmental effect because fathers who are more permissive of disinhibited behavior in their children are more likely to be disinhibited themselves.

Another way of examining the influence of shared family environment was used in a twin study conducted in the Netherlands. The study compared twins who had been raised in a nonreligious home and those who had been raised in a religious home (Boomsma, de Geus, van Baal, & Koopmans, 1999). The Dis subscale had shown significant genetic effects but no effect of shared environment in the total population. However, when the twins were subdivided on the basis of their religious upbringing, the twins raised in a religious background showed 0% effect of genetics for males and only a weak one for females (37%). In contrast, the shared environment effect was 62% for males and 37% for females, both significant. But those raised in a nonreligious environment had the same results as the total population, a significant effect of genetics (61% for females and 49% for males) and practically none (0% for females and 11% for males) for shared environment. Religious upbringing itself was not genetic but purely environmental.

As one would expect, those raised in a religious home had lower scores on the Dis subscale, but there was no difference between the two groups in the variance that might have affected the heritabilities. Few twin studies use this approach, and these results suggest that one may have to assess critical environmental factors within the twin samples to detect heredity–environment interactions like this one. There may be more variation in parental control in religious homes than in permissive nonreligious homes.

Moffitt, Caspi, and Rutter (2006) called this type of interaction *heritability–environment interaction* and distinguished it from *gene–environment interaction*. In the latter, a specific interaction in the DNA sequence interacts with a specific environmental factor. As an example of the latter, Caspi et al. (2002) found that variations in the genotype affecting Type-A MAO expression interacted with childhood maltreatment to influence later expressions in conduct disorder, antisocial personality disorder, and violent crimes.

Twin studies assess broad heritability, including additive, Mendelian, and epistatic types of genetic mechanisms. The last of these depends on specific gene combinations rather than on the sheer number of genes involved in a trait. Parent–child or sibling studies assess only the narrow additive type. Discrepancies between the two methods could be due to the effects of nonadditive genetic mechanisms only found in identical twins because of their identical sets of genes. Many personality traits do show such discrepancies.

Parent–Child Studies

Bratko and Butkovic (2003) analyzed parent–child correlations on sensation seeking (see Table 1.7). The midparent scores' (average of mother and father's SSS scores) correlation with their children's scores on the SSS

TABLE 1.7

Parent–Child and Father–Mother Correlations on the
Sensation Seeking Scale (SSS) and Its Subscales

Relationship	TAS	ES	Dis	BS	Total SSS
Father–Child	.25**	.26**	.27**	.18	.33**
Mother–Child	.02	.15	.24**	.11	.16
Midparent–Child	.24*	.25**	.32**	.19	.31**
Father–Mother	.15	.26**	.46**	.31*	.44**

Note. TAS = Thrill and Adventure Seeking, ES = Experience Seeking, Dis = Disinhibition, BS = Boredom Susceptibility. From "Family Study of Sensation Seeking," by D. Bratko and A. Butkovic, 2003, *Personality and Individual Differences, 35,* p. 1564. Copyright 2003 by Pergamon Press. Reprinted with permission. *$p < .05$. **$p < .01$.

is a measure of narrow heritability, and in this case ($h = .31$) it is about half of the heritability estimate from the twin studies ($h = .59$) described previously. These results suggest that there are either nonadditive genetic factors involved in sensation seeking or biasing factors in the twin studies.

In a previous study (Kish & Donnenwerth, 1972), mothers' scores alone did not correlate at all with children's scores, but the fathers' and daughters' scores on the SSS General were significantly correlated ($r = .39$). In the more recent study (Bratko & Butkovic, 2003), this correlation was also significant for the Total score ($r = .36$). Fathers' TAS scores did not correlate significantly with their sons' Total scores ($r = .28$), but the father–son correlation on the TAS subscale itself ($r = .38$) was significant.

Assortative Mating

There are two opposite sayings regarding the personality attractions between those who marry: *like attracts like* and *opposites attract*. The first is probably truer for attitudes, interests, and values, but there is little evidence for either in studies of personality resemblance or differences between spouses. Personality trait correlations between spouses are usually low or close to zero (Ahern, Johnson, Wilson, McClearn, & Vandenberg, 1982; Donnellan, Conger, & Bryant, 2004; H. J. Eysenck, 1990). Sensation seeking is an exception. Correlations have been found between the SSS scores of husbands and wives in the United States, Germany, Israel, and the Netherlands (Bratko & Butkovik, 2003; Farley & Davis, 1977; Farley & Mueller, 1978; Ficher, Zuckerman, & Neeb, 1981; Ficher, Zuckerman, & Steinberg, 1988; Glicksohn & Golan, 2001; Lesnik-Oberstein & Cohen, 1984). Couples in long-term premarital relationships also show a moderate correlation between partners on the SSS (Thornquist & Zuckerman, 1995).

The high degree of assortative attraction and mating for the trait of sensation seeking suggests its biological importance. If it has an evolutionary history, it would explain the continued variation in sensation seeking trait because there would be selective breeding at both ends of the trait distribution. For the female there may be a trade-off between reliability in a mate (low sensation seekers) and attractiveness as a sexual partner (high sensation seekers). D. M. Buss et al.'s (1990) study of mate selection across 37 different cultures found remarkable consistency across gender and culture in the highest three attributes, ranked from highest to lowest: kind, intelligent, exciting personality. The third-ranked trait would likely pertain to sensation seekers. Linton and Wiener (2001) compared personality and a measure of potential mating success (PMS) in a male sample. Dis correlated with PMS in the single heterosexual sample, and TAS correlated with PMS in the attached heterosexual sample.

Molecular Genetics

The completion of the human genome project has opened new possibilities for the identification of specific genes involved in personality and its disorders. During the past 2 decades, the search for major genes involved in psychiatric disorders has dominated research efforts, with little success in finding replicable results. The problem is that nearly all of these disorders are polygenic and may involve contributions from many genes of small effects. There is always the possibility of finding genes with major effects, but even these will require very large samples of patients afflicted with the disorder.

More recently, attention has turned to finding genes associated with normally distributed personality traits. One of the first fruits of this research was the discovery by Ebstein et al. (1996) in Israel of an association between the gene for the dopamine 4 receptor (DRD4) and the Cloninger (1987b) scale, called Novelty Seeking (NS). NS correlates highly ($r = .68$) with the ImpSS scale (Zuckerman & Cloninger, 1996). Although there are a number of forms of the gene, ranging from 2 to 10 repeats of the base sequence, the most common forms in Western populations, including the Israeli, are a short form, with four repeats, and a long form, with seven repeats. The longer forms were associated with high scores on the NS scale, and the shorter forms with low to medium scores on this scale. This finding was followed by many attempts to replicate it, although some used other personality scales. Prolo and Licinio (2002) summarized the studies to that date with successful replications in 11 out of 21 groups. Schinka, Letsch, and Crawford (2002) did a meta-analysis of these groups and concluded that there was no overall effect contrasting the seven-repeat allele with shorter repeats, but studies comparing all short and long sequences yielded a small but significant effect.

Given the polygenetic nature of this and other personality traits, a combination of related genes might yield a larger effect. Comings, Saucier, and MacMurray (2002) found that four dopamine receptor genes acted in an additive manner to contribute 5.25% of the variance of NS. Noble (1998) reported similar additive effects for the dopamine 2 receptor (DRD2) and DRD4.

Interactive genetic effects are entirely likely, given the evidence for epistatic genetic variance in many of the behavior genetic studies of personality. One study found such evidence for genetic interaction (Strobel, Lesch, & Brocke, 2003). The DRD4 long allele form by itself was not associated with high NS, but when the short allele of the serotonin transporter gene and an allele of the catechol-O-methyltransferase (COMT) were present, the association of DRD4 with NS was significant. What gives one more confidence in the role of the DRD4 in sensation seeking is the association of the gene with forms of behavior found in high sensation seekers, like heroin and alcohol abuse, gambling, and attention-deficit/hyperactivity disorder (Ebstein & Kotler, 2002).

The long form of the gene in newborn infants is associated with orientation to novel stimuli, an early measure of the strength of the approach mechanism (Ebstein & Auerbach, 2002). In an earlier section, I described the results showing stronger OR responses in high than in low sensation seekers. There was also an interaction of the DRD4 with the serotonin (5-HT) transporter promoter. The short form of the 5-HT promoter is associated with anxiety in humans (Munafò et al., 2003). The investigators found that the long form combines with the long form of the DRD4 to enhance the infants' ORs, whereas the short form of the promoter combined with the short DRD4 reduces orientation and increases negative emotionality and distress.

Ebstein and Auerbach (2002) interpreted their findings in a manner consistent with my humoral model of sensation seeking that was shown in Figure 1.10: Dopaminergic pathways mediate approach behavior and impulsive sensation seeking, whereas serotoninergic pathways inhibit such behavior. The strength of the approach mechanism and ImpSS depends on the relative reactivity of dopaminergic and serotonergic systems, which act in reciprocal opposition.

NEW FORMS OF SENSATION SEEKING SCALES

Since the development of SSS–II, SSS–IV, and SSS–V, new forms have been developed for different reasons. Some are merely attempts to shorten the scale (e.g., Hoyle, Stephenson, Palmgreen, Lorch, & Donohew, 2002), although the form 40-item SSS–V takes only about 20 minutes.

Some, like Form VI (SSS–VI; Zuckerman, 1984a), are put in a different form to separate desire or intention from actual behavioral experience. The older forms confound the two types of items. The ImpSS scale was developed from factor analyses of sensation seeking items with items from other personality trait scales and is in a true–false, rather than forced-choice, form (Zuckerman, Kuhlman, Joireman, Teta, & Kraft, 1993). It also combines impulsivity and sensation seeking items, as the title of the scale implies.

Cloninger's (1987b) NS Scale (a true–false form) resembles the ImpSS scale and is highly correlated with it. Of all the modified forms, it has received the most attention from researchers, particularly in the psychiatric and psychobiological fields. Arnett's (1994) Inventory of Sensation Seeking (AISS) represents a new conceptualization of sensation seeking, including two major factors: novelty and intensity.

Some of the criticisms of the standard sensation seeking scales are valid. The original scales (II, IV, V) contained some now-anachronistic terms, like *hippies*, *jet-setters*, and *swingers*, that are unfamiliar to younger generations. I made some attempt to modify the test by either substituting other terms or including a definition of the older term in the item (Zuckerman, 1996a). The forced-choice form is unnecessary because social desirability did not prove to be a problem with this scale as it is for scales measuring neuroticism or psychopathology. Despite these drawbacks, the scale has established its validity in many hundreds of studies, and most subjects do not find much problem in taking the forced-choice form. The Likert-type form used in some of the new forms has its own response-set problems, like the tendency to use extremes or middle points on the scales. Likert-type scales are used to get some range of scores on short forms using a small number of items. Of course, this limits the representativeness of the items selected and, therefore, the content validity. The SSS was designed for late adolescents and adults only. Russo et al. (1993) constructed a children's scale, which can be used from ages 9 to 14. There are also child versions in Spanish (Pérez, Ortet, Pla, & Simó, 1986) and Swedish (Björk-Åkesson, 1990). The Spanish version is for children 11 to 15 years of age, and the Swedish scale is designed for children between 12 and 15 years old.

There have been many translations of the SSS and new forms in other languages. Translations are tricky because equivalent terms from two languages are sometimes difficult to ascertain. Back-translations are desirable to make sure the translated items are still close to their originals in English. It is reassuring that the same four-factor structure has appeared in most of the translations. Some of these scales are described in Appendix I of Zuckerman (1994). Newer translations are mentioned in the text as they are used in research.

Readers may want to consider these new scales if they see an advantage in them for particular populations, economy of time, or their appropriateness for particular kinds of research. One cannot automatically assume that findings on the older sensation seeking scales will hold for the new scales. I attempt to describe some of the validity studies done with these newer scales, but details can be found in the subsequent chapters on different types of risk taking.

Sensation Seeking Scale Forms II and IV General Scale

The General Scale was the first SSS scale to be developed. I include it here because I am often asked for a shorter form for the SSS. Those in search of a scale that is shorter than the 40-item SSS–V might consider the 22-item SSS–II General Scale (Zuckerman et al., 1964), which was carried over into SSS–IV (Zuckerman, 1971). The items were selected from those loading most highly on the first unrotated factor from an item factor analysis and confirmed with item–total correlations. Internal (alpha) coefficients in SSS–II range from .68 to .74. In SSS–IV, the alphas range from .68 to .80. Retest reliability after 1 week is .89; after 3 weeks, .89; and after 6 to 8 months, .75.

The experimental scale (SSS–I), from which the SSS–II General Scale was derived, included mostly items from the future TAS, ES, and BS subscales, but not from the Dis subscale. One cannot get subscale factor scores from the General form. It correlates .74. with the SSS–V Total score, which is balanced with 10 items for each of the four factors. Much of the earlier research on volunteering, drinking, drugs, and extreme sports was done using the SSS–II General Scale. Details on reliabilities and interscale correlations of SSS–IV and SSS–V and can be found in previous volumes (Zuckerman, 1979a, 1994). A copy of SSS–IV can be found in Zuckerman (1979a), and a copy of SSS–V (including some revisions in item wording) is contained in Zuckerman (1994). A copy of SSS–V and its unpublished manual can also be obtained from the author.

Sensation Seeking Scale Form VI

The older forms of the SSS included two types of items referring to behavior. One type expressed a desire to engage in some type of activity. Most of the TAS items were of this type because it was assumed that most younger persons would not have had the opportunity to engage in sports like skydiving, scuba diving, or flying an airplane but that the intention to do so would indicate a TAS tendency that might be expressed in other ways, like reckless or fast driving. Another type of item was put in terms of actual experiences, for instance, "I like wild, uninhibited parties." Most of these items were on the Dis subscale. Most items on the ES and BS scales are expressed as preferences not easily translatable into behavioral expressions.

The separation of items expressing desire or intention from those describing experience could be useful. Although I expected intention and experience scales to be substantially correlated, it is possible that some persons are "latent sensation seekers" with a strong desire to do sensation seeking kinds of things but are restrained from doing so by life circumstances, like family responsibilities or economic circumstances. They would have high scores on desire or intention but low scores on experience. Sensation seeking declines with age, particularly on TAS and Dis subscales. But in some cases, this decline is more precipitous than in others. Depression or negative life experiences might create a discrepancy between intentions for the future and experiences from the past. This kind of information could be useful for clinicians. The experience scales of the SSS–VI resemble omnibus risk-taking scales that are described in chapter 2.

The SSS–VI (Zuckerman, 1984a) consists of four subscales: TAS Intentions (TAS-Int), Dis Intentions (Dis-Int), TAS Experience (TAS-Exp), and Dis Experience (Dis-Exp). Each item on the intentions subscales has a corresponding item on the experience subscales. For instance, "I would like to try skydiving" (TAS-Int) and "I have gone skydiving" (TAS-Exp). Norms are provided for each subscale so that discrepancy scores can be calculated by subtraction of T scores. There are 64 items on the experience scales and 64 on the intentions scales, for a total of 128 items. Items are in the form of 3-point Likert-type scales. Retest reliabilities for the four subscales are high (.84–.93). Internal reliabilities are high for TAS-Int, Dis-Int, and Dis-Exp (α = .83–.94) but are lower for TAS-Exp, probably because of its more restricted range. A copy of the scale and college population based norms are included in Zuckerman (1994).

Impulsive Sensation Seeking

The ImpSS scale is part of a five-factor personality scale, the Zuckerman–Kuhlman Personality Questionnaire (ZKPQ; Zuckerman, 2002; see also Zuckerman et al., 1993). The scale is a 19-item true–false form. The five primary subscales in the ZKPQ were derived from factor analyses of scales including the subscales of SSS–V and a variety of impulsivity scales (Zuckerman, 1991; Zuckerman, Kuhlman, et al., 1988). All of the subscales of the SSS and impulsivity scales loaded on a factor along with H. J. Eysenck's P scale. At the opposite pole of this factor were scales for socialization, restraint, responsibility, and inhibition of aggression. We therefore named the factor Impulsive Unsocialized Sensation Seeking. Later item factor analyses also found this factor including all scale elements, except for the items representing socialization. We therefore shortened the name of the scale to Impulsive Sensation Seeking (ImpSS). Aggression and Inhibition of Aggression loaded on another factor (Aggression–Hostility [Agg-Host]) in a five-factor analysis. Aggression represents the unsocialized aspect of the broader factor found in three factor analyses. The other three subscales in the ZKPQ are Sociability, Neuroticism–Anxiety (N-Anx), and Activity.

Alpha reliabilities for the ImpSS are .77 for men and .81 for women in an American college population. The ZKPQ has been translated into Spanish, Catalan, German, Chinese, and Japanese. Reliabilities of ImpSS in these translated scales range from .68 to .83, and all but the lowest of these are in the range of .76 to .83 (Zuckerman, 2002). Retest reliabilities for 3 to 4 weeks in American students is .80. Men score significantly higher than women. Factor analyses of the items within the scale revealed two subfactors: Impulsivity and Sensation Seeking. The type of impulsivity in those items is the "nonplanning" sort. The "Imp" in ImpSS does not think ahead to possible complications when acting on impulse. One may easily engage in risky behavior if one does not think about the risks. The items in the SS part are a combination of Dis and ES types. Unlike items on the SSS–V, there are no specific activities mentioned in the items except for a liking of "wild parties." Most of the items are stated in general terms like "I sometimes do 'crazy' things just for fun." The alpha reliabilities of the Imp subscale are .74 for males and .77 for females. Those for the SS subscale are .64 for males and .68 for females.

The ImpSS is meant to be used as part of the five-factor ZKPQ because it is often a combination of ImpSS with other factors that distinguishes groups. Generalized risk takers, for instance, score high on ImpSS, Agg–Host, and Sociability (Zuckerman & Kuhlman, 2000). Prostitutes score high on ImpSS and Aggression subscales (O'Sullivan, Zuckerman, & Kraft, 1996). Severity of drug abuse and addiction and treatment outcomes among cocaine abusers is related to ImpSS, Agg-Host, and N-Anx (S. A. Ball, 1995). If the ImpSS scale is used out of the context of the entire ZKPQ, it would be desirable to scatter the items among other types of items so that the basic trait is not as obvious as it would be if all the items were grouped together.

ImpSS is not a substitute for the SSS–V, because it does not include the four subscales of the latter. It does correlate highly with the SSS–V Total score ($r = .66$) but only moderately with the subscales TAS, ES, and Dis ($rs = .43–.45$) and lower with BS ($r = .37$). If only an overall measure of sensation seeking is desired, then the ImpSS may serve. But if other research and theoretical considerations indicate a need for one of the SSS–V subscales, then use of ImpSS alone may be less effective. ImpSS should be useful in research on drugs, drinking, and sex, because unlike the SSS–V, it does not confound the item content with the activities predicted and includes a subscale, Impulsivity, which is often involved with sensation seeking in these activities.

Novelty Seeking Scale

Cloninger (1987b; Cloninger, Svrakic, & Przybeck, 1993) has a psychobiological model for personality from which he developed questionnaire measures. He is the only other test designer to make sensation seeking, or *novelty seeking* (NS), a major personality factor rather than a facet of some other factor like Extraversion in the Big Five. NS was originally regarded as one of the three major personality factors, the others being Reward Dependence and Harm Avoidance, and was part of the Tridimensional Personality Questionnaire (Cloninger, 1987b). More recently, the test was expanded to include additional dimensions of personality: persistence, self-directiveness, cooperativeness, and self-transcendence. NS is described as having a "heritable bias in the activation or initiation of behaviors such as frequent exploratory activity in response to novelty, impulsive decision making, extravagance in approach to cues of reward, and quick loss of temper and active avoidance of frustration" (Cloninger et al., 1993, p. 977).

One can see the similarity in definition of NS to SS, particularly ImpSS. The items in NS include impulsivity items of the nonplanning type, as in the ImpSS. The correlation between a 20-item form of NS and ImpSS was .68 (Zuckerman & Cloninger, 1996). NS also correlated highly ($r = .55$) with the SSS–V Total Scale. NS correlated significantly with all of the SSS subscales but most highly with ES and Dis ($rs = .46, .43$).

More recently, Cloninger et al. (1993) constructed four facet scales for the NS: (a) exploratory excitability versus rigidity, (b) impulsiveness versus reflection, (c) extravagance versus reserve, and (d) disorderliness versus regimentation. Harrod (personal communication, 1996) correlated the ImpSS and SSS–V Total score with the NS scale. The SSS Total score correlated highly with NS1 and NS4, and these two facets of NS correlated most highly with Dis and ES among the SSS subscales.

Short Forms for the Sensation Seeking Scale

As previously described, the 22-item SSS–II General Scale can still be used as a shortened form. However, this scale was developed before the four subfactor scales were constructed for the SSS–IV and SSS–V.

Huba, Newcomb, and Bentler (1981) developed a brief form selecting four forced-choice item pairs from each of the SSS subfactors, removing items in which alcohol or drug use was mentioned. The items were put into Likert-type form. Internal consistencies ranged from poor to adequate

(.43–.70). Not much follow-up has been done on this scale, but another group of investigators criticized the deficiencies of the scale and developed one of their own (Hoyle et al., 2002).

Hoyle et al. (2002) selected items from the four SSS–V factors in which the content was appropriate for young and older adolescents and avoided mention of alcohol or drug abuse, dated colloquialisms, or activities unfamiliar to most adolescents. Each of the primary dimensions of sensation seeking is represented by two items, and responses are in a 5-point Likert form ranging from *strongly agree* to *strongly disagree*. No attempt is made to score the subfactors. There is only a total score, adding the weighted responses for eight items, referred to as the Brief Sensation Seeking Scale (BSSS).

Internal consistencies for White and Asiatic/Hispanic groups fell between .74 and .79, whereas those for African American groups were somewhat lower (.68). African American groups scored lower than other groups, particularly because of their lower TAS and ES item scores. There were no ethnic differences on the Dis and BS items. This pattern of ethnic differences is similar to those found for the SSS. Validity consisted of correlations between the BSSS and attitudes toward, and usage of, tobacco, alcohol, and various types of drugs. All of these correlations were significant in all ethnic groups but were generally higher for White than for African American adolescents. The specific results are discussed further in the chapter on drug risk taking.

In a preceding section, I described the development of the ImpSS scale as part of the five-factor ZKPQ scale. Aluja et al. (2006) decided to develop a short form of the ZKPQ using the data from four countries: the United States, Spain, France, and Germany. The data from outside the United States were collected by using translations from the English version into the languages of those countries. The goal was to find a subset of 50 items (10 for each subscale) that loaded on the designated factors in all four countries. They were successful in finding the equivalent five factors among the larger 89-item test and a sufficient number of items loading on the designated factors in all countries. This 50-item cross-cultural short form (ZKPQ-50-CC) more or less guarantees equivalence for the test in these countries and languages. The 10-item ImpSS scale is of particular interest for this book in that it represents the essence of the impulsive sensation seeking factor across countries. The 10 items are listed in Exhibit 1.1. Although only 2 of the 10 items (Items 1 and 9) are from the impulsive facet of the ImpSS, as designated in the longer form, the other sensation seeking items reflect a tendency to engage in spontaneous novelty seeking behaviors without worry about possible risks. Alpha coefficient reliabilities of the short ImpSS scale ranged from .72 to .74 in the four countries. The correlation between the short and long forms of the ImpSS in the total sample was .87.

EXHIBIT 1.1
Short Impulsive Sensation Seeking Scale Based on Item Factor Analyses Done on Translated ZKPQs in Four Countries

1. I often do things on impulse.
2. I would like to take off on a trip with no preplanned or definite routes or timetables.
3. I enjoy getting into new situations where you can't predict how things will turn out.
4. I sometimes like to do things that are a little frightening.
5. I'll try anything once.
6. I would like the kind of life where one is on the move and traveling a lot, with lots of change and excitement.
7. I sometimes do "crazy" things just for fun.
8. I prefer friends who are excitingly unpredictable.
9. I often get so carried away by new and exciting things and ideas that I never think of possible complications.
10. I like "wild" uninhibited parties.

Note. ZKPQ items as presented in Aluja et al., 2006. ZKPQ = Zuckerman–Kuhlman Personality Questionnaire (Zuckerman, 2002; Zuckerman et al., 1993).

Arnett Inventory of Sensation Seeking

Unlike the sensation seeking scales that merely attempt to shorten the standard SSS forms and correct the item content wording, the AISS is also based on a revised construct of sensation seeking (Arnett, 1994). The original definition of *sensation seeking* included both novelty and complexity as characteristics of stimuli sought by high sensation seekers, but it did not include intensity. As described in earlier sections of this chapter, the findings on the HR OR and the visual and auditory cortical EPs, as well as research on music and media preferences (Zuckerman, 2006b), indicated the importance of intensity as well as novelty of stimuli. The more recent definition of sensation seeking includes both factors (Zuckerman, 1994). However, the selection of items for the four factors in the SSS–IV and SSS–V was based on the empirical results from factor analyses of items. Arnett, however, used qualities of novelty and intensity to devise two different subscales for his AISS. He also rejected the use of any items involving "illegal or norm-breaking behavior" such as many of those in the ES and Dis subscales of the SSS. The Total Scale consists of 10 items for a Novelty subscale and 10 for an Intensity subscale. The items are in the form of a four-point Likert scale.

Internal reliabilities were .70 for the Total score and .64 and .50 for the Intensity and Novelty subscales (Arnett, 1994). A more recent study (Roth, 2003) obtained lower reliabilities: .61 for the Total, .53 for intensity, and .52 for Novelty. The AISS Total correlated .41 with the SSS Total score, and the two subscales correlated even lower (Arnett, 1994). The correlations were practically the same for the two subscales of the AISS. Apparently, the SSS includes some of both in its subscales. The Intensity subscale correlated significantly with TAS and Dis, whereas the Novelty subscale correlated with TAS and ES but not with Dis. Neither intensity nor novelty correlated with BS. Demographic data are consistent with those for the SSS if intensity is equated with Dis and Novelty is equated with ES. Adolescents score higher than adults, and males score higher than females, on the Intensity subscale but not the Novelty subscale. On the SSS, scores on the TAS and Dis decline with age after a peak in late adolescence, and males score higher than females on these subscales. ES shows much less decline with age and does not differ between the genders.

Despite its low internal reliabilities, particularly on the subscales, the AISS is correlated with a variety of types of risky behaviors. These findings are discussed in the next chapters.

Other Tests Highly Related to Sensation Seeking Scale Measures

Variety seeking is part of the definition of *sensation seeking* and is found to be a factor in many kinds of behaviors and preferences. For instance, it is the variety of drugs tried rather than a preference for a specific type of drug that is related to sensation seeking among drug users. Among those sensation seekers who watch television, channel switching is more prevalent among high than low sensation seekers. It is not surprising, therefore, that the SSS General Scale is highly related, close to equivalent, with Garlington and Shimona's (1964) Change Seeker Index and Penney and Rienehr's (1966) Stimulus Variation Seeking Scale. The Need for Change, as measured by Jackson's (1974) Personality Research Form, is also strongly related to the SSS–V Total score.

Novelty seeking has always been a central factor in the definition of sensation seeking, and this is the title Cloninger (1987b) gave to his scale, as discussed in previous sections. Pearson (1970) developed a Novelty Experiencing Scale, which distinguished four types of novelty seeking: external sensation (activities), internal sensation (fantasy and feelings), external cognitive (puzzles, games), and internal cognitive (conceptual problems). All of these four scales were significantly correlated with the SSS General Scale, but only the external sensation scale reached levels of near equivalence (Kohn, Hunt, & Hoffman, 1982). Cognitive experience seeking is not related to sensation seeking as defined by the SSS.

I previously mentioned the confusion between (a) the physiological trait of augmenting–reducing based on cortical EP reactions to different intensities of stimulation and (b) Petrie's (1967) use of the term *augmenting–reducing* to describe individual differences in a psychophysical task, the

Kinesthetic Figural Aftereffect (KFA). Vando (1974) developed a questionnaire called the Reducing–Augmenting (R-A) Scales, designed to identify augmenters and reducers without using Petrie's method. The concept of augmenting–reducing pertains to reactions to intensity of stimulation. One difficulty with the test is that it does not actually correlate with the KFA (Davis et al., 1983). Nearly half of the items on the test are quite similar to those found on the SSS. If endorsed, these are scored as "reducing." Some of the remaining items reflect the preference for intense loud types of music. The remaining two factors are called "General Lifestyle" and "Physical Thrill Seeking." Given the item overlap, it is not surprising that the R-A Scales full scale correlates very highly (rs = .60–.71) with the SSS General and Total scores (Dragutinovich, 1987; Kohn, Hunt, Cowles, & Davis, 1986; Kohn et al., 1982). Because of his theoretical identification with the Petrie (1967) model, Vando called what would be high sensation seekers "reducers" and regarded lows as "augmenters," in contradistinction to the findings in humans, cats, and rats using the cortical EP method. There is a patterning of the KFA scales with the SSS subscales. The R-A Scales musical intensity factor correlates most highly with the SSS Dis; the R-A Scales general lifestyle, with the ES and BS; and the R-A Scales thrill seeking, with the TAS.

It is a peculiarity of personality trait research that many times personality tests with different names measure the same thing, or those with the same name measure different things. Block (1995) referred to this as the "jingle-jangle" phenomenon. The real question is not what a test is named but how relevant it is to the construct it purports to operationalize.

The original SSS was developed to measure the optimal level of stimulation and its corollary the optimal level of arousal. Both novelty and intensity increase arousal, and therefore it could be arousal that the high sensation seeker is pursuing, although that theory of sensation seeking was rejected in Zuckerman (1979a). Arousal is regarded now as an epiphenomena of sensation seeking rather than as its primary motive. Mehrabian (1978) developed the scale Arousal Seeking Tendency (AST); many of the items are similar to those on the SSS. It is not surprising that the AST is highly correlated with the SSS General or Total scales (rs = .56–.71) in studies by Kohn et al. (1982) and Furnham (1984). The SSS Total is also negatively correlated (r = –.54) with the Arousal Avoidance subscale of Apter's (1982) Telic Dominance Scale (Murgatroyd, 1985). More jingle-jangle!

Sensation Seeking and the Big Five

Costa and McCrae (1992a) regarded the Big Five model as the "longitude and latitude" of personality measurement, or the criteria of classification for all other personality tests. However, sensation seeking combined with impulsivity is a major factor in another five, the alternative five (Zuckerman, Kuhlman, et al., 1988). However the majority of personality investigators today seem to subscribe to the Big Five, and they seem to want to know the longitude and latitude of sensation seeking on the Big Five map. McCrae (1987) correlated the SSS–V with the NEO Personality Inventory (Costa & McCrae, 1992b) Openness to Experience (OE), their fifth factor. OE correlated moderately with the SSS Total (r = .45) and significantly with all of the SSS subscales except BS. But by far the highest correlation was with the SSS ES subscale (r =.51). Both OE and the SSS correlated with tests of divergent thinking.

Openness in the Revised NEO Personality Inventory (NEO-PI-R; Costa & McCrae, 1992b) has six subscales: Fantasy, Esthetics, Values, Feelings, Actions, and Ideas. Recalling the study by Kohn et al. (1982) relating sensation seeking to Pearson's Novelty Seeking Scale, one would expect that the strongest correlation would be between sensation seeking and Actions (closest to the NS external sensation scale). Within the SSS, the scale most resembling the NEO-PI-R OE is ES.

McCrae and Costa (personal communication, 1990) reported that the total SSS correlated significantly with all six facet scores for OE, but those with Values were highest, followed by those for Action and Fantasy, and those with Esthetics and Ideas were lowest. Again, the highest correlation of OE Total was with the SSS ES scale (r = .54).

Zuckerman et al. (1993) compared the ZKPQ five, the NEO-PI-R five, and the H. J. Eysenck three scales in a factor analysis. The ZKPQ ImpSS, the NEO Conscientiousness, and the H. J. Eysenck P scale all had strong loadings on a common factor. The OE scale did not load on this factor. ImpSS correlated –.51 with Conscientiousness, .28 with NEO Extraversion, and –.23 with NEO Agreeableness, but zero with NEO OE and Neuroticism (Zuckerman, 2002). The connection between sensation seeking and OE is probably limited to the experience seeking aspect of sensation seeking. The main connection between sensation seeking and the NEO is with the conscientiousness dimension. Sensation seekers are open to new experiences and sensations (but not ideas) if they are novel, intense, and exciting, but within the NEO they are mostly distinguished by their lack of conscientiousness. This does not mean that they are antisocial but that they are impulsive and nonconforming.

DEFINITION OF *SENSATION SEEKING*

Although the theory of sensation seeking, in terms of its biosocial sources, has changed, the definition of the trait in terms of its behavioral aspects has only slightly changed since the first book written on the topic

(Zuckerman, 1979a). The main change was the inclusion of intensity as a characteristic of sensations and experiences that are rewarding for high sensation seekers and nonrewarding or aversive to low sensation seekers (Zuckerman, 1994). The following definition from the 1994 book is unchanged as given in the following statement: "Sensation seeking is a trait defined by the seeking of varied, novel, complex, and intense sensations and experiences, and the willingness to take physical, social, legal, and financial risks for the sake of such experience" (Zuckerman, 1994, p. 27).

It should be noted that in this definition, sensation seekers do not seek risk for its own sake. It is not the riskiness of their activities that make them rewarding. In fact, many or most experiences sought by high sensation seekers are not at all risky. Listening to rock music; partying with interesting, stimulating people; and looking at intensely erotic or violent movies or television involve no risk. However, other types of activities, such as driving very fast, engaging in extreme sports, getting drunk or high on drugs, and having unprotected sex with a variety of partners, do involve risk. In the next chapter, I analyze the nature of risk and why sensation seekers are willing to engage in risky behavior for the sake of the rewards of novel and intense stimulation.

2

SENSATION SEEKING AND RISK

It is only by risking our persons from one hour to another that we live
at all.

—William James, *The Will to Believe*

Although risk can be quantified in terms of population statistics, risk
appraisal is a fundamentally subjective matter for the individual (Slovic,
2000c; Yates & Stone, 1992). One can tell the smoker that his chances of
developing lung cancer are 1 in 10 and that his chance of dying from lung
cancer is 15 times that of nonsmokers, but he cannot really believe he will
be the one who dies. The quote by William James suggests frequent risk in
everyday activities, but most persons feel no risk in getting up and going
out to work or play. To people with agoraphobia, however, the world beyond
their front door is a field of terror. A person with obsessive–compulsive
disorder feels there is a terrible risk of infection in touching a doorknob.
Freud (1926/1959) distinguished between neurotic anxiety and objective
anxiety in terms of the realistic appraisal of threat and its source. Objective
anxiety is realistic in the sense that most other people agree on the riskiness
or threat in an external situation. Neurotic anxiety is due to idiosyncratic
risk appraisal stemming from childhood experiences like separation, threat,
or birth itself. Barlow (1988) suggested that the difference between normal
and pathological anxiety is in the interpretation of arousal rather than
autonomic arousal itself. A situation may elicit negative affect and arousal
because of attentional focus on internal or external cues suggestive of harm
or failure. In a normal person, positive expectancies and affect may also
produce arousal but it is experienced as positive affect and attention is
focused on cues for success.

Apart from extreme phobias, there is a wide range of risk appraisals of activities in many everyday situations. A friend will not drive on an expressway in the city. Another friend will not drive at all if there is the slightest hint of snow because she had some minor accidents in those weather conditions. She makes no distinction between snow flurries and a foot of snow. I would not characterize these friends as phobics, but their risk appraisals are highly personal. There are probably more major accidents on the expressway than on streets in cities, and they are more likely to be severe if not fatal. A little snow on the road increases the chances for slipping if it is icy. These people are just hypersensitive to what is a small increase of risk in the immediate situation. This may be based on a generalized hypersensitivity to risk or specific experiences as in the latter case.

Recently, a widely used anaelgesic drug was said to be a risk for heart attack, and millions of people deriving great benefits from the drug were advised to stop taking it. The risk evaluation was based on a study that showed that 2.5% of those taking the drug at high doses over a long period of time developed heart disease, compared with 1.0% of a control group during the same period. The risk was 2.5 times that of those not taking the drug, a highly significant difference because of the large size of the study sample. But in actuality, the risk was increased only 1.5% for those taking the drug. Risk depends on how you view it.

DEFINITIONS OF *RISK*

One dictionary definition of *risk* is "The possibility of suffering harm or loss; danger" (*The American Heritage College Dictionary*, 1977). But there are many kinds of harm or loss. Yates and Stone (1992) suggested six: financial loss (money), performance loss (for a product), physical loss (which can range from transient discomfort to death), psychological loss (of self-esteem), social loss (esteem of others), and time loss. Horvath and Zuckerman (1993) factor analyzed items on a General Risk Appraisal Scale and found four major areas of risk involved in voluntary activities: crime risk (offenses serious enough to warrant arrest), minor violations risk (e. g., traffic offenses), financial risk (loss of money from gambling or business investment), and sports risk (injuries incurred in sporting activities).

Yates and Stone (1992) defined three characteristics of risk in any activity: potential losses, significance of the losses, and uncertainty of the losses. Potential losses depend on their probability, often a subjective estimate. Significance of losses depends on individual circumstances. Financial risk, for instance, is relative to one's financial resources. Risk of losing $500 may be trivial to a millionaire but a matter of shelter (paying the rent) or survival (eating) to a person living in poverty. Uncertainty of outcome is a major element of risk. Here again, there is a subjective element for many kinds of risk. Life insurance is based on the uncertainty of when one will die. If an outcome is certain, one takes action accordingly. If it is uncertain, one must appraise the likelihood of negative and positive outcomes.

Decisions about whether to accept risks in any activity depend on the benefits, or anticipated positive outcomes, as well as the risks. Betting is a simple example of risk–benefit ratio. Betting the lottery is based on the possibility (however improbable) of winning millions of dollars compared with the risk of losing a small sum of money for the lottery ticket. Most people are aware of the risks of driving a car, but the benefits far outweigh the risks. For those living outside of urban areas, the car is not just a benefit but a necessity. For the activities involving unnecessarily risky sensation seeking behavior, however, the benefits are more obscure, at least to low sensation seekers. Why use a drug that involves physical, legal, and social risks? Why drive recklessly and at excessive speeds when there is no time urgency? The hedonistic rewards of sensation seeking are perceived as benefits only by high sensation seekers. But even if the benefits are understood, why are high sensation seekers not deterred by the risks? The answer, discussed in more detail later in this chapter, is that they either underestimate the risks or are willing to accept them because the benefits are judged to outweigh them.

In subsequent sections of this chapter, I focus on risky activities associated with sensation seeking. These are voluntary rather than involuntary risks. Most people see nuclear power as a beneficial resource, but risky. Those who feel that the risks of catastrophe outweigh the benefits cannot directly influence the risks and can act only indirectly through political action. The nuclear reactors are here, for better or worse. However, those who smoke, drink, drive, ski, or choose risky professions like fire fighting entertain the risks to enjoy the benefits they derive from the activities.

RISK APPRAISAL

The risk of winning or losing on the roll of the dice can be statistically calculated. Records collected by governmental agencies provide objective risk for dying or contracting disease from certain activities like smoking. However, the risk directly influencing behavior is the risk appraisal of the individual that may be at variance with objective indexes of risk.

Death Risk

Premature death is an extreme form of risk and is one of the few kinds for which there are statistical data. Table 2.1 shows some selected activities

TABLE 2.1
Fatality Estimates and Rankings of Perceived Risk for
Some Voluntary Activities

	Fatality estimates[a]		Ranking of risk	
Risky activities	Technical fatality estimates per year	M estimates of students	Experts	Students
Smoking	150,000	2,400	2	3
Alcohol	100,000	2,600	3	7
Motor vehicles	41,000	10,500	1	5
Motorcycles	3,000	1,600	6	6
Mountain climbing	30	70	29	22
Skiing	18	72	30	25
Fire fighting	195	390	18	10
Police work	160	390	17	3

Note. [a]From *The Perception of Risk* (pp.112, 115), edited by P. Slovic, 2000, London: Earthscan. Copyright 2000 by P. Slovic. Originally published in "Rating the Risks," by P. Slovic, B. Fischhoff, and S. Lichtenstein, 1979, *Environment, 21*, pp. 14–20, 36–39. Copyright 1979 by Heldorf Publications. Adapted with permission.

and the annual fatality estimates, derived from government agencies. The table also shows the geometric means of estimates made by students for the same activities. The major source of fatalities are those endangering health, particularly smoking and drinking. The next most deadly are accidents in motor vehicles and on motorcycles. Handguns and electric power are also major sources of fatality, but I do not discuss these here. Note that students markedly underestimate annual fatalities due to smoking, drinking, and driving and overestimate those due to risky sports like mountain climbing and skiing. They also overestimate those involved in fire fighting and police work. Slovic (2000a) compared the rankings of riskiness for these activities by college students and risk experts, and these are also shown in Table 2.1. The relative rankings of risk were fairly close. The students ranked drinking and driving as somewhat less risky than did the experts, and they ranked mountain climbing, skiing, fire fighting, and police work as more risky than did the experts. Students agreed with experts on the high rank of smoking, even if they underestimated the death rate. If one calculates the deaths due to smoking in smokers over 30 years, it would come to about 12%. But most young smokers do not think they will be smoking for 30 years, underestimating the addictive nature of nicotine.

Perceived risks tend to be inversely related to perceived benefits (Slovic, Fischhoff, & Lichtenstein, 2002b). Table 2.2 shows the perceived risks of death and benefits of selected voluntary activities rated on a 0 to 100 scale by respondents. It must be stressed that the risks are only for fatalities, not for legal or social risks. For smoking and most drugs (heroin, barbiturates, morphine, amphetamines), perceived risks outweigh benefits, but for alcohol they are closer, and for caffeine and marijuana, benefits

TABLE 2.2
Perceived Risks and Benefits for Some Voluntary Activities

Activity	Risks	Benefits
Smoking	68	24
Heroin	63	17
Barbiturates	57	27
Alcohol	57	49
Motor vehicles	55	76
Amphetamines	55	27
Morphine	53	31
Fire fighting	44	83
Police work	43	75
Motorcycles	43	43
Caffeine	30	42
Football	30	54
Mountain climbing	28	47
Scuba diving	26	41
Downhill skiing	26	57
Surfing	21	41
Marijuana	21	53
Jogging	14	65

Note. The perceived risk of death and the perceived benefits are on a 0 to 100 scale. From *The Perception of Risk* (p. 143), edited by P. Slovic, 2000, London: Earthscan. Copyright 2000 by P. Slovic. Originally published in *Societal Risk Assessment: How Safe Is Safe Enough?* (pp. 203–204), edited by R. C. Schwing and W. A. Albers, 1980, New York: Plenum Press. Copyright 1980 by Springer-Verlag. Adapted with permission.

outweigh risks. Smoking tobacco is seen as even more risky than using drugs like heroin and barbiturates, with little perceived benefit. Presumably these data are mostly influenced by nonsmokers and nonusers of any of these drugs. A comparison of users and nonusers on perceived risks and benefits would be informative, particularly on perceived benefits.

For sports (football, mountain climbing, scuba diving, downhill skiing and surfing), risks are relatively low and perceived benefits higher; for jogging, benefits far outweigh any risks. Fire fighting and police work are seen as intermediate in risk but highly beneficial.

Novelty and Experience

Slovic, Fischhoff, and Lichtenstein (2000a) found several factors influencing risk appraisal. Voluntary activities were perceived as more beneficial and the risk was more acceptable than were involuntary sources of risk. Catastrophic potential is a major factor for nonvoluntary risks like nuclear power, but the risks for sensation seeking activities are mostly for the individuals engaging in them. Severity of consequences and their controllability are important. The consequence of an unopened parachute for a skydiver is quite severe and certain to be fatal, but careful packing of the chute and training in jumping seem to make the risk controllable. Novelty tends to increase risk appraisal, and familiarity tends to reduce it. This is understandable because fear tends to habituate with noninjurious experience.

Zuckerman (1979b) had subjects rate 116 situations for their novelty, defined by number of times an individual had experienced the situation, and risk of physical, mental, and punishment or loss harm. A substantial correlation (.56) was found between novelty and risk appraisal. However, the scatter plot clearly showed that that the correlation was produced entirely by the relationship at the low end of the novelty dimension or high experience. There were no situations that an individual had frequently experienced that were considered even moderately risky. But among the very novel, nonexperienced situations, an equal number were appraised as low or high risk. Familiarity may breed contempt, but it also makes for tranquility.

Is there a general risk-appraisal tendency? In the previous study (i.e., Zuckerman, 1979b), the ratings for the three kinds of risk, physical, mental, and punishment, were highly intercorrelated: .80, .77, and .74 in men and .78, .61, and .62 in women. In another study, the risk appraisals were classified into six areas: driving, substance use, sexual behavior, safety, social, and delinquency (Bell, Schoenrock, & O'Neal, 2000). The correlations among the six areas were all significant (range = .27–.69 for men and .28–.52 for women). Horvath and Zuckerman (1993) classified risk appraisals into four categories: crime, minor violations, financial, and sports. The correlations were mostly significant (range =.12–.50). The correlations between risks classified by broad types are high, and those classified by areas of behavior are low to moderate. However, there is evidence for a broad risk-appraisal factor.

Gender, Ethnicity, Sensation Seeking, and Risk Appraisal

Many studies have shown that women tend to judge risks as higher than do men for a variety of things. Women estimate risks connected with AIDS, drinking, street drugs, cigarette smoking, and motor vehicle accidents about 10% to 15% higher than do men (Flynn, Slovic, & Mertz, 1994). Similar differences are found for ethnicity, with people of ethnicities besides White estimating risks as higher for a variety of factors including alcohol and drugs. These differences are consistent with the finding that sensation seeking is higher in men than in women and in Whites than in African Americans (Zuckerman, 1979a, 1994).

RISKY BEHAVIOR

In subsequent chapters, I describe studies on sensation seeking in specific areas of risky behavior. In this chapter, the exposition is on studies in which subjects were asked about risky behaviors in several areas and in which general risk taking across areas was related to sensation seeking. We have seen that there is evidence for a general risk-appraisal factor, but we must ask if there is also evidence for a general factor among different types of risky behaviors.

Risk Appraisal, Risky Behavior, and Sensation Seeking

Bell et al. (2000) found that risky behaviors in all six areas (driving, substance use, sexual behavior, safety, social, and delinquency) were significantly intercorrelated for women (rs = .13–.50) and men (rs = .36–.70). The highest correlations for both women and men were between substance use and sexual risk taking. Arnett's (1994) Inventory of Sensation Seeking (AISS) correlated negatively with mens' and womens' mean scores on the six risk perception subscales (rs = −.43, −.48). Using a regression model, Bell et al. found significant influences on mean risky behavior for gender (β = −.34), religion (β = .07), and sensation seeking (β = .53). Greater generalized risky behaviors were highest in male sensation seekers with little or no religious training in their backgrounds.

Horvath and Zuckerman (1993) reported significant negative correlations between the Sensation Seeking Scale Form V (SSS–V) and risk appraisals for crime, minor violations, and sports, but not for financial risks. Zuckerman (1979b) found significant negative correlations between the Total risk appraisal (sum of physical, mental, and punishment risks) and the SSS–V Total, −.42 for men and −.40 for women. Correlations between H. J. Eysenck's (1967) Extraversion, Neuroticism, and Psychoticism scales and total risk appraisal were close to zero. This study used hypothetical situations that were novel for most subjects, thereby controlling for the subjects' actual experience with the situations.

The four types of risky behaviors in the Horvath and Zuckerman (1993) study were significantly intercorrelated. The correlations were relatively low, ranging from .15 to .51, with 4 of them in the .20 to .30 range. The highest correlation was between risky criminal behavior and minor violations. SSS Total scores correlated significantly with risky behaviors for crime (r = .53), minor violations (r = .43), financial risk taking (r = .22), and risky sports (r = .24). A scale for impulsivity was also used in this study. It correlated significantly, but lower than sensation seeking, with all four types of risky behavior.

A multiple regression was done, including reported peer behavior and risk appraisal, as well as the two personality variables, in predicting risky behavior. Peer behavior was the most powerful influence for risky behavior in all four categories of risk. Sensation seeking was next in predictive power, followed by risk appraisal. Impulsivity had little independent predictive power.

Two models were tested against each other. In the first, risk appraisal was in the path of causation between sensation seeking and risky behavior. In the second model, risky behavior mediated the pathway between sensation seeking and risk appraisal. The second model was superior to the first. This result suggests that risk appraisal is a function of experience, that is, perceived risk is lowered by engaging in the risky activity.

Rosenbloom (2003a) used a Risk Evaluation (RE) inventory in which subjects rate the dangerousness of different kinds of activities including sports (parachuting, bungee jumping), health (smoking, unprotected sex), legal (gambling, drug use), and everyday risks (crossing against a red light, cheating in examinations). Both voluntary and forced risks (like undergoing surgery) are included. The Risk Taking (RT) inventory consisted of the same items with actual frequency of experience ratings. The correlations between scales within the RE and RT inventories are not reported. The SSS–V correlated negatively with RE ($r = -.56$), even when RT was controlled ($r = -.38$), and positively with RT ($r = .58$), even when RE was controlled ($r = .42$). Comparisons of levels of each showed that high sensation seekers are higher than low sensation seekers in terms of risk taking and low sensation seekers are higher than highs in terms of risk evaluation.

Gullone, Moore, Moss, and Boyd (2000) also developed a risk appraisal and a risky behavior scale using the same items. Factor analyses, using oblimin rotations (allowing for correlated factors), yielded four factors, which were quite similar for risk appraisal and risky behaviors. Factor 1, Thrill Seeking behaviors, included most risky sports and flying; Factor 2, Rebellious behaviors, included drinking, smoking, drugs, and staying out late; Factor 3, Reckless behaviors, was a reckless and illegal driving factor and included driving and drinking, stealing cars for joyrides, and speeding. It also included having unprotected sex. Factor 4 was labeled Antisocial behaviors, although only cheating and sniffing glue were antisocial; overeating, teasing and picking on people, and talking to strangers were also included, although these could not be described as antisocial behaviors.

The Thrill Seeking risk subscores correlated positively with the corresponding behavior scale, with rs from .59 to .74; Rebellious subscale correlations between risk appraisal and behavior ranged from $-.51$ to $-.57$; Reckless risk appraisal scores correlated $-.2$ to $-.38$ with behavior; and Antisocial appraisal subscales varied from $-.14$ to $-.19$ with behaviors. Although all correlations were significant, those for the Thrill Seeking and Rebellious factors were clearly higher than those for the other two factors. In comparison with other factors in which the risk appraisal–behavior correlation was negative, the one for Thrill Seeking was positive. In other words, the more risky the activity the more likely individuals were attracted to it. I have said previously that although sensation seeking is defined by a tolerance for risk, risk is not the point of it (Zuckerman, 1994). But this may not be true for adolescents looking for thrills through sports. The higher sensation seekers may find the riskiness of the activity part of the attraction to extreme sports. Parachuting may be preferred to volleyball not only for the novel sensations it provides but also because the risk makes it more exciting.

Rolison and Scherman (2002) used a questionnaire containing 19 risk behaviors (not described) and scales for frequency of risk involvement (behavior), perceived benefits of risk involvement, and perceived risks of involvement. An interesting finding was that perceived risks and benefits correlated positively ($r = .28$), suggesting that for these adolescents, at least, the riskier behaviors also yielded the highest benefits. Sensation seeking (using the SSS–V) and Locus of Control (LC) traits were also measured. The SSS, particularly the Disinhibition (Dis) subscale, correlated negatively with perceived risks and positively with perceived benefits. LC did not correlate with any of these three but was removed from the analysis because it acted as a suppressor variable. The multiple regression revealed that the two significant predictors of frequency of involvement in risky behaviors were the Dis subscale and the total perceived risk score. Together they accounted for 50% of the variance in risk taking frequency. Perceived benefits were not independently involved in the prediction.

Risks and benefits are translated into specific negative and positive expectations for a particular kind of risk taking. Benthin et al. (2000) assessed images generated using a free-association test with specific risk-taking activities as stimulus words. The subjects were high school students, ages 14 to 20. Their responses were classified as positive or negative concepts or outcomes. For instance, for "drinking beer," examples of positive concepts were "good taste" and "socially accepted," and examples of negative concepts were "bad taste" and "illegal." Examples of positive outcomes were "fun and pleasure" and "social facilitation." Examples of negative outcome expectations were "cognitive impairment" and "accidents."

Table 2.3 shows the percentage of positive and negative images (concepts plus outcomes) generated by each of the activities as stimuli. For all four substance uses, negative images were more frequent associations than positive images. For the two sexually related stimuli, exercise, and seat-belt use, the positive images were more frequent than the negative images. Despite the preponderance of negative imagery for substance use, about half of the respondents reported participating occasionally or frequently in drinking beer and liquor. Participation in smoking tobacco and marijuana was less frequent. The most frequent positive outcomes in images generated by those using substances were fun and pleasure and social facilitation, with physical arousal or relaxation as secondary images. But for cigarettes, it was primarily social facilitation and relaxation rather than fun. For sexual intercourse, the main positive outcome was primarily fun and pleasure and arousal.

TABLE 2.3

Percentages of Positive (Concepts + Outcomes) and Negative
Associations for Activities

Activities	Positive associations %	Negative associations %
Beer	30	45
Liquor	22	52
Cigarettes	36	73
Marijuana	14	44
Sexual intercourse	47	19
Condom use	55	28
Exercise	54	15
Seat-belt use	52	33

Note. Data from Benthin et al. (2000).

Imagery generated by the activity words were related to behavior in those activities. The subjects had made affective ratings (positive or negative) for each of their associations, and these ratings were used in regression analyses predicting participation in health-related behaviors. Positive affective ratings were more effective than were negative affective ratings in predicting drinking liquor, smoking marijuana, and having sexual intercourse. Negative affective ratings were stronger predictors for cigarette smoking and seat-belt use. The absence of negative ratings predicted risk taking in smoking and nonuse of seat belts. Put another way, benefits were most salient in drinking, drugs, and sex, and associated risks were more influential in smoking and seat-belt use. These findings should be of interest to those designing advertisements designed to reduce risky behaviors.

Zuckerman and Kuhlman (2000) conducted a broad risk-taking study using the Zuckerman–Kuhlman Personality Questionnaire (ZKPQ; Zuckerman, 2002; Zuckerman, Kuhlman, Joireman, Teta, & Kraft, 1993), a five-factor personality test described in chapter 1. The advantage of this test is that in contrast to the SSS–V, it does not include specific item content that might be confounded with the types of risk taking, for instance, drinking, drugs, or sex. The Impulsive Sensation Seeking (ImpSS) scale in the ZKPQ measures a general need for excitement and impulsivity in seeking activities. The six types of risk taking, assessed with a Life Experiences Questionnaire included drinking, smoking, drugs, sex, driving, and gambling.

Table 2.4 shows the correlations among the six types of risk-taking behaviors for male and female college students. Risky drinking, smoking, drugs, and sex were all significantly intercorrelated for both men and women. The only correlation for driving, however, was with drinking (an unfortunate combination in terms of risk). Gambling was correlated with drinking and

TABLE 2.4
Correlations Among Risk-Taking Behaviors

Risk scales	1	2	3	4	5	6
1. Drinking	—	.32***	.31***	.35***	.25*	.37***
2. Smoking	.44***	—	.51***	.31***	-.02	.13
3. Drugs	.35***	.43***	—	.40***	.04	.18
4. Sex	.33***	.29***	.23**	—	.08	.29**
5. Driving	.27***	.11	.09	.11	—	.16
6. Gambling	.07	-.02	-.02	-.02	.06	—

Note. Men ($n = 101$) above diagonal, women ($n = 159$) below diagonal.
*$p < .05$. **$p < .01$. ***$p < .001$.

sex for men but did not correlate with the other types of risk for women. A composite risk-taking measure was formed by adding item mean scores across the six types of risk.

Men scored higher than women on drug risk, risky driving, and gambling and on the composite risk measure. Men scored higher than women on the ZKPQ ImpSS scale, and women scored higher than men on the Neuroticism–Anxiety (N-Anx) and Sociability (Sy) scales. These differences are consistent with those in the ZKPQ norms for college students (Zuckerman, 2002).

The ImpSS scale correlated significantly with drinking, smoking, drugs, and sex, but not with driving or gambling, for both men and women. Drinking also correlated with Aggression–Hostility (Agg-Host) and Sy for both genders. Sy correlated with drugs, sex, and gambling risk for men but not for women.

Gender and the five ZKPQ scales were entered into a multiple regression in prediction of the composite risk-taking score. ImpSS, Agg-Host, and Sy were all significant and independent predictors of total risk taking. Gender was significant only if entered first, but when entered after ImpSS, it was no longer significant, showing that its effect was mediated entirely by the gender difference on ImpSS. The three personality variables each accounted for only 5% to 6% of the variance on risk taking, but the total of all variables accounted for 26% of the variance.

The female and male samples were divided into high, middle, and upper thirds on the basis of the composite risk score and the means for the three ranges are plotted in Figures 2.1 and 2.2 against the T scores from the larger normative groups. The high risk takers are characterized by higher scores on ImpSS, Sy, and Agg-Host for the women and men. The male high and middle risk-taking groups are average on Agg-Host, but the low

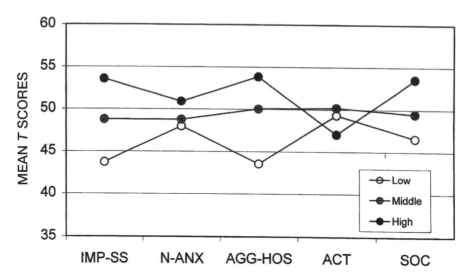

Figure 2.1. Female Zuckerman–Kuhlman Personality Questionnaire (ZKPQ) scale means (*T* scores) for high-, medium-, and low-risk-taking groups on the composite risk score. IMP-SS = Impulsive Sensation Seeking; N-ANX = Neuroticism–Anxiety; AGG-HOS = Aggression–Hostility; ACT = Activity; SOC = Sociability. From "Personality and Risk Taking: Common Biosocial Factors," by M. Zuckerman and D. M. Kuhlman, 2000, *Journal of Personality, 68*, p. 1013. Copyright 2000 by Blackwell. Reprinted with permission.

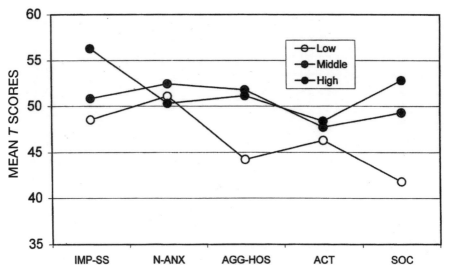

Figure 2.2. Male Zuckerman–Kuhlman Personality Questionnaire (ZKPQ) scale means (*T* scores) for high-, medium-, and low-risk-taking groups on the composite risk score. IMP-SS = Impulsive Sensation Seeking; N-ANX = Neuroticism–Anxiety; AGG-HOS = Aggression–Hostility; ACT = Activity; SOC = Sociability. From "Personality and Risk Taking," by M. Zuckerman and D. M. Kuhlman, 2000, *Journal of Personality, 68,* p. 1013. Copyright 2000 by Blackwell. Reprinted with permission.

risk takers are particularly low in aggression compared with norms. N-Anx and Activity (Act) are not involved in general risk taking.

Arnett (1996) found that his sensation seeking scale, the AISS, given to college students correlated with risky behaviors in driving, sex, drug and alcohol use, and criminal behavior. All of the correlations were significant but low (most rs = .20–.30). A scale of aggressiveness correlated with a more limited number of variables: driving recklessly, number of sexual partners, vandalism, and theft. The correlation of sensation seeking with multiple forms of reckless behavior was .42, and the correlation of aggressiveness was .25. Aggressiveness also correlated with risky driving and sex in the Zuckerman and Kuhlman (2000) study.

In a second study, Arnett (1998) used a risky behavior experience report that included driving (speeding) and other reckless driving habits, binge drinking, smoking marijuana or using other illegal drugs, and risky sexual behavior. Nearly all of the items composing these scales were significantly intercorrelated, with most correlations in the .30 to .50 range. Sensation seeking was positively associated with driving while intoxicated, driving over 80 miles per hour and 20 miles per hour over the speed limit, binge drinking, smoking marijuana, having sex with strangers, and number of sexual partners. Sensation seeking remained significantly related to risky behaviors even after controlling for the influence of gender, age, and education. Religiosity, marital status, and parenthood also accounted for some variance in risky behaviors.

Bradley and Wildman (2002) also studied risky behaviors using the AISS. Their "reckless" risk-taking scale included substance use, reckless sex, and reckless driving. These three types of risk taking were significantly intercorrelated (rs = .46, .50, .32). The weakest correlation was between reckless sex and driving. A separate scale for risky behavior consisted of risky sports and motorbike riding. This correlated significantly with all three reckless behavior scales (rs = .33, .26, .46). Sensation seeking correlated significantly with reckless sex, drugs, driving, the total reckless score, and the risky behavior score. Females scored lower than males on both reckless and risky behaviors. Subjects in their teens scored higher than subjects in their 20s on risky behaviors, but subjects in their 20s scored higher on reckless behaviors. Sensation seeking predicted total reckless and risky behaviors even after demographic and social desirability were controlled.

The study by Lejuez et al. (2002) is unique in that it included a behavioral test along with questionnaire measures of sensation seeking and impulsivity to predict self-reported life behavior. Because the study by Bradley and Wildman (2002) showed some effect of social desirability in interaction with gender, it would be useful to have a behavioral measure of risk taking. The Balloon Analogue Risk Task (BART; Lejuez et al., 2002) involves inflating a balloon portrayed on a computer, with each puff earning money in a reserve. If the inflation goes beyond a certain point, the balloon explodes and all money accumulated in the temporary bank is lost.

The risky behavior report consisted of smoking, drugs, gambling, sex (number of partners), stealing, and seat-belt use when driving. A factor analysis of the risky behaviors found two factors: Delinquency Risk (including stealing, alcohol, and gambling), and Substance Use and Sexual Risk behaviors (including cigarette smoking, number of drugs used, alcohol, seat-belt use when driving, and number of sexual partners). The last factor resembles the core of the factor found in Zuckerman and Kuhlman (2000), which also included smoking, drinking, drugs, and sex.

The BART correlated significantly with all of the risky behavior scales and items, and with four of the five impulsivity and sensation seeking scales. The SSS–V Total correlated with all risky behaviors except number of cigarettes smoked and the use of seat belts. The correlation with the drinking scale was very high ($r = .58$). The impulsivity and constraint scales all correlated with drinking, drugs, gambling, and sex. In multiple regressions, the BART added some significant variance in analyses of both risky behavior factors after controlling for demographic and impulsivity and sensation seeking factors.

The number of accidents children have could be related to their risky sensation seeking behaviors. Potts, Martinez, and Dedmon (1995), using children between the ages of 6 and 9 years old, gave their subjects a sensation seeking scale adapted for children and that used choices of picture portraying activities instead of text items. They also used peer and teacher ratings of risk taking, a risky-behavior checklist filled out by the parents, and an injury-frequency list also filled out by the parents. A pictorial self-report test was also used. The test shows risky situations of a type that are frequent sources of accidents for children. The children are asked to indicate what they would do by placing a figure on the picture at some point from the dangerous area. All but one of the 15 intercorrelations between these measures were significant. All of the measures other than the child version of the SSS were significantly correlated with actual injury frequency. The SSS correlation was only slightly short of significance. Self-, peer, and parent reports confirmed that high sensation seeking children engaged in more risky behaviors. It is not surprising that children who engage in risky behaviors are more likely to have accidents and injuries.

M. K. Wagner (2001) studied four types of risky behaviors in a college sample: alcohol and drug use, risky sexual behavior, reckless driving, and theft and vandalism. The correlations among the four types of risky behavior were all significant ($rs = .18$ to $.35$). Sensation seeking, anxiety sensitivity, and self-reinforcement scales were used as predictors. *Anxiety sensitivity* is defined as fear of the symptoms of anxiety or their consequences (Reiss & McNally, 1985). On the basis of previous research (done on groups with anxiety disorders), M. K. Wagner expected anxiety sensitivity to correlate positively with substance use but negatively with the other kinds of risk-taking behaviors. Sensation seeking was expected to correlate positively with substance use and all four types of risk taking, and it did. But anxiety sensitivity actually correlated positively with substance abuse.

The expectation that anxiety is high in substance abusers is based on the self-medication hypothesis, which suggests that people drink and use illegal drugs to reduce anxiety and depression. Older substance abusers often have high levels of anxiety, but generally as a consequence of substance use and the life stresses it produces rather than as a cause. Withdrawal symptoms also are a source of dysphoria in drug-dependent persons. Adolescents who are abusers but not yet drug-dependent are less commonly anxious or depressed. They use drugs for pleasure and social facilitation rather than for dysphoria reduction. This topic is treated in more detail in the next chapter.

Summary

Risk appraisals in different areas of risk are intercorrelated, as are risky behaviors across different kinds of risk. There is a general factor of risk sensitivity and risk taking that includes most forms of risk taking, particularly smoking, drinking, drugs, sex, reckless driving, and minor criminal behavior. Financial risk, as in gambling, is more peripheral and is involved more in men than women. Sports risk in extreme sports is also related to other kinds of risk in the studies that have included it.

Risk appraisal is a significant factor in the prediction of risky behavior. It is also negatively related to sensation seeking. High sensation seekers tend to estimate risks as lower even in activities they have not experienced to any extent. Sensation seeking is related to risk taking in all kinds of risk areas. This is true of children as well as adolescents and young adults. In fact, the sensation seeking trait may be the common factor that accounts for the relationships among different kinds of risk taking.

Impulsivity and aggression have also been found to be factors in risky behaviors, although to a lesser degree than sensation seeking. Anxiety as a trait does not seem to be involved, at least in adolescent risk-takers. However, anxiety as a state may certainly be involved in the inhibition of impulsive sensation seeking activities. The anticipation of fear may be as much a deterrent to risky behavior as the anticipation of harm. Some studies done in the 1970s explored this possibility using hypothetical situations. These are discussed next.

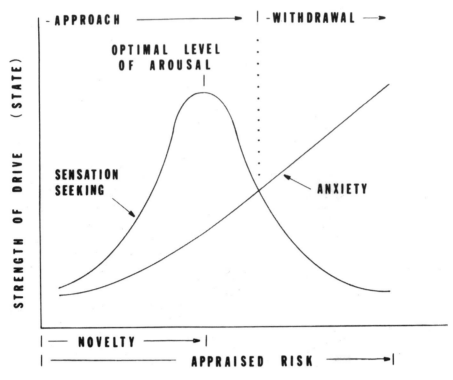

Figure 2.3. Theoretical model showing the relationship between novelty and appraised risk and affective states of anxiety and sensation seeking. State scores from the Sensation Seeking and Anxiety States Scale are on the ordinate. Situations are placed on the abscissa as a function of their mean risk ratings by an independent group. From *Stress and Anxiety* (Vol. 3, pp. 141–170), edited by I. G. Sarason and C. D. Spielberger, 1976, Washington, DC: Hemisphere Publication Services. Copyright 1976 by Hemisphere Publication Services. Reprinted with permission.

INTERACTION OF ANTICIPATED AFFECTS
IN RISK-TAKING BEHAVIOR

Figure 2.3 illustrates a theoretical model showing the relationships between novelty and appraised risk and affective states of anxiety (negative arousal) and sensation seeking (positive arousal; Zuckerman, 1976). This is a generalized model in which the curves shown are expected to be shifted according to levels of trait sensation seeking and trait anxiety.

In the model, anxiety increases linearly as a function of appraised risk. In a conflict model, anxiety increases in spatial or temporal proximity to the risky situation (Dollard & Miller, 1950; Epstein, 1982; N. E. Miller, 1944). In the approach–avoidance conflict, the outcome depends on the relative strengths of conditioned motives (i.e., shared cues associated with shock or food). N. E. Miller (1944) tested the model on rats. It is difficult to test the model in humans because of the difficulty of creating strong motives in the laboratory. Epstein (1982), however, studied a human conflict between a natural fear (falling from heights) and whatever rewards are anticipated as a function of parachute jumping (presumably novel, exciting, or sensation seeking experience).

Fenz and Epstein (1967) measured arousal, using an electrodermal (EDL) measure, and self-ratings of fear at various spatiotemporal points prior to the actual jump, that is, the previous day, reaching the airport on the day of the jump, taking off in the airplane, midpoint altitude, and final altitude for the jump. Novice parachutists showed a sharp gradient of arousal with a sharp increase in EDL after take off, accelerating sharply as the time of the jump drew nearer. Ratings of fear also showed a gradient peaking at the time of the ready signal for the jump. The fear arousal gradients of the experienced jumpers differed from those of the novices. Their arousal levels did not increase after take-off and actually decreased at the final altitude prior to jumping. Their fear ratings peaked at the final checkout before boarding the plane and then decreased steadily to the time of the actual jump. The difference illustrates the extinction of anxiety as a function of actual experience. There was no measure of the strength of positive anticipatory emotions at each stage.

The model shown in Figure 2.3 suggests that positive emotion (sensation seeking) increases with novelty and appraised risk up to some maximal level and then decreases as a function of further appraised risk. At some point, risk appraisal and the anxiety it induces reduce the sensation seeking motive and the positive arousal it produces. Up to that point, the tendency is to approach the situation, but this optimal level of sensation seeking arousal and approach decrease as anxiety increases. At some point where the balance between anxiety and sensation seeking shifts to a dominance by anxiety, avoidance or withdrawal occur. The model suggests that in high trait sensation seekers, the anxiety gradient is lower and the sensation seeking curve is shifted to the right compared with low sensation seekers. The result is that high sensation seekers are more likely to enter into risky situations and low sensation seekers are more likely to avoid them.

To measure anxiety and sensation seeking as states, Zuckerman (1979b) used the Neary (1975) Sensation Seeking and Anxiety States Scale (SSAST; see Zuckerman, 1994, Appendix J). In the SSAST, ratings are made of current feelings on adjectives selected for two scales: (a) anxiety, with words like *frightened, tense, panicky,* and *worried*; and (b) sensation seeking, a kind of surgent, positive arousal indicated by words such as *elated, enthusiastic, adventurous,* and *playful*. Situations were selected along gradients of appraised risk. But because appraised risk differs between high and low sensation seekers, only situations were used for which high and low groups did not differ in ratings of risk.

There were two classes of situation that met these criteria, participation in psychological experiments and travel. For the experiments, the lowest point in the gradient was obtained from the SSAST given in a neutral classroom situation, presumably of low appraised risk. In order of increasing risk for the experimental situations, the mean risk ratings (in parentheses) were social psychology experiment (2.1), hypnosis (3.7), and taking an unknown drug that might "produce unusual effects" (7.4). Previous studies of volunteering had shown that high sensation seekers tended to volunteer for hypnosis and drug experiments, but there were no differences between high and low sensation seekers in volunteering for learning or social psychology experiments (Zuckerman, 1976). However, ratings of risk appraisal for these situations were negative but were not significantly correlated with trait sensation seeking in males; the correlations for females were also low but negative and significant.

For the travel situations, the mean risk ratings were as follows: Europe (1.5), United States (2.1), Asia (3.1), Antarctica (5.2), and the moon (5.4). Note that travel in Europe was rated less risky than travel in the United States. These ratings were made before the current era of terrorism. The correlations between appraised riskiness for each of the situations and trait sensation seeking were all low and nonsignificant.

Subjects were asked to indicate how they would feel if they were about to start traveling in each of the travel situations and how they would feel if they were about to participate in each of the experimental situations, using an abbreviated form of the SSAST. Figure 2.4 shows the anticipatory anxiety and sensation seeking state scores for each situation. For the travel situations, the forms of the affect gradients in relation to degree of riskiness of the situations is as predicted from the model. Anxiety states increase more or less linearly with appraised risk of the situations, whereas sensation seeking states peak earlier in the risk continuum and then decline. For the experiments, the sensation seeking gradient is flatter and lower and the two gradients intersect about midway in the risk continuum closer to the prediction from the model (see Figure 2.3).

Figure 2.5 shows the anticipated state anxiety and sensation seeking for those high or low on trait sensation seeking in the experiment situations. Initially, in the ordinary classroom occasion, there are no differences between high and low trait sensation seekers. But as the riskiness of the situations increases, the state anxiety rises faster in the low sensation seekers. State sensation seeking does not rise in the low trait sensation seekers and falls sharply for the most risky situation (taking an unknown drug). In the high trait sensation seekers, there is a rise in state sensation seeking in the moderate risk experiments and the drop in the most risky experiment is not as pronounced.

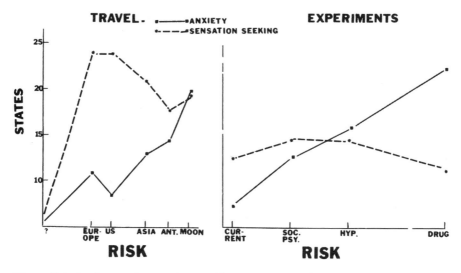

Figure 2.4. Anxiety and sensation seeking state scores in response to hypothetical situations of increasing risk. State scores from the Sensation Seeking and Anxiety States Scale are on the ordinate. Situations are placed on the abscissa as a function of their mean risk ratings by an independent group. ANT. = Antartica; SOC. PSY. = social psychology; HYP. = hypnosis. From *Emotions in Personality and Psychopathology* (p. 176), edited by C. E. Izard, 1979, New York: Plenum Press. Copyright 1979 by Springer-Verlag. Reprinted with permission.

Figure 2.6 contrasts the state anxiety and sensation seeking scores within the trait high and low sensation seeking male subjects. The male data are better than the female data because there is no correlation between the risk ratings of situations and trait sensation seeking in the males, in contrast to the significant negative correlations in the female subjects. Thus, the male data are not confounded with individual differences in risk appraisal.

In low trait sensation seekers, the state anxiety gradient is steeper than in the high trait sensation seekers, and the state sensation seeking falls precipitously in the highest risk situation, thereby producing a crossing of the gradients. In terms of the model (see Figure 2.3), this would indicate avoidance of the hypnosis and drug experiments but more likely participation in the social psychology experiment. In the high trait sensation seekers, the state sensation seeking never falls off, even for the riskiest experiment, and remains higher than the anxiety for the least risky, as well as the most risky, situations. According to the model, this would indicate an approach motive in all experimental situations, even the riskiest. These results are postdictive of the volunteering data for the three kinds of experiments (Zuckerman, 1976).

To summarize these studies of anticipated affects in hypothetical situations, anticipated anxiety increases as a function of riskiness of situations

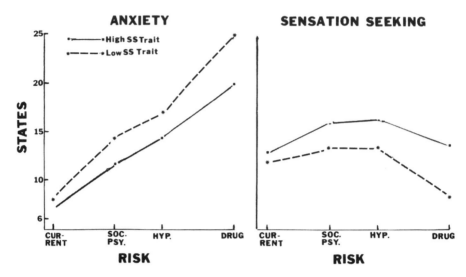

Figure 2.5. Anxiety and sensation seeking state scores of high- and low-trait sensation seekers in response to hypothetical psychological experiments of increasing risk. State scores from the Sensation Seeking and Anxiety States Scale are on the ordinate. Situations are placed on the abscissa as a function of their mean risk ratings by an independent group. SS = sensation seeking; SOC. PSY. = social psychology; HYP. = hypnosis. From *Emotions in Personality and Psychopathology* (p. 178), edited by C. E. Izard, 1979, New York: Plenum Press. Copyright 1979 by Springer-Verlag. Reprinted with permission.

but this increase is more pronounced in high than in low sensation seekers. Anticipated positive surgent affect (sensation seeking) increases with riskiness up to some point but then decreases, but the decrease in low trait sensation seekers is greater than that in high sensation seekers. As a consequence, negative anticipated affect (anxiety) exceeds any expectation of positive affect in the more risky situations for the low trait sensation seekers, which may partially explain why they avoid such situations. In the high trait sensation seekers, positive affect expectations exceed those for negative affect, even in the most risky situations. The results suggest that anticipations of affective reactions, possibly produced by anticipations of harm, play an intermediate, if not a major, role in determining the seeking or avoidance of risky situations. These studies were done in response to hypothetical situations, but the question remains of the actual affective state responses in actual situations.

Mellstrom, Cicala, and Zuckerman (1976) assessed affective reactions and subsequent behavior in three situations that are phobic for some people and interesting for others: approaching and touching a snake, looking down from a high exposed place, and being confined in darkness and silence. In regard to the last two situations, it is interesting that mountain climbers

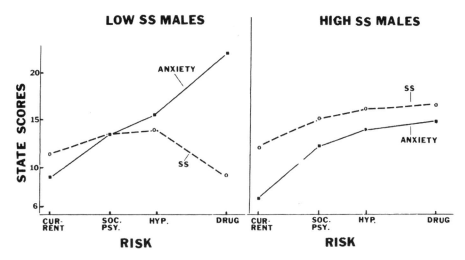

Figure 2.6. Anxiety and sensation seeking state scores of high- and low-trait male sensation seekers in response to hypothetical psychological experiments of increasing risk. State scores from the Sensation Seeking and Anxiety States Scale are on the ordinate. Situations are placed on the abscissa as a function of their mean risk ratings by an independent group. SS = sensation seeking; SOC. PSY. = social psychology; HYP. = hypnosis. From *Emotions in Personality and Psychopathology* (p. 178), edited by C. E. Izard, 1979. New York: Plenum Press. Copyright 1979 by Springer-Verlag. Reprinted with permission.

and rock climbers are high sensation seekers (see chap. 3, this volume) and that high sensation seekers are disproportionately represented in volunteers for sensory deprivation experiments. There are some perceived risks in all three situations. In the snake situation, there is the risk of being bitten, even though the experimenter reassured subjects that it was not a poisonous snake. In the heights situation, in which subjects were asked to go out on an exposed balcony high above street level and look over the parapet, there is the risk of falling to one's death. The risk in the sensory deprivation situation, in which the subject entered a totally dark, quiet room, is more ambiguous, but in sensory deprivation studies, some subjects anticipate mental harm or panic when functionally deprived of visual and auditory input.

The Thrill and Adventure Seeking (TAS) subscale of the SSS was used as a predictor of responses, along with measures of general and specific trait anxiety in the three actual situations. Specific trait anxiety measures were to the specific sources of anxiety in each situation, for instance, fear of snakes in the snake exposure situation. Affective measures were assessed just before entering the situations, and behavioral responses included observers' ratings and performance in terms of time of voluntary exposure and distance of approach to the snake or the parapet in the heights situation.

The TAS correlated significantly and negatively with six indexes of anxiety in the snake situation, including affective state and latency to approach the snake. TAS actually predicted anxiety responses better than general trait anxiety measures but not specific anxiety trait questionnaires. The TAS also predicted 5 of 6 anxiety response measures in both the heights and darkness situations. General and specific anxiety trait were positively related, and sensation seeking was negatively related, to anxiety in actual situations, even though there was no correlation between trait sensation seeking and general anxiety. Both were independent predictors of anxiety in these risky situations. This study supports the role of sensation seeking in approach behavior contrasted with the role of trait anxiety in phobic-type avoidance behavior. The balance between the two major traits and their effects on expectations of outcome may explain some of the individual differences in tendencies to engage in or avoid risky behaviors of the types described in subsequent chapters.

3

SENSATION SEEKING AND RISKY DRIVING, SPORTS, AND VOCATIONS

Truly it may be said that a man drives as he lives.
—Tillmann and Hobbs (1949, p. 329)

The three areas of risk in this chapter are related to physical risk either to oneself or others, but other types of risk are also involved. For instance, in the case of driving there are legal and financial risks in addition to the risk of physical harm in accidents. Engaging in extreme, risky sports is not common, but driving is something done on an almost daily basis by a large part of the population. It is a natural area for the expression of sensation seeking needs in the style of driving.

DRIVING

You are driving on a three-lane highway at a speed only 5 miles above the speed limit, assuming that there is no danger of being stopped and ticketed at that minor level of violation. Your seat belt is securely fastened and you chose this car for its safety features. You are keeping a safe and reasonable distance from the car in front of you, allowing time to brake in case the other car should suddenly slow down or stop. You stay in the middle lane even though traffic is slower than in the left lane. Suddenly a car zooms by on your right and cuts immediately in front of you to cross over to the left lane. He quickly comes up on a car going slower than his desired speed of 80 miles per hour (mph), and he follows him, riding nearly on his bumper until the offender gets out of his lane. You apply your brakes and curse. But after your rage has subsided you ask the question, Why would anyone drive like that? That question will be addressed in what follows.

Driving is risky by objective standards. As shown in Table 2.1 in the previous chapter, it is the third major source of fatality in the United States, being exceeded only by smoking and drinking. But the consequences to health of smoking and drinking are delayed, whereas the consequences of risky driving can be immediate and horrific. Even if one has not personally been involved in a serious accident, the carnage is observable on the road as we are directed around a smashed car or on the evening news, where we see mangled cars and survivors, if any. In a typical year, about 41,000 Americans die in motor vehicle accidents and many more are seriously injured.

Accidents are more common among male than female drivers and are inversely related to age. The highest rates are in young, male adolescents, and this is reflected in increased insurance rates for this group. Adolescent drivers report more risky driving behavior than older drivers, including speeding, following too closely, weaving in and out of traffic, and rapid accelerations (Jonah, 1986; Jonah & Dawson, 1987). It is not coincidental that late adolescents have the highest sensation seeking scores on the Sensation Seeking Scale (SSS) and the Impulsive Sensation Seeking (ImpSS) scale, and males have higher scores than females (Zuckerman, 1994).

Young students tend to underestimate the annual fatality rate from auto accidents and rank the risk somewhat lower than experts do (see Table 2.1, chap. 2, this volume). Lay persons from the general population rate risks from motor vehicles relatively high only below smoking, hard drugs, and alcohol, but they rate the benefits very high, higher than those for nearly all other risky activities (see Table 2.2, chap. 2, this volume). However, this does not explain risky driving, because one can obtain the benefits of driving without taking unnecessary risks.

Theories of Risky Driving

Heino (1996) summarized some of the theories of risky driving. Under *risk homeostasis* theory (Wilde, 1982), each driver has a "target level" of acceptable risk that is balanced with the expected benefits. This target level is compared with the perceived risks of accidents in the given situation. When there is a discrepancy between perceived and target risk, behavior is adjusted accordingly. When perceived risk is higher than the optimal target level, the risk will be reduced by safer driving, but when perceived risk is lower than the target level, driving will be riskier.

This theory resembles the optimal level of arousal theories described in chapter 1, except that risk, not arousal, is the optimized quantity around which behavioral adjustment takes place. It is easy to understand why risk reduction is the outcome of a high perceived level of risk, but why is risk increase an outcome of a low perceived risk level? The positive utilities are not clearly defined. Can risk be both a positive and negative motive? Are some individuals risk seekers and others risk avoiders? Is the target level of risk a fixed quantity or one that varies with the situation or with internal states like the disinhibition produced by alcohol?

The *zero-risk* model (Naatanen & Summala, 1974) suggests that most of the time the subjective risk of the driver is zero and there is a threshold above which the subjective risk suddenly comes into play and can produce inhibitory action like putting on the brakes. There is no optimal level of risk, because all risk is aversive. Individual differences are in thresholds for risk perception.

Is risk intrinsically aversive? There are some forms of sensation seeking in which risk seems to be the main point of the activity. There are those who find the risk in war a stimulant. Caputo (1977), who wrote a book about his experiences as a soldier in the Vietnam war, could have avoided combat but volunteered for a combat unit, explaining that

> There were a number of reasons, of which the paramount was boredom. . . . The rights or wrongs of the war aside, there was a magnetism about combat. You seemed to live more intensely under fire. Every sense was sharper, the mind worked clearer and faster. . . . You found yourself on a precarious emotional edge, experiencing a headiness that no drink or drug could match. (p. 218)

Caputo described an extraordinary optimal level of arousal with lower levels absent of risk as "boredom." Bored youths sometime play Russian roulette, In this game, one puts a single bullet into the six barrel chambers of a revolver, spins the barrel, puts the gun to one's head, and pulls the trigger. If played honestly (without peeking), the chances of dying are one in six. Most of those who play this game are bored but not severely depressed or suicidal. They play this game simply for the high that comes after pulling the trigger with no fatal consequence.

A third theory is called *threat avoidance* (Fuller, 1984), which puts the risk taking into behavioral stimulus–response terms. As with the other two theories, it puts the most stress on the management of risk. Risk is controlled by "potential aversive stimuli," or "threats," such as the sight of a police car or dense traffic. These discriminative stimuli lead to making or not making "anticipatory avoidance responses." This kind of theory could be used to explain individual differences as in the theory of Gray (1982), in which behavioral differences are based on differential sensitivities to stimuli associated with reward and punishment. However, there is little attention to the types of reward that motivate voluntary exposure to risky situations.

My general theory of risk taking (Zuckerman, 1976), described in chapter 2 and shown in Figure 2.3 of this volume, proposes that approach or avoidance reactions are a function of the anticipated and actual states of anxiety and positive affect in the particular situations. Anxiety tends to increase linearly with perceived riskiness, as does positive affect up to a point, but then the positive affect decreases with increasing riskiness. The optimal level of arousal is the point of maximal difference between positive and negative (anxiety) arousal. High and low sensation seekers differ in the height of the anxiety and positive affect gradients in relation to perceived risk and the point at which positive affect begins to decrease as a function of riskiness.

Applying this model to driving, we (Zuckerman, 1994; Zuckerman & Kuhlman, 2000) proposed that novelty and intensity of stimuli produced by speed and reckless driving release dopamine in reward areas of the brain in high sensation seekers, whereas low sensation seekers show a weaker dopamine response and stronger noradrenergic and serotonergic reactions. Noradrenergic arousal is related to anxiety, and serotonergic reaction is related to inhibition of approach. Dopaminergic reactions reinforce the behaviors producing them. However, the high sensation seeker tends to have a lower perception of risk than does the low sensation seeker and therefore is not deterred by it, except in the most extreme situations. Experience without negative outcomes further lowers risk appraisal in the high sensation seeker. The low sensation seekers are particularly sensitized to stimuli and conditioned by experiences that reinforce their fears of catastrophe on the road.

Risky driving includes many kinds of behavior, including speeding, following too closely at high speeds, driving while intoxicated (DWI), frequent and abrupt lane changes, and aggressive driving. Jonah (1997) reviewed 40 studies of sensation seeking and risky driving and concluded that "the vast majority" of these studies showed positive relationships between the two, with correlations in the .30 to .40 range, depending on gender (men were more risk taking), the measure of risky driving, and the form of the SSS used in the particular study. Many studies used abbreviated forms of the SSS, and Jonah noted that of the studies that included the complete SSS, only one failed to find a relationship with risky driving.

Speeding

Speed is the primary goal of sensation seeking drivers, particularly young ones. Much of the reckless driving is a function of the frustration of the driver's desired speed. It is the primary reason for reckless lane changing and close following of the car ahead (i.e., tailgating) when it is going too slow for the driver and he or she cannot change lanes to get around it. The

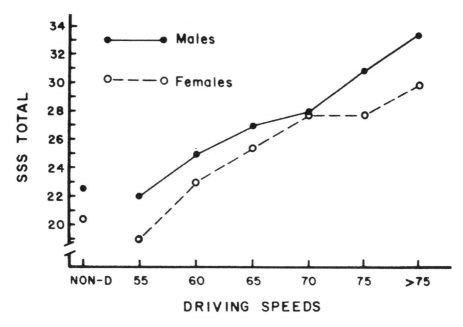

Figure 3.1. Mean Sensation Seeking Scale (SSS) scores as a function of reported driving speeds (miles per hour). NON-D = nondrivers. From "Demographic Influences in Sensation Seeking and Expressions of Sensation Seeking in Religion, Smoking, and Driving Habits," by M. Zuckerman and M. Neeb, 1980, *Personality and Individual Differences,* p. 204. Copyright 1980 by Elsevier Science. Reprinted with permission.

sensation of speed is rewarding, particularly for the high sensation seeker. The drug amphetamine, which increases arousal and elation, is called "speed" in colloquial usage.

Whissell and Bigelow (2003) developed a driving attitude scale and found that the Speeding Attitude subscale (SAS) accounted for most of the strength of the interscale relationships. The SAS correlated with the SSS in three different samples. The items in the SAS reflect a preference for high levels of arousal produced by the sensation of speed. Unfortunately, speed is directly related to accidents involving fatalities. The faster one drives, the greater the chances of losing control of the car in an avoidance maneuver and the longer the braking time in an emergency.

Zuckerman and Neeb (1980) asked subjects at what speed they usually drive on a highway with a 55 mph speed limit on a clear road. The choices were in 5-mph increments from 55 mph to over 75 mph. The results are shown in Figure 3.1. There is a linear increase in the SSS Total, with increments in driving speeds for both men and women. The finding was not produced just by the Thrill and Adventure Seeking (TAS) subscale. The same significant finding was found for all of the SSS subscales. Covariance corrections for age did not change the results.

Significant relationships between driving speed and sensation seeking have been reported by many other investigators including Arnett (1991); Arnett, Offer, and Fine (1997); Burns and Wilde (1995); Clement and Jonah (1984); Furnham and Saipe (1993); Heino (1996); Heino, van der Molen, and Wilde (1996); Jonah, Thiesen, and Au-Yeung (2001); Rosenbloom (2003b); and Ulleberg (2002). Rosenbloom investigated the effects of increasing "mortality salience" by showing a film depicting graves marked with the kilometers per hour driven by the person in the grave. Whereas low sensation seekers showed decreased tendency to risk speeding after seeing the film, the high sensation seekers actually reported increased speeding after the threatening film. Rosenbloom maintained that the subjects were unaware of the link between the film and their reports of behavior, but it is possible that they were, at some level, and that the high sensation seekers were reacting in a defiant way to what they may have seen as an attempt to alter their driving behavior.

Heino (1996) clocked the actual speeds of subjects using a special car with instruments for that purpose. Subjects drove on seven different road sections with different speed limits and other differences such as villages versus open roads. Subjects also made risk ratings for each section of road, and heart rate (HR) was recorded. HR variability has an inverse relationship to arousal and suggests mental effort. There was an overall significant effect of sensation seeking, with high sensation seekers driving faster than low sensation seekers. But there was also an interaction of sensation seeking with road type. Differences were greater on roads that allowed for faster driving such as wide and straight roads with few intersections. High and low sensation seekers did not differ on their perceptions of risk or their HR arousal. This argues against the idea that sensation seekers are risk seekers. It is the sensation reward, not any attraction to risk, that makes them speed. Prior to a second round of the roads, subjects were offered three kinds of incentives to drive more safely. The promise of an uncertain amount of financial reward resulted in a considerable decrease in driving speed and a decrease in perceived risk for the high sensation seekers. Unfortunately, in the real world there are no rewards for safe driving and only occasional punishment for speedy reckless driving.

Burns and Wilde (1995) did a behavioral observation study of the driving of taxi drivers in Canada. Two observers engaged a cab and observed the driving of the cabdriver over a preselected route. The drivers did not know they were under observation. The observers made unobtrusive marks on a checklist recording speed, reactions to stoplights, stop signs, crosswalks, and so on. The records of the observed drivers were obtained from the cab company files. One of the two factors found in the analysis consisted of exceeding the speed limit and changing lanes without caution. Sensation seeking and another measure of risk-taking personality correlated significantly with observed fast and careless driving and with records of speeding violations.

Road rage seems to be an increasing phenomenon in urban life. A sensitivity to frustration by slower driving in some drivers can result in furious reactions of impatient, angry drivers. These exchanges have resulted in deliberate aggressive acts by using their cars as weapons or shooting from their cars. It would not be surprising to find that aggressiveness as a trait is also related to fast and reckless driving. Zuckerman and Kuhlman (2000) found that aggression–hostility was related to reckless driving in both male and female college students. Arnett et al. (1997) reported that both sensation seeking and trait aggressiveness correlated with reports of driving over 80 mph or 20 mph over the speed limit, and racing another car. Adolescents were higher than adults on both personality traits. Jonah et al. (2001) found that not only did high sensation seekers drive faster (over 72 mph on an expressway) and well over the legal speed limit, they also reported a variety of aggressive behaviors like swearing at other drivers, beating drivers at getaways, reporting fun in weaving through traffic and passing other cars, using their horn when annoyed, making rude signs, and being easily provoked and losing their tempers. All of the SSS subscales except Experience Seeking (ES) correlated significantly with aggressive driving. Both aggression and sensation seeking were related to convictions for speeding and dangerous driving, as well as other types of convictions in a Japanese sample of drivers (Matthews, Tsuda, Xin, & Ozeki, 1999).

Risky Driving

Speeding is only one aspect of a broader risky driving factor, although it is the central one. Jonah (1997) reviewed 15 studies of risky driving other than drinking and driving and found that all of them found positive relationships with sensation seeking, particularly in men. Risky driving, as a composite of many specific kinds of behavior, was highly reliable over a 3-month period and was predicted at both times by sensation seeking (Hartos, Eitel, & Simons-Morton, 2002). However, parental behavior factors, like monitoring and control of adolescent children's driving and nonacceptance of their general deviance, like drinking and lying, were also strong factors in predicting reckless driving (Hartos, Eitel, Haynie, & Simons-Morton, 2000; Hartos, Eitel, & Simons-Morton, 2002). The influences of deviant and risky behaviors in peers were also strong predictors of risky driving.

Rosenbloom (2003b), as briefly mentioned earlier, studied the effects of a film emphasizing mortality salience contrasted with the effects of a more neutral film on reports of different kinds of driving risk taking, including the following: adjustment to driving in an unfamiliar vehicle or in an unfamiliar area; speeding; driving under the influence of alcohol; and driving in bad conditions or bad weather. The high sensation seekers reported higher risk taking than lows after both films, but whereas the low sensation seekers showed lower risk taking of all types after seeing the threatening film, the high sensation seekers showed no differences as a function of the films. In fact, as previously described, they increased their reports of speeding after the film! These results suggest that attempts to reduce the risky driving habits of high sensation seekers by emphasizing the mortality risks are unlikely to have much effect. Low sensation seekers are more receptive to such messages, but they are not at high risk to begin with because they are more cautious in their driving habits.

Witte and Donohue (2000) investigated a specific type of risk taking: behavior at train crossings. They found that high sensation seekers experienced more frustration and greater cognitive distortions at crossings and more often made the risky, sometimes fatal, decision to try to "beat the train." They usually do, but in the case of a tie, they lose.

Following Behavior

Following the car in front too closely at high speeds, or tailgating, as we call it in America, is a type of risky driving behavior often involved in accidents. Heino and his colleagues in the Netherlands have studied this behavior observing actual road behavior (Heino, 1996; Heino et al., 1996). Some of the procedure was previously described in response to speeding under free driving conditions on a prescribed route. In the second part of the experiment, the subject was instructed to follow another car with observers in it. In the first phase, the following distance was free for the subject to determine. Then he was instructed to follow at the prescribed distance of 15 meters. After that, he was instructed to follow at distances of 125%, 75%, 50%, and 25% of his preferred distance as measured during the free following phase. Besides the speed and following distance in the free condition measures, a verbally given rating on a 0 to 6 scale of perceived risk was taken from the subject, with instructions to give a new rating whenever there was a change in perceived risk. A heart rate (HR) measure of arousal was continuously measured. Subjects were selected from high and low ranges of the Dutch SSS.

During the free-following phase, the high sensation seekers followed the car ahead at a closer distance than did the low sensation seekers, but they did not perceive this distance as more risky, nor did the low sensation seekers see their longer distance as less risky. In the prescribed following condition, the perceived risk ratings increased for both groups but the increase in perceived risk was larger for the low sensation seekers. The increase in the HR measure of arousal, or mental effort, was only significant for the low sensation seekers in the following condition. Summarizing the results, Heino et al. (1996) stated,

> The results indicate that sensation avoiders [low sensation seekers] and sensation seekers [high sensation seekers] accept the same amount of perceived risk, but that in the case of sensation seekers this perceived risk is achieved at a significantly shorter following distance. (p. 74)

He concluded that the difference between high and low sensation seekers is based on behavioral factors rather than on cognitive differences in risk perception. This is the conclusion reached by Horvath and Zuckerman (1993) in regard to general risk taking.

Traffic Violations and Accidents

Given that high sensation seekers are more likely to engage in risky driving, one would expect that they would have more citations for traffic violations and more accidents. This is true for traffic violations, particularly those for speeding and DWI (Burns & Wilde, 1995; Donovan, Queisser, Salzberg, & Umlauf, 1985). However, the correlations for accidents are less consistent. Some have found no relationship between sensation seeking and traffic accidents (Burns & Wilde, 1995; Jonah et al., 2001; Matthews et al., 1999; D. L. Smith & Heckert, 1998; Whissell & Bigelow, 2003), whereas others have found a relationship (Donovan & Marlatt, 1982; Iverson & Rundmo, 2002). In these two studies with positive findings (Donovan & Marlatt, 1982; Iverson & Rundmo, 2002), aggression–hostility or driver anger (i.e., road rage) was also involved. Matthews et al. (1999) found that aggression, but not sensation seeking, was related to accident involvement. There are several explanations of why risky driving behavior is not always related to accidents. One is the inadequacy of officially reported data. Minor accidents often go unreported by the police. Some people involved in accidents are not the ones causing the accident. It is possible that young drivers who engage in risky driving are also skilled drivers with good reflexes and therefore usually avoid having actual collisions. Sensation seeking alone may not cause accidents but may do so only when it is in combination with aggressive traits.

Ulleberg (2002) used cluster analysis to define personality types. One of these types consisted primarily of men (80%) characterized by high levels of sensation seeking, irresponsibility, and driver-related aggression and low levels of altruism and anxiety. In terms of our factor analyses of personality traits (Zuckerman, Kuhlman, & Camac, 1988; Zuckerman, Kuhlman, Thornquist, & Kiers, 1991), this cluster would correspond to our factor Impulsive Unsocialized Sensation Seeking. Another cluster type had more women and was also high on sensation seeking and driving anger, but unlike the first type, they were also high on aggression and anxiety and low on emotional adjustment. Both of these types had high levels of accidents, but the first type had higher levels of accidents in which they sustained physical injuries. Drivers of the first type, in particular, had nonsafe and risk-taking attitudes toward driving and low levels of risk perception, and despite their accident record, they rated their driving skills more highly than all other groups! They probably blamed their accidents on the drivers in the other car. All drivers were exposed to a traffic safety campaign in school. Most rated the campaign favorably, particularly those clustered in a type characterized by emotional stability, conformity, and low sensation seeking and aggression. However, the unsocialized high sensation seeking group found the campaign "boring" and of little concern to them. This highest risk group had the least favorable response to the campaign targeting them.

Driving While Intoxicated

In the adolescent/young-adult ages (15–24), about half of the drivers admit that they drink and drive, and more than half of the fatal auto accidents among this age group involve alcohol (Rivers, Sarvela, & Shannon, 1996). The reason that alcohol intoxication is such a high risk factor for accidents is that it adversely affects vision, motor reflexes, and judgment. Perception of risk is reduced, and normal control is disinhibited. Given that sensation seeking is related to both drinking and reckless driving, it is not surprising that it is related to DWI. In the Zuckerman and Kuhlman (2000) study, reckless driving was specifically correlated with drinking and not with the other types of risk taking. Jonah (1997) reviewed 18 studies involving sensation seeking and DWI behavior. All but 5 of these reported that DWI increased as a function of sensation seeking scores or that DWI-reported or DWI-convicted offenders had higher sensation seeking scores than control subjects.

Johnson and White (1989) found that a factor combining sensation seeking and impulsivity scales predicted DWI both directly and through a substance abuse factor in a longitudinal study. Stacy, Newcomb, and Bentler (1991) had similar findings using a short form of the SSS that excluded items with drug or alcohol content. They found that sensation seeking predicted DWI self-reported behavior but not DWI arrests in both men and women. The prediction of DWI was direct for men but was mediated through alcohol use for women. Arnett et al. (1997) had adolescent drivers in high school keep a log of their driving activities for 10 days. They found a correlation between reports of DWI and both sensation seeking and trait aggressiveness. Donovan et al. (1985) compared a group arrested for DWI, another group who had four convictions for traffic violations within a year

(CTV) but without DWI, and a control group selected from the general driving population. The two high-risk driver groups (DWI and CTV) were higher than the control group on driving aggression; competitive speeding; and trait sensation seeking, aggression–hostility, and depression. These results suggest that the DWI group is not different from non-DWI reckless drivers on personality factors but that they differ in that an alcohol problem is added to the behavioral problems of the non-DWI reckless drivers. Stacy et al. (1991) found that physical, personal, social, and work-related problems from drinking were highly related to DWI behavior.

Ames, Zogg, and Stacy (2002) added marijuana and other illegal drugs to alcohol in the definition of DWI and investigated the predictors of Impulsive Sensation Seeking (ImpSS, from the Zuckerman–Kuhlman Personality Questionnaire [ZKPQ]; Zuckerman, 2002; Zuckerman, Kuhlman, Joireman, Teta, & Kraft, 1993), memory association relevant to substance use, and self-reported marijuana use in drug offenders from a drug counseling program. ImpSS correlated significantly with DWI, memory association, and marijuana use. Both the SS and the Imp components of ImpSS correlated with DWI. The structural equation model showed both a direct path between ImpSS and DWI and a path mediated through memory association and marijuana use. As other studies have shown, sensation seeking has a direct pathway to risky behavior and does not depend solely on cognitive and substance use mediators.

Fatigue and Vigilance

Becoming drowsy and falling asleep is a major source of accidents in long-distance drivers. Monotonous conditions are particularly aversive to high sensation seekers. Boredom Susceptibility is one of the four factors in the SSS.

Bored subjects in sensory deprivation experiments tend either to become extremely restless and move about more or to fall asleep despite instructions to resist sleep. Brain waves slow, however, and sleep or borderline sleep stages or actual sleep happens. Extraverts are supposed to be especially susceptible to inhibitory states, according to H. J. Eysenck's (1967) arousal theory.

Thiffault and Bergeron (2003) tested subjects in a driving simulator for two 40-minute sessions in which the road environment was repetitive and monotonous in one condition and with visual elements designed to hold attention and maintain arousal in the other. The dependent variable was the variation in steering wheel movements, a sign of sleepiness. Sensation seeking had both a main effect and an interaction with extraversion. Drivers who scored high on sensation seeking, particularly on the ES subscale, and high sensation seeking extraverts were more affected by road monotony, tending to show more variation in steering wheel movements. Sensation seeking was the more powerful of the two predictors.

Verwey and Zaidel (2000) found that extraversion and sensation seeking predicted two different kinds of accidents in a driving simulator. Drivers scoring high on extraversion were more likely to go off the road as a function of falling asleep, whereas those high on sensation seeking did not fall asleep but were more likely to cross solid lane markings. High sensation seekers compensated for their boredom with more risky driving. This study suggests the cause of the higher accident rates of sensation seekers: It is not due to low arousal, as may be the case for extraverts, but to attempts to relieve the monotony of driving by speeding and other kinds of risky driving.

Vigilance and Danger Detection

Fuller's (1984) threat avoidance theory suggests that risk taking is a function of a lack of conditioning or insensitivity to signals of danger. Gray (1982) proposed that sensitivity to signals of punishment characterizes those high in trait anxiety, whereas insensitivity to such signals is characteristic of impulsive personalities.

Rosenbloom and Wolf (2002a, 2002b) put this idea into the paradigm of signal-detection theory. The danger signal is something connected with increased risk of accident and is combined with noise or other risk-irrelevant stimuli. Perceptual sensitivity is success in discriminating between signal + noise and noise alone. A driver may be perceptually sensitive but willing to overlook the increased risk suggested by the danger stimulus. This latter response is called *leniency*. These authors proposed that the TAS and Boredom Susceptibility (BS) subscales of the SSS are the most relevant to risk taking in driving. TAS represents the willingness to take physical risks, and BS represents the drive to overcome monotony in the driving situation by taking risks. Rosenbloom and Wolf investigated their theory in a number of simulated and actual driving situations using subjects of different ages and genders.

In their first study, they used four situations: reaction to the amber traffic light, distance maintenance in following behavior, behavior at traffic merges, and behavior at a pedestrian road crossing. The subjects were 28 drivers who drove professionally, such as bus, truck, and taxi drivers. All agreed to accept a note-taking silent observer who drove with them every day over a period of 3 to 4 weeks. The observations in all situations were translated into signal-detection terms. A "hit," or "success," involved noting the danger stimulus and taking appropriate action like braking; a "miss" was not noting the dangerous stimulus. Taking avoidant action in a situation not calling for it was a "false alarm," and not taking action in such a situation was a "correct rejection." Reactions were classified as "success" or "leniency," the latter being defined as "the willingness to overlook risk."

High TAS scorers showed higher leniency and beta indices of risk taking than did low TAS scorers across situations, but there were no differences in success scores. Although high TAS subjects were not deficient in signal detection, they made more risky decisions in reacting to the signals of danger. BS showed the same result with the beta index but was not a significant predictor of leniency. The correlation of TAS with leniency decreased with age. The role of TAS in risky behavior was particularly strong for the younger drivers, but BS became a stronger factor for the older drivers.

Rosenbloom and Wolf (2000b) examined the choices made by subjects in three age groups—7, 13, and 22 years old—in three situations. All age groups participated in an experiment involving virtual detection of risky signals. A movie showed a series of driving scenes of cars merging in traffic. Subjects had to judge whether there was the sound of a car stopping short or not.

The second experiment involved pedestrians in a road crossing in two busy two-way streets. The subjects had to decide whether crossing was feasible, and their choices were judged correct or not by an observer. The course included stoplights. This was repeated 20 to 50 times, depending on traffic density. The subjects were presumably restrained if they were judged to have made a risky choice. The third experiment involved actual behavior in go-cart driving and was limited to the 13-year-olds. They were rated on how they handled three road dilemmas: merging into traffic, keeping distance from vehicles in front, and responding to the presence of an amber light.

For the virtual simulation situation, neither TAS nor BS significantly predicted success (hits + correct rejections) in detection or leniency (hits + false alarms) for the 7-year-olds. BS, but not TAS, was positively related to both success and leniency for the 13-year-olds. For the 22-year-olds, TAS correlated positively with success and BS correlated positively with leniency. Apparently, the high sensation seekers in this age group were good at detection but also had a bias toward false detection.

In the pedestrian road crossing, the youngest females were more lenient (risky) than the males, but for the older groups, the males were more risk taking in their crossing judgments. TAS was positively correlated with leniency (risky judgments) in all three age groups for men and in two of the three (the oldest and youngest) for women. BS correlated with leniency in only one of the six groups. The correlations were substantial, particularly for the 22-year-olds, in which they were .63 for both genders. There was no gender difference in the go-cart behavior. TAS correlated positively (r = .38) and BS correlated negatively ($-.17$) with leniency. The risky behaviors of merging into traffic without waiting, driving at close distances, and running through amber lights were more characteristic of high TAS sensation seekers. There were no correlations with success. The general trend of all studies is that sensation seekers are not deficient in signal detection but are at traffic risk because of risky judgments and behaviors.

Seat-Belt Use

If one is involved in a collision or other type of accident, the use of a seat belt is the most effective way of preventing fatal or severe injuries. And yet many people do not use seat belts or use them only occasionally. This is why cars began to include warning sounds or passive restraints and reinforce the seat belt with air-bag protection. Many states have instituted laws penalizing nonuse of seat belts. Risk is not the objective of most sensation seeking, so there is no reason that sensation seekers should decline to use this relatively simple mode of decreasing risk.

Wilson (1990) found that in three groups, two groups with driving offenses and one group without, drivers who claimed to use their seat belts all of the time had lower SSS scores than did those who never wore them or wore them inconsistently. However, in a study of college students, no correlations were found between seat-belt use and the SSS Total or any of its subscales (Jonah et al., 2001). A study by Thuen (1994) of 14-year-old Norwegian children found that seat-belt use, in both the front and back seats, was the major variable defining a Safety-Seeking factor. Of course, these younger adolescents were passengers, not drivers, but the Safety-Seeking factor correlated negatively and significantly with the SSS Total and all of its subscales.

Summary

Age and gender are two major factors in risky driving. Nearly every study that compares men and women finds that men are riskier drivers and have more accidents. Comparing young drivers (16–24) with older drivers, Jonah and Dawson (1987) reported that the young drivers are more likely to engage in risky driving, like speeding, driving through yellow lights, changing lanes too abruptly, passing at intersections, following too closely, and DWI. It is not surprising that they are more likely to be involved in accidents. The young drivers are less perceptive of danger in risky situations and less likely to use seat belts, and they place less importance on safety features when buying a new car. They behave as if they were invulnerable and immortal.

Sensation seeking is involved in nearly every type of risky driving behavior, although the relationship with involvement in accidents is less consistent. Sensation seeking drivers perceive themselves as skilled drivers, and this probably reduces their perception of risk in the way that they drive. They may be right in their perception of their driving skills, although unreasonably so if they have been drinking or are otherwise impaired in judgment in a particular situation. Road conditions can also vary as a function of traffic and weather. Risky driving is antisocial and aggressive in that it can involve others, passengers in the driver's car and drivers and passengers in other cars, in accidents. It is not surprising that sensation seeking and aggression are both traits involved in risky driving.

Engagement in risky sports is neither antisocial nor prosocial in that the risks are taken only by the participants themselves. Sports are a minor source of accidents, particularly fatal accidents. But although some sports like parachute jumping and mountain climbing have infrequent accidents, when they do occur, they are usually catastrophic and fatal. This means that only the highest sensation seekers are likely to accept the risk to experience the sensations that provide the rewards of the activity.

SPORTS

Physical play is seen in the young of humans and many other species. Kittens stalk and pounce on inanimate as well as animate moving objects. Dogs chase and retrieve. Some show extraordinary skills in catching Frisbees or balls. Male chimpanzees as well as human children, particularly boys, engage in rough-and-tumble play involving mock wrestling and fighting (Maccoby & Jacklin, 1974). War games, involving play with guns and swords, are popular among boys. Pacifist parents sometimes attempt, with little success, to ban toy weapons, but boys improvise them with whatever materials are at hand.

Play evolves into more formal games, like baseball and football, involving rules and strategies. With increasing age, fewer adults participate in such games with any regularity. However, many develop an intense interest in organized sports, filling stadiums on weekends and avidly following the fate of the small groups of highly selected athletes who constitute professional sports.

As I write this, my local football team, the Philadelphia Eagles, has won the league championship and are on their way to the Super Bowl. The streets and taverns are filled with screaming Dionysians, some of whom paint themselves green or wear sport hats with eagles perched on them. The sport seems to be more arousing for the spectators than for the players.

High sensation seekers regard many life activities, including work and sex, as forms of play. Jacques Cousteau (Davidson, 1972) said of his life work,

It's fun to do things you're not meant to do like going to the moon or living under the ocean. I was playing when I invented the aqualung. I'm still playing. I think play is the most important thing in the world. (p. SM32)

High sensation seekers tend to regard love as a playful game rather than a form of commitment (Richardson, Medvin, & Hammock, 1988).

There are some kinds of children's play that are very risky. Climbing trees, balancing on high ledges, and "daring" competitions are examples. This kind of play can continue into drag racing of cars and extreme forms of more common sports like skiing. Perhaps the most extreme example of risk taking is the adolescent fad for Russian roulette. What is the point? Defiance of death can be highly stimulating, and such activities can be extreme forms of sensation seeking.

Risky Versus Nonrisky Sports

Zuckerman (1983b), in a review of the sensation seeking literature on sports participation, suggested that sensation seeking was primarily related to participation in high-risk sports, somewhat related to participation in medium-risk sports, and not at all related to participation in low-risk sports. High-risk sports included skydiving, scuba diving, mountain climbing, and downhill skiing.

Body-contact sports, like football, were classified as medium risk. Running and gymnastics were classified as low-risk. Turning back to Table 2.2 in chapter 2 of this volume, one can see that perceived risk of death ratings for football, mountain climbing, scuba diving, downhill skiing, and surfing are all low compared with smoking, drinking, and taking drugs, and the perceived benefits of sports far outweigh the perceived risks.

Of course, this classification of sports by risk is arbitrary. There are probably many more injuries in gymnastics than in parachuting, but when something goes wrong in the latter, it is more likely to be fatal. Furthermore, the sports classified as high risk have other qualities that make them attractive to high sensation seekers. They provide novel sensations and experiences not found in the everyday environment, like the free-fall sensations in skydiving and the underwater environment in scuba diving. Subjective risk is minimized by regular participants in these sports who have confidence in their equipment and training.

The TAS subscale of the SSS would be expected to show differences between participants in extreme sports and those in more common sports simply because the items express an interest in such sports. However, most of the studies reviewed by Zuckerman (1983b) showed differences on ES as well as TAS. Most showed differences on the SSS Form IV (SSS–IV)

TABLE 3.1
Mean Sensation Seeking Scale (SSS) Scores of Norwegian Elite and Team Athletes in Selected Sports, Physical Education Students, Teachers, and Military Recruits

Group	n	TAS	ES	Dis	BS	Total
Expedition climbers	9	9.11	8.55	5.88	5.11	28.66
Parachutists/skydivers	20	8.75	6.85	6.50	4.55	26.65
Elite mountain climbers	36	8.25	7.58	5.91	3.55	25.30
White water canoeists	32	8.78	6.44	5.59	4.03	24.78
Karate, males	17	8.00	4.82	5.65	3.82	22.29
Karate, females	14	7.50	5.64	5.29	3.79	22.22
Physical education students, males	43	7.79	5.44	5.37	3.49	22.09
North Sea divers	5	7.80	5.00	4.40	4.80	22.00
Ice-hockey players	19	7.11	4.58	5.68	4.58	21.95
Teachers, males	12	4.83	6.50	6.25	3.83	21.41
Tennis players, males	5	7.60	5.20	6.40	1.80	21.00
Military recruits	28	6.61	4.75	5.82	3.71	20.89
Volleyball players, males	13	5.15	4.00	4.92	4.38	18.46
Volleyball players, females	16	5.44	5.31	4.00	2.44	17.19
Teachers, females	17	3.88	5.25	2.50	2.75	14.38

Note. Groups are arrayed in order of mean scores on the SSS Total. TAS = Thrill and Adventure Seeking; ES = Experience Seeking; Dis = Disinhibition; BS = Boredom Susceptibility. From *Personality and Sensation Seeking in Risk Sport: A Summary*, by G. Breivik, 1991, unpublished raw data. Printed with permission from the author.

General Scale and the SSS Form V (SSS–V) Total score. A few showed differences on Disinhibition (Dis) and BS subscales as well.

Comparisons of Different Sports and Other Groups

Table 3.1 shows data on the SSS collected in Norway by Breivik (1991) on various groups of participants in sports and also on teachers. The expedition mountain climbers consisted of those who had scaled the highest peaks, including Mount Everest. Four of them had been on a fatal climb in which two of the other climbers died. This group and parachutists, elite climbers, and white-water canoeists had the highest SSS scores, not only on Total and TAS but on ES as well. The only distinction between these groups was the high Dis scores of the parachutists.

The next group, consisting of karate participants, physical education students, divers, ice-hockey players, male teachers, tennis players, and military recruits, had essentially normal SSS scores. The last group, consisting of volleyball players and female teachers, had relatively low SSS scores.

Jack and Ronan (1998) reviewed previous studies of different sport participant groups in New Zealand, classified into high-, medium-, and low-risk sports. Of the 13 high- and medium-risk groups studied using all of the

TABLE 3.2

Sensation Seeking Scale (SSS) and Impulsivity (Imp) Means for
Different High- and Low-Risk Sport Groups

	n	TAS	ES	Dis	BS	TAS-Out	SSS Total	Imp
High-risk sports								
Skydivers	11	7.70	7.20	6.50	5.30	19.00	26.70	14.20
Mountain climbers	23	8.43	7.14	5.29	4.33	16.76	25.19	11.05
Hang gliders	26	8.08	5.96	5.46	3.96	15.32	23.28	8.96
Auto racers	34	6.19	4.57	5.51	3.94	14.16	20.38	11.47
M	94	7.41	5.90	5.60	4.14	15.64	23.03	10.87
Low-risk sports								
Swimmers	22	7.91	5.32	6.10	4.59	15.82	23.73	12.19
Aerobics	6	7.00	6.17	6.60	3.00	15.00	22.00	10.33
Golfers	34	6.45	4.35	5.00	3.72	13.06	19.68	10.09
Marathon runners	11	4.45	4.64	2.91	2.00	9.55	14.00	8.55
M	73	6.64	4.86	5.12	3.67	13.54	20.26	10.50

Note. TAS = Thrill and Adventure Seeking; ES = Experience Seeking; Dis = Disinhibition; BS = Boredom Susceptibility; TAS-Out = Total score minus TAS subscale; SSS Total = Total score including all sub-scales. From "Sensation Seeking Among High- and Low-Risk Sports Participants," by S. J. Jack and K. R. Ronan, 1998, *Personality and Individual Differences, 25*, p. 1078. Copyright 1998 by Elsevier Science. Adapted with permission.

SSS subscales, all 13 showed significantly higher TAS scores than control groups, 7 groups revealed higher ES, 4 differed on Dis, and 3 had higher BS scores. These authors then did their own study using subjects who were currently participating in one of eight sport categories: automobile racing, skydiving, hang gliding, mountain climbing, marathon running, swimming, golf, and aerobics. The first four of these were arbitrarily classified as high-risk sports and the last four, as low-risk sports. In addition to the SSS–V, they used the Impulsivity (Imp) subscale from S. B. G. Eysenck and Eysenck's (1977) Impulsiveness, Venturesomeness, and Empathy Scale (IVE).

Table 3.2 shows the means of the eight groups on the SSS and the Imp subscales along with the means for all of the high- and low-risk groups combined. Because the TAS has some confounding with the sports variable and affects the SSS Total, another total measure that excluded the TAS scale was used (TAS-Out). The results comparing high- and low-risk sports groups were analyzed using analysis of covariance with age as a covariate because the low-risk group was younger in age than the high-risk group.

The high-risk sport participants were significantly higher on the SSS Total, TAS-Out, and all of the SSS subscales than were the low-risk sport participants, but among the subscales, the larger differences were on TAS and ES. The scores of the mountain climbers and skydivers in this study are very close to those obtained by Breivik (1991) for elite climbers and parachutists shown in Table 3.1. There was no significant difference between high- and low-risk sports on Imp. There were differences between sports groups within the main risk classifications. Although swimmers were classified as a low-risk group, they were the third highest sensation seeking group. Automobile racers, classified as a high-risk group, fell in the range of two of the low-risk groups. These anomalies suggest that the riskiness of sports is not the sole or even the main feature attracting sensation seekers. Auto racing is probably the riskiest of all of these sports, but participants are not among the highest sensation seekers.

Another study used the SSS and Arnett's (1994) Inventory of Sensation Seeking (AISS) to compare participants in high- and low-risk sports (Zarevski, Marusic, Zolotic, Bunjevac, & Vukosav, 1998). Two items from the TAS subscale were omitted because they pertained to two of the high-risk sports used in the study. High-risk sports were parachuting, scuba diving, hang gliding, speleology (cave exploring), and alpinism (mountain climbing). Low-risk sports were athletics, rowing, bowling, and table tennis. All of the subscales from both the SSS and the AISS differentiated high- from low-risk sport participants, but a discriminant analysis showed that the ES subscale, followed by the TAS and BS subscales, accounted for nearly all of the variance of the discrimination, and a stepwise regression analysis showed that only TAS and ES independently determined the prediction of sports group membership.

Slanger and Rudestam (1997) investigated the risk factor further by subdividing those engaged in risky sports into those who took more extreme risks within the sport. For rock climbing, this means climbing without a protective rope; for skiing, it is skiing of extremely steep, narrow chutes with prominent rocks; for piloting a small airplane, it is flying at low altitude, performing aerobatics, and racing; and for white-water kayaking, it is running rapids rated as extremely dangerous. Another group consisted of those who engaged in the same risky sports but not at such dangerous levels. A control group consisted of those engaged in low-risk sports like bowling and from the sports-oriented general population.

Although those engaged in risky sports scored higher than the samples of the general population on SSS Total, TAS, ES, Dis, and BS, only the TAS subscale was related to differences within the study sample, differentiating the two higher risk samples from those engaged in low-risk sports. Death anxiety did not differentiate between groups, as one might have expected if risk anxiety were the primary factor in risky behavior. Physical self-efficacy, but not total self-efficacy, did differentiate the groups according to risk levels. Those taking the most extreme risks have the highest self-confidence in performing, managing fear, and avoiding mistakes than those at intermediate levels of risk taking, who in turn had higher levels than those engaged in low-risk activities.

Rowland, Franken, and Harrison (1986) compared college athletes engaged in risky sports, such as mountain climbing, skiing, and parachuting, and found they were generally high on SSS scores, but high sensation seekers were also attracted to nonrisky sports or activities like pool, target shooting, and even modern dancing! Chess is a highly cerebral sport or game with no physical risk at all. It is therefore surprising that chess players were found to have higher SSS Total and TAS scores than nonplayers and that those players with more experience had even higher SSS scores (Joireman, Fick, & Anderson, 2002). Chess experience was also associated with the Dis subscale. Rowland et al. found that some sports involving high levels of physical activity like running, jogging, weight lifting, golf, and tennis were more popular among low than among high sensation seekers. However, bicycle riding and swimming did not differ in popularity between high and low sensation seekers.

Some investigators have used the Telic Dominance Scale (TDS; Murgatroyd, Rushton, Apter, & Ray, 1978) to investigate sports participation. The arousal avoidance subscale is inversely related to sensation seeking; that is, low sensation seekers have high arousal avoidance. Kerr and Svebak (1989) found that those engaging in risky sports (canoeing, downhill skiing, motor racing) had lower arousal avoidance than those engaging in safe sports (archery, golf, bowling).

Svebak and Kerr (1989) contrasted those engaging in "endurance" sports requiring strenuous and persistent activity, such as long-distance running, rowing, and jogging, with those involved in "explosive" sports, requiring intense concentration and activity for brief periods of time, such as cricket, soccer, hockey, baseball, and surfing. They found that long-distance runners were higher on the TDS arousal avoidant and planning-oriented scales than tennis or hockey players. These findings are consistent with previous ones showing that long-distance runners are low (McCutcheon, 1981) and tennis and hockey players are average, but not high, on sensation seeking (Breivik, 1991).

Organized Competitive Athletics

Gundersheim (1987) contrasted college team athletes and nonparticipants in organized high school and college athletics on the SSS–IV. There were no differences between male team athletes and nonathletic students, but female athletes scored higher than nonathletes on the SSS General Scale and the TAS and BS subscales. Among the male teams, baseball players were lower than lacrosse and wrestling team participants on the SSS General Scale and TAS subscale. Gundersheim suggested that this difference is due to higher sensation seeking in contact than in noncontact sports. A similar conclusion was reached by Potgieter and Bisschoff (1990), who found that rugby players were higher on the SSS than marathon runners. However, this could be due to the lower sensation seeking of long-distance runners compared with average levels of rugby players.

Schroth (1995) compared college team athletes in different sports and nonathletes on the SSS. Athletes scored higher than nonathletes on SSS Total, TAS, Dis, and BS subscales. Comparing the different teams, they found that male rugby and lacrosse players had higher scores than soccer and crew athletes on SSS Total, TAS, BS, and Dis subscales. No significant differences were found among the female teams (volleyball, soccer, softball, tennis, and golf). The male data supports Gundersheim's hypothesis of higher sensation seeking in participants in contact sports.

Another study compared male and female participants in various team sports and the general college population from the same university on the multifactor ZKPQ (O'Sullivan, Zuckerman, & Kraft, 1998). The male teams were baseball and football, and the female teams were equestrians, field hockey, and lacrosse. According to the body-contact hypothesis, the male football players should have higher ImpSS scores than baseball players and the female hockey and lacrosse players should have higher scores than the equestrians. Compared with the general population college norms, all four teams had higher scores on Activity and lower scores on Neuroticism–Anxiety scales. The male baseball and football teams actually had lower scores than the general students on ImpSS. Females had no differences on this scale. This is the first study using the ZKPQ ImpSS to study team athletes. It could be that the ImpSS is less appropriate for differentiating athletes from nonathletes or contact sports from noncontact sports.

Davis and Mogk (1994) compared elite athletes, subelite athletes, sports enthusiasts from the physical education department who were spectators but not team participants in any sport, and nonathletic control subjects who were not particularly interested in sports either as a spectator or a participant. The elite athletes were members of a national team or professional athletes in swimming, diving, gymnastics, track, squash, boxing, luge, cycling, skiing, or figure skating. Subelite athletes were members of varsity teams or equivalents in the same areas as the elite athletes. The SSS–IV was used along with other tests. Differences on the SSS General Scale among the groups were not significant. TAS was higher in all sport participant and enthusiast groups than in nonathletic control subjects. This was true for ES in the males as well. But for the females, ES was higher in both control groups than for the elite and subelites athletes, resulting in a significant interaction.

Zaleski (1984) compared a risky sports group consisting of racing drivers, mountain climbers, glider pilots, and parachutists with control subjects. The risky sports group was higher on the TAS and Dis subscales.

TABLE 3.3
Sensation Seeking Scale (SSS) and Impulsivity (Imp) Means for Antisocial, Risky Sports, Prosocial Risky Vocation, and Controls

Scales	Antisocial		Risky sports		Prosocial		Control subjects	
	M	F	M	F	M	F	M	F
n	77	43	332	52	170	74	54	58
M age	22.96	29.00	30.83	27.75	29.97	26.49	30.74	29.71
TAS	7.51	6.23	7.86	8.06	7.11	6.35	4.52	4.73
ES	7.03	7.10	6.21	6.96	5.45	5.25	5.31	5.25
Dis	6.75	5.74	5.27	4.59	4.67	3.75	4.70	3.07
BS	5.29	4.97	4.44	3.80	4.20	3.71	4.26	3.60
TAS-Out	19.07	17.82	15.93	15.35	14.32	12.71	14.28	11.93
SSS Total	26.58	24.05	23.79	23.41	21.43	19.06	18.80	16.65
Imp	13.14	13.05	9.55	9.25	8.65	7.28	8.78	8.21

Note. M = male; F = female; TAS = Thrill and Adventure Seeking; ES = Experience Seeking; Dis = Disinhibition; BS = Boredom Susceptibility; TAS-Out = Total score minus TAS subscale; SSS Total = Total score including all subscales. Adapted from "Prosocial and Antisocial Aspects of Personality," by M. Gomà-i-Freixanet, 1995, *Personality and Individual Differences, 19,* p. 129, and from "Prosocial and Antisocial Aspects of Personality in Women: A Replication Study," by M. Gomà-i-Freixanet, 2001, *Personality and Individual Differences, 30,* p. 1406. Copyrights 1995, 2001 by Elsevier. Adapted with permission.

Risky Sports, Antisocial, and Prosocial Activity Contrasts

Gomà-i-Freixanet (1995, 2001) compared men and women involved in risky sports with those with a history of antisocial activities and incarcerated at the time of the study, with those with prosocial risky occupations, and with control subjects not engaged in any risky activities. The risky sports included alpinism, mountain climbing, scuba diving, water skiing, power-boat racing, white-water canoeing, aviation, parachuting, gliding, hang gliding, ballooning, car racing, motorcycle racing, pot holing, and adventuring. The risky prosocial jobs included firefighters, volunteer forest-fire fighters, traffic policemen and policewomen, security guards, prison warders, ambulance drivers, and life savers from the Red Cross. The prisoners in the antisocial groups had committed crimes of armed robbery involving physical risk or risk of death.

Table 3.3 shows the mean SSS scores and that for the Imp subscale from the H. J. Eysenck IVE. Among the males, the antisocial risk takers were higher on all of the SSS subscales and the Imp subscale than all other groups. All three risk-taking groups were higher than the control groups on TAS but did not differ among themselves except on the TAS-Out and SSS Total scores, on which the risky sportsmen were higher than the prosocial and control groups. Among the females, the antisocial subjects were higher than the prosocial and control groups on the SSS Total and on the ES, Dis, TAS-Out, and Imp subscales but did not differ from the risky sportswomen on these subscales, with the exception of the Imp subscale. For women, the only distinction between criminals and risky sports participants was the higher impulsivity in the antisocial group. Sensation seeking was equivalent for both groups.

Gomà-i-Freixanet (1999) compared three different risky sport groups and a control group from the male subjects. The alpinists are an elite group of climbers who tackle the higher mountains and have a notable higher death rate than the less risk-taking mountaineers. These two groups were compared with all of the remaining types of risky sportsmen and control subjects. There were no significant differences in SSS or the Imp subscale between alpinists and other mountaineers, and the ordinary mountaineers were even a little higher on some of the SSS subscales like TAS and Dis, and the Imp subscale. The mountaineers, but not the alpinists, were higher than the other sportsmen on TAS, ES, and the SSS Total. The alpinists, mountaineers, and risky sportsmen were all higher than the control subjects on these same three scales.

Summary

Gomà-i-Freixanet (2004) summarized her own research and the research of other investigators in reference to the different subscales of the SSS and their relationships to levels of risk as follows:

1. The TAS subscale is elevated in sports with high and medium levels of risk and even in some low-risk sports, although less so in the latter.
2. The ES subscale is elevated, along with TAS, only in sports with high levels of risk (showing that there is something more than thrills or adventure in what extreme risk takers, like mountain climbers, are seeking).
3. The BS subscale is high only in the more extreme sports.
4. The SSS Total score and Dis subscale are high in athletes at any level of sport risk compared with nonathletic control groups. Dis relates to the social activities around the sport, celebrations after a day on the slopes, for instance, and being nonconformist and unconventional in general.

I would add that among the high-risk athletes, high Dis scores are found in parachutists but not in mountain climbers. The parachutists get their rewards from brief but intense experiences (free fall) requiring little planning. They tend to be more impulsive than the mountain climbers. Mountain climbers cannot afford to be impulsive. Their climbs have to be carefully planned. There is a need for close coordination during the climb. They literally have to "hang together" if they do not want to "fall apart." However, Dis is elevated in some unlikely low-risk groups like male tennis players and swimmers. Aggressive competitiveness may also be associated with disinhibition.

Specific Risky Sports

Mountain and Rock Climbing

Breivik (1991) and Jack and Ronan's (1998) studies (see Tables 3.1 and 3.2, this chapter) showed that mountain climbers are one of the two highest sports groups on sensation seeking. Their scores on the subscales are high on both TAS and ES, but only average on Dis and BS. Cronin (1991) compared members of a mountain climbing club with control subjects from the same college. The mountain climbers were higher on the SSS Total, TAS, and ES scores. C. J. Fowler, von Knorring, and Oreland (1980) found that experienced mountaineers and others interested in mountaineering scored high on the SSS General Scale, TAS, and the monotony avoidance scale of the Karolinska Scales of Personality (Schalling Asberg, Edman, & Oreland, 1987). The mountaineering groups were also lower on monoamine oxidase, a consistent negative correlate of sensation seeking trait (see chap. 1).

D. W. Robinson (1985) compared elite rock climbers with the American norms and found them to be higher on SSS Total and on the TAS and ES subscales. Levenson (1990) also compared rock climbers with college norms and reported them to be higher on SSS Total, TAS, and ES and lower on Dis.

The findings are fairly consistent in that climbers are higher than control subjects on SSS Total or SSS General Scale and on TAS and ES subscales. They are not impulsive or disinhibited but are in search of a type of challenging adventure in which the reward is novel experience. Each climb is unique in its challenge, and the view from the summit, sometimes above the clouds, can be awe inspiring.

Parachuting and Skydiving

Studies of various sports risk groups (see Tables 3.1 and 3.2) show that parachutists are the highest overall sensation seekers, with the exception of the small group of expedition climbers in the Breivik (1991) data (Jack & Ronan, 1998). In a later study Breivik, Roth, and Jorgensen (1998) studied the reactions of expert and novice parachutists before, during, and after an actual jump. Experts had made on average about 1,000 jumps, whereas novices had made fewer than 10 jumps, on average about 4 jumps. Both groups were higher on the SSS Total and all of its subscales than a control group of Norwegian army recruits. They were also higher on H. J. Eysenck's Extraversion (E) and Psychoticism (P) and lower on Neuroticism (N) than the control group. The only significant differences between experienced and novice jumpers were on the P scale and the ES subscale, on which the experienced jumpers were higher. The SSS Total, TAS, ES, and Dis scores all correlated highly and significantly with the actual number of jumps.

TAS correlated negatively with self-rated anxiety during the jump. The P scale and the BS subscale correlated negatively with HR increases from baselines to that obtained from subjects sitting in the airplane just before exit. The correlations with the P scale were much higher than those with the BS scale.

Their results show that parachutists as a group are high sensation seekers and that those who go on to make many jumps are high on P, a scale related to impulsive antisocial sensation seeking behavior, and ES. TAS contains one item related to the desire to go parachute jumping, so its relationship to the criteria is somewhat confounded. But the parachutists were higher than control subjects on all the SSS subscales, and it was ES rather than TAS that distinguished experienced from novice jumpers. In the Jack and Ronan (1998) study, the skydivers were the highest sport group on an SSS Total score that excluded the TAS subscale. TAS was related to fearlessness during the jump. The combination of P and BS, which was predictive of lower HR arousal just prior to the jump, suggests that it is the impulsive unsocialized type of sensation seeking (Zuckerman, Kuhlman, et al., 1988; Zuckerman et al., 1991) that is related to the lack of fearful arousal during the jump. It is the anticipation of such unpleasant arousal, as well as the possible catastrophic consequences, that prevent most moderate sensation seekers from ever trying parachute jumping. It could be that the impulsive sensation seekers are hypoarousable in many situations and that the arousal that they experience in risky situations is therefore more enjoyable because it brings them up to their optimal levels.

A study of Canadian skydivers confirms the emotional hypoarousal of jumpers (Pierson, le Houezec, Fossaert, Dubal, & Jouvent, 1999). The skydivers scored higher than control subjects on scales measuring blunted affect and anhedonia. The skydivers were also highest on the TAS and BS subscales and borderline significantly higher on ES. These investigators also studied the cortical evoked response potential (ERP) in skydivers, using the oddball paradigm. Skydivers showed higher frontal P3 amplitudes than the control subjects. The greater P3 response was not to target, infrequently presented stimuli, but to nontarget stimuli. Anhedonia with blunted affect is associated with depression and reduced P3 reactions in clinical groups, but in this study the skydivers did not differ from control subjects on measures of depression and trait anxiety. These authors interpreted the reactivity of the ERP in skydivers to an enhanced orienting response to irrelevant as well as relevant stimuli. As described in chapter 1, sensation seekers tend to have stronger orienting reflexes (ORs) to all kinds of novel stimuli if they are novel or intense. The OR does not reflect an emotional response but is an expression of interest associated with approach behavior.

Bungee jumping is a more accessible sport not requiring training or much expense, more like a ride in an amusement park than a sport. It is also regarded as safer, although occasionally the harness on the long rubber band breaks. Michel, Carton, and Jouvent (1997) compared French bungee jumpers with control subjects from the general public. The jumpers were higher than the control subjects on only one subscale, TAS, but ES and BS were positively correlated with the number of jumps they had made.

Downhill Skiing

Downhill skiing is distinguished in terms of risk from cross-country skiing by higher speed and greater risk of accident caused by unanticipated encounters with trees, rocks, or other skiers. Of course, there are different kinds of slopes, with some offering more speed, sensation, and risk than others. Experienced skiers are more likely to graduate to the more challenging slopes. Connolly (1981) found that whereas ordinary skiers differed from nonskiers only on the SSS Total and TAS, ski instructors scored higher on Total, TAS, and ES. Calhoon (1988) studied skiers who were all experienced, including ski instructors and ski patrolmen. These skiers scored higher than college student nonskiers on the Total and all subscales of the SSS.

Skiers in the Netherlands, compared with the Dutch general population, tend to have higher scores on TAS, but a study of skiers making insurance claims for injury due to accidents (compared with skiers filing other types of claims) showed lower TAS scores for the skiers reporting injuries due to accidents (Bouter, Knipschild, Feij, & Volovics, 1988). This finding was contrary to the expectation that high sensation seekers would take more risks and therefore suffer more accidents than low sensation seekers. Bouter et al. (1988) speculated that more experienced high sensation seekers were more familiar with the risks and therefore less accident prone.

These suppositions were confirmed by Cherpitel, Meyers, and Perrine (1998), who found that injured skiers were more likely to be female and weekend skiers with less experience and lower on sensation seeking than a control group of skiers. It is surprising that more control subjects reported drinking in the hour before skiing than injured skiers, although more injured skiers had been drinking 12 hours before skiing. The authors speculated that this could be a hangover effect rather than a result of intoxication. The results indicate that higher sensation seekers may be more likely to ski while intoxicated, but that does not necessarily result in more accidents for them.

Scuba Diving

Heyman and Rose (1979) compared novice scuba divers with same-sex student control subjects. The divers were higher on the SSS Total score. The subscales were not reported in the article. The SSS Total correlated positively with the duration of the first dive and negatively with the depth of the dive.

Low sensation seekers dove to deeper depths but spent less time in the water, whereas high sensation seekers stayed at shallower depths but spent more time exploring their surroundings. Actually, deeper dives are riskier, so experience seeking was probably the dominant motive for the high sensation seekers.

Bacon (personal communication, 1974) compared volunteer salvage divers with college students on the SSS–IV. These professional divers were higher than the control subjects on the General, TAS, Dis, and BS scores. As with skiing, those who make a career out of their sports, like ski instructors, tended to be higher than more novice types in a sport.

Hang Gliding, Paragliding, and Parasailing

These sports have certain kinds of sensation in common: flying high supported only by the wind and some kind of frame for the body. Hang gliders were among the highest sensation seekers in the comparisons by Jack and Ronan (1998). However, this was largely due to their high TAS scores rather than ES or Dis scores. Straub (1982) compared hang gliders and auto racers, in high-risk sports, with bowlers, in a low-risk sport. The gliders were higher than the bowlers on SSS Total and ES. A. M. Wagner and Houlihan (1994) compared hang-glider pilots and golfers and found that the pilots were significantly higher on the SSS Total and all of the subscales as well. Differences were particularly large for the ES and TAS subscales. There was no difference on trait anxiety. Another study compared hang gliders with persons in less risky sports—baseball and wrestling (Rainey, Amunategui, Agocs, & Larick, 1992). The hang gliders were higher than the other groups on SSS Total, ES, and BS.

Franques et al. (2003) compared paragliders with opioid-dependent subjects seeking treatment and control subjects (i.e., college employees). The paragliders scored significantly higher than the control subjects on the SSS Total score and on the TAS, Dis, and BS subscales. The drug-dependent group also exceeded control subjects on Dis and TAS scales. The paraglider group was higher than the drug-dependent group on TAS, whereas the drug-dependent group tended to score higher on Dis. Chirivella and Martinez (1994) contrasted the SSS scores of three groups: parasailing, tennis, and karate participants. The parasailing group was higher than the other two groups on the SSS Total and all of the subscales; the tennis and karate groups did not differ on any of these scales.

Surfing

Surfers and golfers were compared in a study by Diehm and Armatas (2004). Surfers scored higher than golfers on TAS, ES, and Dis, even after differences in age were controlled by covariance. Participants in both sports were divided into competitive and recreational sports persons; however, there was no main effect of level of sport participation and no interactions with type of sport or gender. There was an interaction of sport and gender for Dis. Male surfers and golfers did not differ on Dis, but female surfers were as high as male surfers and higher than female golfers on Dis.

Auto Racing

Remembering that a taste for speed is related to sensation seeking in young drivers, one would expect that those who engage in the risky sport of auto racing would be high sensation seekers. Straub (1982) found that auto racers did exceed control subjects on Total, ES, Dis, and BS scores but did not differ on TAS, in contrast to the hang gliders, who were high on TAS and ES but not on Dis and BS. Auto racers in the Jack and Ronan (1998) study were higher on TAS than golfers and marathon runners but were lower than hang gliders, skydivers, and mountaineers. The racers were also lower than the skydivers and mountaineers on ES. Auto racers seem to be an intermediate group, between high and low sensation seeking sports participants.

White-Water Canoeing

In Breivik's (1991) comparisons of sport groups (see Table 3.1, this chapter), white-water canoeists were the third highest on sensation seeking, just below mountain climbers and parachutists. They showed high scores on TAS and ES, as well as SSS Total. However, Campbell, Tyrrell, and Zingaro (1993) found significant differences between canoeists and norms only on TAS. They were marginally higher ($p < .10$) on ES. TAS scores correlated negatively with state anxiety as they entered the water and with the highest level of river difficulty they would like to attempt. Dis also correlated with the latter.

Interest in Sports

Sports fans get a lot of stimulation from watching their teams play either on television or in the arenas. Is this interest in sports related to sensation seeking? Of course, there is a sex difference in this interest

(Franken, Hill, & Kierstead, 1994). Men were more interested in every sport except figure skating and gymnastics. Women were more interested than men in these two. Interest in football was positively related to Dis in men and women but negatively related to ES in men. Disinhibited behavior is often observed in those watching football in bars or pubs and is associated with drinking. Those interested in seeking sensation through experiences or "through the mind and the senses" (Zuckerman, 1994, p. 31) do not seem to be much interested in the violent sport of football. Dis in men was also minimally but significantly related to interests in boxing, tennis, and golf. Interest in gymnastics was related to TAS in women. Dis was related to engagement in competitive sports in both sexes and to TAS in women. Betting on sports was related to Dis in men only. All of these correlations were quite low, albeit significant, suggesting that sports interests are not a strong indicator of sensation seeking motivations.

Summary

Gomà-i-Freixanet (2004) summarized 25 studies of high-risk sports groups using the SSS–IV or SSS–V, containing the four subscales, in a table. Of the 25 studies, the high-risk sports group was higher than a control group on TAS (20), ES (13), Dis (10), BS (9), General or Total (22). In 3 studies in which a modified Total, excluding the TAS scale, was used, all 3 still showed the risky sport group to be significantly higher than the control subjects. With little exception, groups engaged in risky sports are high general sensation seekers but particularly high on TAS. The difference on the Total is not just a function of the TAS scale as shown by studies using the General Scale and the TAS-Out Total.

There is variation among different sports. Persons who do mountain climbing, parachute jumping or skydiving, white-water canoeing, hang gliding, or scuba diving are highest on general sensation seeking. Those who do ordinary skiing, swimming, auto racing, karate, ice hockey, or tennis are intermediate on sensation seeking. In general, when sports are confined to one activity, long-distance or marathon runners, golf, and volleyball players tend to be low sensation seekers. However, the main difference is on TAS.

Experts who have more experience in a particular risky sport or even make their living by teaching the sport or engage in competitions tend to be even higher than those with less experience. Those who try a sport once or twice or very infrequently are not necessarily high sensation seekers, although they are not low. Some try a sport like skydiving once, find it unpleasant or simply not what they expected, and never do it again.

Outside of sports, those who engage in other types of risky behaviors like use of drugs often score higher on ES, Dis, and BS even if they engage in no sports at all. Interest in sports, particularly football, may show a weak relationship with Dis, perhaps because of its association with disinhibited behavior in general and particularly when drinking.

RISKY VOCATIONS

Personnel specialists were asked to rank 10 occupations according to the degree of risk taking involved in the job, with *risk taking* defined as placing the safety of oneself or others in jeopardy (Musolino & Hershenson, 1977). The four riskiest occupations in order of their rated riskiness were test pilot, air-traffic controller, police officer, and fireman. The lowest in risk were librarian, civil service–clerical, and accountant. Soldiers were not included, but those involved in combat or risky assignments would have to be among the highest in risk taking.

Military and Paramilitary Vocations

Breivik (1991) compared Norwegian paratroopers with sport paratroopers and ordinary military recruits. The paratroopers were higher than ordinary recruits on SSS Total and TAS, Dis, and BS subscales. They did not differ from civilian parachutists on any subscale except ES, on which the civilian parachutists scored higher. Air force recruits in the Swedish air force were compared with randomly selected army conscripts by Hallman et al. (1990). The pilots were higher than the army draftees on TAS and Dis subscales, as well as on the KSP monotony avoidance scale. American preflight naval cadets were higher on TAS but lower on ES, Dis, and BS than were male college students (Waters, Ambler, & Waters, 1976). The authors suggest that the lower scores on the last three scales could be due to a social desirability (SD) response set because the Dis and ES subscales were negatively correlated with SD. Biersner and LaRocco (1983) had a similar result for American navy divers who scored higher on TAS but lower on Dis and ES than a college student group. However, the divers were older than the student sample, and this could have affected their scores on the Dis subscale in particular, which tends to fall with age.

Israeli psychologists have studied the reactions of soldiers in combat and postcombat periods of their lives. One study compared veterans of the 1973 Yom Kippur War in three groups: (a) soldiers who received medals for bravery in combat, (b) soldiers who were treated for combat stress reactions during the war, and (c) control subjects who fought in the war but won no decorations for bravery and were not treated for combat stress (Neria, Solomon, Ginzburg, & Dekel, 2000). A short form of the SSS was used that did not have subscales. The decorated soldiers were higher on the SSS than the casualties and control subjects, who did not differ from each other. A follow-up of subsequent long-term adjustment showed that low sensation seekers reported more posttraumatic stress disorder (PTSD) symptoms and war-related intrusions and avoidance tendencies than did high sensation seekers.

Another study of soldiers captured in that war also shows the greater resilience and coping capacity of high sensation seekers compared with low sensation seekers (Solomon, Ginzburg, Neria, & Ohry, 1995). Low sensation seekers showed more PTSD symptoms and severe psychiatric symptomatology in general after release. The low sensation seekers reported more feelings of helplessness, loss of control, abandonment, and more suffering in prison than high sensation seekers. The lows relied less on active coping and more on isolation and denial strategies during their imprisonment.

Montag and Birenbaum (1986) compared male applicants for risky security-related jobs in Israel with applicants for less dangerous jobs. Those applying for risky jobs were higher on the SSS Total and the TAS, ES, and BS subscales. Glicksohn and Bozna (2000) compared personality profiles of Israeli bomb-disposal experts and antiterror operatives. The antiterror group scored higher than the Israeli norms for that age group on TAS, but bomb disposal experts were well within the normative range on TAS. Other than this, the two professional risk-taker groups were similar, and both were lower on the less socialized types of sensation seeking embodied in the Dis and BS scales, as well as the H. J. Eysenck P scale. Their scores on neuroticism were also low relative to the norms. Some groups of those who volunteer for risky duties like parachuting or security forces have a generalized sensation seeking tendency, but others seem to have a more narrowly focused need for thrills and adventure and are low in other kinds of sensation seeking. They are nonimpulsive, socialized, prosocial sensation seekers.

Prosocial Sensation Seeking Vocations

Goma-i-Freixanet's (1995, 2001) prosocial groups, whose SSS scores are shown in Table 3.3 of this chapter, differed from control subjects only on TAS and not on the other subscales. However, Zaleski (1984), also comparing a group of men in prosocial risky occupations with control subjects and risky sportsmen, found that those in risky occupations differed from control subjects only on Dis. Like the risky sportsmen, they were higher than the control subjects on Dis. Some of these differences between studies may be due to the different mix of risky prosocial occupations in these studies.

Firefighters and Police Officers

Goma-i-Freixanet, Pérez, and Torrubia (1988) compared Spanish firefighters and students on the SSS. The firefighters were significantly higher on the Total and the TAS and ES subscales of the SSS but were not higher on Dis.

Police work is regarded as risky on the basis of television and movies emphasizing the violence in their work. But many police have never drawn their guns, let alone fired them. Much police work in quiet neighborhoods involves traffic duties and somewhat boring assignments as guards in public events. Gomà-i-Freixanet and Wismeijer (2002) tested police bodyguards and compared them with control subjects and other risk-taking groups. Although they did not differ from Catalan norms on any of the sensation seeking scales, they were higher on TAS and lower on BS than the matched control subjects. A lower boredom susceptibility would almost have to be a requirement for a job that requires long periods of inactivity. They were even lower than prosocial and risky sports groups on this scale, although they did not differ from them on TAS. It is ironic that such men may be attracted to a profession because of its image as a provider of thrills and adventure but then be condemned to a life of boring routine.

The police car chase is a standard part of any police action movie. The real police chases are risky and sometimes result in damage and injury to innocent others as well as to the police themselves. Police administrators feel these high-speed pursuits should be limited to the most serious offenses and where there is a strong need to apprehend the fleer. But just as the movie car chases are popular with audiences because of their exciting effects, the chase is even more arousing to the officers actually involved in it. Homant, Kennedy, and Howton (1994) used departmental records and officers' self-reports to document the extent to which individual officers engaged in high-speed pursuits. They also took the SSS and a risk-taking scale designed for police measuring the willingness to take risks in their job and their attitudes toward such risk. Three quarters of the respondents reported that they had initiated at least one pursuit during the past year, and the mean number of pursuits was about two. The mean SSS Total score for the entire group was close to that for equivalent age norms, but the SSS correlated significantly with both self-reported and official records of high-speed pursuits, and the risk scale correlated with the self-report of pursuits. Both scales correlated significantly with a combined pursuit measure. When the two scales were combined, the multiple correlation with pursuit was .40.

Stressful Occupations

There are some prosocial vocations for which the risk is not to self but to others. The type of environment in which employees work to save lives or prevent accidents can be quite stressful, as in air-traffic control rooms or hospital emergency rooms. Those who are arousal avoidant or stressed by stimulus overload do not find such environments compatible, but high sensation seekers may love the change and excitement during high-peak periods.

Musolino and Hershenson (1977) found that the job of air-traffic controller was second only to test pilot in their rankings of jobs for riskiness. They studied a group of air-traffic controllers and compared them with male clerical civil servants and college students, both occupations rated at the low end of the risk scale. The air-traffic controllers were significantly higher than the civil servant clerical workers and the students on the General Scale and on all of the four subscales of the SSS–IV. The highest subscale was TAS, suggesting that these controllers were likely to seek thrills in physical activities or sports outside of their job. Although burnout is said to be common in this job, there was no correlation of SSS with time on the job.

Medicine offers many different kinds of opportunities, including teaching, research, clinical practice, and most stressful of all, working in an emergency room in an urban setting in which a Saturday evening can bring a flood of wounds and acute illnesses, some of which are life threatening. Irey (1974) compared professionals, physicians, nurses, psychologists, and paraprofessionals with physicians in more traditional roles such as professional practice or teaching. Those working in the crisis intervention settings scored significantly higher than those working in traditional settings on all of the sensation seeking scales. The traditional physicians were particularly low on the SSS, consistent with the finding that English medical students were lower than arts and science and agricultural students on the SSS General Scale (Golding & Cornish, 1987).

Best and Kilpatrick (1977) compared rape crisis counselors and pediatric nurses matched for age and education. The crisis counselors scored higher on Dis and ES subscales of the SSS–IV. The rape crisis counselors were described as "well-adjusted women who are open-minded . . . nonanxious, relatively assertive, profeminist, and whose mood of vigor and activity leads them to seek out and enjoy new experiences" (p. 1133).

Summary

Some vocations, like soldiering and police work, which may seem exciting in everyday activity, can be maddeningly boring. When I was in the U.S. Army after basic training and in routine garrison duties, I became so bored by inactivity and routine that I considered volunteering for the paratroops. I was only dissuaded by learning that I would have to extend my period of enlistment to do this. The quote by Caputo (1977) earlier in this chapter illustrates how the author, driven by boredom, volunteers for assignment to a combat unit because he found a "magnetism" in the exhilaration of combat. Volunteers for risky duty, like paratroops, flyers, divers, and antiterror operatives, tend to be higher on sensation seeking, particularly thrill and adventure seeking, than their fellow soldiers content with the routine of garrison life.

Performance in combat is also related to sensation seeking. Heroes who win medals, if they survive, probably accomplish their feats by taking risks and mastering fear. They focus on the task at hand, such as taking out an enemy position, to the exclusion of emotional appraisals of risk that would immobilize them. Some, like Caputo (1977), probably find gratification of their high needs for stimulation and excitement in combat. Even in prisoner-of-war (POW) situations, high sensation seekers adapt better than low sensation seekers, probably because they find active ways of resisting or coping. The low sensation seekers are more susceptible to combat stress reactions and PTSD after combat or the POW experience.

Firefighters have periods of boredom and inactivity, but their sensation seeking needs are periodically gratified by the excitement of a fire call. Depending on their assignments, police may go for extended periods with nothing but monotonous, inactive duties. Those in car patrols may occasionally relieve the boredom by sought-out confrontations or car chases. High-speed pursuits have been related to individual levels of sensation seeking.

The definition of *physical risk taking* can be extended to those occupations in which there is responsibility for risks to others, as in air-traffic controllers and emergency room and crisis center workers. Persons better suited for such prosocial risky vocations in which there are often high degrees of stress tend to be higher sensation seekers.

4

SENSATION SEEKING AND SUBSTANCE USE AND ABUSE: SMOKING, DRINKING, AND DRUGS

> I get no kick from champagne
> Mere alcohol doesn't thrill me at all
> So tell me why should it be true
> That I get a kick out of you
> Some get their kick from cocaine
> I'm sure that if I took even one sniff
> It would bore me terrifically too
> But I get a kick out of you
>
> —Cole Porter, "I Get a Kick Out of You"[1]

The Cole Porter song expresses a common source of substance abuse in the expression *getting kicks*, although love and sex seem to have superseded alcohol and cocaine in this case. When high school students were asked why they smoked, drank, or did drugs, over 80% replied either "for fun, thrills, or excitement;" "to get away with it;" or "it made me feel good" (Wood et al., 1995). What is it about these substances that makes their users willing to risk so much to enjoy them?

There are three phases of motivation in the use of addictive substances: (a) *curiosity* about their effects fueled by accounts of those who have used them; (b) *pleasure*, a positive arousing effect described as "kicks"; and (c) *avoidance* of pain or discomfort caused by attempts at withdrawal from use. The first phase is associated with initial and occasional use; the second, with substance abuse; and the third, with dependence or addiction. Sensation seeking is associated with the first two phases, but the last one is a physiological or psychological consequence of heavy use and not necessarily related to sensation seeking.

---

[1] From "I Get a Kick Out of You." Words and music by Cole Porter. Copyright 1934 by Warner Bros. Inc. Copyright renewed. All rights reserved. Used by permission.

All drugs of abuse, including nicotine, opioids, ethanol, cocaine, and amphetamines, have their rewarding effects through the release of the neuro-transmitter dopamine in the mesolimbic pathways that mediate natural rewards (sex, food) and electrical rewards through self-induced intracranial brain stimulation (Kalivas, 2002). Other kinds of sensation seeking activities probably stimulate the same "pathways to pleasure," but drugs provide a fast and intense sensation in their initial effects on the brain. Even suppressant drugs such as alcohol or heroin provide an initial "rush" before their physio-logical suppressant effects kick in. This is why alcoholics speak of the initial effects of alcohol as "getting high." However, the high tends to habituate with long-term use and the user tends to try to recover it with increasing dosages, leading to the dependency phenomenon of tolerance. One might say that the addict starts using drugs for pleasure but ends by using them to avoid pain or feel reasonably normal. Sensation seekers are likely to get on at the initial phase because of their novel experience seeking tendency, and some, but not all of them, will progress to abuse or dependence.

In contrast to a model that stresses the primary reinforcement of drugs, the primary socialization theory suggests that personality influences drug use primarily through the socialization process, specifically the development of attitudes toward drugs and attraction to peers who have similar attitudes and who use drugs themselves (Oetting, Deffenbacher, & Donnermeyer, 1998). Specifically in reference to sensation seeking, Oetting et al. stated,

> Thus the biological propensity of sensation seekers for higher activity and for seeking high-intensity stimulation may increase the chances of drug use not because the trait makes drug use more reinforcing, but because sensation seeking influences the socialization process. (p. 1348)

There are alternative ways to express sensation seeking, as in the contrast between thrill and adventure seeking and disinhibition. The choices may be influenced by whether one is attracted to friends and groups who are within social boundaries or outside of them in their indulgence in drugs and sex.

Horvath and Zuckerman (1993) found that both subjects' estimates of their peers' behaviors and their own sensation seeking trait predicted their own risky behaviors but that peer behavior was the most powerful predictor in multiple regression analyses. But I maintain that peer attraction, like assortative mating, is a function of the biological tendencies underlying the trait of sensation seeking. Peer influences are reciprocal among high sensation seekers. Although more moderate or low sensation seekers may sometimes be susceptible to peer persuasion, they are unlikely to persevere in drug use if they find the effects uncongenial or anxiety provoking.

A large study of alcohol and marijuana use in studies of a cohort of young adolescents going from the 8th to the 10th grade examined sensation seeking and actual behavior reported by peers in relation to marijuana and alcohol use (Donohew, Clayton, Skinner, & Colon, 1999). Sensation seeking did not directly affect marijuana or alcohol use but indirectly affected use through drug attitudes and peer influences. Their findings are supportive of the primary socialization theory, but it should be emphasized that this is a very young adolescent group just beginning to experiment with marijuana and alcohol. This is an age in which peer influences are likely to be maximal. Continuance of drug use and drinking habits may be directly influenced by sensation seeking at later ages.

Among those who use drugs, sensation seeking is related more to the number of drugs used than the type of drug favored (Zuckerman, 1983a, 1987a, 1987b, 1994). Polydrug users are higher sensation seekers than are single-drug users. A study of drug preferences among recovering drug users currently abstinent in a therapeutic program compared those who preferred opiates, stimulants, marijuana, alcohol, or polydrug users on the Sensation Seeking Scale (SSS) and the Eysenck Personality Questionnaire (EPQ; H. J. Eysenck & Eysenck, 1975; O'Connor, Berry, Morrison, & Brown, 1995). There were no differences on the Psychoticism (P), Extraversion (E), and Neuroticism (N) scales of the EPQ between the drug preference groups. Only the Boredom Susceptibility (BS) subscale of the SSS showed significant differences.

The opiate user group had a significantly higher mean score than the marijuana- and alcohol-preferring groups; the polydrug group was closer to the opiate-user group and had significantly higher scores than the alcohol-preferring group. Opiate and polydrug users represent a more experienced drug group than marijuana and alcohol primary users, and many continue to use marijuana and alcohol after they have developed opiate preferences.

Drug users usually start by drinking alcohol and smoking tobacco at an early age, then try marijuana, then move on to drugs taken by pill like amphetamines and barbiturates, and finally move to even more potent drugs like heroin and cocaine. The method of ingestion increases the potency and speed to peak effect. Injecting or inhaling the drug provides more potent and immediate kicks than waiting for a pill to reach the brain via the gut-to-blood pathway. Smoking nicotine provides a less intense high than cocaine but one that is direct and controllable through drags on the cigarette.

Segal and Singer (1976; Segal, Huba, & Singer, 1980) studied personality and drug use in a large survey of college students and naval personnel. Subjects were divided into four groups: nonusers of either alcohol or marijuana, users of alcohol only, users of marijuana and/or alcohol but not other drugs, and multidrug users. All items in the SSS with content pertaining to drugs or drinking were removed before analyses. Significant differences between all four groups were found on all of the SSS subscales, but Experience Seeking (ES) and Disinhibition (Dis) subscales were the primary predictors of alcohol and drug use in multivariate analyses that included locus of control and personality need scales from Jackson's (1974) Personality Research Form.

Within the four groups in the study by Segal et al. (1980), the lowest sensation seeking scores were in the abstainer group, followed by higher scores in the alcohol-only group, even higher scores in the group taking the step from legal (alcohol) to illegal (marijuana) drugs, and the highest scores in the multidrug users. Similar results comparing drinkers, marijuana-only users, and polydrug users were obtained by Galizio, Rosenthal, and Stein (1983).

Although these studies suggest a natural progression from alcohol to polydrug use, it should be emphasized that these are cross-sectional, not longitudinal, studies. Because the subjects are in a narrow age range, they represent different groups. Many if not most of those who drink never try marijuana, and many if not most of those who smoke marijuana do not go on to more potent drugs. But sensation seeking, particularly the desire for new experiences and enjoyment of states of disinhibition, is associated with the progression to the more potent and risky drugs.

GENERAL DRUG USE

The use of drugs increases from preadolescence to early adulthood. Sensation seekers generally start using drugs at an earlier age than others. They also are more likely to progress from milder drugs, such as marijuana, to more potent drugs, such as amphetamines, cocaine, and heroin.

High School Age Samples

Many studies have been done in several countries relating sensation seeking to the use of a variety of substances including tobacco, marijuana, alcohol, and other drugs. In this section, I focus on those studies using combined indexes of substance use as the dependent variable. Later sections deal with studies of specific drugs. Most of these studies have been of young adolescents in high school years, the time at which substance abuse begins to be a problem, although hard-drug use is less common. Many of the studies have used shortened sensation seeking scales, eliminating confounding items mentioning drinking or drugs. Others have used similar scales like novelty seeking or thrill seeking.

Wills, Windle, and Cleary (1998) studied nearly 1,000 young adolescents (M age = 14) in the eighth grade in New York schools. Substance abuse was defined by a combined index of cigarette, alcohol, and marijuana use. Novelty seeking (NS) and harm avoidance were both related to substance use, but a multivariate analysis showed that NS alone accounted for the relationship.

Bates, White, and Labouvie (1985) assessed 584 American adolescents, first at age 15 then again 3 years later at age 18. The Dis subscale (with drug and alcohol items omitted) from the SSS was given at both occasions, along with self-reports of alcohol or drug use. Dis was related to alcohol and drug use at both concurrent testings, and changes in Dis from the first to the second testing were related to changes in level, quantity, and effects of alcohol and drug use. Those whose Dis scores rose over the 3 years showed increases in alcohol and drug use, whereas those whose Dis scores dropped leveled out in their substance use.

Pederson, Clausen, and Lavik (1989) had a sample of more than 1,000 Norwegian high school students, aged 16 to 19. A short form of the SSS, excluding all items mentioning drugs, found that the ES and Dis subscales were correlated with the use of alcohol and marijuana in both males and females, and the Dis subscale correlated with tobacco and use of inhalants in males only. L. von Knorring, Oreland, and von Knorring (1987) studied a total population of over 1,200 18-year-old Swedish male military draftees, using a translated SSS that excluded the entire Dis subscale and items in the ES subscale indicating an interest in drug use. Both a heavy alcohol and a mixed drug and alcohol group were higher than abstainer and infrequent usage groups on the Total and Thrill and Adventure Seeking (TAS), ES, and BS subscales from the SSS as well as scales for impulsivity and monotony avoidance. Although Dis is the major predictor of drug use in many studies, it is interesting that its exclusion did not affect the predictive value of the other subscales and the SSS Total score.

Huba, Newcomb, and Bentler (1981) used shortened sensation seeking scales to study alcohol and drug use in a sample of over 1,000 high school students between the 10th and 12th grades. Canonical correlation was used to identify relationships between SSS subscales and types of drug use. A factor identified with Dis was closely related to a substance abuse factor, including beer, wine, hard liquor, marijuana, and hashish. The second SSS factor was primarily ES and secondarily BS. In addition to marijuana and hashish, the associated drug factor included barbiturates, sedatives, amphetamines, cocaine, LSD, and other psychedelic drugs. The third SSS factor was TAS, which correlated positively with use of alcohol and marijuana but negatively with use of cigarettes and hard drugs. Apparently, those inclined toward extreme sports are wary of smoking and drugs that might impair their health.

Andrucci, Archer, Pancoast, and Gordon (1989) compared users and nonusers of a variety of drugs in an adolescent high school population. The

SSS Total and ES and Dis subscales significantly differentiated users from nonusers of amphetamines, marijuana, barbiturates, cocaine, hallucinogens, and narcotics. There was no type of drug used more by low than by high sensation seekers. It is interesting that the drugs used by high sensation seekers included both stimulant and depressant drugs. This reinforces an earlier conclusion that the physiological effect of an illegal drug was not related to its preference by sensation seekers. Sensation seekers like to get "high" and "low" and use both types of drugs sequentially or together. Drinking is common with stimulant drugs; it slows down the effects of the stimulant and enables the user to remain "cool" and later to sleep. Sensation seekers use hallucinogens in search of novel experiences.

The authors used other scales from the Minnesota Multiphasic Personality Inventory (MMPI; Hathaway & McKinley, 1951) but found that the SSS Total scale was "the most effective and powerful predictor of use versus nonuse of alcohol and drugs" (p. 263). For alcohol, it was the sole predictor. Anxiety and depression scales predicted little but barbiturate use, probably for self-medication. Removal of confounding items from the Dis and ES subscales did not affect the results. Within the drug-using group, polydrug users were higher on the SSS Total than single-drug users.

Tobacco, Alcohol, and Marijuana in Middle and High School

A number of large studies in the 1990s and early 2000s used sensation seeking scales as one of the correlates and predictors of the three earliest kinds of substance use: smoking tobacco, drinking alcohol, and smoking marijuana. Use of hard drugs was much less common in these middle and high school populations, so it was not a focus of study. Table 4.1 summarizes the results of six of these studies.

Nearly all of these studies showed significant relationships between sensation seeking and use of tobacco, alcohol, and marijuana. Most of the studies used brief 2- to 12-item sensation seeking scales not containing any items referring to substance use.

A large study of 8th- and 11th-grade students in Delaware used short, three-item scales for Dis and TAS developed by Donohew, Clayton, et al. (1999) to predict tobacco and marijuana use (Kopstein, Crum, Celentano, & Martin, 2001). Those with high Dis scores were 3 times as likely to smoke cigarettes and 6 times as likely to use marijuana as those low on this scale. The odds ratios were significant but less for the high and low groups on the TAS subscale, but TAS was not a significant predictor of use of these substances in a bivariate model containing only the Dis and TAS subscales, or in a multivariable model containing other risk factors. Dis also correlated with other risk variables like skipping school, cheating, and arguing frequently with parents but was independently predictive of substance use.

TABLE 4.1
Studies of Middle School and High School Smoking, Drinking, and Drugs

Study	Subjects	Tests	Results
Wood, Cochran, Pfefferbaum, & Arneklev (1995)	1,159 HS; 9th–12th graders; U.S.	CPI Imp scale; 6-item SSS	SS and Imp predict prevalence of tobacco, alcohol, and drug use
Ames, Sussman, & Dent (1999)	1,074 HS; ages 14–19, M age = 17; U.S.	11 SS items from ImpSS in ZKPQ	SS predicts drug use (tobacco, alcohol, and MJ) at baseline and at 1-year follow-up
Baker & Yardley (2002)	420 HS; M age = 15.5; Canada	12-item SS-Imp scale	Tobacco, alcohol, and MJ use correlate .41–.46; SS correlates with all three .24–.37
Martin et al. (2002)	208 adolescents; ages 11–14; U.S.	Russo et al.'s (1993) scale for children	SS correlates with tobacco and alcohol use in boys and girls, MJ use in boys
Kopstein, Crum, Celentano, & Martin (2001)	1,196 8th graders and 1,369 11th graders	Short TAS and Dis subscales of SSS	High Dis 3 times more likely to smoke, 6 times more likely to use MJ than low Dis; TAS more weakly related to tobacco and MJ
Crawford, Pentz, Chou, Li, & Dwyer (2003)	2,208 7th and 8th graders; 7-year annual follow-up	2-item SS scale	Initial level of SS in middle school predicts rates of increase of alcohol and MJ use in middle school and HS

Note. HS = high school; CPI Imp = California Psychological Inventory Impulsivity subscale; SSS = Sensation Seeking Scale; SS = sensation seeking; Imp = impulsivity; ImpSS = Impulsive Sensation Seeking; ZKPQ = Zuckerman–Kuhlman Personality Questionnaire; MJ = marijuana; SS-Imp = sensation seeking and impulsivity items; TAS = Thrill and Adventure Seeking subscale; Dis = Disinhibition subscale.

Another study using seventh- and eigth-grade high school students also included annual follow-up assessments over a 7-year period (Crawford, Pentz, Chou, Li, & Dwyer, 2003). They used a two-item sensations seeking scale with the following items: (a) "Do you like to take chances?" and (b) "Is it worth getting into trouble if you have fun?" Both sensation seeking and substance use increased over the 7-year period. The initial level of sensation seeking in middle school predicted the initial level of cigarette use in high school (in 1 of the 2 schools), the rate of increase in alcohol use in both middle and high school, and rates of increase in marijuana use during both middle and high school.

Martin et al. (2002) studied young adolescents from 11 to 14 years of age from psychiatric and pediatric clinics in Kentucky, using Russo et al.'s

(1993) Child SSS. The Child SSS was significantly associated with tobacco smoking and alcohol use in boys and girls and with marijuana use in boys alone. Pubertal stage was associated with sensation seeking in both boys and girls and with drug use. Sensation seeking mediated the relationship of pubertal development to drug use. Previous studies have related testosterone to sensation seeking (see chap. 1, this volume).

Baker and Yardley (2002) studied high school students (M = 15.5), using a brief, 12-item scale containing both sensation seeking and impulsivity items (SS-Imp). Tobacco, alcohol, and marijuana use were all intercorrelated (rs = .41–.46). The SS-Imp scale correlated significantly with all three forms of substance use (rs = .24–.37), and the relationships were significant in a multiple regression controlling for demographic characteristics like age and the importance of religious faith.

A survey of nearly 1,600 high school students found that thrill seeking and impulsivity scales predicted the use of tobacco, alcohol, drinking and drunkenness, marijuana and hard drugs, and the frequency of use for all of these but hard drugs (Wood et al., 1995). Ames, Sussman, and Dent (1999) investigated drug use, defined by frequencies of recent cigarette, alcohol, marijuana, and other drug use, in over 1,000 California high school students between 14 and 19 years of age. They used the 11-item sensation seeking subscale from the Zuckerman–Kuhlman Personality Questionnaire (ZKPQ) Impulsive Sensation Seeking (ImpSS) scale (Zuckerman, 2002) as a predictor, along with measures of social influences, outcome expectancies, and attitudes toward drug use. Drug use was tested initially and at a 1-year follow-up. When belief and attitude scales were analyzed with sensation seeking and demographic variables in a multiple regression analysis, only sensation seeking, gender, ethnicity, and baseline drug use remained as significant predictors of follow-up drug use.

In the study previously described, ethnicity was a factor in drug use, with White students using more drugs than Black students. Another study examined the role of ethnicity in the relationships between attitudes, drug use, and sensation seeking (McCuller, Sussman, Dent, & Teran, 2001). As in the previous study, they used items from the sensation seeking subscale of the ZKPQ ImpSS to measure sensation seeking. White ethnicity was associated with sensation seeking and soft-drug use, whereas Latino ethnicity was more associated with peer approval, trait anxiety, depression, and hard-drug use.

A study of an African Black population of over 3,000 adolescents in Zimbabwe used a short sensation seeking scale and a substance abuse scale containing questions on frequency of tobacco, alcohol, marijuana, and inhalants (Eide, Acuda, Khan, Aaroe, & Loeb, 1997). Both sensation seeking and peer use of drugs predicted drug use in the subjects. However, the relation with sensation seeking was found in urban but not rural schools.

A study of about 1,000 7th through 11th graders in the United States and close to 1,000 6th through 10th graders in China used a short form of the SSS and a drug use scale limited to only cigarette and alcohol use (Pilgrim, Luo, Urberg, & Fang, 1999). The American sample included samples of African Americans and European Americans. There were two periods of assessment 1 year apart. In all three ethnic groups, sensation seeking was associated with drug use (smoking and drinking). Sensation seeking had an immediate effect and an effect on subsequent drug use mediated by drug use at Time 1. Use of drugs by friends was related to self drug use in European American and Chinese adolescents but not in African Americans.

Young Adults

Our first studies of the relationship of sensation seeking to drinking and drug use in college students were conducted in the early 1970s, when marijuana, hashish, amphetamines, LSD, and barbiturates were the most popular drugs on campus (Zuckerman, Bone, Neary, Mangelsdorf, & Brustman, 1972; Zuckerman, Neary, & Brustman, 1970). High sensation seekers were more likely to use every type of popular drug than were low sensation seekers. In fact, the only type of drug used to any extent by low sensation seekers was tranquilizers. Cocaine use was rare in these students at this time, but all of them who used cocaine were high sensation seekers.

Table 4.2 shows the percentages of high and low sensation seekers using any illegal drug in the studies conducted at the University of Delaware in the 1970s and a study conducted at a nearby university in 1993. The findings are remarkably stable over the 20-year period, with about two thirds to three quarters of the high sensation seekers using at least one drug and only about a fifth to a third of the low sensation seekers trying a drug. Drug use correlated significantly with the General and all of the SSS subscales for female students and all but the Dis subscale for males. The highest correlation was with the ES subscale, which contained some drug items,

TABLE 4.2
Use of Any Illegal Drugs by High and Low Scorers
on the Sensation Seeking Scale

Study	Sex	High SS %	Low SS %
Zuckerman, Neary, & Brustman (1970)	M & F	74	23
Zuckerman, Bone, Neary, Mangelsdorf, & Brustman (1972)	M & F	57	31
Kumar, Pekala, & Cummings (1993)	M	71	17
	F	66	21

Note. SS = sensation seeking; M = male; F = female.

but the correlations with the other subscales were not much lower. The Dis subscale correlated with alcohol use in both males and females, as did TAS in men and ES in women. At that time, the campus tended to be divided between the "jocks" (athletes) and the "hippies." The former tended to use primarily alcohol and the latter did drugs. Things have changed, and now Dis and ES are both elevated in drug users.

The Segal and Singer (1976) and Segal et al. (1980) studies already discussed were also done in the 1970s and showed significant differences between abstainers, alcohol-only, marijuana-only, and polydrug groups on all of the SSS subscales, with polydrug users the highest and abstainers the lowest. The differences on ES and Dis (with confounding items removed) were the strongest. Marijuana users were higher than alcohol-only users in the college samples. In the 1980s another study similarly classified college students into drug nonusers, marijuana-only users, and polydrug users (Galizio et al., 1983). The General and TAS and BS subscales differentiated between both types of drug users and nonusers, but the ES and Dis subscales differentiated all three groups, with the highest scores in the polydrug users, the lowest in the nonusers, and intermediate scores in marijuana-only users.

Jaffe and Archer (1987) compared the SSS, MMPI, and special drug and alcohol-use scales in predictive efficacy for use of various drugs in a college population. The SSS was the most effective predictor of use of 7 of the 10 classes of drugs and was even more powerful than personality scales specifically designed to predict drug abuse. In this study and another by Douglass and Khavari (1978), the SSS correlated with the extent of polydrug use in indexes combining the different types of drug use. Stacy, Newcomb, and Bentler (1991) also found that the SSS correlated with a measure of polydrug use in a community sample (M age = 27). Within a drug-abusing sample in treatment, the TAS, ES, and Dis subscales correlated with the number of drugs the clients had used in the past, but in a Hispanic sample the correlations were not significant, and in an African American sample only the Dis subscale was correlated with number of drugs. These ethnic differences could be a function of a restricted range of drugs in non-White communities, in which marijuana and heroin or cocaine are the main drugs of use.

M. K. Wagner (2001) studied the relation of sensation seeking and anxiety sensitivity to substance (alcohol and drug) abuse in a college sample. Sensation seeking was significantly related to substance abuse, and so was anxiety sensitivity but in an opposite direction to that predicted by the author. Substance abusers tended to be low in anxiety sensitivity. Studies show high trait anxiety in drug abusers tends to be in drug abusers entering drug programs or in trouble with the law. After these drug abusers have been in treatment, their anxiety scores tend to fall to normal levels (Zuckerman, Sola, Masterson, & Angelone, 1975).

Sher, Bartholow, and Wood (2000) used a large sample of over 3,000 first-year college students tested with Cloninger's Tridimensional Personality Questionnaire (TPQ; Cloninger, 1987b) and Eysenck's EPQ (H. J. Eysenck & Eysenck, 1975). Assessment took place on entry to college and 7 years later. The mean age at Year 1 was 18, and at the 7 year follow-up it was 24.5. Subjects were assessed for diagnostic status regarding drug abuse at both Years 1 and 7 using a trained interviewer and a standardized diagnostic interview (Diagnostic Interview Schedule III-A). NS correlated significantly with current diagnoses of tobacco, alcohol, or drug abuse or dependence, or any of these, at Year 1 and prospectively with diagnoses at Year 7. Harm Avoidance (HA) did not correlate with any of these diagnoses at either occasion. The EPQ N and P scales also correlated with the diagnoses on both occasions, but E did not. Multiple regression covarying out baseline diagnosis and gender showed that only HA in the TPQ and P in the EPQ predicted any substance abuse disorder.

A Danish study used 691 subjects from a community cohort sample who underwent an intensive day of assessment that included the Danish translation of the SSS Form V (SSS–V; Ripa, Hansen, Mortensen, Sanders, & Reinisch, 2001). The mean age of the sample was 32. The SSS Total score correlated significantly with prevalence of smoking and use of alcohol, marijuana, and other drugs. The primary subscales contributing to the correlations with the Total score were ES and Dis, and to a lesser degree BS. TAS had practically no correlation with substance use.

Summary

The studies of young high school adolescents and college age adults have typically used large numbers of subjects sampled from different schools. They almost uniformly show a relationship between sensation seeking and use of marijuana or any illegal drug as well as tobacco and alcohol. Prospective studies also show that SSS-type scales predict alcohol and drug use, abuse, and dependence years later, even controlling for demographic and initial use factors. Concurrent or predictive results are found even when potentially confounding items in the SSS are removed or other SSS-type tests are used that do not contain such items. In the SSS, the Dis and ES subscales have the strongest relationships with drug use, although the other subscales are also related. Although an optimal level of arousal hypothesis predicted a greater affinity of sensation seekers for stimulant than for depressant drugs, sensation seekers are equally attracted to both types of drugs. The disinhibiting characteristics of suppressant drugs, like alcohol, may be the source of their initial attraction for high sensation seekers, although stimulant drugs, like nicotine, are used to counteract the depressant effects of other drugs, like alcohol. Conversely, suppressant drugs may be used to counteract the effects of stimulant drugs, as in using alcohol or barbiturates to sleep after using cocaine or amphetamines. The initial willingness to try new drugs is related to the experience seeking aspect of sensation seeking, and the continued use is a function of the hedonistic pursuit of pleasure with disregard for the risks characteristic of the disinhibition aspect. In the next sections, I focus on specific drugs.

SMOKING TOBACCO

Tobacco smoking has the highest mortality of all of the behavioral sources of ultimate death. What makes it so insidious is that it is perfectly legal given the attainment of the legal age for purchase. Young users know the risks but tell themselves that they will quit before they have used it long enough to develop a fatal disease. In fact, tobacco is more addictive than alcohol or cocaine. In one survey, 60% of tobacco users reported one or more features of active drug dependence compared with 23% of alcohol users and 38% of cocaine users (Anthony, 2002).

In the United States, cigarette consumption per capita reached a peak in 1960 and has been declining ever since. Our first studies of the relation of sensation seeking to smoking in college students were conducted in the early 1970s, and we looked again at the association in the mid-1980s (Zuckerman et al., 1972; Zuckerman, Ball, & Black, 1990). In the 1970s, 45% of male and 40% of female students were smokers, but by the 1980s, 27% of male and 37% of female students were smokers. The gender difference was not significant in the earlier study, but more females were smoking in the later study. National statistics, however, show that in 1999 about 35% of both genders of teenagers smoked (Wright, 2002).

In the 1972 study, two thirds of the high sensation seekers, half of the medium sensation seekers, and about a fifth of the low sensation seekers were smokers. Fourteen years later (i.e., in 1986) at the same university, the percentages of high and medium sensation seekers smoking was cut in half and the percentage of low sensation seekers smoking remained quite low.

The differences among levels of sensation seeking remained significant in both decades, but the general decline in smoking was reflected in the drastically reduced proportions of smoking in the high- and medium-level sensation seekers. Many of the high- and medium-level sensation seekers were not current smokers but had smoked in the past and quit smoking sometime before the sophomore year of college.

During these 2 decades, the relationship between sensation seeking and smoking was found in the general American adult population (Zuckerman & Neeb, 1980), American high school students (Andrucci et al., 1989), British male college students (Golding, Harpur, & Brent-Smith, 1983), a Swiss male general population (Sieber & Angst, 1977), young Norwegian high school students (Pederson et al., 1989), Norwegian army recruits (L. von Knorring & Oreland, 1985), a Dutch general population (Feij, van Zuilen, & Gazendam, 1984), and Israeli adolescents (Teichman, Barnea, & Rahav, 1989). In studies using the SSS, most have found that the General or Total and ES and Dis subscales were the best discriminators between smokers and nonsmokers, even in studies in which items pertaining to drugs other than tobacco or drinking were removed (there are no items directly pertaining to smoking). In the 1990s and 2000s, the relationship is still commonly found, as seen in the studies of multisubstance use in the previous section.

Zuckerman and Neeb (1980) compared SSS scores of past and present nonsmokers and smokers in five categories on the basis of how much they smoked in a day. The main difference was between nonsmokers and smokers, even those who only smoked occasionally, and there were no differences between smokers ranging from a few a day to two or more packs a day. A more recent study compared "chippers" (those who regularly smoke 1–5 cigarettes a day), regular smokers (who regularly smoke 20–40 cigarettes a day), and nonsmokers who do not regularly smoke at all (Kassel, Shiffman, Gnys, Paty, & Zettler-Segal, 1994). They used the General SSS Scale from the SSS Form IV (SSS–IV) and the Dis subscale from SSS–V. They also used extraversion, sociability, and impulsivity subscales of the Eysenck Personality Inventory (H. J. Eysenck & Eysenck, 1964). There was no difference between light and heavy smoker groups, but both were significantly higher than nonsmokers on both the General Scale and the Dis subscale. Heavy smoking is a sign of dependence, and 90% of adolescents who initially smoke, even lightly, go on to heavy smoking and full dependence. It seems that the 10% who remain light smokers are just as sensation seeking as those who become dependent. Sensation seeking may be related to the curiosity about the sensation and the imperviousness to known risks, but it is not the critical factor in determining who becomes dependent or is resistant to addiction.

Zuckerman and Kuhlman (2000) used the ZKPQ (Zuckerman, 2002; Zuckerman, Kuhlman, Joireman, Teta, & Kraft, 1993) in a study of multiple forms of risk taking by college students, including smoking. Smoking was measured with a three-item scale assessing (a) history of smoking in which the highest score was for current smoking with no intention to stop; (b) typical number of cigarettes smoked daily; and (c) frequency of inhaling. The smoking scale total was significantly correlated with the ImpSS in males and females, and additionally with Aggression–Hostility and Sociability in females.

Zuckerman et al. (1990) factor analyzed the items in a smoking questionnaire assessing the situations in which people reported smoking. Five factors emerged from the analysis: (a) Attentive–Coping, (b) Negative Emotion, (c) Alone–Relaxed, (d) Social Situations, and (e) Heavy Smoking across all types of situations. Sensation seeking correlated with smoking in social situations for both men and women and with attentive–coping for men only. Men had higher scores on the attentive–coping factor, presumably an arousal-demand situation, whereas women had high scores on smoking in situations involving arousal of negative emotions, presumably an arousal-reduction need.

Carton, Jouvent, and Widlöcher (1994) compared smokers and nonsmokers using a French translation of the SSS–IV. Smokers were higher than nonsmokers on every subscale except TAS, for which a nonsignificant trend was found. A measure of smoking dependency was correlated with the Dis and ES subscales, suggesting some relationship to amount and compulsivity of smoking.

Biological Predispositions and Mechanisms

Heritability is quite high for smoking initiation and dependence, about 60% to 70% and higher in some studies (R. T. Jones & Benowitz, 2002; True et al., 1997). This is higher than all other disorders, with the exception of schizophrenia (Bouchard & McGue, 2003). The high comorbidity between tobacco and alcohol dependence is due to a shared genetic influence (the genetic correlation between them is .68; True et al., 1999). Genetic influences also mediate most of the correlation between smoking and sensation seeking (Koopmans, 1997). What is inherited?

Nicotine injections stimulate the release of dopamine in the mesolimbic system, particularly in the nucleus accumbens (NA; Damsma, Day, & Fibiger, 1989). The NA is a major center for reinforcing effects of drugs or electrical self-stimulation (in rats). Smoking enables the user to deliver doses of nicotine to the brain with each puff of a cigarette. Very frequent puffs produce nausea, and forcing a smoker to puff and inhale frequently has been used in aversive-conditioning therapy. But under voluntary smoking, the smoker has exquisite control of his or her dose needs at an optimal level of arousal. It is this control over the positive reinforcement effects of nicotine that makes use of a nicotine patch, providing a constant rate of infusion, an inferior gratification for the smoker.

Sensation seeking may affect the initial attraction to smoking through a sensitization to the nicotine brain reinforcement effects. A study of nonsmokers that administered a dose of nicotine using a nasal spray showed that high sensation seekers on the ES and Dis subscales (the two on which smokers differed from the nonsmokers) experienced a stronger "head rush" and subjective sense of vigor, confusion, arousal, pleasant response, and tension than low sensation seekers (Perkins, Gerlach, Broge, Fonte, & Wilson, 2001). However, in experienced smokers, there was little difference in subjective response to the dose of nicotine, but the high sensation seekers showed a higher heart rate increase in response to nicotine. Sensation seeking smokers may start out by using tobacco for its positive or novel subjective effects but end by using it solely as a source of arousal.

Netter, Hennig, and Roed (1996) used drugs that stimulate or inhibit the dopaminergic system. Although hormonal response to the stimulating drug was not related to sensation seeking, craving for nicotine was induced by the dopamine-releasing drug in high sensation seekers in contrast to lows. Although this study did not show a relationship between reactivity in response to the dopamine stimulant, a later study classified subjects as "pure" stimulant responders and pure responders to the dopamine antagonist drug (Reuter, Netter, Toll, & Hennig, 2002). High sensation seeking (as scored on the TAS and ES) was associated with high response to the stimulant drug (and low response to the antagonist drug), whereas low sensation seeking was associated with the reverse pattern, that is, high response to the antagonist and low response to the stimulant. The pure stimulant responders, who tended to be high sensation seekers, showed high craving for tobacco after the release of dopamine by the stimulant. Dopamine release tended to increase their incentive motivation to smoke. Extraverts and low sensation seekers, in contrast to high sensation seekers, were more responsive to the antagonist drug and craved tobacco to increase their arousal levels. The two studies from the University of Giessen in Germany agree in suggesting that sensation seeking increases motivation to smoke after being primed by something activating dopamine release. This may have something to do with the urge to smoke at parties and before and after having sex.

Smoking has relaxing as well as stimulant effects, and the former could be related to stimulation of opioid receptors. Krishnan-Sarin, Rosen, and O'Malley (1999) showed that naloxine, an opioid receptor blocker, showed naloxine dose-dependent increases in withdrawal signs and increases in the urge to smoke or nicotine craving. Persons with low levels of natural opiates (endorphins) may be predisposed to crave nicotine in cigarettes. A group of Swedish investigators studied the relationships between endorphins and personality in a group of patients with chronic pain (Johansson, Almay, von Knorring, Terrenius, & Astrom, 1979). The patients with low levels of endorphins were higher on all of the SSS subscales, but particularly Dis and BS, than patients with high endorphin levels. The craving for opiates in high sensation seekers, which is discussed in a later section, could be a function of an attraction to drugs that compensate for their own natural deficits.

Smokers have a 40% reduction in monoamine oxidase Type B (MAO-B), the enzyme that inhibits the catabolism of dopamine and allows more of it to be stored in vesicles in the prenaptic neurons. However, there is strong evidence that smoking itself lowers MAO (J. S. Fowler, Logan,

Wang, & Volkow, 2003; Whitfield et al., 2000). Current smokers have lower MAO than nonsmokers, but previous smokers do not differ from nonsmokers. MAO levels vary inversely with the number of cigarettes smoked (Whitfield et al., 2000) or a metabolite of nicotine in the plasma (J. S. Fowler et al., 2003). One cigarette does not decrease MAO, and 1 week of abstinence does not increase it, but 4 weeks of abstinence leads to full recovery of normal MAO levels. Nonsmoking cotwins of smokers show normal levels of MAO. Whitfield et al. (2000) reported that the association between alcohol dependence and MAO does not persist when smoking levels are taken into account. These findings raise questions about the clinical and personality correlates of MAO.

af Klinteberg, von Knorring, and Oreland (2004) reviewed the literature with attention to the problem of smoking and MAO. They did a large study comparing nonsmokers, ex-smokers, irregular smokers, and regular smokers (L. von Knorring, Oreland, & Winblad, 1984). Although MAO levels were lower only in the group of regular smokers, correlations between MAO and sensation seeking scales were significant in all groups. They also point out the relationships between MAO and behavior in other species and in human infants. These are undoubtedly nonsmokers. Garpenstrand et al. (2002) found that the low MAO levels found in criminal offenders persisted even when samples were confined to offenders and control subjects who smoked. They maintain that MAO is related to personality traits that predispose to clinical disorders, like sensation seeking does to antisocial personality disorder.

Low MAO-B levels are reliably associated with high sensation seeking, as was described in chapter 1. Smoking was not controlled in these studies. In normal samples, only about a third of the high and 15% of the low sensation seekers are smokers (see Table 4.2). Still, this could account for the significant but weak correlation between sensation seeking and MAO. The tendency of low levels of MAO to make the dopaminergic neurons more reactive to nicotine, and other drugs to be discussed, may account for some of the increased prevalence of smokers among high sensation seekers. It is interesting that nicotine itself does not inhibit MAO at concentrations reached during smoking, but other substances in tobacco leaves do (J. S. Fowler et al., 2003).

Summary

Tobacco smoking is the greatest long-term health menace among all substances that foster dependence. Prevalence of smoking in the general, high school, and college populations has fallen during the last decades, but the relationship to sensation seeking remains in adolescents and adults.

Sensation seeking acts through curiosity and risk tolerance. It determines who will initiate smoking but not who will become addicted, but that is a moot point because 90% of those who initiate smoking to any degree will become dependent.

Heritability is very high for smoking, both initiation and dependence, and its phenomenal coexistence with drinking is due to a shared genetic influence. What is inherited is a special attraction to the reinforcing properties of nicotine mediated by dopamine in the mesolimbic system. Sensation seekers have this property of the system. A similar mechanism, perhaps accounting for the relaxing, arousal-reduction properties of nicotine, may act through the stimulation of opioid receptors. Low levels of the enzyme MAO-B, a regulator of dopamine storage and sensitivity of its neurons, are another link between smoking and sensation seeking. MAO is low in both smokers and sensation seekers but more research is needed to assess the direct role of smoking in MAO reduction. This may be a two-way relationship. MAO levels are a reliable trait and may predispose people to both smoking and sensation seeking, as well as heavy drinking and the use of other drugs. Once smoking begins, it may further reduce MAO, just as alcohol further disinhibits behavior in already disinhibited sensation seekers. Another possibility, discussed in chapter 1, is that MAO influences behavior through its regulation of monoamines, particularly dopamine.

DRINKING ALCOHOL

Apart from tobacco, alcohol is usually the first drug used, although it is not typically called a "drug." *Substance use or abuse* is the general term used to cover alcohol and illegal drugs. In the late 1990s, 47% of the general population and 58% of those aged 18 to 25 were at least occasional drinkers (Wright, 2002). About half of all high school seniors used alcohol. There has been a steady decline in use from 1980, at which time 72% of seniors used alcohol. After tobacco, alcohol is the second most frequent cause of deaths—accidents, in the case of the young, and disease, in older persons. Alcohol-related accidents are the leading cause of death in young adults between 17 and 24 years of age. Alcohol leads to major health complications for middle-aged and older abusers. It is a major factor involved in crimes of violence.

Men are heavier drinkers than women in both the American general population (Slater, Basil, & Maibach, 1999; Wright, 2002) and college populations (Forthun, Bell, Peek, & Sun, 1999). Alcohol use peaks in the 18 to 25 age range and declines thereafter (as does sensation seeking). It is lower in Blacks than in Whites, higher in large metropolitan areas, and varies positively with adult educational levels. Those with college backgrounds drink more than those with high school or less education (Wright, 2002).

Preadolescence and Early Adolescence

Personality in preadolescence predicts later drinking problems. M. C. Jones (1968, 1971) studied 10-year-old boys and girls who were followed up 30 years later. Boys who later became problem-drinking men were described by others as rebellious, undercontrolled, hostile, manipulative, self-indulgent, sensuous, negativistic, expressive, assertive, talkative, and humorous, in contrast to their peers who became moderate drinkers or abstainers. The picture is one of extraverted, impulsive sensation seeking. The girls who became problem-drinking women had some of the same traits as the problem-drinking men, but they resembled the total abstainers in depressive and distrustful traits suggestive of neuroticism.

Cloninger, Sigvardsson, and Bohman (1988) used behavioral observations of boys at 11 years of age to predict alcoholism at age 27. High novelty (sensation) seeking and low harm avoidance at age 11 were strongly predictive of alcohol abuse at age 27. As in the study by M. C. Jones (1968), boys who were later to become alcoholic showed impulsive sensation seeking and no sign of anxiety or neuroticism (harm avoidance).

Webb, Baer, and McKelvey (1995) studied environmental and familial factors, parental and peer attitudes toward alcohol use and actual use among older peers, sensation seeking, and tolerance of deviance among fifth- and sixth-grade students (about 10–11 years old). The children were asked about their own intentions to use alcohol in the future. The strongest factor distinguishing intenders from nonintenders at both grade levels was alcohol use by older peers. The second strongest factor at the fifth grade was sensation seeking, although it became nonsignificant at the sixth grade. Attitude toward drinking, tolerance of deviance, and rejection of parental authority, in addition to older peer use, became more predictive of intentions to drink at the fifth grade. Apparently rebelliousness, regardless of sensation seeking needs, became of more importance in determining intentions at the sixth grade.

Andrew and Cronin (1997) studied 9th-, 10th-, and 11th-grade high school students, using the SSS–V (with drug and drinking items excluded) and Arnett's (1994) Inventory of Sensation Seeking (AISS), which includes subscales for novelty and intensity but no items referring to drugs or drinking. All of the SSS–V subscales and the Total score were significantly correlated with frequency and quantity of drinking, binge drinking, and intoxication. The intensity subscale of AISS was also correlated with all drinking measures, but the novelty subscale was not related to any of them.

College Age

Much of the research on early alcoholism has been done on college students because of their convenience to academic psychologists. This is true for many areas of psychological study. How representative are college students of the noncollege young population? About 25% of Americans graduate from a 4-year college, and perhaps another 25% attend college part time or short of a 4-year degree. College students cannot therefore be regarded as an atypical sample. Slutske (2005) answered this question by comparing alcohol use and its disorders among college and noncollege students in the same age range (19–21) in a large, representative American sample. College students exceeded noncollege subjects on yearly, monthly, and weekly alcohol use and binge drinking, but daily drinking was more common among noncollege subjects, although rare in both groups. These differences were mostly in the female, rather than in the male, part of the sample. Women who are in college drink more on a weekly and monthly basis than their peers who are out in the community. Young adults in college were more likely to be diagnosed with alcohol abuse, although there was no difference in alcohol dependence. Overall the similarities in drinking are more impressive than the differences. The typical college student is more likely to engage in sporadic but intense drinking on Fridays, Saturdays, and holidays, including Spring Break (Del Boca, Darkes, Greenbaum, & Goldman, 2004).

Another large-scale community study, involving 2,910 subjects, divided their sample into five categories: nondrinkers, light, moderate, episodic, and heavy drinkers (Slater et al., 1999). Using the short SSS developed by Donohew, Palmgreen, and Lorch (1994), they found that scores increased significantly from nondrinkers to episodic drinkers. Heavy drinkers were high on sensation seeking but not as high as episodic drinkers.

Zuckerman and Kuhlman (2000) measured drinking in college students using a two-item scale: one item on weekly drinking and the other on maximum drinks for any day. The ZKPQ was used for personality. Drinking correlated with the ImpSS subscale and also with the subscales for aggression and sociability in both males and females. In another study, the ImpSS scale predicted initial quantities of drinking in college freshmen (Del Boca et al., 2004).

Most studies of drinking focus on heavy or problem drinkers. Watten (1996) studied abstainers compared with moderate to strong drinkers among Norwegian college students. Using the AISS, containing no drinking or drug items, and measuring sensation seeking in terms of novelty and intensity, Watten found that the abstainers were lower on both dimensions of sensation seeking, and less sociable and more respectful in coping styles. They also were higher on a social desirability scale.

Numerous studies have documented the relationship between sensation seeking and drinking, particularly for men (Baer, 2002; Ham & Hope, 2003; Zuckerman, 1979a, 1994). Although many of the earlier studies used the entire SSS–V, which included some drinking items in the Dis subscale, most later studies excluded these items or used new sensation seeking scales like the ImpSS that do not include such content. Many of these have already been discussed. In the more recent studies that I discuss next, I focus on the cognitive mechanisms and social influences that may mediate the relationship between the personality trait and drinking behavior.

Sensation Seeking: Social and Cognitive Factors

A study investigating the social environmental setting in college as a mediator of gender, ethnic, and personality effects on student drinking used the ImpSS, which contains no items with drinking or drug content (Kahler, Read, Wood, & Palfai, 2003). ImpSS correlated significantly with frequency of drinking, quantity of alcohol drunk, and frequency of drinking to intoxication. The mediational model showed that in two large samples, ImpSS influenced alcohol use directly and in a pathway mediated by their friends' approval of drinking. Another pathway was through the involvement of those high in ImpSS in fraternities and sororities, which in turn were associated with heavy alcohol use.

The same group of investigators also studied the role of motivation along with ImpSS (Read, Wood, Kahler, Maddock, & Palfai, 2003). ImpSS affected alcohol use and problems through enhancement of motives to increase or maintain positive affective states, or sheer hedonism.

Do high- and low-intensity drinkers drink in different situations? College students were studied using the SSS–V and social context of drinking scales by a group in Maryland (Beck, Thombs, Mahoney, & Finger, 1995). One of the main situational motives for drinking in college students was social facilitation involving drinking at bars, at parties, and with friends or others. Other motives were peer acceptance, relief of emotional pain, family celebratory drinking, and a mode of seeking sex. High-intensity drinkers were defined as those who drank every week, drank at least five drinks on a typical occasion, and became drunk at least once a month. High-intensity drinkers had higher scores on almost every situational–motive area but were especially high on social facilitation and disinhibition in both men and women. However, male high-intensity drinkers differed from females in that they were more likely to drink for sex seeking motives. Drinking to reduce emotional pain (e.g., depression) was more common for women.

A study of English high school students examined their drinking habits in terms of anticipated risks and benefits using a short sensation seeking scale without drinking items (Hampson, Severson, Burns, Slovic, & Fisher,

2001). The subjects were relatively heavy drinking for their age, with 38% drinking more than five drinks on a single occasion (48% for beer). Sensation seeking correlated significantly with alcohol consumption ($r = .39$), positively with perceived benefits of drinking ($r = .47$), and negatively with perceived personal risk in drinking ($r = -.43$). A path model suggested that sensation seeking indirectly affected alcohol-related risk taking through its effect on perceived benefits and risks.

Fromme, Stroot, and Kaplan (1993) developed a questionnaire of outcome expectancies for drinking. Benefits included sociability, tension reduction, courageousness, and enhanced sexuality. Negative factors were cognitive and behavioral impairment, negative feelings, taking undue risks, and acting aggressively. Positive expectancies correlated positively with quantity and frequency of drinking, but negative expectancies did not. Katz, Fromme, and D'Amico (2000) used a similar measure of expectancies, along with the ImpSS measure of impulsive sensation seeking to predict drinking in freshman college students at one point in time and 6 months later. Sensation seeking was related to risk and benefit expectancies and to heavy drinking, but unlike other studies previously discussed, sensation seeking was directly related to heavy drinking and was not mediated by expectancies.

Stacy (1997) used cognitive measures like word association to assess alcohol memory activation in college students. He also measured previous alcohol use, alcohol outcome expectancy, acculturation, and the ImpSS scale from the ZKPQ. As might be expected, previous alcohol use was the strongest predictor of later alcohol abuse, 1 month later. Memory activation, alcohol outcome expectancy, and ImpSS were also significant predictors of later alcohol use.

Alcohol Abuse and Dependence

The *Diagnostic and Statistical Manual of Mental Disorders* (4th ed.; American Psychiatric Association, 1994) distinguishes between normative use of alcohol (or other drugs), abuse, and dependence. *Abuse* is recurrent use leading to recurrent legal or interpersonal problems in school or home or at work and irresponsible use, as when driving an automobile. *Dependence* is the substitute for the older term *addiction*. It indicates the development of a high tolerance with the necessity for increased dosages and unpleasant withdrawal symptoms (physical or emotional) when the substance is unavailable or the person tries to cut down or stop usage.

The lifetime prevalence rates of alcohol disorders are high, particularly in males, in which they range from 24% to 33% for abuse and dependence in large-scale community studies. There is a high comorbidity between alcohol disorders and other drug disorders. Mood and panic disorders are also found in a significantly high percentage of alcoholics, although generally in men they are reactive to the alcohol abuse and dependence rather than an antecedent personality trait. Antisocial personality disorder is a frequent correlate of chronic alcoholism disorder, but it has been suggested that this constitutes one type of the disorder contrasted with another type with depression and anxiety.

Cloninger (1987a) defined two types of alcoholism. People with *Type 1* alcoholism had a relatively late age of onset (after 25), frequent psychological dependence or loss of control over drinking, and guilt or fear about dependence. People with *Type 2* alcoholism had an earlier age of onset (before 25), spontaneous alcohol seeking, and frequent fighting and arrests when drinking. Type 1 alcoholics drink compulsively because of dependence and are ashamed of their addiction. Type 2 alcoholics drink because they enjoy it without guilt, and they tend to become antisocial and disinhibited when drunk. Type 1 alcoholics have more neurotic features, and Type 2 more antisocial personality features. Type 1 characterizes both men and women, whereas Type 2 consists primarily of males. Cloninger (1987a) described the personality of Type 1 and Type 2 alcoholics on his primary dimensions of personality. Type 1 alcoholics are low in novelty seeking and high in harm avoidance and reward dependence, whereas Type 2 alcoholics are high on novelty seeking (sensation seekers) and low on harm avoidance and reward dependence. Other studies have shown that novelty seeking, but not harm avoidance, is related to the frequency of drinking and problem drinking among young psychiatric patients (Galen, Henderson, & Whitman, 1997) and the likelihood of relapse in detoxified male (but not female) alcohol dependents (Meszaros et al., 1999).

Sannibale and Hall (1998) found it difficult to classify alcohol abusers using Cloninger's criteria. Some items of the dichotomy were supported but others were not. Specifically, on the gender difference, more women than men were classified as Type 1, but contrary to the type distinction, similar proportions of men and women were found to be Type 2. Type 2s were almost all below the age of 25, as predicted, but nearly half of the Type 1 alcoholics were also younger. Contrary to the typology, Type 2 alcoholics had more alcohol dependence than Type 1 individuals. Type 2 individuals did show more antisocial and sensation seeking behavior when drinking and general signs of antisocial personality disorder, and they scored higher on the SSS–V than Type 1 individuals.

A study conducted in India used the single criterion on age of onset to classify alcoholics and found contrasts largely confirming the Type 1–2 dicohotomy (Varma, Basu, Malhotra, Sharma, & Mattoo, 1994). The early-onset (Type 2) alcoholics tended to become aggressive and generally disinhibited when drinking, whereas the late-onset alcoholics were anxiety prone and guilt ridden (Type 1). The early-onset alcoholics had a large proportion of first-degree relatives with alcohol disorders, indicating a stronger genetic factor, as predicted by Cloninger. They scored significantly higher than late-onset types on a modified SSS Total and on the BS subscale but not on the other subscales. The early-onset types scored higher on a psychopathy scale, whereas the late-onset types scored higher on an anxiety scale. In another study, conducted in Australia, age of onset of alcohol-use disorders was correlated negatively with all of the SSS–V subscales and the Total score and with measures of antisocial personality disorder and diagnosis of this disorder (Sannibale & Hall, 2001).

Most studies find that sensation seeking is linked with antisocial tendencies in the Type 2 alcoholic. Whiteside and Lynam (2003) classified alcoholics as those with or without antisocial personality traits and compared both types with a nonalcoholic control group. Alcoholics with antisocial traits scored higher than those without such traits and the control group on a short sensation seeking scale. There was no difference between the alcoholics without antisocial traits and the control subjects. The antisocial alcoholics also scored higher on other types of impulsivity, such as lack of premeditation and perseverance.

Just as alcohol users in normal populations are not as high on sensation seeking as drug users (Segal et al., 1980), problem drinkers without antisocial traits or use of drugs are not as high as drug abusers (Kilpatrick, Sutker, & Smith, 1976). Kilpatrick et al. (1976) compared young male veterans on substance abuse and regular wards of Veterans Administration hospitals in four groups: regular drug users, problem drinkers, occasional drug and alcohol users (the modal kind in this population), and nonusers of either alcohol or drugs. The drug abusers scored higher than the problem drinkers on all of the SSS–IV subscales except BS. Both the drug abusers and the problem drinkers scored higher than occasional users and control subjects on the BS subscale. A group of older people with chronic alcoholism scored higher on the BS and Dis subscales than an age-equivalent control group of veterans from the same hospital (Kilpatrick, McAlhany, McCurdy, Shaw, & Roitzsch, 1982). There are no drinking items on the BS subscale. Why does it differentiate between drinkers with and without alcohol problems?

Part of the reason for drinking may be to deal with boring, monotonous lives. Such "lives of quiet desperation" may not bother most persons enough to require alcohol to pass the time. But those with a special susceptibility to boredom may not be able to deal with empty, lonely time without alcohol.

A study of female substance abusers from the community and not in treatment used cluster analyses to classify types of substance abusers by personality types (Conrod, Pihl, Stewart, & Dongier, 2000). Five types were reliably identified: anxiety sensitive, introverted, hopeless, sensation seeking, impulsive, and those with "low personality risk." Those with a diagnosis of alcohol dependence were more likely to be high on sensation seeking and impulsive clusters, whereas those with diagnoses of antisocial personality or cocaine dependence were high only on the impulsive cluster.

Genetics

Both excitement seeking (measured by a composite of Dis and BS subscales of the SSS) social deviance and alcohol consumption and problems showed significant effects of genetics and nonshared environment among a large sample of Finnish twins (Mustanski, Viken, Kaprio, & Rose, 2003). Shared environment played no role in the personality factor but had a small but significant effect on consumption. Social deviance was primarily related to problems with alcohol, whereas excitement seeking was correlated equally with both consumption and problems. Genetic correlations showed that the genetic factors made the major contribution to the association between these two personality factors and consumption of alcohol. Koopmans (1997) also found that although genetic factors explained only a small proportion of the total variance in alcohol use, these genetic influences were mediated through the genes involved in sensation seeking.

Many studies have been done on the genetics of alcohol abuse and dependence. Twin studies done in the early 1990s show high concordance in alcoholism (abuse or dependence) in monozygotic twins and heritabilities of .36 to .54 in male twins (Caldwell & Gottesman, 1991; McGue, Pickens, & Svikis, 1992; Pickens et al., 1991). However, in the same studies there was little evidence of significant heritability in female twins. Kendler, Heath, Neale, Kessler, and Eaves (1992), however, did find substantial heritability in females (h = .56). A very large study of about 2,500 Swedish male twins born between 1902 and 1949 yielded a moderate heritability of .54, with only slight evidence of a shared environment effect (.14) and a slightly larger effect (.33) of nonshared environment (Kendler, Prescott, Neale, & Pederson, 1997).

Adoption studies comparing the rates of alcoholism among adoptees as a function of alcoholism in biological parents (who had no social contact with the children) showed a significant influence of alcoholism in biological parents on alcoholism in male adoptees (Goodwin, Schulsinger, Knopf, Mednick, & Guze, 1977; Sigvardsson, Bohman, & Cloninger, 1996). These results were not found for female adoptees (Goodwin et al., 1977; Sigvardsson et al., 1996). Sigvardsson et al. (1996) found that genetic factors played a role in Type 1 alcoholism (Cloninger, 1987a) only in interaction with lower socioeconomic status, but genetic factors alone played a significant role in Type 2 alcoholism. Type 2 alcoholism is primarily found among males, particularly those with antisocial types of behavior and early onset of alcoholism. This would explain why the genetic factors in alcoholism seem more prominent in males where they are mediated by those genes involved in sensation seeking and social deviance.

Molecular genetic studies of alcoholism are summarized in several book chapters (Comings, Saucier, & MacMurray, 2002; Ebstein & Kotler, 2002; Enoch & Goldman, 2002; Zuckerman, 1999). There are two kinds of genetic influences in drinking and vulnerability to alcoholism. The first concerns the capacity to metabolize alcohol. Heavy drinkers who are most at risk for developing alcoholism have a tolerance for alcohol and show little immediate motor or gastrointestinal effects until they reach high levels of alcohol blood concentrations. Sons of alcoholic fathers showed less impairment on cognitive and behavioral tasks and rated themselves as less intoxicated than sons of nonalcoholic fathers after drinking a fixed amount of alcohol, even though the blood alcohol levels in the two groups were similar (Schukitt, 1988). Many more of the sons of alcoholic fathers than the control subjects developed alcoholism, and their initial levels of behavioral reactivity to alcohol at age 20 predicted the number of alcohol dependence symptoms 8 years later (Schukitt & Smith, 1996). The capacity to "hold your liquor" represents a genetically influenced risk factor for alcoholism.

Some drinkers develop facial flushing, headache, palpitations, tachycardia, and nausea after only one or two drinks. The latter group has a protection against becoming alcoholic because their reaction to alcohol is rapid, allowing for aversive conditioning like that produced by antabuse or disulfiram.

The crucial factor differentiating these two extreme reactions lies in genes regulating the metabolism of alcohol. Gene variants for metabolism of alcohol in the liver by the enzyme acetaldehyde dehydrogenase (ALDH) account in part for the lower rates of heavy drinking and alcoholism in Asian relative to European populations (Ebstein & Kotler, 2002). A gene variant that produces a deficiency in ALDH activity is found in about half of Japanese and Chinese samples, but only about 2% of Japanese alcoholics, suggesting that the gene variant confers a protection against heavy drinking and alcoholism. The same gene variant accounts in part for differences in light-drinking and heavy-drinking Israeli Jews and probably for lower rates of alcoholism among Jews in general than persons descended from northern European populations.

Other genetic factors involve genes putatively involved in antisocial and sensation seeking personality traits defining Type 2 alcoholism. One of these is the A1 form of the dopamine-2 receptor (DRD2) gene. This allele is associated with the readiness to drink alcohol solutions in mice. Mice lacking the DRD2 consume less alcohol than those possessing it. Positive reactions to alcohol in rodents are associated with explorativeness, fearlessness, and aggressiveness, characteristic of the Type 2 alcoholic in humans.

Many studies have been done on this candidate gene in humans. About half confirm an association with alcoholism, whereas half of them are nonconfirmatory. This is typical in one-gene studies of traits or disorders that are polygenic. However, a meta-analysis of 15 studies containing about 1,000 alcoholics and 900 control subjects found that the former had a higher prevalence and frequency of the A1 allele of the DRD2 than the latter (Noble, 1998). Furthermore, the allele was more prevalent in the more severe than the less severe alcoholics. The prevalence of the A1 in severe alcoholics (48%) was 3 times as frequent as in the control subjects (16%).

DRD2 along with dopamine-1 receptor (DRD1) and dopamine-4 receptor (DRD4) contribute to about 5% of the variance in the novelty seeking trait (Comings et al., 2002). The DRD4 has also been independently associated with novelty (sensation) seeking, but as with other trait–gene studies, there is not consistent replication of the association (see chap. 1). Similarly, the DRD4 has been associated with alcoholism in some but not many other studies. There is some evidence of an interaction between the DRD4 and the protective ALDH2 gene variant in alcoholism in a Japanese population (Muramatsu, Higuchi, & Hayashida, 1996). In alcoholics with the protective ALDH2 gene, the presence of a variant of the DRD4 gene may override the normally protective effects of the ALDH2 gene variant.

The short form of the serotonergic transporter gene, associated with depression, anxiety and impulsive behavior, is also found with increased frequency in French and German alcoholics and in early-onset, antisocial (Type 2) Finnish alcoholics (Enoch & Goldman, 2002). As usual there were also some nonconfirmatory studies. A particular form of a gene associated with GABA receptors has also been associated with alcohol dependence and antisocial (Type 2) alcoholism. This form is also associated with a lower level of response (tolerance) to acute effects of alcohol.

Biological Mechanisms

Alcohol acts as an agonist for GABA-A receptors and an antagonist for N-methyl D-asperate (NMDA) receptors. Glutamate (glutamic acid) is an amino acid that serves as a neurotransmitter in both very simple and advanced organisms. It is the principal excitatory neurotransmitter in the brain. Alcohol acts to inhibit activity in NMDA receptors, thereby reducing excitation. GABA is an inhibitory neurotransmitter. Alcohol acts on the GABA-A receptors as a stimulant, thereby also increasing their inhibitory effects. The net result of both of these effects is sedation, which increases with dosage of alcohol, producing incoordination and sleepiness at the high doses. However, at low doses, alcohol seems to have a stimulant effect, producing euphoria and activity. Part of this effect is due to *disinhibition*, which is the reduction of social anxiety and therefore greater enjoyment of social interaction with less restraint. Another part of the effect is due to the fact that alcohol, like stimulant drugs, increases dopaminergic activity in the mesolimbic system and the release of dopamine in the nucleus accumbens, a site of major reward effects.

Low levels of platelet MAO-B are associated with sensation seeking and tobacco use as previously discussed. MAO is also reduced in heavy alcohol users or alcohol-dependent subjects, particularly males (La Grange, Jones, Erb, & Reyes, 1995; Major & Murphy, 1978; Sullivan et al., 1990; L. von Knorring, Palm, & Anderson, 1985). Type 2 alcoholics in particular show this relationship. Low MAO persists during periods of abstinence, suggesting that alcohol itself does not reduce MAO, but most alcoholics smoke, and tobacco has been shown to reduce MAO levels. In fact, Whitfield et al. (2000) found that subjects with alcohol dependence and still drinking had lower MAO levels than nonalcohol dependent control subjects, but this result was not significant when smoking status was controlled.

Another reinforcing effect of alcohol is due to its activation of an endogenous opioid. The body produces beta-endorphin, which acts like an external opiate to produce relaxation and, at high doses, sedation. Subjects with a family history of alcoholism are lower in baseline levels of beta-endorphin than those without a history, but a dose of alcohol produces a rise in beta-endorphin in the family-risk subjects, bringing them up to the level of the low-risk subjects (Gianoulakis, Angelogianni, Meany, Thavundayil, & Tawar, 1990). Plasma beta-endorphin is more responsive to alcohol in the high- than in the low-risk subjects (Gianoulakis, Krishman, & Thavundayil, 1996). It is possible that the low levels of endorphin in the children of alcoholics constitute part of the genetic risk, making them more vulnerable to the reinforcing effects of alcohol. A group of Swedish investigators found that among chronic pain patients, those with low levels of endorphins were higher on all of the sensation seeking scales than those with high levels of endorphins (Johansson et al., 1979). Significant negative correlations were found between endorphins and the Dis and BS subscales of the SSS. Thus, low levels of endorphins may be one of the factors explaining the tendency to drink heavily and the vulnerability to alcohol abuse among high sensation seekers. The hypothesis of vulnerability to drugs produced by a lack of some naturally produced neurotransmitter or hormone is called the *endogenous deficit theory* (Zuckerman, 1986b). Another theory of this type links alcohol to low serotoninergic activity. Experimental treatments that increase serotonergic functions reduce alcohol consumption.

There are many biological mechanisms that might explain the reinforcing effects of alcohol, and the role of each one is unknown. Possibly, some of the individual differences in types of alcoholics might be based on the specific mechanisms. Type 1 alcoholics, with their negative affects, might respond more to the sedating, anxiolytic mechanisms, as in the effect of alcohol on endogenous opiates and GABA, whereas the Type 2 might be more responsive to the stimulation of the mesolimbic system through release of dopamine.

Summary

The personality of the prealcoholic male during preadolescence and adolescence suggests impulsive and aggressive sensation seeking. The pre-alcoholic personality of females is similar, except that there are also neurotic, depressive traits as well. This difference in personality is carried over into behavior and emotions after becoming an alcohol abuser or dependent. Two major types of alcoholism have been postulated. Type 1 has a late onset, is predominantly among females or equally divided between genders, and includes strong guilt and depression in reaction to or preceding the alcohol dependence. The other type (Type 2) is predominantly among males with antisocial and sensation seeking traits and behaviors. The association of sensation seeking, impulsivity, and aggression with Type 2 has been con-firmed in several studies.

Sensation seeking influences attitudes toward drinking, perceptions of benefits and risks of drinking, and the actual amount of drinking in college students. The association of sensation seeking and drinking is found even when confounding items in the SSS are not used in the studies. Both male and female college students drink more heavily than their noncollege peers. Binge drinking is characteristic among many college students. High sensation seekers tend to perceive more benefits and fewer risks in drinking than do low sensation seekers. One of the benefits perceived by males is greater sexual access to females. This perceived benefit for males is associated with a greater risk for females.

The association between sensation seeking and alcohol consumption is mediated by genetic factors. Heritability of alcoholism (abuse and depen-dence) is moderate in men, but the findings in women are mixed. Most twin and adoption studies show little heritability of alcoholism in women except in interaction with lower social class. Three kinds of genetic influ-ences are seen at the molecular genetic level. One type consists of genes that regulate the metabolic capacity to dispose of alcohol. Some alcoholics lack a gene that creates a limit to tolerance through unpleasant physiological reactions to too much alcohol. Other genetic factors, like those affecting the responsivity of dopamine receptors to alcohol, increase the vulnerability to alcoholism by making alcohol more reinforcing through release of dopa-mine in reward areas of the brain. The DRD4 receptor gene is related to both sensation or novelty seeking and alcoholism in some, but not all, studies. Other factors may be involved in the genes that regulate receptors for neurotransmitters or peptides that have sedative, antianxiety properties.

Alcohol stimulates receptors for GABA, which has inhibitory effects, and inhibit NMDA receptors, which have excitatory effects. The next effect is relaxation and sedation, although the initial effects may contribute to euphoria through disinhibition of inhibitory areas of brain. Another effect is through the release of endogenous opiates that have been shown to be low in high sensation seekers in one study. A deficit in production of endogenous opiates may create an even stronger vulnerability to dependence on external opiates like morphine and heroin.

HEROIN AND COCAINE

Despite the fact that alcohol, opiates, and cocaine have different physiological and psychological effects, there is a high degree of comorbidity among them. Nearly two thirds of opioid abusers, who are also dependent, have a lifetime history of cocaine dependence, and half have a history of alcohol dependence (Brooner, King, Kidorf, Schmidt, & Bigelow, 1997). Alcoholism is even more frequent in cocaine abusers, with 62% having a history of alcoholism (Rounsaville et al., 1991). Predominant use of either heroin or cocaine at any given time depends on availability and price of the particular drug as well as individual differences in drug preferences. Steady users of only one drug are rare in the addict population (Spotts & Shontz, 1986)

In the 1970s, the potent opiate heroin was the main type of hard-drug use (excluding marijuana). Craig (1982, 1986) reviewed personality studies and reported that sensation seeking was high in heroin users in most studies. Platt and Labate (1976) surveyed prisoners in a youth detention facility and found that heroin users were higher on the General and ES subscale of the SSS–IV. Skolnick and Zuckerman (1979) compared hard-drug (mainly heroin) and soft-drug users in a treatment facility and found that soft-drug users were higher on SSS General and the BS subscale than hard-drug users. Soft-drug users were generally polydrug users, and many subsequent studies have shown that polydrug users are higher than single-drug users and that sensation seeking correlates more with the number of drugs than with the class of drug used. Carrol and Zuckerman (1977) rated drug histories for the relative amount of depressant versus stimulant drug use. Stimulant drug use correlated positively, and depressant drug use correlated negatively with the ES subscale, but Dis correlated positively with stimulant and depressive drug use. The correlations were all low. We might say that experience seeking, a measure of the need for novel experience, is related to experimentation among drugs, whereas disinhibition reflects the need for intense experience produced by any drug acting on the mesolimbic dopaminergic system.

Spotts and Shontz (1986) attempted to control the problem of overlap in type of drugs used by selecting chronic drug users who had used only one drug for 2 to 27 years. From over 1,000 potential subjects heavily using drugs and not in programs or incarcerated, they were able to find only 9 for each of the four types of drugs. The nonuser group, matched closely with the users, was easier. All groups were matched for age, sex, IQ, and socioeconomic status and were compared on the SSS. Amphetamine users were the highest on the General and all SSS subscales, as one might predict from an optimal level of arousal theory. However, cocaine users were lowest on SSS, and opiate and barbiturate users were close to the nonuser control subjects. Cocaine is a stimulant drug and therefore would be expected to attract high sensation seekers. But these were all chronic users of one drug. Cocaine users start out using it as a "party drug," but after years of use, many become asocial and use the drug just to feel "normal." Without it, they become depressed. Their lower SSS scores may indicate this switch in the effects of cocaine at the high doses reached over years of addiction.

Patkar et al. (2002, 2003) compared 149 middle-aged African Americans attending an outpatient cocaine treatment program with 44 control subjects. The cocaine patients were significantly older than the control subjects (37 vs. 33 years), which would tend to make their sensation seeking scores lower. Despite this age difference, the abstinent cocaine users scored higher than control subjects on the SSS–V Total score and the Dis and TAS subscales. They also were higher on aggression, depression, and impulsivity scales.

S. A. Ball (1995) used a sample of 450 patients seeking outpatient treatment for cocaine abuse, with a mean age of 29.4, using the ZKPQ five-factor scale of personality. He compared these patients with the college norms for the ZKPQ, but this is an inappropriate comparison because the mean age was only 19 and this was almost entirely a White population and more highly educated than the general population. There are, as yet, no general American population norms for the ZKPQ except for the ImpSS scale. McDaniel and Zuckerman (2003) randomly selected subjects from the metropolitan areas of Baltimore and Washington, DC. African Americans constituted 25% of the sample in contrast to 64% in S. A. Ball's group of cocaine users. I compared the control subjects in the 25 to 34 age range, roughly equivalent to S. A. Ball's sample, on the ImpSS. The mean for cocaine users (9.40) was significantly higher than that for community control subjects (8.63; $t = 2.78$; $p < .01$).

Within the cocaine-using group, ImpSS correlated significantly with severity of alcohol and drug abuse, and psychiatric disturbance. Patients scoring high on ImpSS reported earlier first use of cocaine and a strong family history for alcohol and drug abuse. Anxiety and aggression–hostility also correlated with these measures of addiction severity and psychiatric impairment.

S. A. Ball, Carroll, and Rounsaville (1994) studied another sample of cocaine users, applying for treatment, using the General Scale from the SSS–IV. They compared the General Scale with factors within the drug-abusing population. Apart from cocaine, the SSS was related to lifetime use of amphetamines, opiates, hallucinogens, sedatives, and solvents. The high sensation seeking group is clearly a polydrug-using group. The SSS was also related to a history of alcohol abuse and/or dependence, antisocial personality, conduct, attention-deficit/hyperactivity, and depressive disorders. High sensation seeking was also related to early age of onset of first use of cocaine and alcohol, age of abuse of the substances, and severity of symptom scores for these two. The authors concluded that sensation seeking fits into the Type 2 schema, which they extended from alcohol to drug disorders (S. A. Ball, Carroll, Barbor, & Rounsaville, 1995).

In the S. A. Ball (1995) study, the ZKPQ N-Anx and Agg–Host scales, in addition to the ImpSS scale, were also correlated with severity of drug and alcohol abuse. These three scales of the ZKPQ were substantially inter-correlated, unlike college student samples, in which they are minimally correlated. A study of another treatment sample of chronic cocaine users, using independent scales for sensation seeking, hostility, and impulsivity, showed that sensation seeking and hostility were both related to frequency of cocaine use and severity of addiction to alcohol (H. W. Murray et al., 2003). Sensation seeking and impulsivity were both related to addiction to alcohol. In appraising drug users, it is important to look at other personality variables besides sensation seeking.

Genetics

Twin studies of drug abuse in general have shown some genetic influences in males with nearly equal influence of shared environment (Gynther, Carey, Gottesman, & Vogler, 1994; Pickens et al., 1991; Tsuang et al., 1996). However, a twin study that broke down the analysis into specific drugs found that most of the genetic influence of heroin (and other opiate) abuse is specific to heroin itself and not shared with other drugs, whereas the major genetic influence on stimulants and sedatives is shared across drugs (Tsuang et al., 1998). The shared genetic factor underlies abuse of all five categories of drugs but is relatively less influential in heroin abuse. There is some influence of shared and nonshared environments in all drug categories.

A study of siblings of cocaine and opioid abusers indicated increased risk for alcoholism, drug abuse, and antisocial personality disorder in the siblings of both types of abusers (Luthar, Anton, Merikangas, & Rounsaville, 1992). Rates of drug abuse in parents of both opioid and drug users were not high, but rates of alcoholism and major depression were elevated relative to that of the general community (Luthar, Merikangas, & Rounsaville, 1993). However, another study showed a strong association between the predominant type of drug disorder in probands and their relatives (Merikangas et al., 1998). Opioid disorders are found with relatively greater frequency in relatives of opioid patients and cocaine disorders in the relatives of cocaine patients, indicating some specificity for type of drug (whether of genetic or environmental sources). But the even stronger influence of antisocial personality, particularly in the relatives of the opioid abusers, suggests an influence through personality. Family studies cannot separate the influence of familial genetic and shared environmental influences, but adoption studies can.

An adoption study showed two pathways to drug abuse or dependency in adopted children (Cadoret, Yates, Troughten, Woodworth, & Stewart, 1995). One pathway went directly from alcohol abuse or dependency in the biologic parent to drug abuse or dependency in the adoptee. This is probably a genetic factor common to alcoholism and drug abuse. The other pathway is from antisocial personality in the biological parent to aggressivity and antisocial personality in the adoptee to drug abuse or dependency in the adoptee. There are several gene candidates that could mediate either pathway.

The DRD4 receptor gene in the long-form allele, which has been associated with novelty seeking, has been also found in greater prevalence in heroin addicted individuals in three different studies in Israel and China (Ebstein & Kotler, 2002). The DRD2 receptor A1 and B1 alleles have been associated with cocaine-dependent and polydrug abusers (Noble et al., 1993; S. S. Smith et al., 1992). Because drug abusers of both opiates and cocaine have been shown to be high sensation seekers, these studies suggest that one or both of the genes may account in part for the greater vulnerability of the sensation seeker.

Biological Mechanisms

The association of dopamine receptor genes with drug abuse suggests that this neurotransmitter is central to the rewarding effects of drugs. What cocaine and heroin have in common is their capacity to release dopamine or inhibit its uptake in the medial forebrain bundle (MFB), where electrical self-stimulation in rats can maintain responding over long periods, rivaling natural rewards like food, drink, and sex. There is some differentiation in the loci where the drugs act. Stimulants, like cocaine, have their effect in the nucleus accumbens (NA) at the upper end of the MFB, whereas the opiates, including heroin, act at the lower end in the ventral tegmental area (VTA; Bozarth, 1987). Of course, almost every other class of drugs has its major euphoric or arousal effects in the MFB. Chemical lesions that deplete dopamine in the MFB disrupt intravenous self-stimulation of amphetamine or cocaine.

The difference between the sedating and stimulating properties of opiates and stimulants are based on other sites of action. Opiates act on the μ-opioid receptors in the brain, and stimulants act on the dopamine reuptake transporter for dopamine (Kopnisky & Hyman, 2002). Stimulant drugs also act on the ascending noradrenergic system, which produces increased arousal. They also increase serotonin transmission. Opiates have their reinforcement effects not only through dopamine release in the NA and independent action on the receptors for the endogenous morphines (endorphins) but also through inhibiting GABA interneurons in the VTA, thereby disinhibiting their control over dopaminergic activity.

Until recently, the studies of brain actions of the drugs were confined to other species, particularly rats. More recently, brain imaging methods have been used to study drug effects in humans. Martin-Soelch et al. (2001) used positron emission tomography scans to study the sites of activation by reward in the brain of humans. These studies showed activation by reinforcement stimuli in mesostriatal and mesocorticolimbic areas (including the MFB) and found increased activation by positively reinforcing stimuli. Similar results were found in nonhuman primates. A group of opiate addicted individuals differed from control subjects in that their activation was only in response to monetary reinforcement, whereas control subjects also responded to nonmonetary reinforcement (signals of correct response). The opiate addicted subjects also had higher sensation seeking scores than the control subjects. Their hypothesis is that sensation seekers need more stimulation to activate brain reward areas like the striatum and MFB. Figure 4.1 shows their hypotheses regarding sensation seeking motivation and dopamine as instigators of drug use.

Low MAO levels are another link between dopamine, sensation seeking, and opiate addiction. I have previously discussed MAO in relation to smoking and alcohol use. Garpenstrand et al. (2002) assessed MAO in prisoners with a diagnosis of opiate abuse. They clearly had lower MAO levels than prisoners without this diagnosis. However, the role of smoking has to be considered because it accounted for the lower MAO in alcoholics. But even when only smokers were used in the analyses, MAO was still lower in those with the opiate abuse. The MAO effect was not observed in those with substance abuse other than opiates, that is, alcohol, nonopiate sedatives, marijuana, or amphetamines.

Low serotonergic reactivity seems to be a characteristic of high sensation seekers, as was described in chapter 1. Clinical studies show that low serotonin activity is found in impulsive and aggressive persons as well as

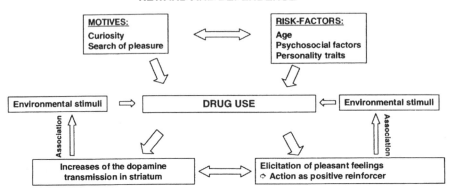

REWARD AND DEPENDENCE

Figure 4.1. Schematic demonstrating the development of drug dependence according to the hypothesis that it is a dopamine-dependent disorder. The motives and risk factors interact to induce first drug intake. Personality traits related to drug dependence are sensation seeking and impulsivity. Sensation seeking induces a need for stronger stimulation and interacts directly with curiosity and the search for new sensation leading to drug use. Then drug-related stimuli receive positive motivational value through the increase in dopamine transmission in the striatum. Because the effects of drugs on dopamine transmission are not subject to habituation, repeated exposure affords the stimuli excessive motivational value. From "Reward Mechanisms in the Brain and Their Role in Dependence: Evidence From Neurophysiological and Neuroimaging Studies," by C. Martin-Soelch et al., 2001, *Brain Research Reviews, 36*, p. 147. Copyright 2001 by Elsevier Science. Reprinted with permission.

those in depression. A study of African American cocaine abusers used the paroxetine binding method to assess serotonergic activity (Patkar et al., 2003). The group of over 100 cocaine patients had higher scores on Total and Dis and TAS subscales of the SSS and higher scores on aggression, impulsivity, and depression scales than control subjects. Paroxetine binding correlated substantially and negatively with SSS Total and all subscale scores in the cocaine group and significantly, but not as highly, in the control subjects. Serotonergic activity also correlated substantially with impulsivity in the cocaine abusers. Serotonin receptors in the NA inhibit release of dopamine, therefore insensitivity of these receptors in high sensation seekers would increase dopaminergic reactions to the stimulant drugs.

Summary

Alcohol, opiates, and cocaine are not exclusive in the history of addicts. At different times or at the same period, most addicts have used one or the other or both. The shared usage is due in part to common genetic and physiological sources; in part to a shared personality profile that includes sensation seeking, impulsivity, and aggression; and in part to environmental influences and availability of particular drugs. Sensation seeking is more highly related to the number of different drugs used than to the particular drug favored by the user. Both young heroin and cocaine users tend to be high sensation seekers, but this is not the case for older, chronic drug-dependent addicts. Among cocaine users, sensation seeking is related to the severity of the cocaine addiction and its consequences, abuse of alcohol and other drugs in addition to cocaine, psychiatric disturbance, and an antisocial personality.

There is a common genetic factor for all drugs as well as less important specific genetic factors, but the specific factor in heroin is relatively stronger than the general factor. Some specificity for type of drug is found in family studies, but an antisocial personality factor underlies general drug use. In the parental generation, alcohol use predominated but is associated with both alcohol and drug use in their adopted away children. But another pathway to drug dependence in the children is the inheritance of an antisocial personality. Specific genes for dopamine receptors are associated with opiate abuse (DRD4) and cocaine abuse (DRD2). DRD4 has also been associated with novelty seeking in some, but not all, studies.

All addictive drugs that initially produce strong acute reward effects (euphoria) do so through release or reuptake inhibition of dopamine in the MFB, particularly the NA. The opiates also have reward effects through their direct action on opiate receptors in the brain. These natural (endogenous) morphine pathways also account for the sedation and analgesic effects of high doses. Effects on other monoamines, norepinephrine, and serotonin produce general arousal or, in the case of serotonin, disinhibition.

Low MAO levels are found in opiate users, as they are in high sensation seekers and users of tobacco and alcohol, but in this case they cannot be accounted for by smoking alone. Low serotonergic activity is a characteristic of high sensation seekers shared with cocaine users.

PSYCHEDELIC DRUGS

Psychedelic drugs include hallucinogens like LSD, dissociative drugs like PCP, and amphetamine analogues such as 3,4-methylenedioxymethamphetamine (MDMA, or "ecstasy"). Some of these drugs are found in natural sources like certain mushrooms and cacti and were used in ancient times to induce visions and dissociated states in religious rites. During the 1960s and 1970s, use of hallucinogens like LSD were common among college students rebelling against the conventional middle-class mores and political stances of the authorities. Timothy Leary, a Harvard psychology professor, urged the youth to "turn off"(to the conventional culture) and "turn on" (use LSD to enhance awareness). Many followed his advice, despite the risk of "bad trips" sometimes requiring psychiatric treatment and aftereffects like recurrent hallucinations without the drug. In group discussions in a therapeutic community where I worked, I discovered that habitual heroin users regarded LSD and other hallucinogenic drugs as more risky than heroin because the results are so unpredictable, or as one client said, "man, they can mess up your mind."

The essence of motivation to use these drugs is experience seeking, or basic sensation seeking in the form of a desire to experience novel states or sensations. It is surprising that so little personality research has been done on psychedelic drugs specifically. What research there is simply includes them in broad categories of abuse. Most psychedelic drug users are polydrug users, so it is difficult to separate the particular personality characteristics associated with this class of drugs from the other drugs they are using. As previously described, polydrug users are typically high sensation seekers.

Psychedelic drugs are usually used in social settings. Users can share their experiences and intensified feelings and support one another in case of bad trips. MDMA use has developed recently as a party drug at "raves," where partiers dance for long stretches and party for 6 to 8 hours at a time. The amphetamine component of the drug sustains the energy required for this manic marathon. There is a dangerous element to this drug that causes neurotoxic damage to the central serotonergic system after repeated doses in animals (Abraham, McCann, & Ricaurte, 2002). There are dose-related memory problems in chronic users and reported psychological problems such as depression and anxiety after prolonged use. Extreme dosage can cause hyperthermia and dehydration, so users are advised to drink large quantities of water when on the drug. However, many drink alcohol or use other drugs despite the dangers involved in mixing drugs.

A study looked at the personality characteristics of regular ecstasy users, most of whom also used marijuana, comparing them with regular marijuana users who did not use ecstasy and nonusers of regular drug or alcohol use of any type (Daumann, Pelz, Becker, Tuchtenhagen, & Gouzoulis-Mayfrank, 2001). Ecstasy users scored higher than both control groups on the nonplanning type of impulsiveness and the ES subscale of the SSS. They were also higher than the nonusers, but not the MJ users, on measures of anxiety and psychoticism. The marijuana-only users had higher scores than nonusers on the TAS subscale of the SSS.

Benschop, Rabes, and Korf (2003) studied ecstasy users in three European cities using 702 subjects, of which two thirds were regular ecstasy users interviewed and tested at parties or raves. They also contrasted ecstasy users who took advantage of free testing of the drug pills to determine their actual content. Testers did not differ from nontesters, but both groups of ecstasy users were significantly higher than nonusers on the ImpSS scale of the ZKPQ. The main reason given for first use of ecstasy was curiosity (over 80% of users). Main reasons for not using the drug were on principle, lack of need, fear of physical or psychological harm, unknown effects, and negative reports by others who used the drug. Those who used the testing service were more concerned about whether they were getting the drug they paid for than worried about contaminants or dosage (the test did not determine dose).

The biochemical effect of ecstacy is due to increased serotonergic transmission (Abraham et al., 2002). MDMA also releases dopamine, although this effect is less pronounced than the serotonergic effect. Like other stimulant drugs, MDMA causes extreme arousal of the sympathetic nervous system, accounting for increased heart rate and hyperthermia and hyperactive motor behavior. In humans, it also causes increased alertness and euphoria. Persons in couples therapy report increased communication, emotional sensitivity, and closeness. But more like hallucinogens, it can produce altered visual and auditory sensations. Like LSD, it can produce (usually transient) psychotic effects.

Psychedelic drugs are attractive to sensation seekers looking for novel and arousing internal experiences. The drug ecstasy is particularly attractive to high sensation seekers because its amphetamine content enables them to enjoy all-night partying and dancing at raves. It has its effects through increased serotonergic and dopaminergic release, producing positive feelings and some hallucinogenic effects as well.

Smoking, drinking, and the use of drugs are all related to sensation seeking. The role of this trait is probably mediated through genetic and biological mechanisms as well as peer influences. The pathway to addiction starts with curiosity piqued by peers and consequent expectations of rewards and minimization of risks in high sensation seekers.

5

SENSATION SEEKING AND SEX

There is nothing safe about sex. There never will be.
—Norman Mailer, *International Herald Tribune*, January 24, 1992

Passion makes the world go round. Love just makes it a safer place.
—Ice-T, *The Ice Opinion*

According to Norman Mailer, *safe sex* is an oxymoron, but Ice-T believes that love (and monogamy?) make it safe. Perhaps Mailer is using a narrower definition of *sex*, equating it with untamed, pure sex outside of a loving relationship like marriage. Someone once said "passion is a disease and marriage is its cure." Zsa Zsa Gabor quipped, "Personally, I know nothing about sex because I've always been married."

Sex may be the most intense sensation experienced or a comfort like a cup of tea at bedtime. During the peaks of sensation seeking and testosterone in adolescence, most young males are preoccupied with sexual images and desires. Romantic love feeds on frustration of desire. Predictable gratification of desire brings inevitable habituation of passionate arousal. Desire remains, but as a banked fire that may flare up at times but is never out of control. As in other realms of sensation seeking, high sensation seekers seek more intense sensations and arousal and use variety to maximize arousal. One prediction that follows from this is that they will have more sexual partners before, during, and after marriage. Variety of sexual activities within a relationship may suffice for a time, but eventually the need for intense arousal may overcome the risks to the primary relationships. Freud (1920/1955) observed that the greatest pleasure is the quenching of a stronger excitation, or to put it simply, the pleasure of orgasm is proportional to the intensity of arousal.

Sexual expression is a function of anticipated pleasures and perceived risks. The research on sex and sensation seeking began in the 1970s during a time dubbed the "sexual revolution." In the late 1940s and early 1950s, Kinsey's surveys of sexual behavior in America opened the drapes to cast some light on what people were actually doing (Kinsey, Pomeroy, & Martin, 1948; Kinsey, Pomeroy, Martin, & Gebhard, 1953). During the 1960s, Masters and Johnson (1966) showed the actual physiological processes involved in sexual arousal. Effective contraception in the form of the birth control pill reduced the risks of pregnancy. The availability of legal abortion in the 1980s also reduced the fear of pregnancy among those whose religious and moral beliefs allowed for this contingency. Antibiotics reduced the fear of gonorrhea and syphilis. The result was a real increase in premarital sex, particularly among young women. More openness about sex in the media and increased access to pornography also fueled the sexual desires of the young. Kinsey et al. (1953) reported that about 50% of females had coitus before they were married. A survey conducted in 1995 found that 75% of all married women had premarital coitus.

The 1980s brought new risks in the form of treatment-resistant kinds of sexually transmitted diseases (STDs) like herpes and the deadly HIV leading in most cases to AIDS. The latter has particularly impacted sexual activities in the gay community, where its effect is most pronounced. Despite these risks, and risks of pregnancy in heterosexual women, many persons practice unprotected sex. Sensation seekers may be among those who are willing to take risks for the sake of intensified sensations in unplanned encounters. Impulsive sensation seekers are at particular risk because of their characteristic lack of restraint in situations of potential pleasure.

Other than physical and health risks, there are other more psychological risks associated with sex, like fear of loss of reputation among women and fear of performance among men. Another type of risk is women's fear of being "used" by men and fear of commitment by men. These two kinds of fear stem from different attitudes of most (but not all) men and women toward the significance of sexual relations. Although younger women in Western cultures have changed in the direction of more permissiveness to premarital sex, recent surveys have shown persisting gender differences in attitudes toward sex and the lowering of social and emotional criteria that make sexual relations acceptable.

ATTITUDES TOWARD SEX

Zuckerman, Tushup, and Finner (1976) studied the relationships between sensation seeking and attitudes toward sex in college students, using two types of attitude scales. One asked what kinds of sexual activities were permissible on the basis of closeness of the social relationship, ranging from *all right with a near stranger* (1) to *only permissible in marriage* (5). The other asked what was permissible in terms of emotional involvement ranging from *no emotional involvement* (1) to *being in love* (5). Powerful sex differences were found on these scales. Female students generally required higher degrees of social and emotional involvement to have sexual relations. All of the Sensation Seeking Scale (SSS) subscales except Boredom Susceptibility (BS) were highly correlated with permissiveness in criteria for sexual relationships for both men and women. As would be expected, Disinhibition (Dis) correlated more highly than the other subscales, but the differences in correlations among the subscales were not large. Even the Thrill and Adventure Seeking (TAS) subscale, which has no items pertaining to interpersonal interactions, correlated with sexual permissiveness. In general, men set fewer criteria for engaging in sex, whereas women demanded more social and emotional involvement (Zuckerman et al., 1976). But high sensation seeking women were more like average men in attitudes toward sex.

In a more recent study of college students, Gaither and Sellbom (2003) found strong gender differences relating to sexual permissiveness. For instance, on the item "When it comes to sex, physical attraction is more important to me than how well I know the person," men scored significantly higher than women, with a strong effect size of .74. In another study, women scored significantly higher than men on a scale stressing the importance of emotional closeness in sexual satisfaction (Hill & Preston, 1996).

Garos and Stock (1998) developed a Sexual Behavior Index, which is actually a scale of attitudes toward sexual behavior. Four subscales were developed through factor analysis. Discordance items reflect conflict or insecurity about sex; Permissiveness items indicate a permissive attitude; Sexual Stimulation shows comfort with sex; and Sexual Obsession items show a preoccupation with sex and difficulty with impulse control. The Zuckerman–Kuhlman Personality Questionnaire (ZKPQ; Zuckerman, 2002; Zuckerman, Kuhlman, Joireman, Teta, & Kraft, 1993) was the personality test used, and the Impulsive Sensation Seeking (ImpSS) scale was divided into its two components, impulsivity and sensation seeking. Both impulsivity and sensation seeking correlated with Sexual Obsession in both men and women, but it is surprising that they did not correlate with Permissiveness or Sexual Stimulation. The results may have had something to do with the mixed sample, which included respondents in addiction treatment centers and community counseling centers as well as college students. Those in treatment may have been high on both depression and anxiety, causing them to view their sexual behavior as obsessive rather than normally permissive.

Hendrick and Hendrick (1986) developed scales to measure six "styles" of love. The *Ludus* type is a more playful, less committed type of love, with more autonomy for partners. The *Storgic* emphasizes friendship rather than passion. The *Pragmatic* type of love is based on estimates of the long-term potential of the partner as a parent, achiever, and helpmate. The *Manic* type is actually an anxious, dependent, possessive type of love. *Eros* is a passionate romantic type of love. *Agape* is a selfless, devoted kind of love. Men were higher on the Ludus type of love, and women scored higher on the Storgic, Pragmatic, and Manic types.

Richardson, Medvin, and Hammock (1988) related these love scales to sensation seeking. The Ludus scale correlated positively with the SSS Total, and all of its subscales. The Pragmatic scale correlated negatively with the SSS Total and the TAS and Dis subscales. Agape correlated negatively with ES and Dis subscales. The Ludus scale also correlated negatively with scales of liking and loving, measures of relationship satisfaction, and the length of current and past relationships and correlated positively with number of past relationships. The results suggest that high sensation seekers do not make good partners in terms of the durability or satisfaction in the relationships. They are generally in it for the sensual gratification without deeper emotional commitments.

RELATIONSHIP SATISFACTION

Thornquist, Zuckerman, and Exline (1991) studied couples "going steady" in college and found that sensation seeking was negatively related to relationship satisfaction in men and women, on the basis of their own and their partners' SSS Total scores. The combination of two high sensation seekers was particularly bad for relationship satisfaction, but the combination of two low sensation seekers resulted in more satisfaction. Discrepancies in sensation seeking have been reported to be related to dissatisfaction in sex and the relationship among college students who have been on an intimate basis with their partners for more than a year (Donaldson, 1989). Wiederman and Hurd (1999) found that students involved in *extradyadic* sex (outside of their primary relationship) had less belief in the association between sex and love or marriage, a ludic-type love style, and high sexual sensation seeking.

Discrepancies in sensation seeking were also related to marital dissatisfaction in couples coming for marital therapy (Ficher, Zuckerman, & Neeb, 1981). When the wife was higher, the husbands had more complaints of impotence and hypertension. Gibson, Franken, and Rowland (1989) studied marital satisfaction in a general population and found that high sensation seeking women had lower marital satisfaction regardless of the sensation seeking levels in their husbands.

A study conducted in the Netherlands examined the relationships between the interactional behavior preceding actual sex and sexual sensation seeking (Vanwesenbeeck, Bekker, & van Lenning, 1998). The latter is measured by a scale developed by Kalichman et al. (1994) that measures specific sensation seeking through uninhibited sex. Three types of interactional behavior factors were found: *Anxious Insecurity*, indicating an uncertain passive attitude (e.g., "I do not know how to deal with sex"); *Proactive Control*, a manipulative attitude (e.g., "I use all my charm to influence my sexual partner"); and *Defensive Control* (e.g., "I let it be known what I do not want in sex" and "I talk about the necessity of contraception"). Anxious Insecurity and Defensive Control are more common in women, representing opposite patterns of dealing or not dealing with a potential sexual situation. Proactive control is found to a greater degree in men. Proactive control was significantly related to sexual sensation seeking in both men and women, and in men only to attitudes of gender conservatism, acceptance of violence and rape myths, and acceptance of adversarial beliefs in relations between men and women. Proactive control in men would increase the risk of rape and unwanted and unprotected sex for women, whereas defensive control in women would reduce that risk.

RISKY SEX

Nearly all studies of general sexual behavior rely on self-report, either from interviews or questionnaires. When subjects know in advance that the topic of the study is sex, those choosing to participate may not be representative of the larger population. This was a question raised by critics of the Kinsey reports. High sensation seekers tend to volunteer for experiments or other activities perceived as risky but offering unusual sensations or experiences (Zuckerman, 1979b, 1994). Bogaert (1996) compared volunteers for a study in which they knew in advance that they would be filling out sexuality and personality questionnaires and viewing a sexually explicit film with nonvolunteers who were not told of the specific nature of the study beforehand. The volunteers were more experienced in sex with more partners, had a greater variety of sexual activities, and were attracted to sexual novelty. They also has higher SSS Total scores. However, despite the mean difference on the SSS, the standard deviation was the same in both groups. In most studies, subjects are informed in advance if sexual questionnaires are involved and offered the chance to withdraw or not fill out the forms. Perhaps because of perceived social pressures, few take advantage of the opportunity to decline participation by leaving or not filling out the questionnaires. In a sign-up situation, however, the bias may operate to select more sexually experienced and higher sensation seeking subjects.

Risky Sex in Predominantly Heterosexual Populations

Our first studies of sexual behavior were conducted with a college population during the 1970s and used a sex experience questionnaire inquiring about frequency of experience with specific types of heterosexual activities and numbers of sexual partners (Zuckerman, Bone, Neary, Mangelsdorf, & Brustman, 1972; Zuckerman et al., 1976). Table 5.1 shows the correlations between sensation seeking scales from the SSS Form IV (SSS–IV) and reported sexual experience. Dis is the only one of the SSS subscales with items containing any reference to sex, but these items refer to attitudes toward sexual behavior rather than actual experience. The General Scale contains none of these items. It is interesting, however, that frequency of activities and number of partners in males correlates with the General and all of the SSS subscales in both studies. In fact, many of the subscales with no references to sex correlate more highly with sexual experience than does the Dis subscale itself. For women in the first study, the sex activities scale correlated with a more restricted range of subscales: ES, Dis, and BS. In the second study, however, the sex activities scale correlated with the General Scale and all of the subscales except BS. Number of partners correlated significantly only with ES and Dis for the women. The sex activities scales ranged from open-mouth kissing to oral and manual stimulation to coitus in the conventional missionary (male superior) and various

TABLE 5.1
Correlations Between SSS Form IV (SSS–IV)
and Heterosexual Experience

SSS–IV	Heterosexual activities[a]				Heterosexual partners[b]	
	Males (n = 38)	Females (n = 60)	Males (n = 82)	Females (n = 71)	Males (n = 120)	Females (n = 131)
General	.51**	.15	.39**	.29*	.40**	.27
TAS	.44**	.16	.42**	.35**	.47**	.20
ES	.37*	.32*	.45**	.37**	.35**	.28*
Dis	.33*	.43**	.39**	.33*	.42**	.29*
BS	.36*	.29**	.23*	.20	.25*	.20

Note. TAS = Thrill and Adventure Seeking; ES = Experience Seeking; Dis = Disinhibition; BS = Boredom Susceptibility. From *Behavioral Expressions and Biosocial Bases of Sensation Seeking* (p. 189), by M. Zuckerman, 1994, New York: Cambridge University Press. Copyright 1994 by Cambridge University Press. Reprinted with permission. [a]Data are from two studies: Zuckerman et al. (1972) and Zuckerman et al. (1976). [b]Number of heterosexual partners; data are from both studies.
*p < .05. **p < .01.

other positions. High sensation seekers had more experience with everything beyond kissing. About 60% of the high and 30% of the low sensation seekers had coital experience. At this time, we did not ask about protection factors like use of condoms, but number of partners is a major risk factor studied in the subsequent research.

Hoyle, Fejfar, and Miller (2000) reviewed all studies relating major personality traits to sexual risk taking up through March 1999. Sexual risk taking was defined by three variables: number of partners, unprotected sex, and high-risk sexual encounters such as having sex with a stranger. A total of 53 studies were found, of which 38 used sensation seeking as the primary predictor of risky sex. They excluded studies that used only a single subscale or a small quantity of items from the SSS. Sensation seeking was correlated with all three categories of sexual risk taking. The mean effect sizes across studies was equated with the mean of correlations. For sensation seeking, these effect sizes were .25 for number of partners, .13 for unprotected sex, .21 for high-risk encounters, and .19 for overall sexual risk taking. The effect of sensation seeking in relation to risky sex was higher among college student (.24) and high-risk populations like gay men (.27) than among noncollege typical risk populations (.13), but even in these the effect sizes are modest.

The correlations for other personality variables, like extraversion and neuroticism from the Eysenck Personality Questionnaire (EPQ; Eysenck & Eysenck, 1975) and NEO Personality Inventory (NEO-PI; Costa & McCrae, 1992b), with overall risk taking were generally much lower than those for the SSS, with the exceptions of low agreeableness in the NEO-PI, low constraint in the Multidimensional Personality Questionnaire (Tellegen, 1985), and aggression–hostility and neuroticism–anxiety in the ZKPQ (only one study with this last instrument).

I do not review the individual studies in the studies reviewed by Hoyle et al. (2000) but take up where they left off in 1999 and into the 2000s. These studies do not lend themselves to a meta-analysis like that done by Hoyle et al. and are discussed in more detail. The new studies have the advantage of using large numbers of subjects, with many of them sampled across wide populations. However, many of them have certain methodological deficiencies. One type of problem in some large population studies is that they do not break down their data by gender or sexual orientation. Males and females differ in risky sexual behaviors such as numbers of partners, use of prostitutes, use of alcohol and drugs before or during sex, and their role in use of condoms. They also differ in sensation seeking, with males being higher. In some studies, gender is entered as a variable in regression equations, but it is rarely directly controlled by partial correlation.

Although large population studies inevitably contain some men and women who are gay and lesbian, these are usually not analyzed separately from heterosexual men and women. Sexual risk taking is different in hetero-sexual populations. In a later section, I discuss studies done on exclusive homosexual or bisexual samples, but in the large community samples, they often constitute a significant source of error variation.

Different forms of sensation seeking scales have been used in these studies, most of which are shorter forms than the standard SSS. Shorter forms are usually less reliable, and reliability puts limits on validity. Most studies have removed items referring to attitudes toward permissive sex, but Kalichman (Kalichman et al., 1994; Kalichman & Rompa, 1995) developed a Sexual Sensation Seeking Scale (SSSS) that has been widely used, particularly in studies of gay men. Some items are sensation seeking items made more specific, for example, "I like to have new and exciting sexual experiences and sensations." These express a desire for novelty, excitement, and a strictly physical approach to sex. But at least one item confounds the scale with the criteria for risky sex, that is, "I enjoy the sensation of intercourse without a condom." Kalichman also has a short Nonsexual Experience Seeking Scale (NSES), but it is heavily loaded with thrill and adventure seeking type items rather than the SSS type of experience seeking and disinhibition items. It would have been better if the NSES items were simply variations of the items in the sexual sensation seeking scale without reference to sex. But despite the differences in item content, the SSSS and NSES are highly correlated (.60–.62; Kalichman & Rompa, 1995). A third test they developed is called the Sexual Compulsivity Scale. The items suggest difficulty in controlling sexual urges and problems caused by them. This scale correlates .55 to .70 with the SSSS and .43 to .57 with the NSES.

Young Adolescent Populations

The largest study in this population is an HIV-prevention study, with nearly 3,000 ninth-grade students (ages 14–15) from 17 high schools in two Midwestern cities (Donohew et al., 2000). These researchers used their own sensation seeking scale, consisting of four items from each of the four subscales of the regular SSS, with simplified wording to fit the reading comprehension levels of their population and modifications to make it more culturally sensitive. An 11-item scale of impulsivity was also used. Median splits were used to divide the sample into high and low sensation seeking groups and high and low impulsivity groups.

Both high sensation seeking adolescents and high impulsive adolescents were more likely to have had sex, used alcohol and marijuana, intended to have sex in the near future, had unwanted sex under pressure, and had unwanted sex when drunk. The results were mostly the same for boys and girls, with the exception that the high female sensation seekers were more likely than the lows to have said "no" to sex on some occasions. Another result contrary to expectation is that high sensation seeking adolescents and impulsive adolescents were more likely to have had a condom, although not necessarily to have used one. The results were additive for sensation seeking and impulsivity so that the least risk-taking group was low on both traits and the most sexually risk-taking group was high on both.

Most of the previously described results depend on the difference between those who had any sexual experience and those who did not. Nearly half of the sample (45%) did have some sexual experience. More restricted findings were obtained when the sample was limited to those who were sexually active.

High sensation seeking adolescents and high impulsive adolescents were more likely to have used alcohol or drugs before having sex. In addition, high impulsive adolescents reported that they never refused unsafe sex, and had sex with five or more partners during their lifetime. Although these are behaviors that should make sex more risky, sensation seeking and impulsivity were not related to condom use, treatment for STDs, or pregnancy.

Xiaoming et al. (2000) studied patterns of initiating sex and drug-related activities among a sample of 261 urban, low-income African American adolescents who were 9 to 15 years at baseline assessment and 13 to 19 by the end of the study. A 44-item modified version of the SSS–IV was used at baseline and at each of four periods of assessment. At baseline, 54% had sexual experience, rising to 80% 4 years later. The proportion of those not using condoms did not increase or decrease during the 4 years, varying from 26% to 35% at different periods of assessment. Mean sensation seeking did not change over time. Sensation seeking and risky sex were higher in those who engaged in both sex and drug taking compared with those who were only sexually active. Among those who first experienced sex and later used alcohol and drugs, high-risk sex scores were the same before and after alcohol and drug use. Those who engage in sex and use drugs tend to be higher sensation seekers than those who only do drugs, but alcohol and drugs do not seem to be causal factors in risky sex. Rather, the subset of those who are high sensation seekers tend to do drugs *and* engage in risky sex.

Miles et al. (2001) studied 738 pairs of adolescent twins (1,476 subjects) ages 13 to 21 (M age = 15.5) from middle and high schools. The subjects were interviewed concerning various types of risk taking, including sex. Two dichotomous variables involved risky sex: *sexual promiscuity*, defined as having more than three partners, and birth control use assessed in those who were sexually active. *Sensation seeking* was defined in terms of self-reported risky behaviors and attitudes toward risk rather than an actual sensation seeking scale. Sexual promiscuity correlated highly with marijuana use and low but significantly with other types of risk taking including riding a motorcycle, not using seat belts in cars, having a risk-taking attitude, and taking dangerous dares. Lack of birth control use among sexually active subjects correlated with all of these except seat-belt use and riding a motorcycle.

Genetic analyses showed moderate genetic influence for some sensation seeking and risky behaviors, including taking dangerous dares, riding a motorcycle, and using marijuana, but little or no genetic variance for the two sexual variables. Instead, sexual promiscuity had moderate shared familial variance (.38) and nonfamilial environmental variance (.53). Nonshared environmental variance was much higher for birth control use (.87). Only marijuana use had substantial shared family environmental influence with sexual promiscuity.

College Populations

Gaither and Sellbom (2003) used Kalichman's (Kalichman et al., 1994; Kalichman & Rompa, 1995) SSSS in a study of sexual behavior in a college sample of 546 students. Men scored higher on the SSSS than women, with a medium effect size for the difference. The SSSS correlated with the number of sexual behaviors (including oral sex) ever, number of "one-night stands," age of first experience of vaginal intercourse (negative correlation), frequency of masturbation, and number of recent sexual partners (last 3 months) for both men and women. Significant correlations found only in women included unprotected sex experiences and receptive anal sex experience. All of these findings were inflated by the inclusion of those with no sexual experience, and when these subjects were removed from the sample, most of the correlations were reduced. The higher correlation of the SSSS with unprotected sex in women than in men is probably due to the usual role of women as the decision makers regarding sexual accessibility and the conditions for it. High sexual sensation seeking women are more likely to be risk takers in sex.

Similar results were found in a smaller sample of students attending a technical training college (Arnold, Fletcher, & Farrow, 2002). Students who used condoms most of the time were lower on the SSSS than those who rarely used them.

E. S. Cohen and Fromme (2002) investigated the relationship between sensation seeking and expectancies using the 19-item ImpSS from the ZKPQ and a large college sample. ImpSS correlated significantly with positive and negative outcome expectations and with frequency of high-risk sexual behavior at two points in time a little over 1 year apart. Structural equation modeling showed that ImpSS affected risky sexual behavior indirectly through its effects on expectancies, particularly positive outcome expectancies. In another study, this group found similar relationships between sensation seeking and risky sex mediated by positive expectancies, using only the sensation seeking items from the ImpSS (Katz, Fromme, & D'Amico, 2000).

Community Populations

Stacy, Newcomb, and Ames (2000) used a cognitive measure of sexuality in addition to sensation seeking in predicting risky sexual behavior in a community sample. The cognitive measure was a homograph free association using ambiguous words with either sexual or neutral meanings as stimuli. A short SSS with four items for each of the four factors was used. The sample was divided into a high-risk and a low-risk group on the basis of the number of sexual partners during the last 4 years and whether they had been tested for HIV infection. The sexual preferences of subjects were not included, but it is likely that the high-risk sample included more gay men than the low-risk sample. Sensation seeking correlated with polydrug use, the association test, number of sexual partners, and engaging in unprotected sex in both high- and low-risk samples. Undesired drug-related sex correlated with sensation seeking only in the high-risk sample, although polydrug use correlated with all three kinds of risky sex behavior in both samples. Hostility and conscientiousness were also used in the study, but sensation seeking was the only personality trait that predicted sexual behaviors. Sensation seeking was related to the cognitive variable memory association, but both of these were independent predictors of risky sex. Gender was involved because men were high sensation seekers and more involved in some forms of risky behaviors.

J. D. Miller et al. (2004) used the Big Five personality factor model in predicting risky sexual behavior in a longitudinal study. Sensation seeking is only directly represented in the Big Five by a facet (subscale) of the major scale of Extraversion called "excitement seeking." However, comparisons of the two models have shown that impulsive sensation seeking is most highly related (inversely) to Conscientiousness in the Big Five (Zuckerman, et al., 1993). At the major factor level, some of the risky sexual behaviors were related to low Agreeableness and Conscientiousness and high Extraversion. High levels of the subscale excitement seeking were related to using alcohol and drugs in conjunction with sex and beginning sex at an early age. The first of these showed an interaction with gender, with the relationship primarily found in women.

Another study using the Revised NEO Personality Inventory (NEO-PI-R; Costa & McCrae, 1992b) had disadvantaged, primarily African American subjects of both sexes from a rural area of Arkansas as subjects (Trobst, Herbst, Masters, & Costa, 2002). High-, medium-, and low-risk groups were designated on the basis of their condom use or nonuse and other risky sexual practices. Having recent sex without a condom occurred in 90% of the high-risk sample, 59% of the medium-risk group, and 0% of the low-risk group. The high-risk group had higher Neuroticism and lower Agreeableness and Conscientiousness scores, as in the previously mentioned study. But in this study, there was no relationship of risky behavior with the facet score of excitement seeking. Impulsiveness within the Neuroticism factor was related to sexual risk taking.

Stein, Newcomb, and Bentler (1994) limited their sample to young adult women in the community. They used an alternative form of the SSS, with all drug-use or sex items omitted. Sensation seeking correlated positively with polydrug use and negatively with social conformity, and all three variables correlated with risky sexual behavior, extent of sexual experience, and number of abortions. Sensation seeking is part of a general nonconformity problem behavior factor that also includes drug use and risky sex behavior.

R. Jones (2004) studied young urban women, primarily African American and Latino. This population accounts for more than half of the HIV infection in the 18- to 29-year-old-age group. She used an adaptation of the SSS, modified for use with those in this demographic sample. The women in the study were limited to those who had either a primary sexual partner, a nonprimary partner, or both. Condom use was lower with primary partners. Consistent condom use was found in about a fifth of relations involving the primary partner and half of those involving a nonprimary partner. Sexual risk behavior involved not only precautions like condom use but also knowledge about the risky behavior of the male partners. Sexual risk taking was predicted by three variables: sensation seeking, sexual imposition (pressure to have sex by the partner), and dyadic trust (nontrust related to risky sex). Sensation seeking remained significant even when the influences of the other two factors were controlled.

Prostitutes are a group of women who constitute a major risk source of HIV infection because of their relations with large numbers of male partners. A second source of infection is from drugs, because many of them are drug injectors. Although they can lower their risk by requiring customers to use condoms, many simply demand a higher fee from customers who refuse to use condoms. This is not a wise risk–benefit ratio.

O'Sullivan, Zuckerman, and Kraft (1996) studied a particularly high-risk-taking group of prostitutes operating along a highway leading out of a city in Delaware. Most operated without the protection of pimps on a road where a serial killer had murdered some of their colleagues a couple of years earlier. The ZKPQ was used as a personality measure. A control group consisted of university service employee women only slightly older and more educated (more high school graduates) than the prostitutes. The prostitutes were interviewed and tested during work breaks and were paid for their participation in the study. They scored significantly higher than control subjects on the ImpSS, Aggression–Hostility, and Neuroticism–Anxiety subscales of the ZKPQ, but when age and education were controlled, only the ImpSS scale retained significance, although the difference for aggression approached significance. Within the prostitute group, those who used co-caine or those who were polydrug users were higher on ImpSS than those who did not use drugs or who only used one drug other than cocaine.

Because prostitutes are a high-risk group for HIV infection, their clients are also at risk. Xantidis and McCabe (2000) studied the male clients of "female commercial sex workers" in Australia tested in a brothel setting with a brief 11-item SSS. Reasons for patronizing prostitutes given by more than 60% of these men included some sensation seeking ones: a liking for variety and a desire for "new experiences." Clients scored significantly higher than control subjects on the SSS.

The last two studies to be discussed used large samples of both unse-lected, predominantly heterosexual men and women from the community and gay men. Kalichman and Rompa (1995) used their own sexual and nonsexual experience seeking and sexual compulsivity (SC) scales in inner-city community and gay samples. In the gay men sample, all three scales correlated with four types of risky behavior: drug or alcohol use before sex, number of sexual partners, and unprotected sexual intercourse. In the inner-city sample, sexual sensation seeking and SC correlated with unprotected intercourse and number of sexual partners, but nonsexual sensation seeking did not correlate with unprotected intercourse. There was minimal correla-tion of any of these personality variables with alcohol or drug use before sex.

McCoul and Haslam (2001) did a similar study but with heterosexual and homosexual men drawn from a more middle-class, educated urban community. They used only impulsivity and sexual sensation seeking scales. Among heterosexual men, both impulsivity and sexual sensation seeking correlated significantly with frequency of unprotected sex, but only sexual sensation seeking correlated with number of partners. But among the gay men, neither of these traits correlated with either form of sexual risk taking. The authors attribute these differences of their results from those in the previous study to the differences in social class and to the likely better knowledge of their partners' HIV status and ability to apply this knowledge regardless of sensation seeking tendencies.

Kalichman, Cain, Zweben, and Swain (2003) studied a high-risk popu-lation in which the risks had ended in a sexually transmitted infection for which they were asking for treatment at a clinic. This was an exclusively heterosexual sample of men, mostly low-income African Americans. Kalich-man's nonsexual sensation seeking scale was used along with measures of alcohol and drug use and expectancies. Unprotected sexual intercourse and sex with alcohol use were the only types of risky sexual behavior examined in the study. Sensation seeking and alcohol use and expectancies correlated low but significantly with unprotected intercourse with casual partners. Sensation seeking had both direct and indirect relationships with unpro-tected sex. The indirect relationship was through its association with alcohol outcome expectancies, which mediate alcohol use in sexual contexts and unprotected sex.

Bryan and Stallings (2002) studied a younger population consisting of a selected sample of adolescent boys (M age = 16) in treatment for substance abuse and delinquency and an unselected sample of adolescents from the community. Risky sexual behavior was assessed using only two questions: one regarding frequency of sexual intercourse and another on contraception use during intercourse. Cloninger's (1987b) three-factor Tridimensional Personality Questionnaire was used for personality assessment. The treatment sample was higher than the control subjects on novelty seeking, harm avoidance, unprotected intercourse, conduct disorder, and substance use. All of these differences were expected except for the one on harm avoidance. Novelty seeking correlated with conduct disorder and substance abuse but did not correlate with unprotected sex in either group.

Summary

Sensation seeking in premarital sex is related to three kinds of risky behaviors: having sex with multiple partners, having unprotected sex (without condoms), and having sex with strangers. The likelihood of all of these types of risk taking is increased by the use of alcohol and other drugs prior to having sex. Drugs act as disinhibitors and stimulants. By reducing anxiety, they reduce thoughts of potential risks. Most studies show that specific sexual sensation seeking and more generalized nonsexual sensation seeking are related to risky kinds of sexual behaviors. Sexual sensation seeking places a value on the intensity of sexual experience, whereas SC carries the feeling of unwanted compulsion and negative self-regard. Regardless of the differences between these motive traits, the three are highly intercorrelated and often have equivalent effects on risky sexual behaviors.

RISKY SEX IN GAY MALE POPULATIONS

AIDS is the major pandemic of the century. Entire nations in Africa are experiencing a decimation of their populations by this deadly disease. The source of the disease in the HIV is known, and its transmission mechanism through semen and blood is also known. The virus can be spread sexually through unprotected anal or vaginal intercourse. The gay population is particularly vulnerable to the infection. The first U.S. cases were reported in the gay population on the West Coast, and by 2000 more than a quarter of a million men who have sex with men (MSM) had died of AIDS (Wolitski, Valdiserri, Denning, & Levine, 2001). Another half million were estimated to be infected with HIV. MSM were a particularly vulnerable group because of their typically large number of sexual contacts. The habit of "cruising" for sex in urban centers in bars and bathhouses resulted in large numbers of anonymous partners. It is estimated that only 5% to 7% of American men have had sex with another man during adulthood, but they constitute about 70% of currently HIV-infected men and account for 42% of all new infections. In one large survey of major metropolitan centers, 18% of MSM surveyed reported that they were HIV seropositive, compared with 1% of the overall population.

Public campaigns warning of the consequences and personal experiences with AIDS deaths in friends within the MSM population led to significant reductions in risky behaviors, including promiscuity and unprotected anal sex, during the 1980s. However, the discovery of a treatment, using antiretroviral drugs, which has extended lives of people with HIV and has controlled the HIV infection, may have resulted in increases in HIV infection and other STDs in urban centers in the last 5 years. Increases in unprotected anal intercourse with partners whose serostatus is unknown have also increased, particularly among the young MSM (Stall, Hays, Waldo, Ekstrand, & McFarland, 2000). Nearly half of MSM have returned to unprotected anal intercourse. This is particularly alarming because about one fifth of seropositive men in one study reported that they recently engaged in unprotected insertive anal intercourse with a partner who was seronegative or whose serostatus was unknown. If the retreat from safe sex is due in some part to a decreased risk estimate as a result of new treatments, it is somewhat naive. The treatments are costly, are lifelong, have multiple side effects, and will probably lead to drug-resistant strains of HIV.

To what extent is sensation seeking a factor in this Russian roulette kind of sexual behavior? Sensation seeking may play a role in two ways. The reluctance to use condoms in risky forms of sex is because of the claim of MSM that they reduce the sensations and spontaneity of sex, important considerations for high sensation seekers. Sensation seeking is associated with drug use, as discussed in the previous chapter. Many studies suggest that the use of alcohol and other drugs in conjunction with sex lowers inhibition and risk appraisal, thus fostering risky sex (Leigh & Stall, 1993). Specter (2005) suggested that the increase in use of crystal methamphetamine in all-night parties and sexual marathons has increased the prevalence of risky sex in MSM. The drug is reputed to remove inhibitions about having unprotected anal sex and to increase the intensity of the sexual experience and the capacity for having multiple partners in a single night.

Before reviewing the literature on the relationship of sensation seeking to risky sex, we must ask the question, Are MSM sensation seekers as contrasted with exclusive heterosexual men? Zuckerman and Myers (1983) compared homosexual and heterosexual male college students and members of a gay church with members of a church organization affiliated with the university. Unfortunately, the campus church group rated themselves as more conservative on religion and politics than the gay church group, so their comparison on sensation seeking is problematic. The SSS Form V (SSS–V) was used, but items biased toward a heterosexual orientation were modified to make them neutral regarding sexual orientation. The gay students did not differ from the heterosexual students on the SSS Total or any of its subscales. The gay church members, however, were higher than the control church group on the SSS Total and the ES and Dis subscales. Given the difference in attitudes of the two church groups, we were inclined to give more weight to the student groups, who were more closely matched on demographic variables, and we concluded that gay and straight people as general populations do not differ in sensation seeking, but this conclusion needs replication on larger, more representative samples.

Kalichman et al.'s (1994) SSSS is specific to sensation seeking through sex, but the items are not specific to either heterosexual or homosexual sex. McCoul and Haslam (2001) compared 112 heterosexual and 104 homosexual men recruited by advertisement notices and groups attending talks in the New York metropolitan area. Although hardly a representative sample, it is more of a community one than a study restricted to college students or church members. The homosexual group did score significantly higher on the SSSS than the heterosexual group. But the question of general sensation seeking remains open.

Table 5.2 summarizes 11 studies in which one or more of the sensation seeking or SC scales are related to at least one of three types of sexual risk taking in MSM: numbers of sexual partners, frequency of unprotected anal sex, and the use of alcohol and/or drugs in conjunction with sexual activity. Five of the 11 studies are by Kalichman and his colleagues. The precise correlations or beta weights in multiple regression are not given. Most of the correlations are in the .20 to .30 range, thus accounting for only 4% to 9% of the variance in the particular kind of risk taking. Nonsignificant correlations were all positive, in the same direction, and in many cases not much lower than significant correlations. Most studies used Kalichman's SSSS with or without his NSES or SC scales. Three studies used my SSS–V or some of its subscales. The subsample sizes were 99 subjects or more for all but 1 study (Parsons, Bimbi, & Halkitis, 2001) and ranged up to 589 (Bancroft et al., 2003). Various methods of recruiting subjects were used, but all relied on volunteers recruited from advertisements or places where MSM congregate, like bathhouses and gay bars, possibly biasing the findings in the direction of higher sensation seeking and sexual-risk-taking subjects (Bogaert, 1996). Oral sex, protected and unprotected, was also examined in some of these studies, but it is not discussed here because it is practiced by nearly all MSM, and although it may pose some risk for HIV infection, it is much less than the risk from anal sex. Some studies make a distinction

TABLE 5.2

Studies of Sensation Seeking and Sexual Compulsivity in Relation to
Risky Sexual Behaviors Among Men Who Have Sex With Men (MSM)

Study	Samples, sources	Test(s) used	Sexual partners	Anal sex without condoms	Alcohol, drugs, sex
Kalichman et al. (1994)	100 MSM; ads; *M* age = 34; 67% W	SSSS NSES SCS	X *ns* *ns*	X *ns* *ns*	X *ns* *ns*
Kalichman & Rompa (1995)	269 MSM; ads, gay bars; *M* age = 36; 63% W	SSSS NSES SCS	X X X	X X X	X X X
McCoul & Haslam (2001)	104 MSM; ads, lectures; *M* age = 36; 96% W	SSSS	*ns*	*ns*	—
Kalichman, Weinhart, Di Fonzo, Austin, & Luke (2002)	197 HIV+ MSM; *M* age = 41; 72% AA	NSES	—	X	X
Schroth (1996)	100 MSM	SSS–V	X	*ns*	—
Chng & Géliga-Vargas (2000)	302 MSM; *M* age = 32; gay bars; 24% AA, 19% W, 25% Asian	SSSS	—	X	—
Kalichman, Heckman, & Kelly (1996)	99 MSM; ads; *M* age = 36; 69% W, 21% AA	SSSS NSES	X X	X X	X X
Kalichman, Tannenbaum, & Nachimson (1998)	176 MSM; Gay Pride Parade	SSSS	X	X	X
Dolezal, Meyer-Bahlburg, Remien, & Petkova (1997)	117 MSM; *M* age = 37	SSS–IV	X	X	X
Parsons, Bimbi, & Halkitis (2001)	50 MSM Internet advertisers	SC SSSS	X *ns*	X *ns*	— —
Bancroft et al. (2003)	509 MSM; gay bars, bathhouses	SSS–V: Dis, BS	X	X	—

Note. ads = advertisements; SSSS = Kalichman's Sexual Sensation Seeking Scale; NSES = Kalichman's Nonsexual Experience Seeking Scales; SCS = Kalichman's Sexual Compulsivity Scale; SSS = Sensation Seeking Scale; SSS–IV = Sensation Seeking Scale Form IV; SSS–V = Sensation Seeking Scale Form V; Dis = Disinhibition; BS = Boredom Susceptibility; W = White; AA = African American; X = significant relationship, *ns* = nonsignificant relationship.

between insertive and receptive anal sex, and the insertive type is less risky for the insertor, but most of the studies show no difference between these two types of activity in relationships with sensation seeking. These details are discussed later as the individual studies are presented.

Number of sexual partners is a major risk factor for HIV infection and STDs in general. Many MSM try to avoid HIV by staying in a monogamous relationship with a partner who is HIV negative. Of course, this depends on the partner remaining monogamous in his sexual activity. In nine studies in which this variable was examined, the tendency to have multiple partners or being nonmongamous was related to either sexual or nonsexual sensation seeking measures in seven studies and to SC in one study. SSSS was not significantly related to number of partners in two studies.

Unprotected anal sex is a second major risk factor for HIV infection. This kind of risky behavior is engaged in by about half of the MSM population, and among those risk takers, about half reported they engaged in this behavior with a partner whose HIV status was unknown (Wolitski et al., 2001). This is particularly risky when one considers the report that a minority (perhaps a fifth) of HIV-seropositive men reported engaging in unprotected anal intercourse with a partner who was HIV seronegative or whose serostatus was unknown. Engaging in unprotected anal sex was related to sensation seeking measures in 8 of 10 studies in which it was measured and was nonsignificant in 2 of the 10. In a study in which the group was broken down into those who were the insertive partner and those who were the receptive partner in anal sex, the significant correlations were practically the same for the two roles (Kalichman & Rompa, 1995). This is not surprising, because when asked to classify their preferences as "tops" (insertors), "bottoms" (receptives), or "versatiles" (engaging in both roles) in anal intercourse, more than half of the subjects classified themselves as versatiles and about 40% of the other two groups occasionally assumed the opposite role (Hart, Wolitski, Purcell, Gómez, & Halkitis, 2003).

The third type of risky behavior is the use of alcohol or drugs in sexual situations. The correlations with sensation seeking were significant in all six of the studies that examined the relationship. Several of the studies examined the relationships to alcohol and drugs separately. The correlations with alcohol were significant in all of the studies, but in two studies (Kalichman, Heckman, & Kelly, 1996; Kalichman, Tannenbaum, & Nachimson, 1998) the correlation with drug usage was inconsistently significant.

In the first study, in which Kalichman et al. (1994) reported on the development of their three scales, Sexual Sensation Seeking Scale (SSSS), Non-Sexual Experience Seeking Scale (NSES), and Sexual Compulsivity Scale, they found that whereas both the SSSS and NSES correlated significantly with ratings of the pleasurableness of foreplay activities, only the

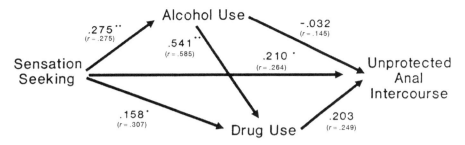

Figure 5.1. Path analysis of a three predictor recursive model of sensation seeking, alcohol use, and drug use in relation to frequency of unprotected anal intercourse. Numbers in parentheses are zero-order correlation coefficients between variables, and numbers outside parentheses represent standardized regression coefficients. From "Sensation Seeking as an Explanation for the Association Between Substance Use and HIV-Related Risky Sexual Behavior," by S. C. Kalichman, T. Heckman, and J. A. Kelly, 1996, *Archives of Sexual Behavior, 25*, p. 149. Copyright 1996 by Springer Publishing Company. Reprinted with permission.
*p < .05. **p < .01.

SSSS correlated with the pleasure of anal intercourse without a condom, and only the NSES correlated significantly with pleasure in anal intercourse with a condom. The SC scale did not correlate with any of the ratings of pleasure for any of the activities. They then divided their sample into a high-risk group (participating in unprotected anal intercourse) and a low-risk group (not engaging in this risky behavior). A discriminant function showed that the group engaging in unprotected anal intercourse was higher on the SSSS but not on the NSES or the SC scales. They were also higher in drug and alcohol use. The SSSS was significantly correlated with number of sex partners, anal intercourse without condoms, and alcohol use (but not drug use), whereas the NSES and the SC scales did not correlate with any of these risky activities. These differences between the SSSS and the other two scales in predicting risky behavior were not found in a second study (Kalichman & Rompa, 1995). In this study of 296 MSM recruited from ads, gay bars, and social groups, all three scales were related to all three types of risky behaviors. In a third study by this group, both the SSSS and the NSES were again generally related to the three types of risky behaviors on both of two testing occasions (Kalichman et al., 1996). Path analysis and hierarchal regression analyses showed that sensation seeking accounted for the relationship between substance use and high-risk sexual behavior. The results of the path analysis are shown in Figure 5.1. The direct effect of sexual sensation seeking accounted for 80% of its total association with unprotected anal sex, whereas only 8% of the relationship was mediated through alcohol use and only 12% was mediated through drug use. The path analysis using the NSES showed similar results. When alcohol and drug use were controlled through partial correlation, both types of sensation seeking remained significant, but when sensation seeking was partialed out, nearly all of the correlations between substance use and frequency of unprotected anal intercourse became insignificant. The results suggest that the personality trait is primary and a common source for both substance use before sex and risky sexual behavior.

Another study by Kalichman and colleagues of men who were HIV seropositive also showed that the nonsexual sensation seeking trait (as measured by the NSES) and alcohol use in sexual contexts were related to unprotected anal intercourse (Kalichman, Weinhart, DiFonzo, Austin, & Luke, 2002). Sensation seeking also affected alcohol use through its relation to outcome expectancies for alcohol. High sensation seekers believed that alcohol increases sexual desire and performance and reduces their concern about safe sex. Those men who used either alcohol or other drugs (marijuana, powder or crack cocaine, nitrate inhalants) during their most recent intercourse were less likely to use condoms during that intercourse. This was a dangerous effect of substances, given the fact that all of these men were HIV positive.

Kalichman et al. (1998) also showed that sexual sensation seeking and alcohol and drug use before sex predicted numbers of male sex partners in a broader sample of MSM among whom only a minority were HIV seropositive. As in the previously discussed study, sensation seeking had a direct relationship with the risky behavior, promiscuity in this case, and an indirect effect through its relationship with alcohol and drug expectancies.

Three of the studies used the Zuckerman SSS–V. Dolezal, Meyer-Bahlburg, Remien, and Petkova (1997) used a convenience sample from New York City, eliminating potential subjects who practiced drug injection. They eliminated items in the SSS that were not appropriate for a homosexual sample or that asked specifically about drug or alcohol attitudes. Total sensation seeking was significantly correlated with alcohol and drug use during sex, but was related to the practice of both receptive and insertive anal sex, even when alcohol and drug use during sex were controlled in multiple regression. The latter two variables were also related to these risky sexual behaviors, but their influence typically dropped to marginal significance when sensation seeking was included in the models predicting unprotected anal sex.

An overall risky sex index was calculated using monogamous versus nonmongamous relationships, and the consistent versus inconsistent use of condoms during anal sex. The highest risk rating was for nonmonogamous men practicing receptive and/or insertive anal sex without consistent condom use. The risk index was significantly predicted by sensation seeking and either alcohol or drug use during sex. Similar results were obtained for oral sex.

The Kinsey Institute sponsored the largest of these studies, with 589 MSM recruited from gay bars, bathhouses, and fitness centers (Bancroft et al., 2003). The Dis and BS subscales of the SSS–V were used as sensation seeking measures. The sexual attitude items were not removed from the Dis subscale. The Dis subscale correlated positively with a scale measuring the "propensity for sexual excitement" (SE) and negatively with a scale measuring the "propensity for sexual inhibition" (SIPC) due to the threat of performance consequences (like becoming infected with HIV). Dis was low but positively correlated with items measuring the tendency to have increased sexual interest and response when in an anxious or depressed mood. Risky anal sex was increased with SSS Dis and decreased in relation to SIPC and a scale for anxiety. Similar results were obtained for risky oral sex. Number of casual partners was increased with Dis, SE, and negative moods. Recent tendency to engage in cruising was increased by Dis and negative moods. A measure of long-term risk taking, beyond the 6-month retrospective recall, was also increased by Dis and SE and decreased by SIPC. Dis was a significant predictor for all risk types of behavior, but SSS BS was not. Dis was also related to active or inactive sexual groups; Dis was higher in active groups. The inclusion of the sexual attitude items in the Dis suggests a positive attitude toward risky sexual activities, like having many partners.

The third study to use the SSS was the one by Schroth (1996). The SSS Total correlated significantly with number of sexual activities and sexual partners but not with number of risky sexual behaviors like anal sex without condoms.

Most of the studies described here have used populations that were predominantly of one ethnicity or another. For instance, in Kalichman et al. (1996), the sample was 69% White and 21% Black, whereas in Kalichman et al. (2002), it was 72% Black and 23% White. Chng and Géliga-Vargas (2000) examined the influence of ethnicity and gay identity as well as sexual sensation seeking in risky sexual behavior in MSM in a sample nearly evenly distributed among African Americans, Latinos, Whites, and Asians. Ethnic identity was not a significant predictor of unprotected anal intercourse, but gay identity was. Those with an undefined gay identity were more likely to engage in unprotected anal intercourse than those with a defined gay identity.

Sexual sensation seeking was a strong predictor of unprotected anal intercourse. The highest sensation seekers were 12.7 times as likely to engage in unprotected anal intercourse than the lowest sensation seekers. HIV status was also a significant predictor of risky behavior. Men with unknown HIV status reported the highest rate (77%) of unprotected anal sex; men with HIV negative, the lowest rate (46%,); and men who were HIV positive had an intermediate rate (57%). Of the seropositive men, 57% continued to engage in unprotected anal sex, considerably higher than the 28% reported in the study by Kalichman et al. (2002).

Special MSM Populations

Many MSM have turned to Internet chat rooms to seek partners (Stall et al., 2000). This can be a risk-reduction strategy because they allow time to assess the HIV status of the potential partner and their sexual preferences and precautions before the heat of the moment in face-to-face encounters in bars or bathhouses. Those who are HIV positive can seek out other partners who are also infected, and those who are HIV negative can require partners who are also negative, assuming honesty in their contact.

Parsons et al. (2001) studied a group of men who used the Internet to advertise their "escort" services. These men are more select than "street hustlers" in their choices of partners. However, they had large numbers of sexual contacts: an average of 46 with work sex partners and 24 with casual partners, many without condom protection, in the recent 3-month period. HIV status was reported to be negative in 80% of the group, positive in 16%, and undetermined in 4%. SC was significantly related to the number of unprotected receptive anal sex occasions with both work and nonwork partners and to frequency of unprotected insertive anal sex with work partners. Although sexual sensation seeking was highly correlated with SC, it was not significantly related to risky sex behaviors.

Ross, Mattison, and Franklin (2003) studied 1,169 men who attended three gay "circuit parties." Circuit parties are occasions in which drug use and sexual activity, often under the influence of drugs, are common. Attendees were asked their reasons for attending the parties. The reasons grouped into two factors, Celebratory (to have fun, to dance, to enjoy music, to be with friends) and Sensation Seeking (to have an intense gay experience, to be wild and uninhibited, to party, to use drugs, and to have sex). Celebratory reasons were more commonly given than sensation seeking ones. Sensation seeking, but not social, reasons were correlated with the incidence of unsafe sex in the past year and a relatively strong relationship with ecstasy use at the party.

Parsons and Halkitis (2002) contrasted men who sought sexual partners in public service environments (PSEs), such as parks, and commercial sex environments (CSEs), such as bathhouses and sex clubs. Those who went to PSEs had higher scores on SC, whereas those who went to CSEs had higher scores on sexual sensation seeking and depression and lower levels of perceived responsibility to protect sex partners from HIV infection. Men going to CSEs reported more acts of unprotected anal sex than those who did not go to CSEs. No significant differences in unprotected sex were found between men who went to PSEs and those who did not. Both groups of men had more nonprimary sexual partners than those who did not go to either PSEs or CSEs. Men who went to PSEs reported an average of 17 sex partners, and those who went to CSEs said they had an average of 24 partners in the most recent 3 months. Those who went to CSEs reported more drug use, including amphetamines, hallucinogens, GHB, and nitrates ("poppers"), than those who did not go to CSEs. Those who went to PSEs reported more use of barbiturates only. The PSE seekers seem to be more neurotic (compulsively driven), whereas the CSE seekers are more sensation seeking through sex and drugs.

Summary

MSM are a population especially at risk for HIV transmission or infection, especially if they engage in unprotected anal sex with a partner of positive or unknown HIV serostatus. There is a conflict between the desire for the more intense sensations perceived in sex without condoms and the risk of an incurable disease or other STDs. High sensation seekers among MSM are generally more willing to take the risks for the sake of the added sensations. This is a concrete expression of the definition of *sensation seeking*: "the seeking of varied, novel, complex, and *intense* sensations and experiences, and the willingness to take physical . . . risks for the sake of such experience" (Zuckerman, 1994, p. 27).

BIOLOGICAL CONNECTIONS BETWEEN RISKY SEX AND SENSATION SEEKING

Testosterone is a major factor in regulating sexual desire and arousal in men and women. Daitzman and Zuckerman (1980) found that young males who scored in the upper range of the SSS Dis subscale had higher levels of testosterone than those scoring in the lower range. Both Dis and testosterone correlated with amount of heterosexual experience and number of heterosexual partners in these college student subjects. The findings relating sensation seeking, particularly Dis, to plasma testosterone were replicated by Aluja and Garcia (2005); Aluja and Torrubia (2004); Bogaert and Fisher (1995); and Gerra et al. (1999) but not by Dabbs, Hopper, and Jurkovic (1990), who used testosterone from saliva rather than plasma.

In both male and female rats, dopamine activity is increased in the nucleus accumbens, the nexus of reward response in the brain, during both anticipatory and consummatory phases of sex (Melis & Argiolas, 1995; Pfaus, Damsma, Wenkstern, & Fibiger, 1995). The dopamine released before and during sex is above that produced by activity alone. Dopamine release in the striatum is more reflective of physical activity. Drugs such as amphetamines that are frequently used during risky sex increase sexual activity in the rat and decrease the postejaculatory interval before sexual activity is resumed. This could account for the association of methamphetamine and multiple sex partners on the same occasion in MSM, as in bathhouses and sex clubs.

The evidence relating dopamine activity to sensation seeking is mixed, as described in chapter 1. However, a recent study found that novelty seeking is associated with a high level of dopamine, as indicated by response to a dopamine agonist (Stuettgen, Hennig, Reuter, & Netter, 2005). High dopaminergic reactivity to sexual stimulation, perhaps sensitized by high levels of testosterone, may be what connects sensation seeking to risky sexual behavior, particularly variety of sexual partners.

EVOLUTIONARY SIGNIFICANCE

Sexual sensation seeking is an adaptive advantage in evolution for men for obvious reasons. Sex is a drive fueled by the hormone testosterone and restrained or channeled by society. Freud's thesis was that culture arose from the sublimations of the restrained, diverted, and transformed sex drive. Sublimation is a questionable concept, but he was right in that unrestrained sexuality is risky because it threatens the interpersonal bonds that make culture possible. Any society that tolerated incest and rape would be unstable.

Evolution is not regulated by the needs of society, although it must find solutions to the problems of survival that work for everyone. Evolution is driven by the reproductive success or failure of the individual. When the need for novelty and variety extends into the realm of sexuality, it may result in more reproductive success for a man, but within a society, it flouts the rights of other men and threatens the survival of the Don Juan.

Nature encourages reproduction by providing intense pleasurable sensations in the sexual act, peaking at orgasm. An intense approach–avoidance conflict is created when desire is directed at a novel but forbidden sexual partner. Sensation seekers tend to fixate on the anticipated hedonic benefits and minimize or ignore anticipated risks in many kinds of situations, whether in sex, skydiving, or mountain climbing.

6

SENSATION SEEKING AND CRIME, ANTISOCIAL BEHAVIOR, AND DELINQUENCY

Because that's where the money is.
> —Willie Sutton's (attributed) answer to the question,
> "Why do you rob banks?"

Willie Sutton was a notorious bank robber from the 1920s through the early 1950s. His answer is a rational one for a thief. Great risks are balanced by the opportunity for great gains. But it is not the complete story for criminal motivation, particularly for adolescent delinquency and for crimes like unprovoked aggression, rape, car theft, and vandalism. Impulsive destructive acts can be sources of pleasurable excitation for otherwise idle and bored adolescents, and the risks may add to the pleasure rather than work against it. In other words, sensation seeking may be a motive for some individuals in some situations. Adolescents in lower socioeconomic (SE) classes do not have the opportunities for adventure and excitement available to middle-class children, like travel, scuba diving, surfing, rock climbing, racing their own cars, and so forth. Sex, drugs, and crime are their more accessible sources of sensation seeking, and sex and drugs may not be enough for some. Of course, some middle-class children also engage in criminal sensation seeking.

In the previous chapters, I discussed sensation seeking in driving, sports, drugs, sex, and gambling. As we have seen, risk taking in these areas is correlated across activities. Some of them involve antisocial behavior, as in driving under the influence of alcohol or drugs and possession of drugs,

169

but in this chapter I focus on forms of criminality or antisocial behavior other than these. It is not surprising that crime, delinquency, and aggression are correlated with alcohol and drug use as well as gambling, risky sex, and general social nonconformity (Newcomb, Galaif, Carmona, & Vargas, 2001; Willoughby, Chalmers, & Busseri, 2004). Sensation seeking is associated with a general deviance factor that includes drug use, sexual risks, and law abidance (Newcomb & McGee, 1991). Alcohol and drugs have a disinhibiting effect on behavior, and drugs and gambling require money to sustain them. Alcohol and drug use not only predicts arrests in juvenile offenders but also robustly predicts recidivism (Stoolmiller & Blechman, 2005). Horvath and Zuckerman (1993) found a substantial correlation between criminal risk taking, such as shoplifting, selling drugs, and vandalism, and nonfelonious violations, such as traffic offenses and violations of social rules. Both of these also correlated with financial risks, as in gambling, and sports risk taking. Risk appraisals in these areas were also correlated.

Arnett (2000) described a period of "emerging adulthood" from ages 18 to 25, distinct from adolescence and early adulthood, and characterized by growing independence from childhood norms, values, and expectations and a delay in accepting the responsibilities of adulthood. Risky behaviors such as unprotected sex, substance use, and risky driving behaviors peak during this period (Arnett, 1992). Crimes such as rape, robbery, assault, and theft also peak during this period (Wright, 2002). One-year prevalence rates for antisocial personality disorder (APD) peak in the 18- to 29-year-old range and decline thereafter (Robins & Regier, 1991). This is true for the behavioral component of APD but not for the personality component (Harpur & Hare, 1994). Sensation seeking also peaks during this period, although the absolute peak is in the late adolescent years (16–19).

Gender differences in crime are also parallel to those in sensation seeking. Robbery and assault are about twice as common in men than in women, and the jail population consists of 7 to 8 times as many men as women. In community studies men were 5 to 7 times more likely than women to receive a lifetime diagnosis of APD (Kessler et al., 1994; Robins & Regier, 1991). Gender differences are prominent in sensation seeking, particularly in the late adolescent and emerging adult groups and specifically on the Thrill and Adventure Seeking (TAS), Disinhibition (Dis), and Boredom Susceptibility (BS) subscales, most characteristic in physical and social risk taking.

GENERAL ANTISOCIAL BEHAVIOR AND DELINQUENCY

Antisocial behavior can be studied in children as young as 6 years old. Kafry (1982) showed children aged 6 to 10 years old pictures of children engaged in antisocial behavior including playing with matches, hitting peers or adults, shoplifting, and truancy. They were asked to indicate which of these behaviors they actually did. The author developed a children's form of the Sensation Seeking Scale (SSS) that correlated significantly with the number of pictured antisocial activities that they claimed doing themselves.

Horvath and Zuckerman (1993) found that sensation seeking and impulsivity both correlated with self-reports of criminal behavior by college students, although the correlation for sensation seeking (.53) was much higher than that for impulsivity (.36), and the beta weight in a multiple regression was twice as high for sensation seeking as for impulsivity. But the importance of personality factors may be more relevant for a college population, where felonious crime is less common than for a lower SE neighborhood where gangs and crime are more common and peer influence is more prevalent.

Lynam et al. (2000) compared the relationship of impulsivity to criminal offending in male adolescents in poor neighborhoods and in better neighborhoods in Pittsburgh. The poorest area, in contrast to the better ones, was largely African American, with mostly single-parent families, and with inhabitants living in poverty and public housing. The impulsivity measure was a composite of behavioral measures and observer, caregiver, and self-reports. The effect of impulsivity on both theft and violent crimes was stronger and significant in the poorer neighborhoods and nonsignificant in the highest SE neighborhoods. This finding is in direct opposition to the hypothesis that personality may play a greater role in areas of the city where crime is less prevalent. The authors suggest that because external social control is weaker in the poor neighborhoods, individual self-control is more important.

Krueger et al. (1994) reported on the relationship between delinquency and personality in a large 18-year-old complete cohort group from a community in New Zealand. Delinquency was assessed by a variety of methods including self-report, informant reports, police contacts, and court convictions. The four methods were all significantly intercorrelated. Naturally, the great majority of offenses are never recorded in police and court records. Self-reports and informants' reports correlated .48, but police contacts and court convictions were much more highly intercorrelated, .78. Self-reports correlated .42 and .36 with police reports and convictions, respectively. The personality test used was the Multidimensional Personality Questionnaire (MPQ; Tellegen, 1985), which consists of 10 scales grouped into three major factors. Subjects were classified into "abstainers" from any kind of delinquency; "normative delinquents," who engaged in the typical, less serious types of delinquency; and "versatile" delinquents, who engaged in many more types of delinquency than their peer group. Previous studies showed the versatiles to be distinguished from other normative adolescent delinquents by the persistence of their antisocial behavior over the life course (Moffitt, 1993).

Comparing the versatile with the normative delinquents, the versatiles scored lower on the three scales composing the constraint factor of the MPQ: harm avoidance (–sensation seeking), control (–impulsivity), and traditionalism (–socialization). They also scored lower on social closeness and higher than the normative delinquents on aggression and alienation subscales of the MPQ.

Delinquency/Self-Reported Behavior

Investigators have used a variety of self-report delinquency measures in their studies of sensation seeking. Studies using the full SSS, with all of its subscales, have generally shown significant relationships between the Total score and all of the subscales except TAS and the extent of delinquent behavior in high school and college students (Pérez & Torrubia, 1985; Simó & Pérez, 1991). However, Pfefferbaum and Wood (1994) found that the thrill seeking and risk-taking scales were significantly related to both property and interpersonal delinquency, whereas self-control and socialization scales were negatively correlated with delinquency of both types. When asked the reasons for their specific delinquent acts, 38% of those engaging in property delinquency but only 11% of those in interpersonal delinquency gave "fun" or "thrills" as their motive. The major motive for interpersonal delinquency was "anger" or "revenge."

A study of nearly 2,000 Black and White adolescents found that a scale consisting of some items from the SSS TAS scale and an impulsivity scale were significantly correlated with both property and violent crimes (Cooper, Wood, Orcutt, & Albino, 2003). Thrill seeking predicted a higher order problem behavior factor among White adolescents but not among Blacks.

Romero, Luengo, and Sobral (2001) used the SSS and an Impulsivity (Imp) scale in a study of three groups: school-attending adolescent males and females and male adolescents institutionalized for delinquency. The Imp and all four SSS subscales were significantly correlated with self-reported antisocial behavior in all three groups, but the correlations with Imp and SSS Experience Seeking (ES) and Dis were higher than those with TAS and BS.

Longitudinal Studies

Moffitt (1993), who has been engaged in longitudinal studies of a population, has observed that there are two types of delinquents. In one type, the antisocial behavior is adolescent limited, whereas in another type, it is life-course persistent. The *Diagnostic and Statistical Manual of Mental Disorders* (3rd ed.; *DSM–III*; American Psychiatric Association, 1980) definition of APD demands that the onset of the disorder must appear before or by age 15 (conduct disorder) and persist beyond age 18, corresponding to the life-course persistent type if it meets other diagnostic criteria. H. R. White, Bates, and Buyske (2001) added a third type, escalating delinquency, and found that the persistent delinquents were higher on the SSS Dis than nondelinquent, adolescent-limited, and escalating delinquent groups. The persistent delinquents were lower than nondelinquent and escalating delinquents on a harm avoidance scale. All three delinquent groups were higher than nondelinquents on an impulsivity scale but did differ among themselves on this scale. Impulsivity, as a factor in delinquency, may be more modifiable than disinhibitory sensation seeking.

A study of children at ages 3 to 5 revealed that a lack of control, or impulsivity, at these early ages in interaction with the condition of having only one parent predicted convictions for nonviolent crimes at age 18 (Henry, Caspi, Moffitt, & Silva, 1996). The child's control trait alone, without moderation by paternal presence or absence, predicted convictions for violent offenses.

Personality was rated in kindergarten children using Cloninger's (1987b) theory as a guide. Novelty seeking, called "impulsivity" in this study, predicted early onset of delinquent behavior (self-reported) at ages 10 to 13 (Tremblay, Pihl, Vitaro, & Dobkin, 1994).

Newcomb and McGee (1991) assessed a sample of nearly 600 male and female subjects while in high school, 1 year later in late adolescence, and 4 years later when subjects were in their early 20s. They used a short version of the SSS but one that included the subscales. All of the subscales were significantly correlated with stealing episodes or law abidance at all times of assessment, but the correlations with TAS, ES, and BS were small, whereas those with Dis were much higher. TAS directly predicted stealing episodes during the third period of assessment. Sensation seeking in total predicted stealing episodes during the second period of evaluation.

W. R. White, Labouvie, and Bates (1985) used only the Dis and ES subscales from the SSS in prediction of delinquent behavior over 3-year periods of adolescence from 15 to 21 years of age. Both scales correlated with concurrent reports of delinquency, but only Dis predicted future delinquency.

A short-term longitudinal study used different kinds of impulsivity scales in predicting antisocial behavior (i.e., vandalism, theft, aggression, rule violations, and drug abuse) in 1,226 adolescents in the community (Luengo, Carrillo-de-la-Peña, Otero, & Romero, 1994). Impulsivity in general predicted each of the separate kinds of antisocial behaviors as well as the total antisocial behavior score. The Barratt (1985) impulsivity scale distinguishes between different expressions of the trait: nonplanning, motor impulsivity, and cognitive impulsivity. All types correlated significantly with all types of antisocial behavior, but the correlations with cognitive impulsivity were minimal compared with those for motor impulsivity and nonplanning. *Cognitive impulsivity* refers to rapid thinking and decision making. Nonplanning, or acting without thinking of the possible consequences of behavior, and motor impulsivity are the types involved in impulsive sensation seeking.

A group with low levels of delinquency at both time periods was compared with a group going from no delinquency at Time 1 to minor delinquency at Time 2 and a third group going from minor delinquency at Time 1 to major delinquency at Time 2. All impulsivity scales except cognitive impulsivity showed increases in scores across the three groups, with the lowest scores in the consistently nondelinquent group and the highest scores in those moving from minor to major delinquency. Cognitive impulsivity scores were the same for all three groups.

Personality, Risk Appraisal, and Peer Influences

Cognitive approaches to risk taking suggest that risk appraisal is an important factor in antisocial behavior. The role of nonplanning impulsivity in delinquency indicates that the relationship between sensation seeking and delinquency might be mediated by a tendency to minimize or ignore the riskiness of antisocial behavior. Horvath and Zuckerman (1993) developed a General Risk Appraisal Scale by factor analyzing risk appraisals of a variety of activities. They were asked how risky the activity would be if they actually engaged in it. One of the four factors was criminal risk, including activities such as shoplifting, selling drugs, and vandalism. Risk appraisal for criminal activity correlated significantly with financial, minor violations, and sports risk appraisal.

Peer influence (i.e., "bad company") is often cited as a major determinant of delinquent behavior. This explanation has been even more salient since the biometric genetic studies that show little influence of shared family environment, leaving the environmental influences to nonshared environment such as the different friends siblings may have. These studies will be described later in this chapter. Horvath and Zuckerman (1993) assessed this factor by asking their college student subjects to estimate how many of their peers engaged in the various risky activities. They were also asked how often they engaged in the same activities. The SSS and S. B. G. Eysenck and Eysenck's (1977) impulsivity scale were also used as predictors of the subjects' own self-reported behaviors.

Figure 6.1 shows the correlations among the various predictors of criminal behavior and self-reported criminal behavior in the Horvath and

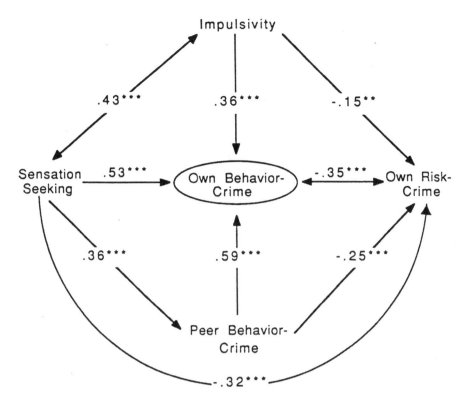

Figure 6.1. Correlations among sensation seeking, impulsivity, reported peer behavior, appraised riskiness of criminal behavior, and subject's own criminal behavior in a college population. From "Sensation Seeking, Risk Appraisal, and Risky Behavior," by P. Horvath and M. Zuckerman, 1993, *Personality and Individual Differences, 14,* p. 47. Copyright 1993 by Elsevier Science. Reprinted with permission.
$**p < .01.$ $***p < .001.$

Zuckerman (1993) study. All variables correlated significantly with criminal behavior. Risk appraisal of criminal activities correlated negatively with behavior, as expected. A multiple regression showed that peer behavior was the major predictor ($\beta = .43$), followed by sensation seeking (.27), impulsivity (.13), and risk appraisal (−.15). Together, the four variables accounted for 50% of the variance in criminal behavior.

Correlation cannot distinguish cause and effect. Does risk appraisal mediate the relationship between sensation seeking and criminal behavior, or is it a result of engaging in criminal behavior without negative consequences? A LISREL analysis attempted to answer these questions by testing the fit of two alternative models, one of which places risk appraisal as a mediating trait and the other suggests that risk appraisal is lowered by actual criminal behaviors. The second model provided a better fit than the first. Sensation seeking influences behavior, and that in turn influences risk appraisal. The cognitive factor is not primary but is a secondary result of behavior.

Incarcerated Delinquents

All of the previously discussed studies have defined delinquency by self-reports or other methods in subjects from the general population or high school and college populations. Institutionalized delinquents are those who have been arrested and convicted of crimes on the basis of evidence independent of their own admissions.

Thorne (1971) reported that institutionalized female, but not male, delinquents scored higher than schizophrenics on the SSS General Scale. Karoly (1975) found no significant differences between female delinquent and nondelinquent high school students on the SSS General Scale. Both of these studies used the earlier form (II) of the SSS, which did not contain subscales. Ono and Murayama (1980) found that Japanese imprisoned male delinquents scored higher than university students on the ES subscale, although the difference on the Dis subscale approached significance.

Farley and Farley (1972) compared high and low scorers on the SSS General Scale within a group of incarcerated female delinquents (14–17 years old) and found that the high scorers had made more escape attempts, incurred more punishments for disobedience, and engaged in more fighting than the low sensation seekers. Similar results were later found for male delinquents (Farley, 1973). English and Jones (1972) also found that high sensation seekers among incarcerated delinquents made more escape attempts.

Romero et al. (2001) compared a group of imprisoned male delinquents with a group of males in high school or vocational training college on the Eysenck Personality Questionnaire (EPQ; H. J. Eysenck & Eysenck, 1975), SSS–V, and an impulsivity scale. Large significant differences were found for the EPQ Psychoticism (P) and the Imp scales, a moderate difference for the Extraversion (E) scale, and significant but weaker differences on the SSS ES and BS subscales, with the incarcerated delinquents scoring higher on all of these scales. Differences on TAS and Dis were not significant.

Antisocial Versus Positive Risky Behaviors

Sensation seeking and impulsivity are usually related to antisocial kinds of behavior, and in previous chapters, I discussed that sensation seeking, at least, is related to more positive or social kinds of risky behavior, as in sports or sex. The issue is whether sensation seeking is characteristically higher or different in form (pattern of subscale scores) in antisocial and positive or neutral social kinds of activities.

Hansen and Breivik (2001) attempted to answer this question by giving a Swedish version of the SSS and a survey of specific kinds of risky activities to 360 Norwegian adolescents between 12 and 16 years of age. The Swedish SSS (Björk-Åkesson, 1990) contains four subscales. The Swedish TAS is similar to the SSS TAS and measures the seeking of excitement through risky physical activities. New Experience Seeking (NES) is somewhat similar to the SSS ES but measures the desire for novel activities. Activity measures the desire to "do wild things" and resembles the SSS Dis subscale. Outgoingness measures the desire to be the center of attention and does not resemble any particular SSS subscale.

The risky behavior scales were divided into two types. The negative risk behaviors ranged from mild social pranks, like ringing the doorbell and running, to criminal behavior, such as shoplifting, vandalism, stealing, or pickpocketing. The positive risk items were physical activities ranging from riding roller-coasters to bungee jumping, skiing downhill at high speeds, mountain climbing, and other activities associated with sensation seeking in previous studies. SSS Total correlated with both negative and positive risky behaviors for both boys and girls. The only difference in subscale patterns was that NES did not correlate with negative risky behaviors. All the other subscales correlated about equally with negative and positive risk taking. The ES subscale is associated more with the need for novelty than for intensity of experience and can find expression in many things that are not frightening or arousing, such as travel, friends, music, and media.

Fischer and Smith (2004) conducted a similar type of study. Their negative risk scale contained use of drugs, driving under the influence, and criminal activities like shoplifting, vandalizing, and other kinds of rule violations like cheating on exams and plagiarizing, not uncommon in student populations. The positive risk taking included sports, roller coasters, and mild risks like going on a blind date. The negative and positive risk-taking scales were positively and moderately correlated ($r = .42$). Their sensation seeking scale consisted of the 11 SS items from the Impulsive Sensation Seeking (ImpSS) scale of the Zuckerman–Kuhlman Personality Questionnaire (ZKPQ; Zuckerman, 2002; Zuckerman, Kuhlman, Joireman, Teta, & Kraft, 1993). They also included the deliberation subscale of the Revised NEO Personality Inventory (Costa & McCrae, 1992b) Conscientiousness scale. Sensation seeking was positively correlated with both types of risk taking, but lack of deliberation (impulsiveness in the nonplanning form?) correlated only with negative types of risk taking.

In this section of the chapter, I focus on aggressive types of antisocial behavior. Aggression is a personality factor distinct from Impulsive Unsocialized Sensation Seeking in the alternative-five model (Zuckerman, 2002; Zuckerman, Kuhlman, et al., 1988; Zuckerman, Kuhlman, Joireman, Teta, & Kraft, 1993; Zuckerman, Kuhlman, Thornquist, & Kiers, 1991). However, sensation seeking becomes a prominent motive and trait in that part of the criminal population that has traits of APD or psychopathy (Zuckerman, 1994, 2002, 2005). Those with APD exhibit impulsive criminal behavior that is motivated by the need for excitement rather than more rational motives like money.

Gomà-i-Freixanet (1995, 2001) compared males and females incarcerated for armed robbery crimes with violence with sportsmen and sportswomen engaging in risky sports; those engaged in risky prosocial jobs such as police, firefighting, and ambulance driving; and control subjects not engaged in risky sports or vocational activities. These results were discussed in regard to risky sports in chapter 3 and the mean results on the SSS, and the S. B. G. Eysenck and Eysenck (1977) Impulsivity scales were shown in Table 3.3 (chap. 3, this volume).

The aggressive male criminals were significantly higher than all other three groups on the SSS Total, the Total minus the TAS subscale, and all the SSS subscales except ES, on which they did not differ from the risky sports group. They were also higher than all other groups on the impulsivity scale and lower than all groups on a socialization scale. The aggressive female criminals were significantly higher than the female prosocial risk takers and control subjects on all of the SSS Total, Total minus TAS, and all of the subscales except BS, on which they did not differ significantly from the other groups. Unlike the male group, the female aggressive criminal group did not differ from the risky sports females on any of the scales except impulsivity and socialization. On these scales, they scored higher on the former and lower on the latter than all other groups. Male aggressive criminals tend to be higher sensation seekers than those taking risks in nonantisocial (sports) or prosocial activities, but female aggressive criminals do not differ from women engaged in risky sports, although they do exceed those in prosocial risky occupations. The major difference between risk-taking criminals and risk-taking sportswomen is that the criminals are more impulsive and less socialized.

Predicting Violence

A short-term, 1-year prediction study with 870 adolescents, 14 to 19 years at baseline assessment and 16 to 18 at follow-up, was done using the

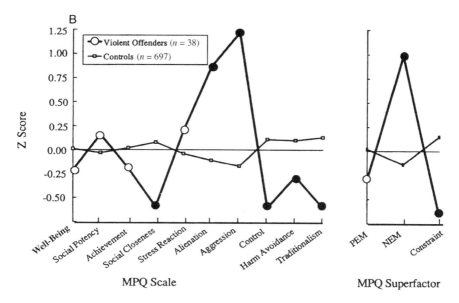

Figure 6.2. Multidimensional Personality Questionnaire (MPQ) profiles of violent offenders and healthy controls. PEM = positive emotionality; NEM = negative emotionality. From "Personality Differences Predict Health-Risk Behaviors in Young Adulthood: Evidence From a Longitudinal Study," by A. Caspi et al., 1997, *Journal of Personality and Social Psychology, 73*, p. 1057. Copyright 1997 by the American Psychological Association.

11 sensation seeking items from the ZKPQ ImpSS scales as one of the predictors (Sussman, Simon, Dent, Steinburg, & Stacy, 1999). Violence perpetration was based on self-admitted use of weapons to injure or threaten someone or physical aggression against others. The base rate of aggression was high in this population: 58% reported having attacked someone physically in the past year, and 16% used weapons to do so. Sensation seeking predicted violence but only to a modest degree. Current drug use, attitudes toward police, and identification with other perpetrators and gangs were much stronger predictors. It is regrettable that the investigators did not use the full ImpSS scale, because impulsive items in combination with sensation seeking items would probably have strengthened the prediction.

The long-term, ongoing longitudinal study of a population cohort in New Zealand used the MPQ at age 18 to predict violent crime and other risky behaviors at age 21 (Caspi et al., 1997). Violent crime was determined by actual records of conviction for such crimes. The MPQ includes a Constraint factor composed of scales for harm avoidance (sensation seeking reversed), control (impulsivity reversed), and traditionalism (socialization). The Negative Emotionality factor includes scales for aggression, alienation, and stress reaction (neuroticism). Figure 6.2 shows the MPQ profile for violent offenders. This group scored lower than control subjects at age 18 on harm avoidance, control, and traditionalism, and higher than control subjects on aggression and alienation but not on stress reaction. This combination of aggression and impulsive sensation seeking is commonly found among antisocial individuals.

Fight Seeking

When I was in the Army taking basic training, a sergeant was trying to stop us from using the word *gun* to describe our rifles. In a dramatic demonstration, he raised his rifle and shouted, "This is a rifle," and then grabbing his crotch, "This is a gun." Raising his rifle again, he explained, "This is for fighting," and then grabbing his crotch again, "This is for fun." The implication was that fighting is a serious business compared with sex. However, many males regard fighting also as fun and seek every opportunity to do so.

Joireman, Anderson, and Strathman (2003) explored the "aggression paradox" of fighting for fun or to gratify sensation seeking needs. They preface their article with a line from a song by Elton John: "Saturday night's all right for fighting. Get a little action in." Joireman et al.'s general aggression model is shown in Figure 6.3. In this model, the likelihood of aggression in an aggression-provoking situation is increased by personality traits of sensation seeking, impulsivity, consideration of future consequences, and trait hostility and anger. Person and situation variables interact to produce states of hostility and anger in persons high on impulsive sensation seeking who do not consider possible future consequences of aggression.

All of Joireman et al.'s (2003) studies used college students as subjects. In their first study, they used the ZKPQ, which contains a scale for impulsive sensation seeking (ImpSS) as well as one for aggression–hostility (Agg-Host). They also gave subjects a scale for consideration of future consequences (CFC). CFC correlated negatively with ImpSS and Agg-Host as predicted. CFC was more highly correlated with the Imp subscale of ImpSS. A multiple regression analysis suggested that CFC mediated the relationship between ImpSS and Agg-Host. It should be noted, however, that none of these correlations was very high; none exceeded .29.

In a second study, Joireman et al. (2003) found that the SSS subscales of Dis and BS were significantly correlated with aggression questionnaire subscales of hostility, anger, and physical and verbal aggression. The TAS subscale was correlated only with aggression scales, and the ES subscale correlated with none of the aggression or anger scales. The Dis subscale was the strongest predictor of physical aggression ($r = .46$), whereas the BS subscale was the best predictor of verbal aggression ($r = .37$).

The third study used conceptually defined situations, asking subjects how they would respond to situations "likely to produce anger." In addition

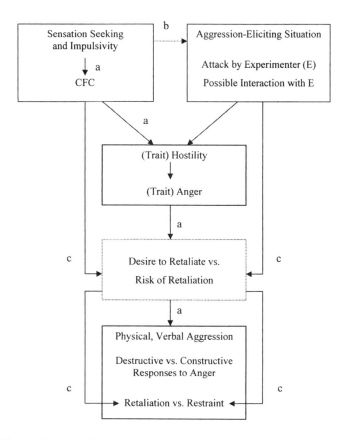

Figure 6.3. Application of a general aggression model in a study by Joireman, Anderson, and Strathman (2003). Solid boxes indicate aspects of the model that authors manipulated or measured directly; dashed boxes indicate underlying processes assumed to be operating. CFC = consideration of future consequences. From "The Aggression Paradox: Understanding Links Among Aggression, Sensation Seeking, and the Consideration of Future Consequences," by J. Joireman, J. Anderson, and A. Strathman, 2003, *Journal of Personality and Social Psychology,* *84,* p. 1288. Copyright 2003 by the American Psychological Association.

to the SSS and CFC scales, Joireman et al. (2003) used a separate scale of impulsivity (Imp) as a predictor. They tested models for the pathways from personality traits to self-predicted physical and verbal aggression through the mediation of CFC. The SSS Dis subscale and the Imp scale predicted hostility, anger, and physical and verbal aggression through the mediation of CFC as predicted. However, the BS subscale was not mediated by CFC and had a direct pathway to physical and verbal aggression and to anger in physical and verbal aggression in women. The final model for physical aggression is shown in Figure 6.4.

The hypothesized attraction of high sensation seekers to situations involving the opportunity for physical or verbal aggression was also tested

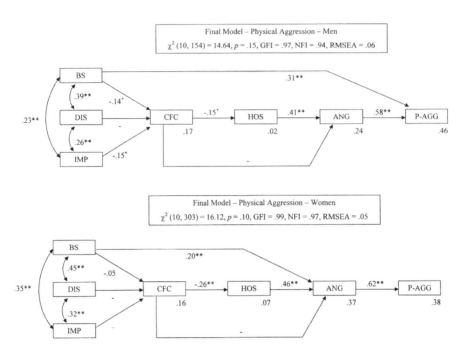

Figure 6.4. Final path models for physical aggression in men and women. Squared multiple correlations for each endogenous variable are shown below the variable. Path coefficients are standardized regression coefficients. GFI = goodness-of-fit index; NFI = normed-fit index; RMSEA = root-mean-square error of approximation; BS = boredom susceptibility; DIS = disinhibition; IMP = impulsivity; CFC = consideration of future consequences; HOS = hostility; ANG = anger; P-AGG = physical aggression. From "The Aggression Paradox: Understanding Links Among Aggression, Sensation Seeking, and the Consideration of Future Consequences," by J. Joireman, J. Anderson, and A. Strathman, 2003, *Journal of Personality and Social Psychology, 84,* p. 1294. Copyright 2003 by the American Psychological Association. [+]*p* < .10. *******p* < .01.

in this study. A separate group of students was asked whether they would like to participate in several different kinds of studies. Two of these options included the possibilities of a noninjurious type of play aggression (a fight with padded mallets) and verbal aggression (an argument with another person). The Dis, BS, and TAS subscales of the SSS correlated positively with a stronger desire to engage in both types of aggression.

The fourth study used an experimentally controlled situation in which subjects were provoked by a rude experimenter. Only the CFC scale was used in this study. Aggression was assessed by a postexperimental evaluation of the experimenter. The possibility of the experimenter reacting to his evaluations was varied from none to uncertain or immediate. CFC interacted with the likelihood and timing of future interactions with the experimenter.

Low CFC individuals moderated their negative evaluations in the situation of anticipated immediate interaction with the instigator of aggression but did not moderate them in situations of certain future interactions.

High sensation seekers who are bored or enjoy disinhibition and are adventurous are attracted to situations in which aggression is likely. Those who have little concern for future consequences of their behavior are more likely to become hostile and angry and to engage in aggression in such situations.

Swett, Marcus, and Reio (2005) developed the Fight Seeking Scale (FSS) using both specific fight seeking questions and sensation seeking items, the latter on the assumption that sensation seeking is an integral part of fight seeking. In spite of the dichotomous combination of items, the Total scale had a relatively high index of internal consistency ($\alpha = .81$), suggesting high correlations between all items.

Subjects were divided into high and low fight seekers on the basis of their scores on the FSS. It is not surprising that high scorers on the scale reported 4 times as many fights as low scorers. The high FSS subjects were mostly male (83% vs. 17% female) and were involved in fights with strangers and alcohol-related fights. They did not use avoidance strategies like disengagement or finding less risky sources of excitement. They were more likely to engage in verbal arguments that escalated into physical aggression. They claimed that fights were usually started by others and that their opponents suffered more damage than they did. They reported feeling calmer after the fight.

It is unfortunate that they did not analyze the fight seeking and sensation seeking parts of the scale separately in regard to self-reported aggression. However, the high internal consistency of the scale items reinforces other findings that aggression–hostility and sensation seeking traits are both involved in actual behavioral aggression.

In the traditional Western movie, there is usually at least one free-for-all barroom fight. It is probably no accident that fights often occur in or near establishments or parties where alcohol is imbibed in large quantities. Alcohol is a powerful disinhibiter of sexual or aggressive impulses, and heavy drinkers are usually persons who are impulsive and disinhibited even when not drinking.

Leonard, Quigley, and Collins (2003) recruited subjects through telephone surveys and newspaper advertisements. Subjects were classified into those who experienced violence, those who merely observed violence, and those who neither observed nor experienced violence in or outside of a bar. Those who experienced violence were twice as likely as those who merely observed it to drink more often and more heavily. Males experiencing aggression were lower on Agreeableness and higher on Openness to

Experience scales of the NEO. Agreeableness and anger traits distinguished the two groups among the female subjects. Sensation seeking was not measured in this study.

Sports Rioters

Social facilitation of aggression is a phenomenon often observed in riots at sports events. In Europe, there are groups of football (soccer) fans who go to games with the full intention of fight seeking before, after, or during the game. Ice hockey is a sport in which fighting between players is almost expected and fans often join in.

G. W. Russell and Arms (1998) asked male ice-hockey fans about the likelihood of their joining in a fight started by fans of the opposing team. Sensation seeking was measured by a combination of the TAS and BS subscales. Impulsivity, anger, aggression, and psychopathy were measured as traits. All of these were significantly correlated with the reported likelihood of involvement in a fight at the game. The subjects' saying that they were highly motivated to attend games to "watch the fights" was related to their admitted willingness to become involved in fights at the games.

In a review of the literature on the topic, G. W. Russell (2003) cited other studies in Canada and Finland also showing significant relationships between likelihood of involvement in sports riots and sensation seeking. Aggression, anger, impulsivity, and psychopathy were also predictors of a proclivity for riot involvement in some of the other studies.

PSYCHOPATHY

The concept of a psychiatric disorder characterized by antisocial behavior emerged in only the 19th century. Prior to that, such individuals were considered deficient in moral judgment or victims of brain disease. In the 19th century, diagnostic terms such as *mania without delusion, moral insanity, moral imbecility, lucid insanity, mental degeneracy,* and *psychopathic inferiority* were used. The gist of these diagnostic conceptions was that there was an abnormal lack of restraint and inhibition of antisocial impulses and a proclivity to engage in antisocial behavior that could not be explained by delusional thinking, psychosis, or "normal" criminal motives like profit or revenge.

Cleckley (1976) defined the characteristics of the psychopath in detail with illustrative case histories. His description included characteristics such as a poverty or absence of any strong emotions (whether positive or negative), unreliability, insincerity, untruthfulness, lack of insight, and unresponsiveness in general interpersonal relationships. Other traits described a generalized pattern of "inadequately motivated" antisocial behavior and "fantastic and uninviting behavior," with or without drink; an impersonal "trivial and poorly integrated sex life"; and the "failure to follow any life plan." Neurosis or psychosis were ruled out as explanation for this behavior disorder.

The syndrome was renamed *antisocial personality disorder* (APD) and was grouped with other personality disorders in the *DSM–I* (American Psychiatric Association, 1952). It was described in the *DSM–I* and *DSM–II* (American Psychiatric Association, 1968) in personality terms such as *callous*, *hedonistic*, *irresponsible*, and *impulsive*. But in the *DSM–III* (American Psychiatric Association, 1980), the definition was almost entirely in terms of behavior, with a specific behavioral criterion for each descriptor. Criticized for overspecificity, the committees made modifications in the *DSM–III–R* (American Psychiatric Association, 1987) and *DSM–IV* (American Psychiatric Association, 1994). *Impulsivity*, *aggressiveness*, and *irresponsibility* are personality descriptors, but the preponderant criteria are behavioral life patterns like the failure to conform to social norms for lawful behavior, chronic lying, and exploitation of others for profit or pleasure. The antisocial behavior must have begun by age 15 and extended to age 18 and older. Thus, it must be consistent over time and not limited to childhood, adolescence, or adulthood.

Psychopathy Check List

Hare and Cox (1978) used Cleckley's (1976) criteria to construct a Psychopathy Checklist (PCL). The PCL is based on case records and an interview with the offender (it is mostly applied to incarcerated criminals). The technique uses a skeptical attitude toward the self-view of the psychopath, which is redolent with rationalization and self-justification. Rather, the observer is told to diagnose the underlying attitudes and emotional reactions, or lack of them. Harpur, Hare, and Hakistan (1989) factor analyzed the PCL items and found two replicable factors. The first factor, Selfish, Callous, and Remorseless Use of Others, describes the personality of psychopathy in terms of the characteristic style of interpersonal relationships, which is exploitative without love, empathy, or genuine attachment. The second factor, Social Deviance, is more behavioral but includes traits like sensation seeking ("need for stimulation and proneness to boredom"), impulsivity, and lack of socialization ("irresponsibility," "poor behavior controls"). This factor resembles the factor found repeatedly in our factor analyses of personality scales: Impulsive Unsocialized Sensation Seeking (Zuckerman, 1989).

Harpur et al. (1989) correlated prisoners' ratings on the PCL with various personality scales including Minnesota Multiphasic Personality Inventory (MMPI; Hathaway & McKinley, 1951), EPQ, California Psychological Inventory (Gough, 1956), Karolinska Scales of Personality (Schalling, Asberg, Edman, & Oreland, 1987), and the SSS. Selected correlations are shown in Table 7.2 of the Harpur et al. article. The MMPI Psychopathic Deviate (Pd) and Hypomania (Ma) subscales compose the two scale elevations characteristically found in people diagnosed with psychopathy. A variety of anxiety scales were also included. These generally correlated negatively with Factor 1, although the EPQ Neuroticism (N) scale correlated positively with Factor 2 on the PCL. Sensation seeking, socialization, and the EPQ P scales correlated with Factor 2, as did the MMPI Pd and Ma subscales.

Harpur, Hart, and Hare (1994) found that only the Agreeableness scale of the NEO was correlated (negatively) with the PCL in prison inmates, but the subscales of excitement seeking and hostility were also correlated with the PCL. One would have expected the Conscientiousness factor to be correlated with the PCL. It was not correlated at all in the prison sample, although it was in a student sample.

Other Psychopathy Measures

In another study, the extended form of the Revised NEO containing subscales for the five major factors was given to patients in a psychiatric hospital (Bagby, Costa, Widiger, Ryder, & Marshall, 2005). The patients were primarily those with mood and anxiety disorders but with some having schizophrenia or abusing substances. A self-report instrument backed by an interview for some subjects was used to make diagnoses on the *DSM–IV* personality disorders, including APD.

A primary APD diagnosis correlated positively with the impulsiveness subscale of the Neuroticism factor. Within the Extraversion factor, the APD diagnosis correlated positively with excitement (sensation) seeking. Within the Conscientiousness factor, the APD diagnosis correlated negatively with deliberation (low cognitive impulsiveness) and dutifulness. APD correlated negatively with altruism, compliance, and modesty in the Agreeableness factor and negatively with fantasy, activity, and ideas in the Openness factor .

Summary

As found for criminal and antisocial behavior in general, the extreme group diagnosed as APD is characterized by sensation seeking, impulsivity, and lack of socialization. One could argue that psychopathy is the extreme on the major personality factor called Impulsive Unsocialized Sensation Seeking (Zuckerman, 1994) or "Psychoticism" in the Big Three (Zuckerman, 1989). However, sensation seeking alone does not define psychopathy. It requires the additional traits of aggression and impulsivity. Put another way, most high sensation seekers are not psychopathic, but most psychopaths are high sensation seekers.

BIOSOCIAL BASES OF ANTISOCIAL BEHAVIOR, CRIME, AND PSYCHOPATHY

The explanations for criminality and the antisocial personality are often dichotomous: either all genetic ("bad seed") or all environmental ("deprived childhood"). The vulnerability hypothesis (Zuckerman, 1999) is an interactional one. We might say, bad seed (genetics) without enough rain (education, resources) and sun (love).

Genetics

The idea of a genetic basis for crime runs contrary to long-standing psychological and sociological theories attributing crime solely to poverty; disorganized and dysfunctional families; and parental neglect, rejection, or abuse. When criminal behavior is found in both parents and children, it is usually attributed to the effect of bad parenting or bad role models. Of course, these theories ignore the occasional delinquent child emerging from a stable, loving family or a nondelinquent, responsible child emerging from a dysfunctional family. Furthermore, two siblings in the same family and neighborhood environment may be contrasted in their levels of responsibility and law abidingness. As in the gangster movies of the 1930s, one child (often played by James Cagney) turns out to be a psychopathic criminal, whereas his brother (often played by Pat O'Brien) becomes a priest or a policeman. Of course, these are extreme portrayals, and similarity in antisocial behavior is more common. But dissimilarity is not uncommon and not easily explainable in terms of shared environment.

Only a genetic analysis using twins or adopted children can sort out the real contributions of genes, shared environments, and nonshared environments. Nonshared environment can include the influences of teachers, friends, gangs, and others specifically affecting one child in the family and not the others.

Twin Studies

Studies conducted between 1941 and 1977 showed a very high concordance for juvenile delinquency for both identical and fraternal twins (Ishikawa & Raine, 2002, Table 4; Zuckerman, 1999, Table 5.2). This pattern suggests a strong influence of shared environment, with only a weak influence of genetics. In studies of adult criminality, however, the concordance ratios (identical to fraternal) are close to the 2:1 ratio, suggesting a relatively stronger genetic influence in adult criminality (Ishikawa & Raine, 2002), with little or no influence of shared environment.

Lyons et al. (1995) studied the differential heritability of juvenile and adult antisocial traits using the large twin sample in the Vietnam veteran study. Subjects were interviewed using the symptoms for APD from the *DSM–III–R*. The symptoms were divided into those occurring before age 15 (juvenile) and those after age 15 (adult), although it also included the adolescent period. Correlations between juveniles' and adults' antisocial behavioral traits for both identical and fraternal twins were moderate (.39–.42). The juvenile trait scores correlated .39 for identical twins and .33 for fraternal twins—no major difference. Genetic variance (heritability) was .07; shared environment, .31; and nonshared environment, .62. In contrast, the adult antisocial scores correlated .47 for identical twins and .27 for fraternal twins. Genetic variance was .43; shared environment, .05; and nonshared environment, .52. Using diagnostic thresholds for dichotic analyses of conduct disorder and adult APD, 26% of the former and 66% of the latter was genetic in origin. For shared environment, 56% of childhood conduct disorder was a function of this source of variance, whereas only 21% of APD could be accounted for by these family and other shared environment factors.

The same set of genetic and shared environment influences accounted for variation in juvenile and adult antisocial behavior. The greater heritability for adult antisocial behavior was due to an increase in the genetic influence on the adult trait rather than a different set of genetic factors in adulthood. Many personality traits show a higher heritability in adolescence and adulthood than in childhood. In those whose traits are more strongly genetic, behavior from childhood to adulthood is more consistent. The major impact of shared environment, including family, is in childhood. Peer and neighborhood as well as family influences may potentiate or inhibit antisocial behavior during childhood, but genetic influences emerge from total familial influence to become the predominant one determining whether antisocial behavior will be limited to childhood and early adolescence or will persist into adult life. The more persistent type of antisocial tendencies probably reflect the greater genetic influence in this type compared with the childhood or adolescent limited delinquency.

Lyons et al. (1995) hypothesized that personality characteristics like sensation seeking and impulsivity mediate the relationship between genes and antisocial behavior. This is a distinct possibility because the characteristic peak in sensation seeking is in late adolescent and young adult ages.

Using another large twin cohort, Jacobsen, Prescott, and Kendler (2002) investigated sex differences on the development of antisocial behavior during three age epochs: childhood (before 15), adolescence (15–17 years), and adult (18 years and older). The Lyons et al. (1995) study did not include a separate adolescent group, lumping the adolescent in with the adult group. The Jacobsen et al. study used a self-report scale for antisocial behavior.

Like Lyons et al. (1995), Jacobsen et al. (2002) found that genetic factors increase in importance with age and that shared environment factors are more important during childhood. These changes occurred during the adolescent period and remained during the adult period. Because fraternal twin same-sex and opposite-sex correlations were nearly equal, it was concluded that there were no qualitative sex differences in genetic or shared environmental influences on antisocial behavior. However, there were some quantitative sex differences in interaction with age. The influence of genetic factors during childhood was greater for females than for males, and shared environment influences were greater for males. These sex differences diminished in adolescence, and by adult age heritabilities were similar for males and females.

It may seem paradoxical that genetic factors are stronger in females than in males in childhood and not different in strength from males during adolescence and adult ages, despite the fact of a much higher prevalence of the symptoms of conduct disorder and APD in males (Kessler et al., 1994; Robins & Regier, 1991). This paradox may have two explanations. One is the threshold effect. Because antisocial behavior is less common in females, it may take more genetic influence to make them antisocial. The reason that the sex difference in genetic influence disappears by adolescence may be the emergence of the genetically influenced testosterone factor, which peaks in that period in males.

Blonigen, Carlson, Krueger, and Patrick (2003) examined the type of genetic mechanisms involved in antisocial behavior using an older twin sample than in the previously discussed studies; their subjects were in their early 40s. A self-report instrument, the Psychopathic Personality Inventory (Lillienfeld & Andrews, 1996), was used as a measure of antisocial behavior. The Total score and all subscales were significantly correlated between identical twins but not significantly, and sometimes negatively, correlated between fraternal twins. The identical twins correlation on the Total score was .46 but was only −.26 (not significant) for fraternal twins. The subscales with the highest correlations were social potency, fearlessness, and impulsive nonconformity. Sensation seeking was not assessed in this scale. Correlational and model fitting suggested that antisocial behavior in this middle-aged group was a function of genetic epigenetic behavior and therefore emergent from a unique combination of genes. This was not a conclusion from previous studies that had much larger samples. They concluded that antisocial behavior is a function of normally distributed traits inherited in an additive fashion, as are most traits.

Adoption Studies

Most twin studies do not measure environmental factors directly and rely on purely statistical methods to translate twin similarities and differences into appraisals of genetic and environmental effects. The adoption method more clearly separates these effects by contrasting the influences of biological and adoptive parents. The former includes the genetic (and prenatal) influences, and the latter includes the social (shared environment) influences including the family. Unlike the twin studies, the adoption studies cannot assess the epistatic influences of the biological parents.

The adoption studies of criminality have been described more fully in a previous book (Zuckerman, 1999). The Danish research contrasted the risk of conviction for criminal offenses in children as a function of the criminal histories of biological parents, separated from the children soon or shortly after birth, and the adoptive parents who have no genetic relationship to the child but who provide the family of rearing, therefore the shared environmental experience. The result is a 2 × 2 table from which genetic and social factors can be analyzed as independent or interaction effects.

The Danish study by Mednick, Gabrielli, and Hutchings (1987) showed a twofold increase in risk for criminal convictions for sons of biological parents with criminal records but no significant effect in sons of adoptive parents with criminal records. The interaction effect in which both the biological and adoptive fathers had criminal records was small but significant, with an increase above that for the cases in which the biological father alone had a criminal record. Biologically related siblings raised in different homes had a concordance rate of 20%, which was twice as high as that for nonrelated adoptees raised in the same family.

The Danish study looked only at parental criminality as a factor in biological and environmental influences. A Swedish longitudinal study analyzed the congenital and postnatal influences in more detail (Bohman, 1996; Cloninger & Gottesman, 1987). *Congenital* refers to variables describing the biological parents in addition to the presence or absence of a criminal record, and *postnatal* included many factors of the adopting parents, including occupational level and child-rearing practices. In this study, there was a strong additive effect of risk from the two sets of antecedent variables. High postnatal risk factors alone doubled the percentages of crime risk for male adoptees (6.7%) compared with those with neither type of familial factor (2.9%), but the presence of a congenital risk factor without postnatal factors quadrupled the risk (12.1%). The additive effect of both congenital and postnatal factors increased the risk markedly above the effect of either congenital or postnatal factors alone to 40%! A partitioning of variance showed 59% of petty criminality explained by genes only, 19% by environment only, 14% by gene–environment interaction, and 7% by gene–

environment correlation. The rates of criminality in women were much lower, but the pattern of interaction of prenatal and postnatal influences was similar.

An American study also used a longitudinal analysis predicting childhood and adolescent aggressivity, conduct disorder, and adult APD from parental alcoholism, prenatal alcohol exposure, and APD in the biological parents, and adverse home environments in the adoptive parents (alcohol or drug abuse or dependence, marital problems, separations, divorce), as gleaned from interviews of the adoptive parents (Cadoret, Yates, Troughton, Woodworth, & Stewart, 1995). Regression analyses and model fitting showed that three variables predicted APD in the children: APD in the biological parent, prenatal alcohol exposure, and adverse home environment provided by the adoptive parents. Unlike the results of the Scandinavian studies, the adoptive home environment was the strongest factor of the three and APD in the biological parent was the weakest, albeit significant, factor. Although the interaction of biological and family environment factors was not significant for APD in the children, it was significant for childhood and adolescent aggression and diagnosis of conduct disorder in children.

Prenatal Environmental Risk

The influence of prenatal alcoholism in the mothers points up an environmental type of risk that is counted as part of the genetic one in studies in which only the diagnostic characteristics of the biological parents are considered. A biological mother who is more likely to use drugs and drink heavily as well as to neglect her nutrition during pregnancy poses a threat to brain development of the fetus. Birth complications can also cause brain injuries also potentially affecting subsequent social behavior in children.

Raine, Brennan, and Mednick (1994) studied the effects of recorded birth complications and postnatal maternal rejection on risk for criminality in children. Neither factor alone accounted for an increased risk of criminality, but in interaction the pre- and postnatal factors increased the rate of violent offenses in late adolescence to 47%, as contrasted with 20% in those with neither or only one of the two risk factors.

Summary

Both twin and adoption studies show that both genetic and environmental factors influence antisocial behaviors in childhood and early adolescence, with environment being more important. However, in late adolescence, particularly in males, genetic factors increase and shared environment factors decrease in relative importance, at least in twin studies.

The role of family environment in adoption studies depends on how widely family environment is defined. When it is limited to the record of criminality in biological and adoptive parents, the influence of the social, rearing environment is relatively weak compared with the role of the biological–genetic factor. However, when the rearing environment is defined more broadly in the terms of the kinds of adverse influences, its role in risk appears larger and even more predominant in the American study. Large interaction effects were seen in both the American and Swedish adoption studies. The finding that the combined effects of genetic predisposition and adverse family environment are stronger than either alone suggests a diathesis–stress model for antisocial behavior (Zuckerman, 1999).

Social Class and Education

Twin studies give a relativistic picture of the genetic–environmental influences, with the substantial remainder attributed to nonspecific environment after the effects of genetic and shared environment are removed. In adoption studies, about 20% of the risk for criminality is genetic, with another 20% added by the interactive effect. What about those who become criminal without predisposed genetic or environmental factors in their background?

Poverty or social class is recognized as a major source of crime, although its effects may be mediated through family disorganization and unemployment, conditions that are more prevalent in lower socioeconomic (SE) classes. Some would insists that lower SE and crime are related genetically. In the Danish study (Mednick et al., 1987), criminality in children was related to the SE class of the biological parent, partly confirming this viewpoint. However, criminal risk in children was also related to the SE class of the adoptive parents, indicating an independent environmental effect of class. This result is in a state with a welfare system that narrows the range of SE class compared with American society. In the Swedish longitudinal study (Cloninger & Gottesman, 1987), the trait of aggressiveness in boys interacted with social class of their parents in producing criminality when they became adults. An aggressive boy raised by educated, higher SE parents is much less likely to commit a crime than one of equal aggressiveness but raised by parents with less education.

In a U.S. study, Robins (1978) found that social class was particularly important in African Americans. When degree of early antisocial behavior was held constant, social class was unrelated to later antisocial behavior in Whites, but in African American children, social class of parents was significantly related to antisocial behavior in grown children. The differences in environment and family structure in African Americans is probably wider than it is between lower and middle-class Whites.

Arousal and Arousability

The first theory of sensation seeking was based on the idea of individual differences in optimal levels of cortical arousal (Zuckerman, 1969a). Theories of extraversion, psychopathy, and criminality (Eysenck, 1967, 1977) were also based on the idea that some persons sought high levels of stimulation to compensate for constitutionally low levels of arousal or arousability.

Conditioning

H. J. Eysenck's (1977) theory of criminality proposed that criminal behavior is due to a deficiency in classical conditioning, resulting in a failure to acquire the normal inhibition associated with punishment or an insensitivity to conditioned signals of punishment. This deficit could be based on a low level of basal cortical arousal or arousability in response to conditioned stimuli. The specific deficit in fear conditionability rather than general conditionability could be related to a deficit in autonomic system arousal. In this respect, the primary psychopathic type of criminal has a pathological absence of fear, whereas the secondary psychopathic type may have an excess of anxiety or neuroticism.

H. J. Eysenck's (1977) general theory for criminality suggests that criminals should be high on E, N, and P, although the most consistent findings are on psychoticism (H. J. Eysenck & Eysenck, 1976). In fact, Zuckerman (1989) suggested that the psychoticism dimension, as measured by the P scale, is really a measure of psychopathy rather than psychoticism per se. Psychoticism is the major correlate of sensation seeking within Eysenk's triad and is the best marker for the dimension Impulsive Unsocialized Sensation Seeking derived from three dimensional factor analyses of many types of scales (Zuckerman et al., 1991).

The paradigm most used for conditioning involved the skin conductance response (SCR) to a stimulus (conditioned stimulus; CS), like a neutral tone, which precedes shock or a very loud tone (the unconditioned stimulus; UCS). Conditioning is assessed by the size of the response (conditioned response) to the CS after a number of CS–UCS pairings. It should be noted that this is an aversive conditioning paradigm. H. J. Eysenck's (1977) theory actually applied to conditioning in general, including reward as well as aversive conditioning. Gray (1981) suggested that criminal behavior is a function of an impulsivity dimension based on sensitivity to signals of reward and insensitivity to signals of punishment.

The first review of studies of conditioning by Hare (1978) supported the idea that criminals, particularly those diagnosed as psychopathic, showed weaker aversive conditioning than control subjects. They also demonstrated a weaker SCR in a pseudoconditioning paradigm in which the anticipatory increase in SCR in a gradient of time before shock or a loud noise was lower for psychopathic criminals than for nonpsychopathic criminals or normal control subjects. Raine (1997) reviewed later studies and confirmed that psychopathic individuals and juveniles with conduct disorder showed poorer conditioning than control subjects.

Cortical Arousal and Arousability

The hypothesis of low cortical arousal in psychopathy has been tested using the electroencephalogram (EEG). The older literature (Syndulko, 1978) noted frequent EEG abnormalities in psychopaths, the most common one being an excess of slow-wave activity. A more recent review (Ishikawa & Raine, 2002) tended to support this finding, particularly among the more violent psychopathic individuals. Greater activity in slow waves (theta, delta) and slowing of alpha activity in adolescence are predictive of convictions for crimes in later adolescence or young adulthood (Mednick, Volavka, Gabrielli, & Itil, 1981; Satterfield, 1987; Volavka, 1987). These differences are usually found in the frontal and temporal lobes.

Raine, Buchsbaum, and LaCasse (1997) did a positron emission tomography (PET) study of murderers. The murderers were divided into those with and without a dysfunctional home background, or one with abuse, neglect, family conflict, and poverty. Psychopathic individuals who emerge from a healthy home background may have more severe and biologically based disorders than those who come from dysfunctional homes in which antisocial behavior is socially normative. The murderers from normal, middle-class homes had lower prefrontal glucose metabolism (low arousal) than both the murderers from dysfunctional homes and control subjects. Both types of murderers had lower right prefrontal arousal than control subjects.

New findings also suggest greater right than left frontal activation in psychopaths as opposed to the normal greater left frontal activation. Language function is in the left hemisphere. Hare and McPherson (1984) proposed the hypothesis that the left hemisphere in psychopaths is not as specialized for linguistic processing as in normals. The result could be the peculiar discrepancy between behavior and verbal expressions of feeling and intention found in psychopathic individuals.

Cortical evoked potentials (EPs) have been used to study the brain's arousability in response to stimuli. A summary of the EP studies of criminal behavior revealed that studies relating the auditory and visual EP N1 component to psychopathy yielded largely negative or inconsistent results (Ishikawa & Raine, 2002). However, inmates with diagnosed APD and college students and alcoholic individuals with histories of aggressive behavior showed small P3 EP amplitudes. The N1 component of the EP is related to selective attention, and the P3 is related to controlled cognitive processing and detection of novelty.

In chapter 1, I described the augmenting or reducing of the EP as related in many studies to sensation seeking, particularly the disinhibition scale. Most of these studies used the amplitude of the EP wave between N1 and P1, which increased as a function of increases in stimulus intensity in high sensation seekers (augmenting) and decreased or showed no change at the highest intensities in low sensation seekers (Zuckerman, 1990, 1994, 2005). Impulsivity is also related to augmenting of the EP. Nonpsychopathic criminals also show augmenting of the visual EP, although psychopathic individuals do not (Raine, 1997; Raine & Venables, 1990). A recent study of impulsively aggressive college students also showed them to have a reduced P1 amplitude and a larger N1 amplitude in response to visual stimuli (Houston & Stanford, 2005). They also showed EP augmentation in response to increasing intensities of visual stimuli and shorter latencies than control subjects for all EPs. The combined traits of sensation seeking, impulsivity, and aggressiveness may be what mediates augmenting in criminals as well as noncriminals. The short latencies of EPs may be related to cognitive impulsivity.

Skin Conductance

Two measures of skin conductance taken in unstimulated, resting conditions have been interpreted as measures of tonic sympathetic system activity. Skin conductance level (SCL) taken from the palmar surface of the hand is one of these, and spontaneous fluctuations of SCL unrelated to external stimulation or nonspecific skin conductance fluctuations (NSSFs) is another. The underarousal hypothesis of antisocial behavior has been applied to autonomic as well as cortical activity.

Hare (1978) reviewed studies of SCL in psychopathic criminals and found that most were in the direction of lower SCL for psychopathic prison inmates but many were not significant. Combining results showed a weak tendency toward lower basal arousal in psychopathic criminals. The same mixed results were obtained in studies of NSSFs.

Ishikawa and Raine (2002) reviewed later studies of SCL in relation to criminality. Only a minority of studies on SCL and NSSFs were significant, and the significant findings applied only to nonpsychopathic criminals and children with conduct disorder.

Studies of the relationship of these measures of basal sympathetic system arousal in relation to sensation seeking have also yielded primarily nonsignificant findings. However, a study that used the ImpSS scale of the ZKPQ rather than the SSS used in prior studies found that high sensation seekers were lower in SCL than low sensation seekers and that serious crime delinquents were lower in SCL than control subjects (Gatzke-Kopp, Raine, Loeber, Stouthamer-Loeber, & Steinhauer, 2002). The Imp component of the ImpSS was not related to SCL. There was no significant interaction between sensation seeking and delinquency status.

SCRs to nonaversive stimuli such as tones or lights of low to moderate intensities have been used as measures of arousability. The SCR to a novel stimulus is called the *orienting reflex* (OR). The OR is a measure of strength of focal attention. If the stimulus is repeated in a series, the OR becomes weaker with each presentation and finally disappears. This process is called *habituation* and represents a kind of learning not to respond to predictable events. Initial studies of the SCR OR in relation to sensation seeking showed a stronger OR in high than in low sensation seekers, with rapid habituation on the second presentation of the stimulus (Neary & Zuckerman, 1976). Findings in other laboratories were mixed in results. However, a series of studies by B. D. Smith, Perlstein, Davidson, and Michael (1986) showed that SCR ORs were particularly strong in high sensation seekers when the stimuli were of a content of interest to them or of an intense sexual or aggressive nature (B. D. Smith, Davidson, Smith, Goldstein & Perlstein, 1989).

Ishikawa and Raine (2002) reported a weaker SCR OR only in antisocial persons with coexisting schizoid or schizotypal personality traits. Ordinary antisocial groups do not show weaker ORs. However, strong ORs in males with antisocial tendencies or inherited dispositions are associated with resistance to developing a criminal career. It may be that a stronger OR in high sensation seekers is also associated with a tendency to seek sensation through noncriminal activities rather than antisocial behavior. A strong attentional capacity may facilitate better academic performance and general information-processing capacity.

Hare (1978) found little difference between psychopathic and non-psychopathic prisoners in SCR to tones of moderate intensity but more psychopathic prisoners had weaker SCRs to tones of high intensity (120 dB). Fung et al. (2005) also found a weak SCR in response to high intensity white-noise bursts in psychopathy-prone adolescents. This would explain their poorer conditioning when high-intensity tones are used as the UCS. However, Raine (1996), reviewing studies of responses to aversive stimuli, concluded that there is no evidence supporting the idea that psychopathic individuals are underresponsive to aversive stimuli. Some of the inconsistencies in these findings may be due to the failure to separate primary and secondary psychopathy. Only the former is associated with a lack of fearfulness and other signs of a deficit in general emotional reactivity.

Heart Rate

Tonic levels of heart rate (HR) could also be viewed as an index of level of sympathetic system activity. Hare (1978) stated that earlier investigators had failed to show any difference in HR related to psychopathy. However, Venables (1987) and Raine (1996) and Ishikawa and Raine (2002) reported consistent findings of lower tonic HR in child and adult groups with delinquent or antisocial behavior. Raine noted that the effect (lower rather than higher HR) is specific to antisocial disorders. Ishikawa and Raine said that "low resting heart rate is perhaps one of the best replicated biological markers of antisocial behavior, particularly among children" (p. 215). Some investigators found lower tonic HR in high sensation seekers than in lows (Ridgeway & Hare, 1981; T. N. Robinson & Zahn, 1983), but others have not, and one study even found a higher HR for high sensation seekers.

Tonic HR interacts with psychosocial risk factors to increase the risk for antisocial behavior. Boys who have low HR are more likely to become adult violent offenders if they come from a large family or have a poor relationship with their parents (Farrington, 1997). Other social risk factors interacting with low HR are low SE status, mother being a teenager when pregnant, and separated from a parent by age 10.

HR ORs are influenced by stimulus intensity. The HR OR is a deceleration of HR over the few seconds after the stimulus. However, the HR change is biphasic. An acceleration of HR may occur after an intense or aversive stimulus, in which case it represents either a defensive reflex (DR) or a startle reflex. As described in chapter 1, high sensation seekers, particularly those high on the Dis subscale, tend to exhibit a stronger OR (HR deceleration) on the first presentation of a moderate intensity tone than do low disinhibiters. Low disinhibiters tend to exhibit an HR acceleration, characteristic of a DR, to tones of moderate intensity (Orlebeke & Feij, 1979; Ridgeway & Hare, 1981). Greater DRs (HR acceleration) were seen in low disinhibiters, particularly at tones of high intensity (Zuckerman, Simons, & Como, 1988).

Hare (1978) found no consistent differences between psychopathic inmates and control subjects in HR ORs or DRs in response to tones ranging from 80 to 120 dB. However, in HR responses during anticipation of an aversive stimulus, psychopathic individuals demonstrated stronger increases in HR than nonpsychopathic individuals (Hare, 1978; Ishikawa & Raine, 2002). This is in direct contrast to the weak SCRs of psychopathic individuals in anticipation of aversive stimuli. Hare interpreted HR acceleration in anticipation of punishment to be an adaptive process enabling the individual to inhibit attention to cues that might otherwise be distressful. The SCR reflects the reduction in stress resulting from this "tuning out" of the aversive CS. Why this kind of defensiveness should occur in low sensation seekers more than in highs is not clear, because the Dis subscale is a positive correlate of psychopathy.

Biochemistry

Chapter 1 described the highly replicable relationship between the enzyme monoamine oxidase (MAO) and sensation seeking. High sensation seekers tend to have low platelet MAO Type B (MAO-B) levels. The relationship is supported by correlations of MAO-B with many types of behavior characteristic in high sensation seekers and with disorders characterized by high sensation seeking and impulsivity, including attention-deficit/hyperactivity disorder, APD, borderline personality disorder, alcoholism, drug abuse, pathological gambling, and bipolar mood disorder (see Table 1.4, chap. 1, this volume). MAO-B is also associated with delinquency and criminality, particularly crimes involving violence and aggressiveness (Alm et al., 1994; Belfrage, Lidberg, & Oreland, 1992; Coursey et al., 1979; Garpenstrand et al., 2002; af Klinteberg, 1996; Lidberg, Modin, Oreland, Tuck, & Gillner, 1985; Stalenheim, 2004; A. L. von Knorring, Bohman, von Knorring, & Oreland, 1985; Yu et al., 1984).

Garpenstrand et al. (2002) found low MAO-B levels in criminal offenders imprisoned for violent crimes including homicide, assault, armed robbery, and rape. Diagnosis by *DSM–IV* criteria showed personality disorders present in 56% of the prisoners, primarily APD, borderline disorder, and paranoid disorders. Smoking has been shown to reduce MAO levels, so the authors compared only smokers among the prisoners and control subjects. The difference between offenders and control subjects was significant even when smoking was controlled by covariation. Another study, controlling the smoking confound, found that novelty seeking fully mediated the relationship between low MAO and externalizing behavior in incarcerated delinquents (Ruchkin, Koposov, af Klinteberg, Oreland, & Grigorenko, 2005).

The mechanism by which MAO affects behavior is not known. MAO does not have a direct effect but acts as a catabolic regulator of monoamines, particularly dopamine (Deutch & Roth, 1999; Murphy, Aulakh, Garrick, & Sunderland, 1987). af Klinteberg, von Knorring, and Oreland (2004) discussed the various possible mechanisms for the association between MAO activity and impulsivity, sensation seeking, and psychosocial disturbances, involving these traits. But because no connection between platelet MAO and brain MAO has yet been found, they speculated that platelet MAO may be a genetic marker for the capacity of some central nervous system neurotransmitter, particularly serotonin. The common genetic control could be through common gene promoter sequences. One candidate is the AP-2 DNA-binding transcription factor family. AP-2 brainstem levels are correlated to monoamine expression in the forebrain. Males and females homozygous for the long form of the AP-2ß had lower platelet MAO activity as compared with those with one or two short alleles. Therefore, they hypothesized that the connection between MAO and personality is an indirect one based on the genetic correlation between MAO and AP-2. This is an interesting theory that still raises the question of the monoamine neurotransmitters in the final route to personality traits that are involved in antisocial activities.

The discovery that MAO has a role in both sensation seeking and violent criminality pointed to the role of the monoamine neurotransmitters that MAO regulates or is related to at the genetic level. The transmitter receiving the most attention is serotonin. As described in chapter 1, serotonin reactivity is low or insensitive in high sensation seekers, probably reflecting the impulsive, disinhibitory nature of the trait. The metabolite of serotonin (5-HIAA) is reduced in impulsive murderers and arsonists as well as those who make impulsive and violent suicide attempts (Brown et al., 1982; Brown, Goodwin, Ballenger, Goyer, & Major, 1979; Coccaro et al., 1989; Lidberg et al., 1985; Volavka, 1995; Zalsman & Apter, 2002; Zuckerman, 1999). The direction of aggression, toward others or oneself, is less important than the impulsive and violent nature of the acts. This is consistent with studies of animals that suggest a primary involvement of serotonin in behavioral inhibition and a deficit in capacity to delay impulsive approach response in situations of approach–avoidance conflict (Soubrié, 1986).

In studies of reactions to serotonergic agonists, men diagnosed as APD show a blunted serotonergic response (Moss, Yao, & Panzak, 1990), as do those diagnosed as having borderline personality disorder. A similar blunted serotonergic response to agonists is found in high sensation seekers (Hennig, 2004; Netter, Hennig, & Roed, 1996) and in those high on impulsivity and aggression (Hennig, 2004). In a group with personality disorders, the serotonergic responses to an agonist were inversely related to measures of aggression, assault, irritability, and impulsiveness in both clinician and self-reports (Coccaro et al., 1989).

The catecholamines epinephrine and norepinephrine (NE) assayed from urine are low in men who have been arrested and have strong psychopathic traits (Lidberg, Levander, Schalling, & Lidberg, 1978; Woodman, Hinton, & O'Neill 1977). Low levels of urinary epinephrine in Swedish boys at age 13 predict aggressive, destructive, and bullying behavior during early adolescence and criminal activity at adult ages (Magnusson, 1988; Olweus, 1987). Epinephrine is actually a hormone produced in the adrenal medulla and a stimulant for general arousal of the sympathetic branch of the autonomic nervous system. NE is produced both in the periphery and in the brain, where it is a neurotransmitter. NE activity produces arousal in both the autonomic and central nervous systems. Peripheral autonomic NE, as assessed by its metabolite 3-methoxy-4-hydroxyphenylglycol (MHPG) in plasma or urine, is increased by anxiety producing treatments, such as painful stimulation, stressful movies, or dangerous natural situations

(Forsman, 1982; Frankenhauser, 1979). Anxiety-inducing drugs like Yohimbine increase plasma MHPG in both anxiety patients and normals (Charney, Heninger, & Breier, 1984). Animal studies show that stress- or anxiety-producing situations produce rises in brain NE and firing activity of noradrenergic neurons in the brain (Charney & Drevets, 2002; Gray, 1982).

The low levels of both epinephrine and NE would be consistent with the fearlessness said to be characteristic of psychopathic individuals and disinhibited criminals in general. Ballenger et al. (1983) found that NE in the cerebrospinal fluid (CSF) was negatively related to sensation seeking but not to a self-report scale of assaultiveness. In fact, plasma MHPG, the NE metabolite, was positively correlated with this physical aggression scale. Brown et al. (1979) reported a positive correlation between CSF levels of MHPG and aggressiveness in a group of people with personality disorders but could not replicate the finding in a later study (Brown et al., 1982). A group of male arsonists had lower levels of CSF NE, as well as serotonin, than control subjects (Virkkunen, Nuutila, Goodwin, & Linnoila, 1987). The findings for the role of central NE in aggression are mixed, and the relationship to sensation seeking depends on the particular index of noradrenergic activity. High levels may be related to impulsive emotional types of antisocial behavior as opposed to a general state of low arousal when not provoked.

Cortisol is a stress-related hormone produced by the adrenal cortex. Cortisol in CSF is negatively related to the SSS Dis subscale as well as other indicators of impulsive antisocial personality like the psychoticism scale (Ballenger et al., 1983). Low levels of urinary cortisol have been found in psychopathic and violent prisoners (Virkkunen, 1985) and in children with conduct disorder symptoms, particularly those involving aggression (Oosterlaan, Geurts, Knol, & Sergeant, 2005). Corticotrophin, the hormone in the pituitary that releases cortisol from the adrenal cortex, is also related to psychopathic personality (Virkkunen et al., 1994).

Testosterone provides another common link between sensation seeking and antisocial behavior. Plasma testosterone levels are high in sensation seekers, particularly those of the disinhibitory type, as reported in chapter 1. Criminals as a group do not have higher testosterone levels than more law-abiding control subjects, but those among them, women as well as men, who have committed violent crimes usually have higher levels of this hormone (Volavka, 1995; Zuckerman, 1999, for reviews of these studies).

Summary

Antisocial behavior in general, but particularly that associated with violent crime and psychopathic personality, is related to low levels of arousal in both psychophysiological and biochemical indices of arousal, such as catecholamines or cortisol, or arousability. But sensation seeking is not related to arousal or arousability by moderate intensities of stimulation. In fact sensation seekers show strong orienting reactions to novel stimuli. High sensation seekers and criminals also have a greater cortical response to high intensities of stimulation representing the capacity to process such stimuli. But low sensation seekers show stronger autonomic reactions (defensive reflex) to intense (emotional or sensory) stimuli. Behavioral inhibition mediated by serotonin is weaker in sensation seekers and offenders with psychopathic personalities. The low levels of MAO found in sensation seekers and criminal offenders, particularly violent ones, may also be related to a disinhibition produced by the serotonin deficit, as a function of a genetic correlation between the enzyme and the neurotransmitter.

The finding of some genetic and biological bases of the connection between sensation seeking and illegal types of risky behavior does not mean that these kinds of behavior cannot be prevented or changed by treatment. Biology is *not* destiny. Genes are in constant interaction with environmental events and changing these events or their expectations can change behavior or divert the unhealthy personality expressions into healthier forms of behavior. The next chapter discusses the research on prevention and treatment.

7

PREVENTION AND TREATMENT OF UNHEALTHY RISK-TAKING BEHAVIOR

. . . check impulse; quench appetite; keep reason under its own control.
—Marcus Aurelius Antoninus, *Meditations*, II

It is difficult to change a basic personality trait like sensation seeking. However, it is entirely possible to change the ways in which it is expressed or to prevent unhealthy expressions, like smoking, excessive drinking, drug use, and risky sex, that create risks to the personal health of the risk taker as well as negative social consequences. Other forms of sensation seeking, like risky sports or vocations, also entail physical risk. No one would propose a prevention or therapy program to treat these heroic sensation seekers. Prosocial risky vocations like firefighting are valuable to society, and society indeed encourages the brave souls who want to do such work.

Psychologists and others have attempted to treat unhealthy risky behaviors using basic principles of behavior change. Communication researchers have attempted to devise messages in the media to prevent the behaviors before they become habitual or addictive. The tasks of prevention and treatment are not easy. Simple information, reasoning, and appeals to fear of negative consequences are not enough to dissuade a high sensation seeker from trying some risky behavior that promises an intense reward. Once established, a habit that provides reward is difficult to extinguish because of the negative emotional and physical state produced by withdrawal of that reward. Immediate successes are common for those in any kind of program, but long-term restraint is difficult to achieve, particularly after the program ends.

In this chapter, I describe the results of prevention and treatment programs, with a particular interest in the personality and environmental influences on individual successes and failures. Researchers in these areas have not paid a great deal of attention to the mediation of personality in the outcome of these programs, with a few notable exceptions like the work of Donohew, Bardo, and Zimmerman (2004) in drug prevention. Smoking is a potent risk to health and, as discussed in chapter 4, a type of risk more characteristic of high than low sensation seekers.

SMOKING

Smoking initiation is influenced by both genetic and shared environmental factors, but genetic factors are even more influential in determining individual differences in the amount of smoking, the crucial factor in addiction (Koopmans, Heath, van Doornen, & Boomsma, 1997). The genetic influence in the initiation of tobacco use is largely mediated by the genes involved in sensation seeking (Koopmans, Boomsma, Heath, & van Doornen, 1997). Of course, the shared environmental influences are important in modeling smoking. Cigarette smoking is prevalent in about a quarter of American men and women over the age of 12 and 40% of the 18- to 25-year-old population (McGeveran, 2006). In a large study of smoking initiation in seventh through ninth graders in two states, the children reported that a third of their fathers and mothers and about a quarter of their siblings and best friends smoked (D. M. Murray et al., 1992). There is likely to be some role model for smoking in either the home or in the school. Sensation seeking probably interacts with social influences through selection of models on the basis of their perceived positive or negative characteristics.

Apart from real, live models, there are the models seen in the media. Sargent et al. (2002) counted the number of tobacco use occurrences in popular movies and found a relationship between smoking prevalence and the incidence of smoking in movies seen by students in fifth through eighth grades. The relationship remained significant, even when statistically controlled for gender; grade; friend, sibling, and parent smoking; sensation seeking; rebelliousness; and self-esteem. High exposure to tobacco use in movies increased the number of positive expectations of smoking and the perception that most adults smoke.

It did not increase the perception that most teenagers smoke, probably because most of the smoking models in the movies were adults. Even though the advertising of smoking by the tobacco companies has been restricted, the potent influences of the media are still sources of smoking in the young.

Prevention of Smoking

Given the great health risks of smoking and the difficulty of stopping smoking because of the potent addictive qualities of nicotine, the importance of prevention has been recognized by federal and state authorities and a great deal of research has been done on smoking prevention. One type involves media advertisements to publicize the health risks of smoking. Indeed, every pack of cigarettes must contain a health warning. Not all of these are as blatant as what I found on a can of English pipe tobacco. In letters one-inch tall on one side of the can, it read, "Smoking kills," and on the other side, "Smokers die younger."

Once started, smoking can become addictive quickly, so it is more effective to stop the initiation of smoking early in adolescence, before most smokers start. A study of signs of drug dependency in cocaine, marijuana, alcohol, and tobacco users found that tobacco use was by far the most addictive (U.S. Department of Health and Human Services, 2000). Of more than 8,000 smokers, 34% exhibited three or more signs of dependence, contrasted with 8% of alcohol drinkers, 17% of marijuana users, and 18% of cocaine users. Friend and Levy (2002) examined studies of the effects of mass media messages in several states on smoking prevalence and per capita cigarette consumption. Compared with the reduction in the rest of the country, the groups exposed to antismoking messages showed an overall reduction of about 10%. However, youth-oriented interventions had more mixed results, and smaller community-level research programs were less effective. These media studies are confounded by other concurrent changes in the states sponsoring media campaigns, such as increases in cigarette prices by taxation, restrictions on ads by tobacco companies, restriction of smoking in public places, and enforcement of age restrictions on cigarette purchases.

More controlled studies have been conducted using antismoking programs within schools. Although they are called *prevention studies* because they start at the school grades when prevalence is low, there are some who are already smoking (10%–16%) at the outset of the study. There are typical increases in smoking prevalence in all groups between the seventh and ninth grades (D. M. Murray et al., 1992).

Bruvold (1993) describes four types of intervention programs used in the schools. The *rational* type simply provides factual information about drugs, their effects and consequences, through lectures and displays. The *developmental* type has less focus on drugs per se but attempts to reduce the affective factors that presumably influence susceptibility to drugs, including increasing self-esteem, decreasing alienation, and developing decision-making and interpersonal skills, as well as through lectures, discussions, group problem solving, and role playing. The *social norms* approach has similar goals but attempts to provide alternatives to drug use by going outside the classroom to encourage participation in community-improvement projects, vocational training, tutoring, and recreational activities. The *social reinforcement* type is more directly behavioral and attempts to develop abilities to resist social pressures to use drugs and skills in resisting such pressures, through discussion, behavior modeling, role playing, and practice.

Bruvold (1993) did a meta-analysis of smoking prevention programs as described in 94 studies. The programs were classified into the four categories previously described. Changes in knowledge, attitudes, and smoking behavior were measured and effect sizes determined. The rational method showed significant effects for knowledge but not for attitudes or behavior. The social reinforcement produced significant effects for attitudes and behavior; the social norms and developmental approaches also produced significant behavioral changes at posttest and follow-up, but the effect sizes were weaker and mixed in direction for the developmental approach. The analysis showed that the traditional methods involving primarily lectures (rational and developmental) do impart information about drugs but that mere knowledge does not translate into attitudinal and behavioral changes.

Rooney and Murray (1996) also did a meta-analysis of smoking prevention programs with stricter criteria for inclusion of studies. Studies were included only if they were "social" or "peer-type" programs not focused exclusively on health consequences or alternative strategies and had a control or comparison group. The comparison groups were the usual type of school drug education involving primarily the rational or lecture method. They also used an adjustment for errors in the unit of analysis. Their analysis of 90 studies meeting their criteria for inclusion found a statistically significant but small effect size of .10 or a reduction in smoking of 5%. They noted larger treatment effects for treatments that targeted the younger sixth graders, that had lower attrition rates, that were concentrated in a short period of time or offered booster sessions, and that included a trained teacher and an untrained same-age peer leader. Under optimal conditions, 20% to 30% reductions of smoking were found.

D. M. Murray et al. (1992) examined the results of four types of prevention programs in two states, Minnesota and Wisconsin. This was a prospective study of 48 school units randomly assigned to one of four conditions. Baseline assessment was done in the sixth grade, interventions in the seventh grade, and follow-up observations were made in the seventh, eighth, and nineth grades. The three treatment groups were based on the social influences model. Teachers were trained in workshops to administer the programs, and a member of the project staff visited the schools to ensure that quality of the program was maintained. The control treatment was the usual drug reduction program in the schools, presumably consisting of lectures. Over 8,000 students from 81 schools participated in the study. At baseline in the 6th-grade, smoking prevalence was quite low (0.6%–3.8%). Smoking prevalences increased from the seventh to ninth grades in all four groups, but none of the interventions was more effective in reducing tobacco use below that of the control group. The failure could be associated with the short number of sessions in the treatments (3–6), but the previously discussed meta-analyses showed that shorter treatments were not detrimental to outcome and in some cases were an advantage.

Sussman, Dent, Burton, Stacy, and Flay (1995) described the development and results of the Project Towards No Tobacco Use prevention program conducted in 48 junior high schools in 29 Southern California school districts. Schools were randomly assigned to participation in the different treatment programs. The treatment programs were based on the social influence model. The *normative social influence* program was designed to help students maintain their group status quo without conforming to group influences to smoke. The *informational social influence* program attempted to counteract the assumed prevalence of smoking and focused on how to achieve desired social images without smoking. A third treatment emphasized the *physical consequences* of smoking. A combined treatment involved all three components. All treatments involve active student participation as in role-playing exercises and practice of techniques of resistance to smoking social influences. The standard program of each school was used as a control group. Treatment effects were assessed posttreatment and at 1- and 2-year follow-ups from seventh to ninth grades.

An analysis was done of the 2-year follow-ups from seventh to ninth grades. All program conditions showed less trying of cigarettes than the control condition and did not differ among themselves in effectiveness. However, the combination of treatments was superior to all other conditions as well as the control condition in reducing weekly smoking; the separate treatments did not differ from each other or the control condition. The physical consequences treatment was more effective for smokeless tobacco and superior to all other treatments for prevention of this form of tobacco intake. The differences, even when significant, were not dramatic. For instance, trial cigarette use increased 16% in the combined treatment and 23% in the standard care control group, and weekly smoking increased 4% in the combined treatment compared with 9% in the control group.

One of the most widely used drug prevention programs is Project Drug Abuse Resistance Education (DARE). This program addresses alcohol, marijuana, and other illegal drugs, as well as cigarette smoking. Lynam et al. (1999) studied the effects of participation in DARE of 1,002 sixth graders followed up over 10 years to an average age of 20. The studies already discussed used relatively short follow-ups, so this study is of interest in terms of long-term effectiveness of such programs. The DARE program was delivered by police officers in 1-hour sessions over a period of 17 weeks.

Like the programs already described, it trains in resistance to social pressures, decision-making skills, information on drugs, and choosing healthy alternatives to drug use. For cigarette smoking, the preprogram cigarette use was significantly related to age 20 use, but the effect of the DARE program was nonsignificant. The same result was true for alcohol, marijuana, and illegal drug use.

Apparently, those who start smoking or using drugs early are going to keep using them and increase their use of them, whereas those who are already resistant to drugs are less likely to start using them. Treatment programs such as DARE cannot counteract the initial differences between individuals in susceptibility to smoking, drinking, or drug use. Small but significant short-term effects of such programs seem to have no lasting qualities. Sensation seeking may be one of the mediators of the individual differences in susceptibility to smoking. Unfortunately, it is rarely included in prevention or treatment studies. Peer influences may be stronger factors in low than in high sensation seekers, or high sensation seekers may be more invulnerable to antismoking programs.

Smoking Cessation: Treatment and Self-Initiated Attempts at Cessation

Is information about the risks of smoking sufficient to make smokers stop? For most smokers, the answer would seem to be "no." However, the Surgeon General's Report in 1964 (U.S. Public Health Service, 1964) on the medical risks of smoking reversed what was an accelerating trend in cigarette consumption from 1905 to 1964 to a decelerating annual per capita consumption of cigarettes that continues to the present. Per capita consumption in 2000 was about half of that in 1960 (Wright, 2002). There is no way to determine how much the reduction in cigarette consumption is due to prevention of smoking in the young and how much to cessation of smoking in those already smoking. However, the American Cancer Society (1986) estimated that over 90% of 37 million people who stopped smoking since the Surgeon General's Report have done so without the aid of treatment programs. Still, smoking remains the single major cause of death due to disease. For this reason, a great deal of research has been done on ways to reduce the prevalence of smoking.

In 1980, Leventhal and Cleary reviewed research and theory on treatment of "the smoking problem." Intervention attempts fall into two major classes: the therapy or doctor–patient model and those following a public health, community, or public opinion model. In the therapy model, the most popular approaches were behavior therapies, operant procedures, aversive conditioning, sensitization or desensitization, contracting, and self-monitoring techniques. More recently, cognitive therapies have been tried.

Physician intervention involving mainly health advice and other information dissemination programs have been used. Pharmacological methods involving the substitution of the source of nicotine from cigarettes to patches or gum have also been tried. Studies of hypnosis and sensory deprivation use suggestion or simple removal of the cues maintaining smoking.

Leventhal and Cleary (1980) discussed the results at that time. Although a variety of methods produced decreases in smoking during treatment, there was a high drop-out rate and dropouts were often excluded from the denominator in evaluating therapy results. This would tend to exaggerate the effectiveness of therapy, because dropouts were probably treatment failures. Although therapy results in a temporary stopping of smoking, the relapse rate is quite high by 6 months and even higher 1 year after the end of treatment. The typical persistent quitters amount to only 10% to 25% of the pretherapy base. Those figures have not changed much in current studies, as I discuss later in this chapter. The results are often statistically significant in comparisons with control subjects because of the large numbers of subjects but are clinically insignificant in effect size. No particular therapy was said to work better than any other, and none were superior to simple interventions by medical practitioners.

Leventhal and Cleary (1980) also discussed the public health model of combating smoking through mass communication and laws restricting the advertising and locales of smoking. Communication studies often use fear-arousing methods showing the health consequences of smoking. Fear-arousing methods are usually ineffective in the long run because they elicit denial or undesirable avoidance, such as not going for medical exams and having periodic chest X-rays. In high sensation seekers, fearful messages may instigate a daring fatalistic attitude. Fear-arousing messages have more effect in less educated persons and those with low self-esteem. Programs undertaken by schools are effective in increasing antismoking attitudes, but behavioral effects are "usually nonexistent, and when they do appear are usually of small magnitude" (p. 378). Community studies have only a minor effect on smoking. Antismoking campaigns at the time did stimulate smokers to switch to filter cigarettes and those claiming lower tar and nicotine levels. However, smokers increased their cigarette consumption to get the nicotine levels they needed. At the time of this review, restrictions on tobacco advertising and legal restrictions on smoking in travel, work, and public places were just starting. Laws restricting smoking in public places, the promotion of smoking through advertising, and increases in the price of cigarettes through taxation all seem to have significant effects on the prevalence of smoking in communities (Jamrozik, 2004).

Once smoking starts, it quickly moves to addiction. There is no nicotine abuse diagnosis in the *Diagnostic and Statistical Manual of Mental Disorders*

(4th ed.; *DSM–IV*; American Psychiatric Association, 1994), only nicotine dependence. Between 50% and 80% of those who smoke develop nicotine dependence, with withdrawal symptoms when they try to stop. Nearly all who smoke through age 20 years become regular, daily smokers. Of those who successfully quit, less than 25% do so on their first attempt. Relapse is the rule for most smokers attempting to quit either on their own or through cessation programs. The relapse rates of smoking over time are nearly identical to those for heroin, with most relapses occurring within the first 4 months after quitting (Hunt, Barnett, & Branch, 1971). The minority of long-term successful quitters consist mainly of those who have quit on their own outside of treatment. It is important to understand their characteristics to develop better programs for those who cannot quit on their own.

Marlatt, Curry, and Gordon (1988) recruited a sample of individuals who indicated that they intended to quit smoking. At the end of the critical 4-month period, 16% were still abstinent, 12% were mostly abstinent, 51% had relapsed to former levels of smoking, and 21% had never quit. These figures were quite similar for 1- and 2-year follow-ups, except that relapse increased to 60% for 3 years. The mainly abstinent total of 20% is a familiar figure in the literature on smoking cessation and a standard for comparison for active treatment programs.

Marlatt et al. (1988) compared those in the different outcome groups. Comparing those who attempted to quit with those who never really tried to quit, they found that attempters were more common among men than women, and in those more educated who had higher incomes and had a higher desire to quit. Comparison of abstainers and nonabstainers at a 1-month follow-up showed fewer abstainers had been in prior treatment for smoking and that fewer of their friends, acquaintances, and those they lived with were smokers. The former finding suggests that those in treatment may be harder core smokers, and the latter findings suggest that it is more difficult to quit when exposed to smoking stimuli among friends and family. Another factor is the easy availability of cigarettes if the quitter has not hoarded or bought any since quitting.

At the 2-year follow-up, long past the immediate temptations just after quitting, the abstainers were found to be significantly younger, with fewer years of smoking experience, probably indicating a greater degree of addiction in the nonabstainers. The most significant predictor of long-term abstinence was the self-rated desire to stop smoking. It is not surprising that this internal motivation is a strong factor, but what determines it? There has been little study of personality in determining this kind of motivation. However, health risk is an external factor that could increase motivation for quitting.

Schachter (1982) reported a much higher percentage of successful self-initiated quitters than reported in intervention studies; almost two thirds were successful! He surmised that successful quitters may have achieved abstinence after many previous attempts to stop. But his sample was relatively small and specialized. One of his two samples consisted of the psychology department at Columbia University! Using a much larger sample of over 5,000 smokers from 10 studies, S. Cohen et al. (1989) found self-quitting rates of 8% to 25% and a median of 14%, a slightly lower rate than that found in treatment studies (20%). Contrary to Schachter's hypothesis about the cumulative effect of repeated quitting attempts, S. Cohen et al. found no relationship between number of previous attempts and success in quitting. They did find a difference in quitting success between light and heavy smokers. Naturally, the light smokers were more successful. This result suggests that success in achieving abstinence is a function of the severity of the nicotine addiction. This suggests that nicotine replacement therapy (NRT), using nicotine chewing gum, might be more successful than psychological or behavioral treatments.

An early study showed that use of nicotine gum was more successful than psychological treatments (Raw, Jarvis, Feyerabend, & Russell, 1980). At 1 year posttreatment, 38% of those using nicotine gum had ceased smoking compared with only 14% of those receiving psychological treatment. Another study by the same group, using a randomized controlled trial with nicotine gum compared with placebo gum, showed a clear superiority of the gum to placebo, with 38% of those chewing the active gum abstinent at 6 months and 1 year compared with only 16% in the placebo group. Most subjects stopped using the nicotine gum after 6 months, and only 7% of them developed a longer term dependence on the gum. A study conducted in France showed both nicotine gum and acupuncture groups were superior to a control group in quitting, although the differences were markedly diminished by high relapse rates in all groups after 13 months (Clavel, Benhamou, Huertas, & Flamant, 1985). Raw, McNeill, and West (1999) reviewed studies of NRT and reported that nicotine replacement doubled cessation rates compared with controls irrespective of the adjunctive therapies. However, NRT therapies are much less successful in women than in men, possibly because of increased anxiety and weight gain after cessation of smoking (Reynoso, Susabda, & Cepeda-Benito, 2005).

Another major review of NRT therapy for smoking cessation included 123 studies involving over 35,600 subjects (Silagy, Lancaster, Stead, Mant, & Fowler, 2005). This study compared different forms of NRT including gum, transdermal patches, nasal spray, inhalers, and nicotine tablets. All five forms of NRT were more effective than placebos or no NRT, and the benefits were apparent throughout the 6- to 12-month period of follow-up. However, the percentage abstinent in NRT after 12 months was only 17% compared with 10% in the control subjects. Specific rates achieved for the different techniques of NRT were 17% for gum, inhaler, and tablets; 14% for patches; and 24% for intranasal spray. The spray may have been slightly more effective than the other methods because it delivers nicotine quickly and directly on demand and is therefore closest to actual smoking. The effectiveness of NRT appeared to be independent of the intensity of additional support programs.

Advice to quit smoking coming from a personal physician could be more effective than antismoking campaigns in the general community. A large study of over 6,000 smokers in England compared various types of physician advice with a control group of smokers getting no advice (Jamrozik et al., 1984). The intervention groups achieved a 1-year abstinence rate of 15% compared with 11% for the control groups. Although significant, the difference is not impressive. In addition, the difference was significant only in the middle to upper social classes, but advice was not effective in the two lower socioeconomic classes.

Another large-scale physician intervention program in England showed that a brief intervention had no effect compared with the usual medical cursory advice to stop smoking, but a brief intervention supported by backup from a smokers' clinic did increase abstinence, particularly in those supplementing their efforts with nicotine gum (M. A. H. Russell, Stapleton, Jackson, Hajek, & Belcher, 1987). Again, the difference was not impressive, with the total abstinent at 1 year of 8% in the control subjects and 9% in the brief intervention compared with 13% in the supported brief intervention. The great majority of smokers remained smokers at 1 year postintervention.

Of course, the motivation to quit in general medical patients is probably no more than in the general population of smokers, and medical advice to the contrary, there is still not enough motivation to counteract the power of the addiction. A study of men who were identified as at high risk for heart disease, not only by heavy smoking habits but also by high cholesterol and blood pressure, was undertaken involving over 8,000 smokers in the United States (Ockene, Hymowitz, Sexton, & Broste, 1982). A special intervention (SI) group received a full range of informational and behavioral techniques for cessation, including self-monitoring, gradual change, stimulus control, behavioral contracts, and relaxation techniques. The control group consisted of those receiving the usual care (UC) with minimal advice or intervention. At 1 year, 40% of SI and 21% of UC groups reported abstinence. Differences appeared mainly in the 1st year and were maintained through the 4 years of the study. They were largely confirmed by blood tests for nicotine presence.

Another kind of motivated smoking cessation study was conducted with pregnant women (Windsor et al., 1985). But in this study, the intervention methods consisted only of self-help guided by manuals on how to stop smoking, which were intended to increase motivation and the use of specific techniques to counteract the urge to smoke. The most intensive of these achieved a quit rate of only 14% compared with 2% of the controls and 6% of a less intensive self-help schedule. Apparently, motivation alone is not sufficient to reach a significant proportion of smokers without some behavioral modification that goes beyond mere information giving.

Curry, Ludman, and McClure (2003) conducted a recent review of studies of self-administered treatments for smoking cessation. They found no evidence that self-help manuals, like those used by Windsor et al. (1985), are effective. However, in studies in which self-help is combined with adjuncts such as written feedback and outreach telephone counseling, there was an increase in abstinence rates.

Behavioral methods have been prominent in attempts at smoking cessation. Lando (1977) used a broad-spectrum treatment, including 1 week of aversive conditioning (rapid smoking to the point of nausea), contractual management, booster sessions, and group sessions in which problems of self-control were discussed and alternative therapies such as chewing gum (nonnicotine) instead of smoking were suggested. Subjects made self-contracts promising certain rewards or punishments for abstinence or slippage. Control subjects just had the 1 week of aversive conditioning with no support beyond that. At 6 months posttreatment, 76% of the active treatment group was still abstinent compared with 35% of the control subjects. The relapse was high in the control group after only 2 months, showing only a brief effect of aversive conditioning without maintenance by other behavioral methods and group support.

Summary

Both genes and environmental influences from parents, siblings, and friends as well as media influences are factors affecting the likelihood of smoking. Attempts have been made to counter the environmental influences and prevent smoking from starting in preadolescents and adolescents and to stop it if already started. Merely imparting information about the negative consequences of smoking through lectures does not prevent youth from starting to smoke and does not get them to quit smoking. A combination of various methods in schools involving more active participation of students does show some reduction in the increases in smoking prevalence normally occurring with age. Although statistically significant, the effects of these programs are weak.

Active treatments for smoking depending on voluntary participation usually have high drop-out rates, and even in those persisting in treatment, relapse rates are high. There are treatment effects above those in untreated smokers, but as in prevention, the differences are small. Many smokers eventually quit on their own without treatment. These are usually lighter smokers with less severe addictions. Nicotine replacement methods have been more successful, with or without adjunctive treatments, at least in men.

Physician interventions with their patients are a little more effective than nonmedical advice unless the patient's motivations are enhanced by high-risk factors like high cholesterol and high blood pressure. But such heightened motivation only facilitates abstention if the worried patient is treated with a full range of behavioral techniques beyond the mere giving of information and advice.

SUBSTANCE ABUSE

Some of the prevention programs concerned with substance abuse have concentrated on one type of substance such as alcohol or marijuana, whereas others are broad-spectrum programs including smoking, drinking, marijuana, and other illegal drugs. Most of the programs addressed at alcohol are designed to teach moderate use rather than a goal of abstinence. Only 11% of the general American population are alcohol abstainers, whereas 61% can be classified as social drinkers (Helzer, Burnam, & McElvoy, 1991). Programs attempt to discourage the type of drinking in the rest who drink heavily, abuse alcohol, or are dependent on alcohol. In most states, the legal drinking age is now 21, but the laws are widely circumvented and flouted by adolescents. Binge drinking is widespread in college, and for those who are vulnerable it is often a prelude to alcohol abuse and dependence. Marijuana use is also widespread among the young, and programs directed against it view it as an entry to major drug use.

Prevention of Drug Use

Tobler (1992) did a meta-analysis of 143 adolescent drug prevention programs, attempting to determine which type of prevention program worked and with what type of population. Only programs with subjects drawn from 6th to 12th grade with prevention as a goal and with quantitative outcome measures and a control or comparison group were included.

Programs were classified into five categories, although some included more than one approach. *Knowledge-only* programs include lecture presentations of the legal, biological, and psychological effects of drug abuse, with limited group discussion. The information was mainly to scare the students with possible negative consequences. *Affective-only* programs are derived from humanistic psychology and address the psychological factors that are presumed to underlie vulnerability to drug use, including low self-esteem and lack of recognition of feelings and values. *Peer* programs assume that the major determinant of drug use is peer example and pressure. These programs use positive peer influences, teaching, and counseling. They may also teach refusal skills to counteract peer pressures, information to counteract false norms of drug taking, assertion training, and interpersonal and intrapersonal skills to impart self-confidence in dealing with peer pressures. *Knowledge plus affective* is a combination of these two approaches. The *alternatives* approach is designed to provide substitute community activities and entertainments for antisocial drug-using ones and to provide training in skills that may be lacking. Some, recognizing the sensation seeking needs in drug use, provide opportunities for physical adventures.

The overall effect size for knowledge alone was moderate (.52), but those for skills in refusal methods, drug use (self-reported), or behavior (reported by school, parents, or authorities or reflected in school grades and attendance) were lower (.24–.27). Attitude change showed the least effect (.18).

Knowledge-only programs affected only knowledge and had little effect on attitudes or use. Affective-only programs were ineffective on all outcome measures. Peer programs had the highest effect sizes for knowledge, attitudes, and self-reported drug use. Strangely, the effect size for behavioral criteria was negative, calling into question the results for self-reported use. Programs providing alternatives had the highest effect size for behavioral indices of drug use, including school grades and attendance, as well as court, parents', and prinicipal's reports of drug use (.56). Programs targeting tobacco use only were most successful, whereas those for alcohol, whether alone or with other drugs, had a dismal average effect size (.17). However, the peer programs targeting alcohol had a better effect size (.30) than the other strategies.

The knowledge-only programs providing information designed to "scare" youths away from drug use had practically no effect. Perhaps the scare tactic is to blame for this failure. High sensation seekers who are the main group at risk for drug use are not easily scared and tend to underestimate the personal risk involved in drug use. They are likely to tune out such messages. However, if messages were deliberately designed to hold their attention, they might be more effective.

Donohew and his colleagues have attempted to design media messages targeting high sensation seekers and tested their effects (Donohew, Bardo, & Zimmerman, 2004; Donohew, Lorch, & Palmgreen, 1991). They first examined the relationship between sensation seeking and drug use among junior and high school students in Kentucky communities (Donohew et al., 2004). Large differences were found between high and low sensation seekers in the prevalent use of marijuana, cocaine, liquor, beer, "uppers," and "downers." Marijuana use, for instance, was 4 times as prevalent in high than low sensation seekers in junior high and 3 times as prevalent in senior high school. Other illegal drugs were used by only very small percentages of low (1%–2%) compared with high (7%–15%) sensation seekers.

The characteristics of video drug ads appealing to high and low sensation seekers were studied in focus groups. High sensation seekers liked messages that were novel, creative, unusual, complex, emotional, graphic, unconventional, fast paced, and suspenseful, with intense sound and hard-edged music and visual effects. Low sensation seekers liked more closure at the end of a story, whereas high sensation seekers liked to draw their own inferences. On the basis of these preliminary researches, two 30-second antidrug public service announcements (PSAs) were developed, one with low-value stimulation and the other with more intense stimulation of the type that was shown to appeal to high sensation seekers. The dependent variable was the indicated intent to call the drug hotline given in the PSA.

There was a significant interaction effect between sensation seeking and message sensation value. For high sensation seekers, the more stimulating PSA resulted in more intent to call the hotline than the low value PSA, but the reverse was true for the low sensation seeker. A similar interaction was found when "users versus nonusers of drugs" was used for the comparison. The largest impact on intent to call the hotline was found in drug-using high sensation seekers exposed to the high stimulating PSA.

Lorch et al. (1994) examined the effects of embedding PSAs in half-hour television programs that were high or low in stimulation value. High sensation seekers paid significantly more attention to the high-stimulation programs and their embedded PSAs than to those in low-stimulation programs. Low sensation seekers paid greater attention to PSAs in low-stimulation programming but also watched a lot of the high-stimulation programs. In the next study, Palmgreen et al. (1995) put high-stimulation PSAs in actual television programs and used surveys of hotline callers to determine who was responding to the PSA. Of these respondents, about three quarters were high sensation seekers and a third reported having used drugs within the past 30 days, compared with 23% of the general population. Recall of the content of the PSA was highest among the high sensation seekers.

Finally, this research group tested the effectiveness of an actual televised high-stimulation antimarijuana message targeted at high sensation seeking adolescents in two Kentucky counties (Palmgreen, Donohew, Lorch, Hoyle, & Stephenson, 2001). There were repeated monthly interviews of 100 randomly selected 7th through 10th graders over a 32-month period, during which the PSAs, embedded in programs watched by high sensation seekers, were shown during 1-month periods in each of the counties.

The low sensation seekers had low levels of marijuana use over the entire period of the study, with no developmental trends or campaign effects. In contrast, the high sensation seekers showed developmental trends over the study, with increasing prevalence of marijuana use over the course of the study. However, during the campaign periods, the use of marijuana started a downward trend that continued in the subsequent months. In one county in which there were two periods of antidrug exposure, the effect of the first campaign showed a wearing-off effect after 6 months. The effects of the campaign were specific to marijuana use; there were no effects on the use of tobacco, alcohol, inhalants, cocaine, or hallucinogens.

The studies of the Kentucky investigators showed the benefits of designing a communication attack on drug use in consideration of the sensation seeking characteristics of drug consumers. Messages that get their attention and do not attempt to scare or preach to them can be effective in reducing drug consumption. Similar attacks should be used for other substances because the effects are highly specific to the targeted drug. This group of investigators has applied a similar strategy to sexual risk taking.

Several large-scale programs for drug abuse prevention emerged in the 1990s. The Life Skills Training (LST) program uses the methods of the peer social resistance skills approach to prevention of adolescent drug use (Botvin & Griffin, 2004). The first component addresses developing personal self-management skills for identifying and resisting media influences and developing self-control skills for dealing with anxiety, anger, and frustration, and impulsive reactions and setting goals for self-improvement. The second component is the development of social skills to enhance interpersonal competence. The third component is specifically aimed at imparting drug information, correct normative expectations about drug use, and resisting media and peer pressures to smoke, drink, or use drugs. The program used cognitive–behavioral techniques, group discussions, classroom demonstrations, and conventional teaching methods. There are 15 sessions in the 1st year of the program, typically during the seventh grade, 10 booster sessions in the eighth grade, and 5 booster sessions in the ninth grade.

The first report of results described the effects during a 3-year study of about 4,500 students attending 56 schools in New York state (Botvin, Baker, Dusenbury, Tortu, & Botvin, 1990). Three groups were compared: (a) teachers trained in a 1-day workshop with feedback provided; (b) teachers trained with videotapes and no feedback; and (c) control subjects not exposed to the program. There was significantly less cigarette smoking and marijuana use in both treatment conditions than in the control condition. No significant effects were found for drinking frequency or amount of alcohol consumed, but the frequency of getting drunk was less in the second experimental condition. This finding is problematic. It is difficult to see how reported drunkenness could be affected by the program without an effect on drinking amount per se. Tests on the skills and information taught by the program showed the expected increase in knowledge and change in attitudes but no effects for the attempted changes in personality traits.

A second study evaluated the long-term effects of the LST program on the subjects when they reached the 12th grade (Botvin, Baker, Dusenbury, Botvin, & Diaz, 1995). No interventions were made during the 10th to 12th grades. There was an attrition of 40% of the original sample but no differences in drug use variables were found between the attrition and staying samples. About 3,600 students remained in the follow-up sample. Effects were examined in a "high-fidelity" portion of the group (2,752 students) who were judged to have been exposed to at least 60% of the program between 7th and 9th grades. Both treatment groups had significantly lower smoking, weekly drinking, heavy drinking, and problem drinking than the control group. Treatment groups had lower rates for weekly marijuana use. Polydrug use was markedly reduced in both intervention groups.

These significant results were not apparent in the full group that included those who had less than 60% participation in the program. Only the drunk variable for alcohol was significant, and marijuana use was not different between treatment and control groups. This discrepancy in results can be interpreted in two ways. One is that full exposure to the program is necessary for results in prevention of drug use. The other is that those with less participation were less motivated and interested in the program, and therefore were the ones more at risk for drug use.

This study of a largely suburban, middle-class population from intact families was followed by one of youths from 29 inner-city middle schools, which selected a high-risk sample from among them (Griffin, Botvin, Nichols, & Doyle, 2003). Risk was estimated from poor grades in school and from their friends' use of alcohol and tobacco. The high-risk sample was predominantly African American and Hispanic and was economically disadvantaged. Base rates of substance use at the seventh-grade baseline were surprisingly low, considering that the sample was partly selected on the basis of peer use of alcohol and tobacco. More than one third of those in both treatment and control groups dropped out of the study before completion. Not unexpectedly, the dropouts were those reporting lifetime smoking, use of marijuana, and polydrug use at the pretest; however, they did not differ from stayers in drinking and inhalant use. One year after the intervention program, those who persisted in the program reported less smoking, drinking, use of inhalants, and polydrug use than control subjects, but the difference in marijuana use was not significant. The investigators claim that the results show the effectiveness of the LST program in a high-risk population, but the high drop-out rate of those most at risk in terms of already using drugs somewhat weakens the claim. However, the aim of the program is prevention, not cessation, so that for those not already involved in drug use at an early age, the program accomplishes its goals.

All Stars is a prevention program designed to reduce adolescent risky behaviors through targeting four mediators linked to drug use (McNeal,

Hansen, Harrington, & Giles, 2004). These are false normative beliefs ("everyone is doing it"), perceived incongruence between drug use and desired lifestyle, commitment to not use drugs, and bonding with school. Three other mediators involving personality characteristics were not targeted in the intervention program but were studied for possible program effects and as mediators predicting behavior: self-esteem, impulsive decision making, and sensation seeking. The subjects were about 1,800 students attending 14 middle schools in two cities in Kentucky. Students were surveyed in the fall of the school year and at the end of the year. Special scales were developed to measure the mediating variables and prevalences of drinking alcohol, smoking, using marijuana, and sexual activity. The last of these is discussed in a subsequent section on risky sex. The program was conducted in some schools by specialists in prevention from outside of the schools and in other schools by the teachers in the schools. Both specialists and teachers were trained for the specific program. Control schools received the usual education from health education classes taught by teachers.

Increases in 30-day prevalence of alcohol, tobacco, and marijuana use occurred in the control group from baseline to final assessment at the end of the school year. Program exposure reduced the increase of use of alcohol, cigarettes, and marijuana and reduced the use of inhalants, but these treatment effects were observed only in the schools in which teachers administered the program. Specialists had no significant effects on these behaviors. Similarly, the teachers had significant effects on all of the targeted mediators, whereas the specialists only affected manifest commitment to abstinence from drugs. Teachers, but not specialists, also affected nontargeted mediators of impulsive decision making and sensation seeking. It would be unusual for this type of program to change a personality trait, especially one that was not targeted. The changes may have been specifically limited to substance use behavior.

Treatment

This section of the chapter focuses primarily on treatment of problem drinking and drug abuse in young adults rather than the older, substance-dependent population. Young adults 18 to 29 have the highest 1-year prevalence rates for alcoholism (Helzer et al., 1991). The types of alcoholism (Type 2; Cloninger, 1987a) and drug abuse (Type B; Feingold, Ball, Kranzler, & Rounsaville, 1996) associated with antisocial behaviors and high sensation seeking have an early onset, before the age of 25. Chronic substance abuse is more likely to be characterized by substance dependency, which is more difficult to treat than abuse.

Vaillant (1983) described the results of treatment programs for alcoholism during the 1970s. One of these was a hospital program using multimodality therapy, disregarding motivation and aiming to move patients from general hospital care to Alcoholics Anonymous (AA) after initial recovery. The results in this clinical sample were compared with four other treatment programs and three pooled "no treatment" studies with follow-up assessments at 2 to 3 years. The results from the treatment and no-treatment samples were nearly identical: 17% to 20% abstinent or social drinking, 13% to 16% improved, and 63% to 67% still abusing alcohol. Longer follow-ups from 7 to 10 years were not much better: The medians for 6 studies were 26% abstinent or social drinking, 27% improved, and 57% still alcoholic or dead. AA is the most prevalent treatment model with the goal of total abstinence. An AA study conducted in Trinidad and Tobago reported a 7-year follow-up of 37% abstinent or social drinking, 16% improved, and 47% with continued alcoholism (Beaubrun, 1967). A behavior modification program with the aim of turning alcoholic individuals into social drinkers reported better results, with 35% abstinent or social drinking, but a larger 50% improved, and only 15% with continued alcoholism after 2 years (Sobell & Sobell, 1976). However, a 10-year follow-up of these findings, by Pendery, Maltzman, and West (1982) disputed their sanguine outcome data. The argument about the efficacy of programs with total abstinence goals compared with those with controlled moderate drinking as a goal persists.

Programs like AA promote the view that alcoholism is a compulsive disease and the drinker has no option other than total abstinence maintained by confession, moral commitment, and faith in God, reinforced by close group support. The cognitive approach maintains that alcoholism is a *thought disorder* maintained by faulty cognitive premises and beliefs that can be changed by *cognitive restructuring* (Steigerwald & Stone, 1999). These authors maintain that AA does incorporate a kind of cognitive restructuring, challenging the alcoholic individual's beliefs in grandiosity, defiance, and isolation. However, the attitude of powerlessness and faith in a higher power seems contradictory to the idea of rationality and control of drinking as the solution to alcoholism. The *matching hypothesis* states that different types of clients will benefit from different types of programs.

The Project MATCH Research Group (1997) undertook a large-scale research project to assess the relative effectiveness of three types of programs and the effects of differences in clients' gender, conceptual level, severity of alcoholism, psychopathologies, sociopathy, and motivations on responses to the different treatments. The three treatments were cognitive–behavioral coping skills therapy (CBT–CST); motivational enhancement therapy (MET); and 12-step facilitation therapy (TSF). TSF is based on the traditional AA program. Nearly 1,000 subjects were recruited from clinical research units around the country. About three quarters were males. All clients met the *DSM–III–R* (American Psychiatric Association, 1987) criteria for alcohol abuse or dependence. Clients were randomly assigned to one of the three treatment programs. Treatments lasted 12 weeks, and continuous monthly drinking estimates were made during the year following treatments.

There were no consistent or clinically significant outcome differences between the three treatment groups on the primary measures, percentage of days abstinent, or number of drinks per drinking day. On the secondary outcome measures, there was only one consistent finding, but one limited to the outpatient clients. On time to first relapse (3 consecutive drinking days), TSF clients had the best outcome, with 24% avoiding any drinking in posttreatment months compared with 15% and 14% in CBT–CST and MET, respectively. Of course, this is a statistically significant difference but is hardly an outstanding success for the total abstinence goal of the 12-step program.

Tests of the matching hypothesis showed few effects in the form of treatment by client–attribute interactions. For percentage of days abstinent, the lower the client's psychiatric severity score, the greater the percentage of days abstinent when treated with TSF compared with CBT–CST. In other words, the less disturbed clients showed more benefit from the total abstinence emphasis of the TSF program. The converse prediction that those high in psychiatric disturbance would do better in CBT–CST was not supported. Those who had less purpose in life and aspired to experience greater meaning were somewhat more responsive to TSF than to other treatments. Conceptual level and sociopathy showed no interaction effects.

College alcohol abuse has become a major problem in recent years (Vicary & Karshin, 2002). The freedom from parental restraints and the wide availability of liquor around most campuses has led to widespread binge drinking, particularly among the more impulsive and sensation seeking types of students. Fraternities and sororities sponsor parties at which binge drinking is the norm. But off-campus residences are also centers of drinking. Many less sensation seeking students are gulled into heavy drinking by the perception that this is the norm, and they seek social acceptance by emulating their peers. For many, this is their first significant drinking experience, and they do not know how to regulate their drinking, leading to drunkenness rather than more limited social drinking. Heavy drinking has a prominent role in date rape and failure to practice safe sex in consensual relations.

Fromme, Marlatt, Baer, and Kivlahan (1994) developed a group intervention for young adult drinkers, the Alcohol Skills Training Program (ASTP). The ASTP is not designed for individuals exhibiting moderate or severe dependence. Unlike most alcoholism programs, it is not designed to produce total abstinence, although clients may choose this goal. For those who do not, the program is intended to return the drinker from a pattern of alcohol abuse, as in sporadic binge drinking, to moderate controlled social drinking. Clients learn to become more aware of their levels of intoxication by measuring and charting their blood alcohol levels (BALs) when drinking; they also note the circumstances, mood, and associates they are with when drinking. They analyze their expectancies from drinking and learn to challenge unrealistic ones. A bar-lab is set up to simulate the normal drinking environment. They learn to moderate their drinking to stay within limits that will keep BALs below .055% and learn how many drinks they may have during 1- to 4-hour time periods. No drinking is to take place before driving. Drinking skills encourage slow drinking. The client learns to recognize the high-risk situations in which they tend to overindulge. Alternative strategies, like relaxation, are taught to deal with stress and anxiety. Group discussions are used to get feedback on their concepts of drinking and its goals.

A study of the ASTP program was done using heavy-drinking college students reporting at least one negative consequence of drinking and interested in changing their drinking behavior (Kivlahan, Marlatt, Fromme, Coppel, & Williams, 1990). Subjects were assigned to a moderation-oriented cognitive–behavioral skills training (ST) group, an alcohol information (AI) class emphasizing the negative consequences of drinking, or a control group receiving assessments only. Measures of drinking were collected at 4-, 8-, and 12-month follow-ups. Self-reports and objective BAL measurements were used to assess drinking. There were reductions in reports of drinks per week of more than 50% in the ST group. But despite the reduction in overall drinking, substantial numbers of subjects in all groups still reported episodes of heavy drinking and BAL tests confirmed this in 40% of the ST group, 58% of the AI group, and 64% of the control group. Many in all groups reported driving after drinking four or more drinks.

Apparently, the ASTP program had minimal effects on binge drinking and driving under the influence (DUI) of alcohol. Heavy episodic drinking is related to sensation seeking, and both of these are related to the likelihood of DUI and other risky driving behavior like not wearing seat belts (van Beurden, Zask, Brooks, & Dight, 2005).

A Canadian group of investigators examined the effects of treatment programs on driving records of patients drawn from substance abuse treatment centers (Macdonald, Mann, Chipman, & Anglin-Bodrug, 2004). This study included cocaine and marijuana abusers as well as alcohol abusers with a control group of nonsubstance abusing drivers. Separate treatments were given for each of the substance abuse types. Treatment models involved cognitive, behavioral, multidisciplinary, and holistic treatments. Although clients were taught how to recognize high-risk situations and cope with them, the programs addressed substance abuse, not specifically driving. The follow-up interval was 7 years. Traffic violations decreased with age for all groups, but there were no time-by-group interactions before and after treatment. However, the average number of collisions after treatment was lower in the alcohol and cocaine groups but did not change in the marijuana or control groups. The alcohol group had significantly more collisions than the control group before treatment but not after treatment. The cocaine group had more collisions than the control group both before and after therapy, although there was a reduction in their accidents after therapy. All groups had markedly more license suspensions than the control group before and after treatment, but there were significant reductions in the incidence of suspensions. These results were based on official records, not self-reports, and thus were not subject to the distortion in self-reports.

Stewart et al. (2005) noted that drinkers have different motivations related to their personality types. In chapter 4, I described the distinction between Type 1 and Type 2 alcoholic individuals made by Cloninger (1987a). The Type 1 is more likely to drink to regulate dysphoric mood, whereas the Type 2 begins drinking early as a form of sensation seeking. Stewart and colleagues selected drinkers among high school students who scored high on Arnett's (1994) Inventory of Sensation Seeking test, the Intensity subscale, an index of Anxiety Sensitivity (AS), or a scale for Hopelessness (H). These subjects were randomly assigned to a treatment or control group. The high sensation seeking subjects reported more frequent drinking and tended to engage in more binge drinking than the high AS or H subjects, but there was no difference between the control group and the intervention group on any of the baseline measures. The intervention was a brief two-session one that addressed specific motives for drinking by different personality types. There was a 4-month follow-up assessment after treatment. The treatment group overall had lower levels of alcohol consumption than the control subjects. The treatment increased rates of abstinence in the AS and H groups but did not affect rates in the SS group. However, binge drinking was reduced in the SS group (68%–48%) but was not affected in the AS or H groups. The AS group alone showed reduced problem-drinking symptoms relative to the control subjects. Although some high sensation seekers did reduce their binge drinking, their overall drinking patterns remained problematic.

More recent pharmacological treatment for alcoholism has taken two primary forms (Volpicelli, Krishnan-Sarin, & O'Malley, 2002). One is the use of disulfiram in the aversive conditioning to alcohol. Disulfiram, like its antecedent, Antabuse, results in severe nausea and other unpleasant reactions in interaction with alcohol. One experience with the combination can produce a conditioned avoidance reaction, perhaps also on the basis of conscious anticipation of the consequences of ingesting alcohol. This treatment depends on motivation because the patient must take the drug regularly to maintain the avoidance behavior. Without supervision, many stop taking the drug. Although some conditioned aversive reactions are created, these can be easily overcome in the absence of subsequent conditioning using the drug.

Another approach is based on the knowledge of the central pharmacological effects of alcohol. Alcohol increases the release of opioid peptides in rats and humans predisposed by their genetics to alcoholism. Opioid antagonists, like naltrexone, block the opioid receptors that mediate the positive effects of alcohol. It seems to reduce levels of craving for alcohol, and when alcoholics do drink, they get less of a "high" from drinking. A study of beer drinkers in a natural setting showed that for most subjects, naltrexone, compared with a placebo, produced decreases in beer consumption and a decrease in positive affect during drinking (Davidson, Palfai, Bird, & Swift, 1999). Most studies show a reduction in drinking levels and percentage of drinking days in those taking the drug. Naltrexone is often combined with cognitive–behavioral approaches.

A study of currently abstinent but previously alcohol-dependent subjects given naltrexone or placebo plus either coping skills therapy or nonspecific supportive therapy was undertaken by O'Malley et al. (1992). Both types of therapy advocated abstinence, but the coping skills therapy taught specific skills in achieving this aim. It is surprising that results for abstinence were best in the naltrexone group receiving only supportive therapy, in which 61% remained abstinent over 12 weeks compared with 28% in the naltrexone–coping skills, 21% in the placebo–coping skills, and 19% in the placebo–supportive group. Relapse rates, however, showed a superiority of both naltrexone groups to both placebo groups in preventing relapse, regardless of the type of adjunct psychological therapy.

Anton, Moak, Wald, and Latham (1999) examined the effects of naltrexone with cognitive–behavioral therapy (CBT) and placebo with CBT. This study showed that naltrexone-treated subjects drank less and took longer to relapse after 12 weekly therapy sessions. Subjects with complete abstinence during the 90-day follow-up were not more frequent in the naltrexone than in the placebo group. Although showing that cognitive therapy without the active drug is less effective than the combination of drug and therapy, the study does not show that the combination is superior to the drug alone and therefore is not in contradiction to the results of previously described study by O'Malley et al. (1992).

Opiate-blocking drugs have also been used in the treatment of opiate abuse, but I do not review these studies here. Any treatment that relies on continued use of a drug is helpful to preventing relapse in clients motivated enough to keep taking the drug without supervision. Cognitive–behavioral methods may provide some help, but without the blocking of the pleasure reinforcement of the drug or some adequate substitute, it may not be enough to achieve lasting abstinence.

Patkar et al. (2004) examined the effects of a 12-week outpatient treatment program on substance abusers, including alcohol, cocaine, and multisubstance abusers. Clients were randomly assigned to either a high-structure behaviorally oriented treatment or a low-structure facilitative treatment. Follow-up assessments were done at 9 months posttreatment. Three subscales from the Zuckerman–Kuhlman Personality Questionnaire (ZKPQ; Zuckerman, 2002; Zuckerman, Kuhlman, Joireman, Teta, & Kraft, 1993) were used pretreatment: Impulsive Sensation Seeking (ImpSS), Neuroticism–Anxiety (N-Anx), and Aggression–Hostility (Agg-Host). The multidrug users scored significantly higher than the alcohol and cocaine groups on the ImpSS and the N-Anx subscales, respectively. They also had more dirty urines on admission and more severe drug use and psychiatric problems. Despite these differences, the three groups did not differ on changes in most of the variables after treatment; all groups showed improvements. The cocaine group had a higher 30-day abstinence rate than the multisubstance groups, and the alcoholic group had a higher rate of alcohol use after treatment and a higher rate of negative urines during treatment.

A second study by this group compared the responses to treatment of a group of African American cocaine-addicted subjects (Patkar et al., 2004) with control subjects, who were screened and excluded for a history of substance abuse, psychiatric disorder, or a positive urine test. This was a 12-week program, although there was a high drop-out rate, and the average client only participated for 4 weeks. The focus of this study was the use of personality measures in the prediction of outcomes. The Sensation Seeking Scale (SSS) Form V (Zuckerman, Eysenck, & Eysenck, 1978), the Barratt Impulsivity Scale (Imp; Barratt, 1985), and the Buss–Durkee Hostility Inventory (BDHI; A. H. Buss & Durkee, 1957) were used as predictors. The SSS Total score correlated negatively and significantly with days in treatment and positively with number of negative urine tests, and drop-out rates. All four SSS subscales were negatively correlated with days in treatment and dirty urines, and three of the four subscales (excluding Boredom Susceptibility) were positively correlated with dropout. The Imp scale correlated negatively and significantly only with days in treatment, and the BDHI correlated only with drop-out rate. The three scales predicted response to treatment even after controlling for pretreatment levels of education and a drug severity score.

S. A. Ball (1995) used the ZKPQ in predicting response to treatment among cocaine-addicted patients. High scores on ImpSS, N-Anx, and Agg-Host were found in those who continued to use drugs during the program, and high scorers had a higher percentage of dirty urine tests. High ImpSS scorers kept fewer treatment appointments and were less likely to stay in treatment for at least 1 month or to complete treatment. As in the study by Patkar et al. (2004), sensation seeking and impulsivity, separately or in combination, are indicators of a poor prognosis for treatment cooperation in cocaine users.

Maude-Griffin et al. (1998) compared the efficacy of CBT and the TSF treatment for urban crack cocaine abusers. Over 80% of the subjects were African American and unemployed. Follow-up assessments were done at 1, 2, 3, and 6 months. Participation was poor, with only 17% of the clients attending at least 75% of the group and individual sessions. CBT clients were more successful in achieving 4 consecutive weeks of abstinence, as verified by urine tests, than TSF clients, but the difference was not great (44% vs. 32%). The superiority of CBT was more pronounced in those clients who had major depression and those who had higher abstract reasoning scores. Among African Americans, those with high levels of religious belief did better in TSF.

Crits-Christoph et al. (1999) conducted a large, multicenter study comparing treatments for cocaine dependence. The sample was predominantly male (77%), 58% were White, and 40% were African American. Most smoked crack cocaine and had been using it for an average of 10 years. The four treatments were (a) individual drug counseling (IDC) plus group drug counseling (GDC); (b) cognitive therapy (CT) plus GDC; (c) supportive–expressive therapy (SET) plus GDC; and (d) GDC alone. The SET therapy was psychodynamic, involving both interpersonal and intrapsychic functions, and analyses of conflicts and defenses. The IDC and GDC were based on the philosophy of the 12-step program, with the idea of addiction as a disease and encouraging behavioral changes, avoiding drug inducing situations, and engaging in healthy behavior. Self-reports of drug use were checked against urine analyses with good agreement between the two assessments ($r = .64$). The hypothesis of the study was that professional psychotherapies (CT and SET) combined with GDC would be more effective than IDC with GTC and GTC alone. The results were just the opposite.

All treatments reduced drug use and achieved some abstinence, but the IDC plus GTC was superior to the other three groups in these effects. By the 6th month, about 40% of the IDC plus GDC group reported cocaine use in the past month contrasted with 58% in the CT plus GDC, 50% in the SET plus GDC, and 52% in the GDC alone groups. Three months of consecutive abstinence were achieved by 38% of the IDC plus GDC, 23% of the CT plus GDC, 18% of the SET plus GDC, and 27% of the GDC alone groups. The lower rate of drug use by the group treated by drug counselors and groups was still evident in the 9- and 12-month follow-up assessments. The superiority of individual plus group counseling to the other treatments might be attributed to the greater experience of the drug counselors and their specific training in dealing with drug abusers.

Summary

As was true for smoking prevention, providing knowledge alone or using scare tactics are not effective in preventing substance abuse. Media influences in antidrug messages depend on the techniques of information presentation. Messages designed to grab the attention of high sensation seekers and embedded in programs that they watch or listen to were more effective in getting them to call a hotline with information about treatment. They also are more effective in getting them to recall the content in the message. Such targeted media messages appear to have lowered the rates of marijuana use in some communities

Cognitive–behavioral intervention programs, involving the teaching of skills necessary to resist peer pressures to use drugs and enabling clients to exert self-control, reduce marijuana and other drug use and drinking in those who do all or most of the program. But these methods have little effect on those who quit the program early. Quitting rates are high in most substance abuse programs, and those quitting are most at risk because they typically started using drugs earlier than others and were already using drugs at the start of the study. The effect rates in the remainder may be exaggerated by this selection factor.

In conventional treatment programs for alcoholic individuals, the long-term results show little effect over the natural course of the disorder, with only a minority (typically about 20%) achieving abstinence over a long follow-up period. Different kinds of psychological treatments show little difference in terms of outcomes. Cognitive–behavioral programs teaching moderate drinking skills have shown some promising initial effects in problem drinkers among college students in reducing the overall level of drinking, but they do not affect the most serious kind of college drinking, episodic binge drinking.

A study directed at the different motivations for drinking in high sensation seekers and in highly anxious and depressed high school students found that binge drinking was reduced in high sensation seekers even though they did not achieve abstinence or anywhere near it. The anxious and depressed students were more likely to achieve abstinence, but binge drinking was not affected. However, binge drinking was more common in high sensation seekers than in anxious and depressed students before treatment.

Sensation seeking and impulsivity are indicators of poor prognosis for treatment in cocaine addiction. High sensation seekers tend to be uncooperative, they quit treatment early, and they test positive for drug use during treatment. A large study comparing the usual type of drug counseling with cognitive–behavioral and dynamic interpersonal therapies, all combined with group counseling therapy, found a superior outcome in clients getting standard drug counseling rather than the theory driven therapies.

Pharmacological treatments for alcoholism involving chemical block-age of opiate receptors reduce the reward effects of alcohol, and thereby reduce drinking. The combination of this treatment with behavioral therapy that is aimed at increasing coping skills actually had less effect than a combination of drug treatment with simple supportive therapy. Possibly, the typical clients in cocaine therapy are not candidates for more subtle therapies. But like all drug treatments, the drug helps in maintaining sobriety as long as the client's motivation is there to keep taking the drug. Therapy that enhances motivation and deals with life problems in a practical way may be more effective in combination with drugs that reduce the drug's reward effects.

RISKY SEX

The risks of unprotected sex are unwanted pregnancies and sexually transmitted diseases (STDs) including syphilis, gonorrhea, chlamydia, herpes, and AIDS. About 4% of female and 10% of male high school students have had sexual intercourse before age 13, and about 62% of both males and females have had sexual intercourse at least once by the senior year of high school (McGeveran, 2006). Close to a third report not using a condom during their last intercourse. This is not to say that the rest have been consistent in condom use. It is not surprising that about 30% of sexually active American adolescent females have had unintended pregnancies (Fisher, 1990). A history of pregnancy is found in about 20% of 9th through 12th grade students (Resnick et al., 1997). Apart from health problems, unwanted pregnancies create risks that go beyond birth in the form of unwanted children at increased risk for abuse and neglect.

STD infections are increasing in adolescents, and HIV infections are rising rapidly. A Canadian study of over 5,500 1st-year college students found the 5.5% of sexually active students reported at least one STD in their history, but this increased with number of partners to a high of 24.2% for those women who had 10 or more partners (MacDonald et al., 1990). The urgency of prevention of these diseases, particularly AIDS, is literally a life-or-death matter. More effective methods of contraception, like the birth control pill, while reducing the risk of pregnancy, increase the risk of disease when they are used instead of condoms (MacDonald et al., 1990). By reducing the inevitability of death from AIDS, the development of new treatments for the disease have led to an increase in sexual risk taking among gay men.

In chapter 5, I discussed the findings that sensation seeking was a predictor of risky sexual behavior among both heterosexual and homosexual individuals. Sensation seeking is nearly always related to the number of sexual partners and the willingness to engage in a variety of sexual activities like anal sex. For homosexual men, sensation seeking correlates with both the frequency of unprotected anal intercourse and the number of partners in this most risky kind of sex for HIV infection (Kalichman, Heckman, & Kelly, 1996). In an HIV-prevention study, the combination of sensation seeking and impulsivity was related to the use of alcohol before sex and the inability to refuse unsafe sex (Donohew et al., 2000). High sensation seekers are more accepting of risky behavior in potential partners and are even more attracted to sexual risk takers than low sensation seekers (Henderson et al., 2005). However, the high sensation seekers rate their chances of getting an STD infection after unprotected sex as lower than do low sensation seekers. Actually, about a fourth of sexually experienced adolescents contract an STD every year, and sensation seekers typically have more sexual experience. Despite this involvement of the sensation seeking motive in risky sex, designers of intervention studies rarely if ever include it or other personality traits as possible moderators of outcome. Bancroft et al. (2003) and Kalichman et al. (1996) argued for its inclusion in prevention studies.

Prevention Programs for Adolescents

Kirby (2002) reviewed the effectiveness of different approaches to reducing unprotected sex in adolescence. Some parents fear that any kind of program teaching safe sex, or even general sex education, will increase the likelihood of their children having sex. There is no evidence that such programs increase the incidence of sexual relations above what it is in untutored students. However, the evidence that such programs decrease the incidence of risky sexual behavior is inconsistent. Only about one third of the programs seemed to effect a delay in the initiation of sex, only about a quarter showed a reduction in the frequency of sexual activity, and only about a third found a reduction in the number of sexual partners. There is more consistency in programs directed at increasing condom use, particularly the specific HIV education programs. The three studies that were most methodologically sound, including large sample size, random assignment to experimental and control groups, and long-term follow-ups, demonstrated that sex and HIV education programs can delay sexual onset, decrease the frequency of sex, and increase condom or contraceptive use, with effects lasting at least 1 year.

A comparison of successful and unsuccessful programs revealed certain characteristics distinguishing the successful programs, including (a) concentrating on reduction of one or more risky sexual behaviors; (b) basing the program on theoretical approaches of proven effectiveness for other kinds of risky behaviors; (c) giving a clear message about condom or contraceptive use; (d) giving information about methods of avoiding intercourse or making it safer; (e) giving instruction in communication, negotiation, and refusal skills in dealing with partners; (f) lasting long enough to complete important components of the program; and (g) selecting teachers who believe in the program and training them.

Political pressures in recent years in the United States have promoted "abstinence only" programs without education in safe sex or the use of protection to minimize the risk in sex. None of these programs that used adequate controls and criteria for outcome showed a replicable effect on sexual behavior, although there was some change in attitudes (Kirby, 2002; Thomas, 1999). The withholding of safe-sex information in such programs is probably based on the mistaken notion that information increases the propensity to initiate sexual behavior. But even if the program is successful in changing attitudes toward premarital sex, there is no correlation between attitudes and actual abstinence in high school adolescents (Fisher, Fisher, & Rye, 1995).

Low-income African American youth are at particularly high risk for pregnancy and STDs, including AIDS (Centers for Disease Control and Prevention, 1996; Conway et al., 1993; Dicks, 1994; Hein, 1989; St. Lawrence et al., 1995). A sample of African American females (M age = 16) was involved in a study of the effectiveness of a program designed to promote condom use (Crosby et al., 2003). A history of pregnancy was reported by 40% of the subjects. Condom use was increased by the program, but a fifth of the sample was already pregnant at either the baseline or 6-month follow-up. Perceived barriers to condom use and the perception of norms supporting or denying condom use among peers were predictors of condom use. However, attitudes toward condom use and knowledge about STD/HIV prevention were not significant predictors.

Another study of low-income African Americans tested the effectiveness of two kinds of programs, an abstinence one and a safe-sex intervention, in a younger group (M age = 12 years) from middle schools in Philadelphia (Jemmott, Jemmott, & Fong, 1998). Interventions were theory based and culture sensitive. Subjects were randomly assigned to either an intervention program or a general health promotion group that served as a control for the targeted intervention groups. At a 12-month follow-up, there was no difference between groups in the percentage who had sexual intercourse, but the safe-sex intervention decreased the frequency of intercourse, particularly unprotected intercourse, among the sexually experienced at preintervention. The abstinence program did not reduce this kind of risky behavior or even decrease the number of subjects having sexual intercourse.

St. Lawrence et al. (1995) compared African American adolescents randomly assigned to an educational program that met only one time (control group) or a 8-week sexual education and behavioral ST program encouraging condom use and resistance to pressures for unprotected sex. Male adolescents in the extended treatment program showed a significant reduction in unprotected vaginal and anal intercourse. Rates for females were low to begin with, but the program reduced the increase in unprotected vaginal intercourse found in the education-only group. The ST reduced the rates of sexual activity in general and deterred the onset of activity for those who were abstinent at the time of entry into the program.

Drug abusers are especially vulnerable to STDs, HIV infection, and AIDS from needle sharing and from the general sexual promiscuity in the population (Darke, Baker, Dixon, Wodak, & Heather, 1992; A. J. Saxton & Calsyn, 1992). Intravenous drug users have the second highest rate of AIDS, second only to gay and bisexual men (Wright, 2002). A study of a predominantly White adolescent substance-dependent population compared three modes of treatment: information intervention only (I); information plus behavioral skills for safer sex (I + B); and information, skills training, and methods for increased motivation (M) through sensitization to the risk (I + B + M; St. Lawrence, Crosby, Brasfield, & O'Bannon, 2002). At the 12-month follow-up, all three programs showed a reduction in the number of sexual partners, with no difference between them. However, the two programs that trained behavioral skills were more effective in reducing unprotected vaginal intercourse, with an increase in condom use during intercourse. The extended programs also increased the percentage of those choosing abstinence. On all of these measures, the program adding sensitization to risk (I + B + M) was even more effective than the other behavioral program (I + B).

St. Lawrence, Crosby, Belcher, Yazdani, and Brasfield (1999) examined the effects of anger management and sexual risk reduction programs conducted with incarcerated male delinquents. At 6 months after release, the subjects in the sexual risk reduction program showed significantly less unprotected vaginal and anal intercourse and fewer sexual partners than the anger management program.

A large-scale college program was designed to reduce unintended pregnancies and decrease risk for STDs by promoting condom use at a large Canadian university (Fisher, 1990). The program involved dormitory-based lectures using videotapes and booklets designed to change students' feelings, thoughts, and fantasies about the use of condoms in sexual intercourse. To increase the availability of condoms, condom machines were installed in washrooms in student dormitories and in the student center. Up until the time of the program, the rate of positive pregnancy tests at the university was a steady 10 per 1,000 women per year. In the 1st year after the lectures were introduced, the rate dropped to 7.3, a 27.7% reduction, and in the next year, after the video and booklets were introduced, it dropped to 6.5, a further 11% reduction. The rate remained at this reduced level over the next 6 years. Although there was no control group, a comparison with abortion rates in the general Canadian population in women of similar age showed no significant reduction. There were no data on STDs, but if condom use was increased, as the evidence suggests, there would likely be a reduction in STD.

Adult Gay Men

In 1988, Stall, Coates, and Hoff reported that the widely accepted connection between risky sexual behavior and AIDS resulted in dramatic decreases in rates of gay men participating in unprotected anal intercourse. Unfortunately, this trend toward safer sex seems to be reversed in the gay population because of the development of drugs that promise interruption of what was the inevitable progression from HIV to AIDS. Younger men not exposed to the full brunt of the AIDS epidemic of the 1980s are now engaging in risky behavior. Earlier studies of gay men found that hearing a safe-sex lecture or reading a brochure, hearing advice from a physician about AIDS, or even counseling were not associated with the practice of safe sex (unpublished studies cited by Stall et al., 1988). Knowledge alone was not sufficient to deter some risk takers from engaging in unsafe sex even before the use of AIDS-controlling drugs.

Kelly, St. Lawrence, Hood, and Brasfield (1989) compared the results of a 12-week program consisting of group sessions providing information about risk practices, training in self-management and assertiveness in resisting pressure to have unsafe sex, with changes in a group waiting to receive the treatment program. At baseline, those in both groups used condoms in only about a fourth of their anal intercourse contacts. At a 4-month follow-up, the treatment groups reported using condoms in two thirds of their anal intercourse occasions compared with the control group that used condoms in only about a fifth of their anal intercourse acts. The improvement in the treatment groups was maintained to an 8-month follow-up. However, 16 months after the program, about 40% of those who were practicing safer sex had relapsed (Kelly, St. Lawrence, & Brasfied, 1991)

Kelly, St. Lawrence, Diaz, et al. (1991) studied the factors related to the relapse into unsafe practices. The most powerful predictor of relapse was their behavior before they began the program, including many partners, frequent unprotected anal sex, use of intoxicants before and during sexual activity, and reporting more pleasurable reward of anal intercourse without a condom and less pleasure with a condom. Relapsers reported less depression than those who continued to practice safe sex. The differences in risky sex before treatment lead to relapse after treatment, suggesting a risk-taking disposition, probably sensation seeking and impulsivity, involved in poor prognosis.

Kelly, St. Lawrence, Diaz, et al. (1991) reported the results of a communitywide survey of gay men in a small Mississippi community before and after exposure to an AIDS prevention program compared with figures from comparison cities. The program used leaders from the gay community as interveners among their peers. The program reduced unprotected anal intercourse and having sex with multiple partners in the intervention city compared with other cities. A 3-year follow-up of cities receiving the interventions showed that reductions in unsafe anal intercourse and sex with multiple partners was maintained over the longer follow-up interval (St. Lawrence et al., 1994).

The use of alcohol and drugs in high-risk sexual behavior suggests a causal relationship because one effect of these drugs is to disinhibit behavior. However, drugs and sex are part of a risk-taking disposition related to sensation seeking and may be simply correlated aspects of that disposition without any causal relationship (Leigh & Stall, 1993; Zuckerman & Kuhlman, 2000).

Summary

Only a third of the programs teaching safe sex actually reduce sexual behavior, but many show increases in the use of condoms as protection against pregnancy or infection. Programs that are more explicit in instructions in condom use and skills in dealing with partners who are reluctant to use them are usually more successful. Knowledge alone, as provided in health classes, may change attitudes but has little effect on sexual behavior. Information combined with skills training is effective. Abstinence-only programs are no more effective in preventing sexual activity among adolescents than safe-sex programs and leave them without information on how to protect themselves if they do begin sexual activity. At the least, safe-sex programs do not increase the number of sexually active adolescents beyond the normal increase with age. Safe-sex programs do decrease the incidence of unprotected vaginal and anal intercourse in those who are sexually active.

Gay men are a high-risk group for AIDS and other STDs because of the practice of unprotected anal intercourse with multiple partners (Ekstrand & Coates, 1990; Wright, 2002). Programs containing risk information, self-management, and skills in resisting unprotected sex increase the use of condoms in anal intercourse. However, there is a high rate of relapse back to unsafe sex, particularly in those who had this pattern before they entered the program.

Sensation seeking and impulsivity are involved in the risky types of sexual behavior but hardly any of the intervention studies have included personality measures. The sensation seeking motive should be addressed in intervention programs. In adolescents, alternative forms of sexual gratification that are less risky, such as mutual masturbation and oral sex, should be suggested as alternatives to coital sex. None of the programs described in this chapter said they include this kind of suggestion, although many adolescents realize there is an alternative to the sexual tension and frustration of total abstinence.

The unhealthy modes of risk taking in the pursuit of intense and novel sensations are probably influenced by a common genetic factor, the one producing a general sensation seeking personality. This is not to say that the modes of sensation seeking are not modifiable or at least displaceable. The particular expressions of sensation seeking are influenced by the specific environmental models and availabilities provided by peers and the media. Family influences are also important, although to some extent these represent genetic correlations rather than purely environmental influences.

Smoking, drinking, drugs, and sex are all correlated at the phenomenal level (Zuckerman & Kuhlman, 2000). Typically, they are all activities present in particular youth groups who attract the higher sensation seekers in any adolescent population. Prevention programs try to counteract the powerful influences of this type of peer culture by providing information on the potentially dangerous outcomes of smoking, heavy drinking, drug abuse, and risky sex. These rational appeals through simple information dissemination by authorities have little effect in reducing risky behaviors, although messages designed to attract the interest of high sensation seekers can at least get them to contact hotlines. More successful prevention programs go beyond mere information provision and engage the potential risk taker in social skills and assertiveness training necessary to resist peer pressures and, in the case of sex, training in safer sex like the use of condoms.

Preaching abstinence alone has little effect in preventing the initiation of sex, and programs teaching safe sex do not increase sexual activity. Abstinence alone leaves the failed abstainer open to pregnancy and STDs. Their message probably only reaches low sensation seekers who are already reluctant to experiment in sexuality. For those already active, they do not generally result in a cessation of sexual activity.

Treatment of those already smoking, drinking, using drugs, and engaging in coital sex involves many of the same methods that are used in prevention programs. As with prevention, information alone is not sufficient to interrupt risky patterns of behavior already established, like smoking, binge drinking, drug use, and risky sex. However, programs that also include training in self-management and interpersonal skills necessary in reducing peer pressures have some success. One problem is the high drop-out rate in such programs, and another is the high relapse rate. Total abstinence is the goal of most smoking and drug-abuse programs, but this is only achieved in a minority of clients, at most about a fifth of those who actually participate in and complete the programs. Reduction in substance use is a more common result of substance abuse programs, and an increase in protected sex or condom use is more common in the safe-sex programs.

Sensation seeking and impulsivity are probably involved in the prognosis for treatment programs. They do predict a negative outcome in the treatment of cocaine abuse, but they have not been widely used in intervention research in other areas. Generally, those more heavily involved in substance abuse and unsafe sexual practices before treatment are most likely to relapse after treatment. Studies of the correlates of risky behaviors described in earlier chapters have shown that more severe addiction and risk taking are related to higher levels of sensation seeking personality. Treatment of this group should attempt to address the motivation of sensation seeking as an obstacle to successful intervention.

In my experience in treating drug abusers in a therapeutic community, the question of postdrug life frequently came up. Giving up drugs and association with those still using drugs left few alternatives for expression of their sensation seeking needs. Socializing at church, working at a monotonous 9-to-5 job, and settling down in a monogamous relationship did not offer a happy prospect for them. Drinking, gambling, motorcycles, and sexual variety offered legal alternatives to drug use but posed their own possibilities for addiction and harm. Very few programs offer healthy substitutes for unhealthy expressions of sensation seeking.

I started this chapter with the assertion that it is difficult to change a basic personality trait like sensation seeking. However, there is one treatment that does change this trait: age. Almost everyone becomes more conservative, cautious, law abiding, and risk aversive with age. These changes are usually attributed to the accumulation of wisdom, but they may also represent changes in biology. The forebrain finally masters the mesolimbic dopamine system. But many change unhealthy and risky behaviors even without the help of therapy. Therapists should find out how they do it.

REFERENCES

Abraham, H. D., McCann, U. D., & Ricaurte, G. A. (2002). Psychodelic drugs. In K. L. Davis, J. T. Coyle, & C. Nemeroff (Eds.), *Neuropsychopharmacology: The fifth generation of progress* (pp. 1545–1556). Philadelphia: Lippincott Williams & Wilkins

Adolfsson, R., Gottfries, C. G., Oreland, L., Roos, B. E., & Winblad, B. (1978). Monoamine oxidase activity and serotonergic turnover in human brain. *Progress in Neuropsychopharmacology, 2*, 225–230.

Ahern, F. M., Johnson, R. C., Wilson, J. R., McClearn, G. E., & Vandenberg, S. G. (1982). Family resemblances in personality. *Behavior Genetics, 12*, 261–280.

Alm, P. O., Alm, M., Humble, K., Lippert, J., Sörensen, S., Lidberg, L., & Oreland, L. (1994). Criminality and platelet monoamine oxidase activity in some former juvenile delinquents as adults. *Acta Psychiatrica Scandinavica, 89*, 41–45.

Aluja, A., & Garcia, L. F. (2005). Sensation seeking, sexual curiosity, and testosterone in inmates. *Neuropsychobiology, 51*, 28–33.

Aluja, A., Rossier, J., Garcia, L. F., Angleitner, A., Kuhlman, M., & Zuckerman, M. (2006). A cross-cultural shortened form of the ZKPQ (ZKPQ-50–CC) adapted to English, French, German, and Spanish languages. *Personality and Individual Differences, 41*, 619–628.

Aluja, A., & Torrubia, R. (2004). Hostility–aggressiveness, sensation seeking, and sexual hormones in men: Reexploring their relationship. *Neuropsychobiology, 50*, 102–107.

American Cancer Society. (1986). *Cancer facts and figures*. New York: Author.

The American Heritage college dictionary (3rd ed.). (1977). Boston: Houghton Mifflin.

American Psychiatric Association. (1952). *Diagnostic and statistical manual of mental disorders*. Washington, DC: Author.

American Psychiatric Association. (1968). *Diagnostic and statistical manual of mental disorders* (2nd ed.). Washington, DC: Author

American Psychiatric Association. (1980). *Diagnostic and statistical manual of mental disorders* (3rd ed.). Washington, DC: Author.

American Psychiatric Association. (1987). *Diagnostic and statistical manual of mental disorders* (3rd ed., rev.). Washington, DC: Author.

American Psychiatric Association. (1994). *Diagnostic and statistical manual of mental disorders* (4th ed.). Washington, DC: Author.

Ames, S. L., Sussman, S., & Dent, C. W. (1999). Pro-drug use myths and competing constructs in the prediction of substance use among youth at continuation high schools: A one-year prospective study. *Personality and Individual Differences, 26*, 987–1003.

Ames, S. L., Zogg, J. B., & Stacy, A. W. (2002). Implicit cognition, sensation seeking, marijuana use, and driving behavior among drug offenders. *Personality and Individual Differences, 33,* 1055–1072.

Andrew, M., & Cronin, C. (1997). Two measures of sensation seeking as predictors of alcohol use among high school males. *Personality and Individual Differences, 22,* 393–401.

Andrucci, G. L., Archer, R. P., Pancoast, D. L., & Gordon, R. A. (1989). The relationship of MMPI and sensation seeking scales to adolescent drug use. *Journal of Personality Assessment, 53,* 253–266.

Anthony, J. C. (2002). Epidemiology of drug dependence. In K. L. Davis, D. Charney, & J. T. Nemeroff (Eds.), *Neuropsychopharmacology: The fifth generation of progress* (pp. 1557–1574). Philadelphia: Lippincott Williams & Wilkins.

Anton, R. F., Moak, D. H., Wald, R., & Latham, P. K. (1999). Naltrexone and cognitive behavioral therapy for the treatment of outpatient alcoholics. *American Journal of Psychiatry, 156,* 1758–1764.

Apter, M. J. (1982). *The experience of motivation: The theory of psychological reversals.* London: Academic Press.

Arnett, J. (1991). Still crazy after all these years: Reckless behavior among young adults aged 23–27. *Personality and Individual Differences, 12,* 1305–1313.

Arnett, J. (1992). Reckless behavior in adolescence: A developmental perspective. *Developmental Review, 12,* 339–373.

Arnett, J. (1994). Sensation seeking: A new conceptualization and a new scale. *Personality and Individual Differences, 16,* 289–296.

Arnett, J. (1996). Sensation seeking, aggressiveness, and adolescent reckless behavior. *Personality and Individual Differences, 20,* 693–702.

Arnett, J. (1998). Risk behavior and family role transitions during the twenties. *Journal of Youth and Adolescence, 27,* 301–320.

Arnett, J. (2000). Emerging adulthood: A theory of development from the late teens through the twenties. *American Psychologist, 55,* 469–480.

Arnett, J., Offer, D., & Fine, M. A. (1997). Reckless driving in adolescence: "State" and "trait" factors. *Accident Analysis and Prevention, 29,* 57–63.

Arnold, P., Fletcher, S., & Farrow, R. (2002). Condom use and psychological sensation seeking by college students. *Sexual and Relationship Therapy, 17,* 355–366.

Arqué, J. M., Unzeta, M., & Torrubia, R. (1988). Neurotransmitter systems and personality variables. *Neuropsychobiology, 19,* 149–157.

Baer, J. S. (2002, March). Student factors: Understanding individual variation in college drinking. *Journal of Studies on Alcohol* (Suppl. 14), 40–53.

Bagby, R. M., Costa, P. T., Jr., Widiger, T. A., Ryder, A. G., & Marshall, M. (2005). *DSM–IV* personality disorders and the five-factor model of personality: A multidimensional examination of domain- and facet-level predictions. *European Journal of Personality, 19,* 307–324.

Baker, J. R., & Yardley, J. K. (2002). Moderating effect of gender on the relationship between sensation seeking–impulsivity and substance use in adolescents. *Journal of Child and Adolescent Substance Abuse, 12,* 27–43.

Ball, L., Farnill, D., & Wangeman, J. (1983). Factorial invariance across sex of the Form V of the Sensation Seeking Scale. *Journal of Personality and Social Psychology, 45,* 1156–1159.

Ball, S. A. (1995). The validity of an alternative five-factor measure of personality in cocaine abusers. *Psychological Assessment, 7,* 148–154.

Ball, S. A., Carroll, K. M., Barbor, T. F., & Rounsaville, B. J. (1995). Subtypes of cocaine abusers: Support for a Type A–Type B distinction. *Journal of Consulting and Clinical Psychology, 63,* 115–124.

Ball, S. A., Carroll, K. M., & Rounsaville, B. J. (1994). Sensation seeking, substance abuse, and psychopathology in treatment seeking and community cocaine abusers. *Journal of Consulting and Clinical Psychology, 62,* 1053–1057.

Ballenger, J. C., Post, R. M., Jimerson, D. C., Lake, C. R., Murphy, D. L., Zuckerman, M., & Cronin, C. (1983). Biochemical correlates of personality traits in normals: An exploratory study. *Personality and Individual Differences, 4,* 615–625.

Bancroft, J., Janssen, E., Strong, D., Carnes, L., Vuladinovic, Z., & Long, J. S. (2003). Sexual risk-taking in gay men: The relevance of sexual arousability, mood, and sensation seeking. *Archives of Sexual Behavior, 32,* 555–572.

Barlow, D. H. (1988). *Anxiety and its disorders.* New York: Guilford Press.

Barratt, E. S. (1985). Impulsiveness subtraits: Arousal and information processing. In J. T. Spence & C. E. Izard (Eds.), *Motivation, emotion, and personality* (pp. 137–146). Amsterdam: Elsevier Science.

Barron, F. (1953). Complexity–simplicity as a personality dimension. *Journal of Abnormal and Social Psychology, 48,* 163–172.

Barron, F., & Welsh, G. S. (1952). Artistic perception as a possible factor in personality style: Its measurement by a figure preference test. *Journal of Psychology: Interdisciplinary and Applied, 33,* 199–203.

Bates, M. E., White, H. R., & Labouvie, E. W. (1985, August). *A longitudinal study of sensation seeking needs and drug use.* Paper presented at the 93rd Annual Convention of the American Psychological Association, Los Angeles.

Beaubrun, M. H. (1967). Treatment of alcoholism in Trinidad and Tobago. *British Journal of Psychiatry, 113,* 643–58

Beck, K. H., Thombs, D. L., Mahoney, C. A., & Finger, K. M. (1995). Social context and sensation seeking: Gender differences in college student drinking motivations. *International Journal of the Addictions, 30,* 1101–1115.

Belfrage, H., Lidberg, L., & Oreland, L. (1992). Platelet monoamine oxidase activity in mentally disordered violent offenders. *Acta Psychiatrica Scandinavica, 85,* 218–221.

Bell, N. J., Schoenrock, C. J., & O'Neal, K. K. (2000). Self-monitoring and the propensity for risk. *European Journal of Personality, 14,* 107–119.

Benjamin, J., Ebstein, R. P., & Belmaker, R. H. (Eds.). (2002). *Molecular genetics and the human personality*. Washington, DC: American Psychiatric Publishing.

Benschop, A., Rabes, M., & Korf, D. J. (2003). *Pill testing ecstasy and prevention: A scientific evaluation in three European cities*. Amsterdam: Rozenberg Publishers.

Benthin, A., Slovic, P., Moran, P., Severson, H., Mertz, C. K., & Gerrand, M. (2000). Adolescent health-threatening and health-enhancing behaviors: A study of word association. In P. Slovic (Ed.), *The perception of risk* (pp. 327–340). London: Earthscan.

Best, C. L., & Kilpatrick, D. G. (1977). Psychological profiles of rape crisis counselors. *Psychological Reports, 40*, 1127–1134.

Biersner, R. J., & LaRocco, J. M. (1983). Personality characteristics of U.S. Navy divers. *Journal of Occupational Psychology, 56*, 329–334.

Björk-Åkesson, E. (1990). *Measuring sensation seeking: Göteborg Studies in Educational Sciences, 75*. Göteborg, Sweden: Acta Universitatis Gothobrugensis.

Blanco, C., Orensanz-Munoz, L., Blanco-Jerez, C., & Saiz-Ruiz, J. (1996). Pathological gambling and platelet MAO activity: A psychobiological study. *American Journal of Psychiatry, 153*, 119–121.

Blaszczynski, A. P., Wilson, A. C., & McConaghy, N. (1986). Sensation seeking and pathological gambling. *British Journal of Addiction, 81*, 113–117.

Block, J. (1995). A contrarian view of the five-factor approach to personality description. *Psychological Bulletin, 117*, 187–215.

Blonigen, D. M., Carlson, S. R., Krueger, R. F., & Patrick, C. J. (2003). A twin study of self-reported psychopathic personality traits. *Personality and Individual Differences, 35*, 179–197.

Bogaert, A. F. (1996). Volunteer bias in human sexuality research: Evidence for both sexuality and personality differences in males. *Archives of Sexual Behavior, 25*, 125–140.

Bogaert, A. F., & Fisher, W. A. (1995). Predictors of university men's number of sexual partners. *Journal of Sex Research, 32*, 119–130.

Bohman, M. (1996). Predisposition to criminality: Swedish adoption studies in retrospect. In G. R. Bock & J. A. Goode (Eds.), *Genetics of criminal and antisocial behaviour* (pp. 99–109). Chichester, England: Wiley.

Boomsma, D. I., de Geus, E. J. C., van Baal, G. C. M., & Koopmans, J. R. (1999). A religious upbringing reduces the influence of genetic factors on disinhibition: Evidence of interaction between genotype and environment on personality. *Twin Research, 2*, 115–125.

Botvin, G. J., Baker, E., Dusenbury, L., Botvin, E. M., & Diaz, T. (1995). Long-term follow-up results of a randomized drug abuse prevention trial in a White middle-class population. *Journal of the American Medical Association, 273*, 1106–1112.

Botvin, G. J., Baker, E., Dusenbury, L., Tortu, S., & Botvin, E. M. (1990). Preventing adolescent drug abuse through a multimodal cognitive behavioral approach:

Results of a 3-year study. *Journal of Consulting and Clinical Psychology, 58,* 437–446.

Botvin, G. J., & Griffin, K. W. (2004). Life skills training: Empirical findings and future directions. *The Journal of Primary Prevention, 25,* 211–232.

Bouchard, T. J., Jr. (1994, June 17). Genes, environment, and personality. *Science, 264,* 1700–1701.

Bouchard, T. J., Jr., & McGue, M. (2003). Genetic and environmental influences on human psychological differences. *Journal of Neurobiology, 54,* 4–45.

Bouter, L. M., Knipschild, P. G., Feij, J. A., & Volovics, A. (1988). Sensation seeking and injury risk in downhill skiing. *Personality and Individual Differences, 9,* 667–673.

Bozarth, M. A. (1987). Ventral tegmental reward system. In J. Engel, L. Oreland, B. Pernor, S. Rössner, & L. A. Pelhorn (Eds.), *Brain reward systems and abuse* (pp. 1–17). New York: Raven Press.

Bradley, G., & Wildman, K. (2002). Psychosocial predictors of emerging adults' risk and reckless behaviors. *Journal of Youth and Adolescence, 31,* 253–265.

Brain, P. F. (1983). Pituitary–gonadal influences on social aggression. In B. B. Svare (Ed.), *Hormones and aggressive behavior* (pp. 1–26). New York: Plenum Press.

Bratko, D., & Butkovic, A. (2003). Family study of sensation seeking. *Personality and Individual Differences, 35,* 1559–1570.

Breivik, G. (1991). [Personality and sensation seeking in risk sport: A summary]. Unpublished raw data.

Breivik, G., Roth, W. T., & Jorgensen, P. E. (1998). Personality, psychological states, and heart rate in novice and expert parachutists. *Personality and Individual Differences, 25,* 365–380.

Breuer, J., & Freud, S. (1955). *Studies on hysteria* (J. Strachey & A. Freud, Trans.). London: Hogarth Press. (Original work published 1895)

Briggs, M., & Briggs, M. (1972). Relationships between monoamine oxidase activity and sex hormone concentration in human blood plasma. *Journal of Reproduction and Fertility, 29,* 447–450.

Brocke, B., Beauducel, A., John, R., Debener, S., & Heilemann, H. (2000). Sensation seeking and affective disorders: Characteristics in the intensity dependence of acoustic evoked potentials. *Neuropsychobiology, 41,* 24–30.

Brooner, R. K., King, V. L., Kidorf, M., Schmidt, C. W., & Bigelow, G. E. (1997). Psychiatric and substance use comorbidity among treatment-seeking opioid abusers. *Archives of General Psychiatry, 54,* 71–79.

Brown, G. L., Ebert, M. H., Gover, P. F., Jimerson, D. C., Klein, W. J., Bunney, W. E., & Goodman, F. K. (1982). Aggression, suicide, and serotonin: Relationships to CSF amine metabolites. *American Journal of Psychiatry, 139,* 741–746.

Brown, G. L., Goodwin, F. K., Ballenger, J. C., Goyer, P. F., & Major, L. F. (1979). Aggression in humans correlates with cerebrospinal fluid amine metabolites. *Psychiatry Research, 1,* 131–139.

Bruvold, W. H. (1993). A meta-analysis of adolescent smoking prevention programs. *American Journal of Public Health, 83,* 872–880.

Bryan, A., & Stallings, M. C. (2002). A case control study of adolescent risky behavior and its relationship to personality dimensions, conduct disorder and substance use. *Journal of Youth and Adolescence, 31,* 387–396.

Buchsbaum, M. S. (1971, April 30). Neural events and the psychophysical law. *Science, 172,* 502.

Buchsbaum, M. S., & Silverman, J. (1968). Stimulus intensity control and the cortical evoked response. *Psychosomatic Medicine, 30,* 12–22.

Burns, P. C., & Wilde, G. J. S. (1995). Risk taking in male taxi drivers: Relationships among personality, observational data, and drive records. *Personality and Individual Differences, 18,* 267–278.

Buss, A. H., & Durkee, A. (1957). An inventory for assessing different kinds of hostility. *Journal of Consulting Psychology, 21,* 343–349.

Buss, D. M., Abbott, M., Angleitner, A., Asherian, A., Biaggio, A., Blanco-Villasenor, A., et al. (1990). International preferences for selecting mates: A study of 37 cultures. *Journal of Cross-Cultural Psychology, 48,* 247–249.

Cadoret, R. J., Yates, W. R., Troughton, E., Woodworth, G., & Stewart, M. A. (1995). Genetic environmental interaction in the genesis of aggressivity and conduct disorders. *Archives of General Psychiatry, 52,* 916–924.

Cadoret, R. J., Yates, W. R., Troughten, E., Yates, W. R., & Stewart, M. A. (1995). Adoption study demonstrating two genetic pathways to drug abuse. *Archives of General Psychiatry, 52,* 42–52.

Caldwell, C. B., & Gottesman, I. I. (1991). Sex differences in the risk for alcoholism: A twin study. *Behavior Genetics, 6,* 563.

Calhoon, L. L. (1988). Explanations in the biochemistry of sensation seeking. *Personality and Individual Differences, 9,* 941–949.

Campbell, J. B., Tyrrell, D. J., & Zingaro, M. (1993). Sensation seeking among whitewater canoe and kayak paddlers. *Personality and Individual Differences, 14,* 489–491.

Caputo, P. (1977). *Rumor of war.* New York: Ballantine Books.

Carrasco, J. L., Saiz-Ruiz, J., Hollander, E., César, J., & Loper-Ibor, J. J., Jr. (1994). Low platelet monoamine oxidase activity in pathological gambling. *Acta Psychiatrica Scandinavica, 90,* 427–431.

Carrol, E. N., & Zuckerman, M. (1977). Psychopathology and sensation seeking in "downers," "speeders," and "trippers": A study of the relationships between personality and drug choice. *International Journal of the Addictions, 12,* 591–601.

Carrol, E. N., Zuckerman, M., & Vogel, W. H. (1982). A test of the optimal level of arousal theory of sensation seeking. *Journal of Personality and Social Psychology, 42,* 572–575.

Carton, S., Jouvent, R., & Widlöcher, D. (1994). Sensation seeking, nicotine dependence, and smoking motivation in female and male smokers. *Addictive Behaviors, 19,* 219–227.

Caspi, A., Begg, D., Dickerson, N., Harrington, H. L., Langley, J., Moffitt, T. E., & Silva, P. A. (1997). Personality differences predict health-risk behaviors in young adulthood: Evidence from a longitudinal study. *Journal of Personality and Social Psychology, 73,* 1052–1063.

Caspi, A., McClay, J., Moffitt, T. E., Mill, J., Martin, J., Craig, I. W., et al. (2002, August 2). Role of genotype in the cycle of violence in maltreated children. *Science, 297,* 851–853.

Centers for Disease Control and Prevention. (1996). *HIV/AIDS Surveillance Report: U.S. HIV and AIDS cases reported through June 1996.* Atlanta, GA: U.S. Department of Health and Human Services, Public Health Services.

Charney, D. S., & Drevets, W. (2002). The neurological basis of anxiety disorders. In K. L. Davis, D. Charney, J. T. Coyle, & C. Nemeroff (Eds.), *Neuropsychopharmacology: The fifth generation of progress* (pp. 901–930). Philadelphia: Lippincott Williams & Wilkins.

Charney, D. S., Heninger, G. R., & Breier, A. (1984). Noradrenergic function in panic anxiety. *Archives of General Psychiatry, 41,* 751–763.

Cherpital, C. J., Meyers, A. R., & Perrine, M. W. (1998). Alcohol consumption, sensation seeking, and ski injury: A case study control. *Journal of Studies on Alcohol, 59,* 218–221.

Chirivella, E. C., & Martinez, L. M. (1994). The sensation of risk and motivational tendencies in sports: An empirical study. *Personality and Individual Differences, 16,* 777–786.

Chng, C. L., & Géliga-Vargas, J. (2000). Ethnic identity, gay identity, sexual sensation seeking and HIV risk taking among multiethnic men who have sex with men. *AIDS Education and Prevention, 12,* 326–339.

Clavel, F., Benhamou, S., Huertas, A., & Flamant, R. (1985). Helping people to stop smoking: Randomized comparison of groups being treated with acupuncture and nicotine gum. *British Medical Journal, 291,* 1538–1539.

Cleckley, H. (1976). *The mask of sanity* (5th ed.). St. Louis, MO: Mosby.

Clement, R., & Jonah, B. A. (1984). Field dependence, sensation seeking, and driving behaviour. *Personality and Individual Differences, 5,* 87–93.

Cloninger, C. R. (1987a, April 24). Neurogenic adaptive mechanisms in alcoholism. *Science, 236,* 410–416.

Cloninger, C. R. (1987b). A systematic method for clinical description and classification of personality variants. *Archives of General Psychiatry, 44,* 573–588.

Cloninger, C. R., & Gottesman, I. I. (1987). Genetic and environmental factors in antisocial behavior. In S. A. Mednick, T. E. Moffitt, & S. A. Stack (Eds.), *The causes of crime: New biological approaches* (pp. 92–109). Cambridge, England: Cambridge University Press.

Cloninger, C. R., Sigvardsson, S., & Bohman, M. (1988). Childhood personality predicts alcohol abuse in young adults. *Alcoholism: Clinical and Experimental Research, 12,* 494–505.

Cloninger, C. R., Svrakic, D. M., & Przybeck, T. R. (1993). A psychobiological model of temperament and character. *Archives of General Psychiatry, 50*, 975–990.

Coccaro, E. F., Siever, L. J., Klar, H. M., Maurer, G., Cochrane, K., Cooper, T. B., et al. (1989). Serotonergic studies in patients with affective and personality disorders: Correlates with suicidal and impulsive aggressive behavior. *Archives of General Psychiatry, 46*, 587–599.

Coccini, T., Castoldi, A. F., Gandini, C., Randine, G., Vittadini, G., Baiardi, P., & Mango, L. (2002). Platelet monoamine oxidase B activity as a state marker for alcoholism: Trend over time during withdrawal and influence of smoking and gender. *Alcohol and Alcoholism, 37*, 566–572.

Cohen, E. S., & Fromme, K. (2002). Differential determinants of young adult substance use and high risk sexual behavior. *Journal of Applied Social Psychology, 32*, 1124–1150.

Cohen, S., Lichtenstein, E., Prochaska, J. O., Rossi, J. S., Gritz, E. R., Carr, C. R., et al. (1989). Debunking myths about self-quitting: Evidence from 10 prospective studies of persons quitting smoking by themselves. *American Psychologist, 44*, 1355–1365

Comings, D. E., Saucier, G., & MacMurray, J. P. (2002). Role of DRD2 and other dopamine genes in personality traits. In J. Benjamin, R. P. Ebstein, & R. H. Belmaker (Eds.), *Molecular genetics and the human personality* (pp. 165–191). Washington, DC: American Psychiatric Association.

Connolly, P. M. (1981). *An exploratory study of adults engaging in the high-risk sport of skiing.* Unpublished master's thesis, Rutgers University, Brunswick, New Jersey.

Conrod, P. J., Pihl, R. O., Stewart, S. H., & Dongier, M. (2000). Validation of a system of classifying female substance abusers on the basis of personality and motivational risk factors for substance abuse. *Psychology of Addictive Behaviors, 14*, 243–256.

Conway, G. A., Epstein, M. R., Hayman, C. R., Miller, C. A., Wendell, D. A., Gwin, M., et al. (1993). Trends in HIV prevalence among disadvantaged youth. *Journal of the American Medical Association, 269*, 2287–2289.

Cooper, M. L., Wood, P. K., Orcutt, H. K., & Albino, A. (2003). Personality and the predisposition to engage in risky or problem behavior. *Journal of Personality and Social Psychology, 84*, 390–410.

Costa, P. T., Jr., & McCrae, R. R. (1992a). Four ways five factors are basic. *Personality and Individual Differences, 13*, 653–665.

Costa, P. T., Jr., & McCrae, R. R. (1992b). *NEO-PI-R: Revised NEO Personality Inventory.* Odessa, FL: Psychological Assessment Resources.

Coursey, R. D., Buchsbaum, M. S., & Murphy, D. L. (1979). Platelet MAO activity and evoked potentials in the identification of subjects biologically at risk for psychiatric disorders. *British Journal of Psychiatry, 134*, 372–381.

Craig, R. J. (1982). Personality characteristics of heroin addicts: Review of empirical research 1976–1979. *International Journal of the Addictions, 17*, 227–248.

Craig, R. J. (1986). The personality structure of heroin addicts. *National Institute on Drug Abuse Research Monograph Series, 74,* 25–36.

Crawford, A. M., Pentz, M. A., Chou, C.-P., Li, C., & Dwyer, J. H. (2003). *Psychology of Addictive Behaviors, 17,* 179–192.

Crits-Christoph, P., Siqueland, L., Blaine, J., Frank, A., Luborsky, L., Onken, L. S., et al. (1999). Psychosocial treatments for cocaine dependence: National Institute on Drug Abuse collaborative treatment study. *Archives of General Psychiatry, 56,* 493–502.

Cronbach, L. J., & Meehl, P. E. (1955). Construct validity in psychological tests. *Psychological Bulletin, 52,* 281–302.

Cronin, C. (1991). Sensation seeking among mountain climbers. *Personality and Individual Differences, 12,* 653–654.

Cronin, C., & Zuckerman, M. (1992). Sensation seeking and bipolar affective disorder. *Personality and Individual Differences, 13,* 385–387.

Crosby, R. A., Di Clemente, R. J., Wingood, G. M., Salazar, L. F., Harrington, K., Davies, S. L., & Oh, M. K. (2003). Identification strategies for promoting condom use: A prospective analysis of high-risk African American female twins. *Prevention Science, 4,* 263–270.

Curry, S. J., Ludman, E. J., & McClure, J. (2003). Self-administered treatment for smoking cessation. *Journal of Clinical Psychology, 59,* 305–319.

Dabbs, J. M., Hopper, C. H., & Jurkovic, B. J. (1990). Testosterone and personality among college students and military veterans. *Personality and Individual Differences, 11,* 1263–1269.

Daitzman, R. J., & Zuckerman, M. (1980). Disinhibitory sensation seeking, personality, and gonadal hormones. *Personality and Individual Differences, 1,* 103–110.

Daitzman, R. J., Zuckerman, M., Sammelwitz, P. H., & Ganjam, V. (1978). Sensation seeking and gonadal hormones. *Journal of Biosocial Science, 10,* 401–408.

Damsma, G., Day, J., & Fibiger, H. C. (1989). Lack of tolerance to nicotine-induced dopamine release in the nucleus accumbens. *European Journal of Pharmacology, 168,* 363–368.

D'Angio, M., Serrano, A., Driscoll, P., & Scatton, B. (1988). Stressful environmental stimuli increase extracellular DOPAC levels in the prefrontal cortex of hypoemotional (Roman high-avoidance) but not hyperemotional (Roman low-avoidance) rats: An in vivo voltemetric study. *Brain Research, 451,* 237–247.

Darke, S., Baker, A., Dixon, J., Wodak, A., & Heather, N. (1992). Drug use and HIV risk-taking behavior among clients in methadone maintenance treatment. *Drug and Alcohol Dependence, 29,* 263–268.

Daumann, J., Pelz, S., Becker, S., Tuchtenhagen, F., & Gonzoulis-Mayfrank, E. (2001). Psychological profile of abstinent recreational Ecstacy (MDMA) users and significance of concomitant cannabis use. *Human Psychopharmacology: Clinical and Experimental, 16,* 627–633.

Davidson, D., Palfai, T., Bird, C., & Swift, R. (1999). Effects of natrexone on alcohol self-administration in heavy drinkers. *Alcoholism: Clinical and Experimental Research, 23*, 195–203.

Davidson, S. (1972, September 10). [Untitled article]. *New York Times*, p. SM32.

Davis, C., Cowles, M., & Kohn, P. (1983). Strength of the nervous system and augmenting–reducing: Paradox lost. *Personality and Individual Differences, 4*, 491–498.

Davis, C., & Mogk, J. P. (1994). Some personality correlates of interest and excellence in sport. *International Journal of Sport Psychology, 25*, 131–143.

Del Boca, F. K., Darkes, J., Greenbaum, P. E., & Goldman, M. S. (2004). Up close and personal: Temporal variability in the drinking of individual college students during their first year. *Journal of Consulting and Clinical Psychology, 72*, 155–164.

Dellu, F., Piazza, P. V, Mayo, W., Le Moal, M., & Simon, H. (1996). Novelty-seeking in rats—Biobehavioral characteristics and possible relationship with the sensation seeking trait in man. *Neuropsychobiology, 34*, 136–145.

Depue, R. A. (1995). Neurobiological factors in personality and depression. *European Journal of Personality, 9*, 413–439.

Deutch, A. Y., & Roth, R. H. (1999). Neurochemical systems in the central nervous system. In D. S. Charney, E. J. Nestler, & B. S. Bunney (Eds.), *Neurobiology of mental illness* (pp. 10–25). New York: Oxford University Press.

Díaz-Marsá, M., Carrasco, J. L., Hollander, E., César, J., & Saiz-Ruiz, J. (2000). Decreased platelet monoamine oxidase activity in female anorexic nervosa. *Acta Psychiatrica Scandinavica, 101*, 226–230.

Dickerson, M., Hinchy, J., & Fabre, J. (1987). Chasing, arousal, and sensation seeking in off-course gamblers. *British Journal of Addiction, 82*, 673–680.

Dicks, B. A. (1994). African American women and AIDS: A public health/social work challenge. In B. A. Dicks (Ed.), *Social work in health care* (pp. 123–143). New York: Haworth Press.

Diehm, R., & Armatas, C. (2004). Surfing: An avenue for socially acceptable risk-taking, satisfying needs for sensation seeking and experience seeking. *Personality and Individual Differences, 36*, 663–677.

Dolezal, C., Meyer-Bahlburg, H. E. L., Remien, R. H., & Petkova, E. (1997). Substance use during sex and sensation seeking as predictors of sexual risk behavior among HIV+ and HIV– gay men. *AIDS and Behavior, 1*, 19–28.

Dollard, J., & Miller, N. E. (1950). *Personality and psychotherapy: An analysis in terms of learning, thinking, and culture.* New York: McGraw-Hill.

Donaldson, S. (1989). Similarity in sensation-seeking, sexual satisfaction, and contentment in relationship in heterosexual couples. *Psychological Reports, 64*, 405–406.

Donnellan, M. B., Conger, R. D., & Bryant, M. (2004). The Big Five and enduring marriages. *Journal of Research in Personality, 38*, 481–504.

Donohew, L., Bardo, M. T., & Zimmerman, R. S. (2004). Personality and risky behavior: Communication and prevention. In R. M. Stelmack (Ed.), *On the psychobiology of personality: Essays in honor of Marvin Zuckerman* (pp. 223–245). New York: Elsevier.

Donohew, L., Clayton, R. R., Skinner, W. F., & Colon, S. (1999). Peer networks and sensation seeking: Some implications for primary socialization theory. *Substance Use and Misuse, 34,* 1013–1023.

Donohew, L., Lorch, E., & Palmgreen, P. (1991). Sensation seeking and targeting of televised anti-drug PSAs. In L. Donohew, H. E. Sypher, & W. Bullenski (Eds.), *Persuasive communication and drug abuse prevention* (pp. 209–226). Hillsdale, NJ: Erlbaum.

Donohew, L., Palmgreen, P. L., & Lorch, E. P. (1994). Attention, need for sensation, and health communication campaigns. *The American Behavioral Scientist, 38,* 310–322.

Donohew, L., Zimmerman, R., Cupp, P. S., Novak, S., Colon, S., & Abell, R. (2000). Sensation seeking, impulsive decision-making, and risky sex: Implications for risk-taking and design of interventions. *Personality and Individual Differences, 28,* 1079–1091.

Donovan, D. M., & Marlatt, G. A. (1982). Personality subtypes among driving while intoxicated offenders: Relationship to drinking behavior and driving risk. *Journal of Consulting and Clinical Psychology, 50,* 241–249.

Donovan, D. M., Queisser, H. R., Salzberg, P. M., & Umlauf, R. L. (1985). Intoxicated and bad drivers: Subgroups within the same population of high-risk men drivers. *Journal of Studies on Alcohol, 46,* 375–382.

Dostoevsky, F. (2003). *The gambler* (C. Garnett, Trans.). New York: Modern Library. (Original work published 1866)

Douglass, F. M., & Khavari, K. A. (1978). The drug use index: A measure of the extent of polydrug use. *International Journal of the Addictions, 13,* 981–993.

Dragutinovich, S. (1987). Stimulus intensity reducers: Are they sensation seekers, extraverts, and strong nervous system types? *Personality and Individual Differences, 8,* 693–704.

Driscoll, P., & Bättig, K. (1982). Behavioral, emotional, and neurochemical profiles of rats selected for extreme differences in active, two-way avoidance performance. In I. Lieblich (Ed.), *Genetics of the brain* (pp. 95–123). Amsterdam: Elsevier.

Driscoll, P., Dudek, J., Martin, J. R., & Zirkovic, B. D. (1983). Two-way avoidance and acute stress induced alterations of regional noradrenergic, dopaminergic, and serotonergic activity in Roman high- and low-avoidance rats. *Life Sciences, 33,* 1719–1725.

Ebstein, R. P., & Auerbach, J. G. (2002). Dopamine D4 receptor and serotonin transporter promotor polymorphisms and temperament in early childhood. In J. Benjamin, R. P. Ebstein, & R. H. Belmaker (Eds.), *Molecular genetics and the human personality* (pp. 137–149). Washington, DC: American Psychiatric Publishing.

Ebstein, R. P., & Kotler, M. (2002). Personality, substance abuse, and genes. In J. Benjamin, R. P. Ebstein, & R. H. Belmaker (Eds.), *Molecular genetics and the human personality* (pp. 151–163). Washington, DC: American Psychiatric Publishing.

Ebstein, R. P., Novick, O., Umansky, R., Priel, B., Osher, Y., Blaine, D., et al. (1996). Dopamine DR receptor (DRD4): Exon III polymorphism associated with the human personality trait of novelty seeking. *Nature Genetics, 12,* 78–80.

Eide, A. H., Acuda, S. W., Khan, N., Aaroe, L. E., & Loeb, M. E. (1997). Combining cultural, social, and personality trait variables as predictors for drug use among adolescents in Zimbabwe. *Journal of Adolescence, 20,* 511–524.

Ekstrand, M. L., & Coates, T. J. (1990). Maintenance of safer sexual behaviors and predictors of risky sex: The San Francisco men's health study. *American Journal of Public Health, 80,* 973–977.

Ellison, G. D. (1977). Animal models of psychopathology: The low-norepinephrine and low-serotonin rat. *American Psychologist, 32,* 1036–1045.

English, G. E., & Jones, R. E. (1972, April). *Sensation seeking in hospitalized drug addicts.* Paper presented at Southeastern Psychological Association, Atlanta, Georgia.

Enoch, M. A., & Goldman, D. (2002). Molecular and cellular genetics of alcohol addiction. In K. L. Davis, D. Charney, J. T. Coyle, & C. Memeroff (Eds.), *Neuropsychopharmacology* (pp. 1414–1423). Philadelphia: Lippincott Williams & Wilkins.

Epstein, S. (1982). Conflict and stress. In L. Goldberger & S. Breznitz (Eds.), *Handbook of stress: Theoretical and clinical aspects* (pp. 49–68). New York: Free Press.

Eysenck, H. J. (1967). *The biological basis of personality.* Springfield, IL: Charles C Thomas.

Eysenck, H. J. (1977). *Crime and personality* (3rd ed.). London: Routledge & Kegan Paul.

Eysenck, H. J. (1983). A biometrical–genetical analysis of impulsive and sensation seeking behavior. In M. Zuckerman (Ed.), *Biological bases of sensation seeking, impulsivity, and anxiety* (pp. 1–27). Hillsdale, NJ: Erlbaum.

Eysenck, H. J. (1990). Genetic and environmental contribution to individual differences: Three major dimensions of personality. *Journal of Personality, 58,* 245–261.

Eysenck, H. J., & Eysenck, S. B. G. (1964). *Eysenck Personality Inventory.* San Diego, CA: Educational and Industrial Testing Service.

Eysenck, H. J., & Eysenck, S. B. G. (1975). *Manual of the Eysenck Personality Questionnaire.* London: Hodder & Stoughton.

Eysenck, H. J., & Eysenck, S. B. G. (1976). *Psychoticism as a dimension of personality.* New York: Crane, Russak, & Co.

Eysenck, S. B. G., Pearson, P. R., Easting, G., & Allsopp, J. F. (1985). Age norms for impulsiveness, venturesomeness, and empathy in adults. *Personality and Individual Differences*, 6, 613–619.

Eysenck, S. B. G., & Eysenck, H. J. (1977). The place of impulsiveness in a dimensional system of personality description. *British Journal of Social and Clinical Psychology*, 16, 57–68.

Farley, F. H. (1967). Social desirability and dimensionality in the Sensation Seeking Scale. *Acta Psychologia*, 26, 89–96.

Farley, F. H. (1973, August). *Implications for a theory of delinquency.* Paper presented at the Sensation Seeking Motive Symposium at the 81st Annual Convention of the American Psychological Association, Montreal, Quebec, Canada.

Farley, F. H., & Davis, S. A. (1977). Arousal, personality, and assortative mating in marriage. *Journal of Sex and Marital Therapy*, 3, 122–127.

Farley, F. H., & Farley, S. V. (1972). Stimulus seeking motivation and delinquent behavior among institutionalized delinquent girls. *Journal of Consulting and Clinical Psychology*, 39, 140–147.

Farley, F. H., & Mueller, C. B. (1978). Arousal, personality, and assortative mating in marriage: Generalizability and cross-cultural factors. *Journal of Sex and Marital Therapy*, 4, 50–53.

Farrington, D. P. (1997). The relationship between low resting heart rate and violence. In A. Raine, P. A. Brennan, D. P. Farrington, & S. A. Mednick (Eds.), *Biosocial bases of violence* (pp. 89–106). New York: Plenum Press.

Feij, J. A., van Zuilen, R. W., & Gazendam, A. (1984). *SBL Handleiding: Spanningsbehoeftiligsth* [Sensation Seeking Scale guide]. Lisse, the Netherlands: Swets & Zeitlinger.

Feingold, A., Ball, S. A., Kranzler, H. R., & Rounsaville, B. J. (1996). Generalizability of the Type A/Type B distinction across different psychoactive substances. *American Journal of Drug and Alcohol Abuse*, 22, 449–462.

Fenz, W. D., & Epstein, S. (1967). Gradients of psychological arousal of experienced and novice parachutists as a function of an approaching jump. *Psychosomatic Medicine*, 29, 33–51.

Ficher, I. V., Zuckerman, M., & Neeb, M. (1981). Marital compatibility in sensation seeking trait as a factor in marital adjustment. *Journal of Sex and Marital Therapy*, 7, 60–69.

Ficher, I. V., Zuckerman, M., & Steinberg, M. (1988). Sensation seeking congruence in couples as a function of marital adjustment: A partial replication and extension. *Journal of Clinical Psychology*, 44, 803–809.

Fischer, S., & Smith, G. T. (2004). Deliberation affects risk taking beyond sensation seeking. *Personality and Individual Differences*, 36, 527–537.

Fisher, W. A. (1990). Understanding and preventing teenage pregnancy and sexually transmitted disease/AIDS. In J. Edwards, R. S. Tindale, L. Heath, E. J. Posavac (Eds.), *Social influence processes and prevention* (pp. 71–101). New York: Plenum Press.

Fisher, W. A., Fisher, J. D., & Rye, B. J. (1995). Understanding and promoting AIDS-preventative behavior: Insights from the theory of reasoned action. *Health Psychology, 14*, 255–264.

Flynn, J., Slovic, P., & Mertz, C. K. (1994). Gender, race, and perception of environmental health risks. *Risk Analysis, 14*, 1101–1108.

Forsman, L. (1982). Consistency in catechoamine excretion in laboratory and natural settings: Correlational and variance component analysis. *Scandinavian Journal of Psychology, 23*, 99–106.

Forthun, L. F., Bell, N. J., Peek, C. W., & Sun, S. W. (1999). Religiosity, sensation seeking, and alcohol drug use in denominational and gender contexts. *Journal of Drug Issues, 29*, 75–90.

Fowler, C. J., von Knorring, L., & Oreland, L. (1980). Platelet monoamine oxidase activity in sensation seekers. *Psychiatry Research, 3*, 273–279.

Fowler, J. S., Logan, J., Wang, G.-J., & Volkow, N. D. (2003). Monoamine oxidase and cigarette smoking. *Neurotoxicology, 24*, 75–82.

Franken, R. E., Hill, R., & Kierstead, J. (1994). Sport interest as predicted by the personality measures of competitiveness, mastery, instrumentality, expressivity, and sensation seeking. *Personality and Individual Differences, 17*, 467–476.

Frankenhauser, M. (1979). Psychoendocrine approaches to the study of emotion as related to stress and coping. In H. E. Howe & R. A. Dienstbier (Eds.), *Nebraska Symposium on Motivation: Beliefs, attitudes, and values* (pp. 123–161). Lincoln: University of Nebraska Press.

Franques, P., Auriacombe, M., Piquemal, E., Verger, M., Brisseau-Gimenez, S., Grabot, D., & Tignol, J. (2003). Sensation seeking as a common factor in opioid dependent subjects and high risk sport practicing subjects: A cross-sectional study. *Drug and Alcohol Dependence, 69*, 121–126.

Freud, S. (1955). Beyond the pleasure principle. In J. Strachey (Ed. & Trans.), *The standard edition of the complete psychological works of Sigmund Freud* (Vol. 18, pp. 7–64). London: Hogarth Press. (Original work published 1920)

Freud, S. (1959). Inhibitions, symptoms, and anxiety. In J. Strachey (Ed. & Trans.) *The standard edition of the complete psychological works of Sigmund Freud* (Vol. 20, pp. 87–156). London: Hogarth Press. (Original work published 1926)

Friend, K., & Levy, D. T. (2002). Reductions in smoking prevalence and cigarette consumption associated with mass-media campaigns. *Health Education Research, 17*, 85–98.

Fromme, K., Marlatt, G. A., Baer, J. S., & Kivlahan, D. R. (1994). The alcohol skills training program: A group intervention for young adult drinkers. *Journal of Substance Abuse Treatment, 11*, 143–154.

Fromme, K., Stroot, E., & Kaplan, D. (1993). Comprehensive effects of alcohol: Development and psychometric assessment of new expectancy questionnaire. *Psychological Assessment, 5*, 19–26.

Fulker, D. W., Eysenck, S. B. G., & Zuckerman, M. (1980). A genetic and environmental analysis of sensation seeking. *Journal of Research in Personality, 14*, 261–268.

Fuller, R. (1984). A conceptualization of drinking behavior as threat avoidance. *Ergonomics, 27*, 1139–1155.

Fung, M. T., Raine, A., Loeber, R., Lynam, D. R., Steinhauer, S. R.,Venables, P. H., & Stoulhamer-Loeber, M. (2005). Reduced electrodermal activity in psychopathy-prone adolescents. *Journal of Abnormal Psychology, 114*, 187–196.

Furnham, A. F. (1984). Extraversion, sensation seeking, stimulus screening, and Type "A" behaviour pattern: The relationship between measures of arousal. *Personality and Individual Differences, 5*, 133–140.

Furnham, A. F., & Saipe, J. (1993). Personality correlates of convicted drinkers. *Personality and Individual Differences, 14*, 329–336.

Gaither, G. A., & Sellbom, M. (2003). The Sexual Sensation Seeking Scale: Reliability and validity within a heterosexual college student sample. *Journal of Personality Assessment, 81*, 157–167.

Galen, L. W., Henderson, M. J., & Whitman, R. D. (1997). The utility of novelty seeking, harm avoidance, and expectancy in the prediction of drinking. *Addictive Behaviors, 22*, 93–106.

Galizio, M., Rosenthal, D., & Stein, F. (1983). Sensation seeking, reinforcement, and student drug use. *Addictive Behaviors, 8*, 243–252.

Garlington, W. K., & Shimona, H. E. (1964). The Change Seeker Index: A measure of the need for variable sensory input. *Psychological Reports, 14*, 919–924.

Garos, S., & Stock, W. A. (1998). Investigating the discriminant validity and differentiation capability of the Garos Sexual Behavior Index. *Sexual Addiction and Compulsivity, 5*, 251–267.

Garpenstrand, H., Longato-Stadler, E., af Klinteberg, B., Grigorenko, E., Damberg, M., Oreland, L., & Hallman, J. (2002). Low platelet monoamine oxidase in Swedish imprisoned criminal offenders. *European Neuropsychopharmacology, 12*, 135–140.

Gatzke-Kopp, L. M., Raine, A., Loeber, R., Stouthamer-Loeber, M., & Steinhauer, S. R. (2002). Serious delinquent behavior, sensation seeking, and electrodermal arousal. *Journal of Abnormal Child Psychology, 30*, 477–486.

Gee, P., Coventry, K. R., & Birkenhead, D. (2005). Mood state and gambling: Using mobile telephones to track emotions. *British Journal of Psychology, 96*, 53–66.

Gerra, G., Avanzini, P., Zaimovic, A., Sartori, R., Bocchi, C., Timpano, M., et al. (1999). Neurotransmitters, neuroendocrine correlates of sensation seeking in normal humans. *Neuropsychobiology, 39*, 207–213.

Gerra, G., Zaimovic, A., Ferri, M., Marzocchi, G. F., Timpano, M., Zambelli, U., et al. (2000). Neuroendocrine correlates of temperament traits in abstinent opiate addicts. *Journal of Substance Abuse, 11*, 337–354.

Gianoulakis, C., Angelogianni, P., Meany, M., Thavundayil, J., & Tawar, V. (1990). Endorphins in individuals with high and low risk for development of alcoholism. In L. D. Reid (Ed.), *Opioids, bulimia, alcohol abuse, and alcoholism* (pp. 229–246). New York: Springer-Verlag.

Gianoulakis, C., Krishman, B., & Thavundayil, J. (1996). Enhanced sensitivity of pituitary β–endorphins to ethanol in subjects at high risk of alcoholism. *Archives of General Psychiatry, 53,* 250–257.

Gibson, K. J., Franken, R. E., & Rowland, G. L. (1989). Sensation seeking and marital adjustment. *Journal of Sex and Marital Therapy, 15,* 57–61.

Glicksohn, J., & Bozna, M. (2000). Developing a personality profile of the bomb-disposal expert: The role of sensation seeking and field dependence–independence. *Personality and Individual Differences, 28,* 85–92.

Glicksohn, J., & Golan, H. (2001). Personality, cognitive style, and assortative mating. *Personality and Individual Differences, 30,* 1199–1209.

Glover, V., Sandler, M., Owen, F., & Riley, G. J. (1977, January 6). Dopamine is a monoamine oxidase-B substrate in man. *Nature, 265,* 80–81.

Goldberg, L. R. (1990). An alternative description of personality: The Big-Five factor structure. *Journal of Personality and Social Psychology, 59,* 1216–1229.

Goldberger, L. (1961). Reactions to perceptual isolation and Rorschach manifestations of the primary process. *Journal of Projective Techniques, 25,* 287–302.

Golding, J. F., & Cornish, A. M. (1987). Personality and life-style in medical students: Psychophysiological aspects. *Psychology and Health, 1,* 287–301.

Golding, J. F., Harpur, T., & Brent-Smith, H. (1983). Personality, drinking, and drug-taking correlates of cigarette smoking. *Personality and Individual Differences, 4,* 703–706.

Gomà-i-Freixanet, M. (1995). Prosocial and antisocial aspects of personality. *Personality and Individual Differences, 19,* 125–134.

Gomà-i-Freixanet, M. (1999). Personality profile of subjects engaged in high physical risk sports. *Human Performance in Extreme Environments, 4,* 11–17.

Gomà-i-Freixanet, M. (2001). Prosocial and antisocial aspects of personality in women: A replication study. *Personality and Individual Differences, 30,* 1401–1411.

Gomà-i-Freixanet, M. (2004). Sensation seeking and participation in physical risk sports. In R. M. Stelmack (Ed.), *On the psychobiology of personality: Essays in honor of Marvin Zuckerman* (pp. 185–201). New York: Elsevier.

Gomà-i-Freixanet, M., Pérez, J., & Torrubia, R. (1988). Personality variables in antisocial and prosocial disinhibitory behavior. In T. E. Moffitt & S. A. Mednick (Eds.), *Biological contributions to crime causation* (pp. 211–222). Dordrecht, the Netherlands: Nijhoff.

Gomà-i-Freixanet, M., & Wismeijer, A. J. (2002). Applying personality theory to a group of police bodyguards: A physically risky prosocial prototype? *Psicothema, 14,* 387–392.

Goodwin, D. W., Schulsinger, F., Knopf, J., Mednick, S., & Guze, S. B. (1977). Alcoholism and depression in adopted-out daughters of alcoholics. *Archives of General Psychiatry, 34,* 164–169.

Gough, H. (1956). *California Psychological Inventory.* Palo Alto, CA: Consulting Psychologist Press.

Graham, F. K. (1979). Distinguishing among orienting, defensive, and startle reflexes. In H. D. Kimmel, E. H. van Olst, & J. F. Orlebeke (Eds.), *The orienting reflex in humans* (pp. 137–168). Hillsdale, NJ: Erlbaum.

Gray, J. A. (1981). A critique of Eysenck's theory of personality. In H. J. Eysenck (Ed.), *A model for personality* (pp. 246–276). New York: Oxford University Press.

Gray, J. A. (1982). *The neuropsychology of anxiety: An enquiry into the functions of the septohippocampal system.* New York: Oxford University Press.

Gray, J. A. (1987). The neuropsychology of emotion and personality. In S. M. Stahl, S. D. Iverson, & E. C. Goodman (Eds.), *Cognitive neurochemistry* (pp. 171–190). Oxford, England: Oxford University Press.

Griffin, K. W., Botvin, G. J., Nichols, T. R., & Doyle, M. M. (2003). Effectiveness of a universal drug abuse prevention approach for youth at high-risk for substance use initiation. *Preventive Medicine, 36,* 1–7.

Gullone, E., Moore, S., Moss, S., & Boyd, C. (2000). The adolescent risk-taking questionnaire. *Journal of Adolescent Research, 15,* 231–250.

Gundersheim, J. (1987). Sensation seeking in male and female athletes and nonathletes. *International Journal of Sport Psychology, 18,* 87–99.

Gynther, L. M., Carey, G., Gottesman, I. I., & Vogler, G. P. (1994). A twin study of non-alcohol substance abuse. *Psychiatry Research, 56,* 213–220.

Hallman, J., af Klinteberg, B., Oreland, L., Wirsen, A., Levander, S. E., & Schalling, D. (1990). *Personality, neuropsychological, and biochemical characteristics of air force pilots.* Unpublished manuscript.

Hallman, J., Persson, M., & af Klinteberg, B. (2001). Female alcoholism: Differences between female alcoholics with and without a history of additional substance misuse. *Alcohol and Alcoholism, 36,* 564–571.

Ham, L. S., & Hope, D. A. (2003). College students and problematic drinking: A review of the literature. *Clinical Psychology Review, 23,* 719–759.

Hampson, S. E., Severson, H. H., Burns, W. J., Slovic, P., & Fisher, K. J. (2001). Risk perception, personality factors, and alcohol use among adolescents. *Personality and Individual Differences, 30,* 167–181.

Hansen, E. B., & Breivik, G. (2001). Sensation seeking as a predictor of positive and negative risk behaviour among adolescents. *Personality and Individual Differences, 30,* 627–640.

Hare, R. D. (1978). Electrodermal and cardiovascular correlates of psychopathy. In R. D. Hare & D. Schalling (Eds.), *Psychopathic behavior: Approaches to research* (pp. 107–143). Chichester, England: Wiley.

Hare, R. D., & Cox, D. N. (1978). Clinical and empirical conceptions of psychopathy and the selection of subjects for research. In R. D. Hare & D. Schalling (Eds.), *Psychopathic behaviour: Approaches to research* (pp. 1–22). Chichester, England: Wiley.

Hare, R. D., & McPherson, L. M. (1984). Violent and aggressive behavior by criminal psychopaths. *International Journal of Law and Psychiatry, 7,* 35–50.

Harpur, T. J., & Hare, R. D. (1994). Assessment of psychopathy as a function of age. *Journal of Abnormal Psychology, 103*, 604–609.

Harpur, T. J., Hare, R. D., & Hakistan, R. (1989). Two-factor conceptualization of psychopathy: Construct validity and assessment implications. *Psychological Assessment, 1*, 6–17.

Harpur, T. J., Hart, S. D., & Hare, R. D. (1994). The personality of the psychopath. In P. P. Costa & T. A. Widiger (Eds.), *Personality disorders and the five-factor model of personality* (pp. 198–216). Washington, DC: American Psychological Association.

Hart, T. A., Wolitski, R. J., Purcell, D. W., Gomez, C., & Halkitis, P. (2003). Sexual behavior among HIV-positive men who have sex with men: What's in a label? *Journal of Sex Research, 40*, 179–188.

Hartos, J. L., Eitel, P., Haynie, D. L., & Simons-Morton, B. G. (2000). Can I take the car? Relations among parenting practices and adolescent problem-driving practices. *Journal of Adolescent Research, 15*, 352–357.

Hartos, J. L., Eitel, P., & Simons-Morton, B. (2002). Parenting practices and adolescent risky driving: A three-month prospective study. *Health Education and Behavior, 29*, 194–206.

Hathaway, S. R., & McKinley, J. C. (1951). *The Minnesota Multiphasic Personality Inventory manual* (Rev. ed.). New York: Psychological Corporation.

Hebb, D. O. (1955). Drives and the CNS (conceptual nervous system). *Psychological Review, 62*, 243–254.

Hein, K. (1989). Commentary on adolescent acquired immunodeficiency syndrome: The next waves of human immunodeficiency virus epidemic? *The Journal of Pediatrics, 114*, 144–149.

Heino, A. (1996). *Risk taking in car driving: Perception, individual differences, and effects of safety incentives.* Unpublished doctoral dissertation, University of Groningen, the Netherlands.

Heino, A., van der Molen, H., & Wilde, G. J. S. (1996). Differences in risk experience between sensation avoiders and sensation seekers. *Personality and Individual Differences, 20*, 71–79.

Helzer, J. E., Burnam, A., & McElvoy, L. T. (1991). Alcohol abuse and dependence. In L. N. Robins & D. A. Regier (Eds.), *Psychiatric disorders in America: The epidemiology catchment area study* (pp. 81–115). New York: Free Press.

Henderson, V. R., Hennessy, M., Barrett, D. W., Curtis, B., McCoy-Roth, M., Trentacoste, N., & Fishbein, M. (2005). When risky is attractive: Sensation seeking and romantic partner selection. *Personality and Individual Differences, 38*, 311–325.

Hendrick, C., & Hendrick, S. S. (1986). A theory and method of love. *Journal of Personality and Social Psychology, 50*, 392–402.

Hennig, J. (2004). Personality, serotonin, and noradrenaline. In R. Stelmack (Ed.), *On the psychobiology of personality: Essays in honor of Marvin Zuckerman* (pp. 379–408). Amsterdam: Elsevier.

Hennig, J., Kroeger, A., Meyer, B., Prochaska, H., Krien, P. Huwe, S., & Netter, P. (1998). Personality correlates of +/− pindolol induces decreases in prolactin. *Pharmacopsychiatry, 31,* 19–24.

Henry, B., Caspi, A., Moffitt, T. E., & Silva, P. A. (1996). Temperamental and familial predictors of violent and nonviolent criminal convictions: Age 3 to age 18. *Developmental Psychology, 32,* 614–623.

Heyman, S. R., & Rose, K. G. (1979). Psychological variables affecting scuba performance. In C. H. Nadeau, W. R. Holliwell, K. M. Newell, & G. C. Roberts (Eds.), *Psychology of motor behaviour and sport* (pp. 180–188). Champaign, IL: Human Kinetics Press.

Hill, C. A., & Preston, L. K. (1996). Individual differences in the experience of sexual motivation: Theory and measurement of dispositional and sexual motives. *The Journal of Sex Research, 33,* 27–45.

Homant, R. J., Kennedy, D. B., & Howton, J. D. (1994). Risk taking and police pursuit. *Journal of Social Psychology, 134,* 213–221.

Horvath, P., & Zuckerman, M. (1993). Sensation seeking, risk appraisal, and risky behavior. *Personality and Individual Differences, 14,* 41–52.

Houston, R. J., & Stanford, M. S. (2005). Electrophysiological substrates of impulsiveness: Potential effects on aggressive behavior. *Progress in Neuro-Psychopharmacology and Biological Psychiatry, 29,* 305–313.

Hoyle, R., Fejfar, M. C., & Miller, J. D. (2000). Personality and sexual risk taking: A quantitative review. *Journal of Personality, 68,* 1203–1231.

Hoyle, R. H., Stephenson, M. T., Palmgreen, P., Lorch, E. P., & Donohew, R. L. (2002). Reliability and validity of a brief measure of sensation seeking. *Personality and Individual Differences, 32,* 401–414.

Huba, G. J., Newcomb, M. D., & Bentler, P. M. (1981). Comparison of canonical correlation and interbattery factor analyses on sensation seeking and drug use domains. *Applied Psychological Measurement, 5,* 291–306.

Hunt, W. A., Barnett, L. W., & Branch, L. G. (1971). Relapse rates in addiction programs. *Journal of Clinical Psychology, 27,* 455–456.

Hur, Y.-M., & Bouchard, T. J., Jr. (1997). The genetic correlation between impulsivity and sensation seeking traits. *Behavior Genetics, 27,* 455–463.

Irey, P. A. (1974). *Personality dimensions of crisis interveners vs. academic psychologists, traditional clinicians, and paraprofessionals.* Unpublished doctoral dissertation, Southern Illinois University, Carbondale.

Ishikawa, S. S., & Raine, A. (2002). Behavior genetics and crime. In J. Glicksohn (Ed.), *The neurobiology of criminal behavior* (pp. 81–110). Boston: Kluwer Academic.

Iverson, H., & Rundmo, T. (2002). Personality, risky driving, and accident involvement among Norwegian drivers. *Personality and Individual Differences, 33,* 1251–1263.

Izard, C. E. (Ed.). (1979). *Emotions in personality and psychopathology.* New York: Plenum Press.

Jack, S. J., & Ronan, K. R. (1998). Sensation seeking among high- and low-risk sports participants. *Personality and Individual Differences, 25*, 1063–1083.

Jackson, D. N. (1974). *Personality Research Form manual.* Goshen, NY: Research Psychologists Press.

Jacobsen, K. C., Prescott, C. A., & Kendler, K. S. (2002). Sex differences in the genetic and environmental influences on the development of antisocial behavior. *Development and Psychopathology, 14*, 395–416.

Jaffe, L. T., & Archer, R. P. (1987). The prediction of drug use among college students from MMPI, MCMI, and Sensation Seeking Scales. *Journal of Personality, 51*, 243–253.

Jamrozik, K. (2004). ABC of smoking cessation: Policy priorities for tobacco control. *British Medical Journal, 328*, 1007–1009.

Jamrozik, K., Vessey, M., Fowler, G., Wald, N., Parker, G., & van Vunakis, H. (1984). Controlled trial of three different anti-smoking interventions in general practice. *British Medical Journal, 288*, 1499–1503.

Jemmott, J. B., Jemmott, L. S., & Fong, G. T. (1998). Abstinence and safer sex HIV risk-reduction interventions for African American adolescents. *Journal of the American Medical Association, 279*, 1529–1536.

Johansson, F., Almay, B. G. L., von Knorring, L., Terrenius, L., & Astrom, M. (1979). Personality traits in chronic patients related to endorphin levels in cerebrospinal fluid. *Psychiatry Research, 1*, 231–239.

Johnson, V., & White, H. R. (1989). An investigation of factors related to intoxicated driving behaviors among youth. *Journal of Studies on Alcohol, 50*, 320–330.

Joireman, J. A., Anderson, J., & Strathman, A. (2003). The aggression paradox: Understanding links among aggression, sensation seeking, and the consideration of future consequences. *Journal of Personality and Social Psychology, 84*, 1287–1302.

Joireman, J. A., Fick, C. S., & Anderson, J. W. (2002). Sensation seeking and involvement in chess. *Personality and Individual Differences, 32*, 509–515.

Jonah, B. A. (1986). Accident risk and risk-taking behaviour among young drivers. *Accident Analysis and Prevention, 18*, 255–271.

Jonah, B. A. (1997). Sensation seeking and risky driving: A review and synthesis of the literature. *Accident Analysis and Prevention, 29*, 651–665.

Jonah, B. A., & Dawson, N. E. (1987). Youth and risk: Age differences in risky driving, risk perception, and risk utility. *Alcohol, Drugs, and Driving, 3*, 13–29

Jonah, B. A., Thiessen, R., & Au-Yeung, E. (2001). Sensation seeking, risky driving, and behavioral adaptation. *Accident Analysis and Prevention, 33*, 679–684.

Jones, A. (1964). Drive and incentive variables associated with the statistical properties of sequences of stimuli. *Journal of Experimental Psychology, 67*, 423–431.

Jones, A. (1969). Stimulus-seeking behavior. In J. P. Zubek (Ed.), *Sensory deprivation: Fifteen years of research* (pp. 167–206). New York: Appleton-Century-Crofts.

Jones, M. C. (1968). Personality correlates and antecedent of drinking patterns in adult males. *Journal of Consulting and Clinical Psychology, 32*, 2–12.

Jones, M. C. (1971). Personality antecedents and correlates of drinking patterns in women. *Journal of Consulting and Clinical Psychology, 36*, 61–69.

Jones, R. (2004). Relationships of sexual imposition, dyadic trust, and sensation seeking with sexual risk behavior in young urban women. *Research in Nursing and Health, 27*, 185–197.

Jones, R. T., & Benowitz, N. L. (2002). Therapeutics for nicotine addiction. In K. L. Davis, D. Charney, J. T. Coyle, & C. Nemeroff (Eds.), *Neuropsychopharmacology: The fifth generation of progress* (pp. 1533–1544). Philadelphia: Lippincott Williams & Wilkins.

Kafry, D. (1982). Sensation seeking in young children. *Personality and Individual Differences, 3*, 161–166.

Kahler, C. W., Read, J. P., Wood, M. D., & Palfai, T. P. (2003). Social environmental selection as a mediator of gender, ethnic, and personality effects on college student drinking. *Psychology of Addictive Behaviors, 17*, 226–234.

Kalichman, S. C., Cain, D., Zweben, A., & Swain, G. (2003). Sensation seeking, alcohol use, and sexual risk behaviors among men receiving services at a clinic for sexually transmitted infections. *Quarterly Journal of Studies on Alcohol, 64*, 564–569.

Kalichman, S. C., Heckman, T., & Kelly, J. A. (1996). Sensation seeking as an explanation for the association between substance use and HIV-related risky sexual behavior. *Archives of Sexual Behavior, 25*, 141–154.

Kalichman, S. C., Johnson, J. R., Adair, V., Rompa, D., Multhauf, K., Johnson, J., & Kelly, J. (1994). Sexual sensation seeking: Scale development and predicting AIDS-risk behavior among homosexually active men. *Journal of Personality Assessment, 62*, 385–397.

Kalichman, S. C., & Rompa, D. (1995). Sexual sensation seeking and sexual compulsivity scales: Reliability, validity, and predicting HIV risk behavior. *Journal of Personality Assessment, 65*, 586–601.

Kalichman, S. C., Tannenbaum, L., & Nachimson, D. (1998). Personality and cognitive factors influencing substance use and sexual risk for HIV infection among gay and bisexual men. *Psychology of the Addictive Behaviors, 12*, 262–271.

Kalichman, S. C., Weinhart, L., DiFonzo, K., Austin, J., & Luke, W. (2002). Sensation seeking and alcohol use as markers of sexual transmission risk behavior in HIV-positive men. *Annals of Behavioral Medicine, 24*, 229–235.

Kalivas, P. W. (2002). The neurocircuitry of addiction. In K. L. Davis, D. Charney, J. T. Coyles, & C. Nemeroff (Eds.), *Neuropsychopharmacology: The fifth generation of progress* (pp. 1357–1366). Philadelphia: Lippincott Williams & Wilkins.

Kaplan, J. R., Manuck, S. B., Fontenot, D. V. M., & Mann, J. J. (2002). Central nervous system monoamine correlates of social dominance in cynomolgus monkeys (*Maccica fascicularis*). *Neuropsychopharmacology, 26*, 431–443.

Karoly, P. (1975). Comparison of "psychological styles" in delinquent and nondelinquent females. *Psychological Reports, 36,* 567–570.

Kassel, J. D., Shiffman, S., Gnys, M., Paty, J., & Zettler-Segal, M. (1994). Psychosocial and personality differences in chippers and regular smokers. *Addictive Behaviors, 19,* 565–575.

Katz, E. C., Fromme, K., & D'Amico, E. J. (2000). Effects of outcome expectancies and personality on young adults' illicit drug use, heavy drinking, and risky sexual behavior. *Cognitive Therapy and Research, 24,* 1–22.

Kelly, J. A., St. Lawrence, J. S., & Brasfield, T. L. (1991). Predictors of vulnerability to AIDS risk behavior relapse. *Journal of Consulting and Clinical Psychology, 59,* 163–166.

Kelly, J. A., St. Lawrence, J. S., Diaz, Y. E., Stevenson, L. Y., Hauth, A. C., Brasfield, T. L., et al. (1991). HIV risk behavior reduction following intervention with key opinion leaders of population: An experimental analysis. *American Journal of Public Health, 81,* 168–171.

Kelly, J. A., St. Lawrence, J. S., Hood, H. V., & Brasfield, T. L. (1989). Behavioral intervention to reduce AIDS risk activities. *Journal of Consulting and Clinical Psychology, 57,* 60–67.

Kendler, K. S., Heath, A. C., Neale, M. C., Kessler, R. C., & Eaves, L. J. (1992). A population-based twin study of alcoholism in women. *Journal of the American Medical Association, 268,* 1877–1882.

Kendler, K. S., Prescott, C. A., Neale, M. C., & Pederson, N. L. (1997). Temperance board registration for alcohol abuse in a national sample of Swedish male twins born 1902 to 1949. *Archives of General Psychiatry, 54,* 178–184.

Kerr, J. H., & Svebak, S. (1989). Motivational aspects of preference for and participation in "risk" and "safe" sports. *Personality and Individual Differences, 10,* 797–800.

Kessler, R. C., McGonagle, K. A., Zhao, S., Nelson, C. B., Hughes, M., Eshleman, S., et al. (1994). Lifetime and 12-month prevalence of *DSM–III–R* psychiatric disorders in the United States. *Archives of General Psychiatry, 51,* 8–19.

Kilpatrick, D. G., McAlhany, D., McCurdy, L., Shaw, D. L., & Roitzsch, J. C. (1982). Aging, alcoholism, anxiety, and sensation seeking: An exploratory investigation. *Addictive Behaviors, 7,* 97–100.

Kilpatrick, D. G., Sutker, P. B., & Smith, A. D. (1976). Deviant drug and alcohol use: The role of anxiety, sensation seeking, and other personality variables. In M. Zuckerman & C. D. Spielberger (Eds.), *Emotions and anxiety: New concepts, methods and applications* (pp. 247–278). Hillsdale, NJ: Erlbaum.

Kinsey, A. C., Pomeroy, W. B., & Martin, C. E. (1948). *Sexual behavior in the human male.* Philadelphia: W. B. Saunders.

Kinsey, A. C., Pomeroy, W. B., Martin, C. E., & Gebhard, P. H. (1953). *Sexual behavior in the human female.* Philadelphia: W. B. Saunders.

Kirby, D. (2002). Effective approaches to reducing adolescent unprotected sex, pregnancy, and child bearing. *Journal of Sex Research, 39,* 51–57.

Kish, G. B., & Donnenwerth, G. V. (1972). Sex differences in the correlates of stimulus seeking. *Journal of Consulting and Clinical Psychology, 38*, 42–49.

Kivlahan, D. R., Marlatt, G. A., Fromme, K., Coppel, D. B., & Williams, E. (1990). Secondary prevention with college drinkers: Evaluation of an alcohol skills training program. *Journal of Consulting and Clinical Psychology, 58*, 805–810.

af Klinteberg, B. (1996). Biology, norms, and personality: A developmental perspective. *Neuropsychobiology, 34*, 146–154.

af Klinteberg, B., von Knorring, L., & Oreland, L. (2004). On the psychobiology of personality. In R. M. Stelmack (Ed.), *On the psychobiology of personality: Essays in honor of Marvin Zuckerman* (pp. 429–451). Amsterdam: Elsevier.

Kohn, P. M., Hunt, R. W., Cowles, M. P., & Davis, C. A. (1986). Factor structure and construct validity of the Vando Reducer–Augmenter Scale. *Personality and Individual Differences, 7*, 57–64.

Kohn, P. M., Hunt, R. W., & Hoffman, F. M. (1982). Aspects of experience seeking. *Canadian Journal of Behavioral Science, 14*, 13–23.

Koopmans, J. R. (1997). *The genetics of health-related behaviors: A study of adolescent twins and their parents*. Enschede, the Netherlands: Ipskamp.

Koopmans, J. R., Boomsma, D. I., Heath, A. C., & van Doornen, J. P. D. (1995). A multivariate genetic analysis of sensation seeking. *Behavior Genetics, 25*, 349–356.

Koopmans, J. R., Heath, A. C., van Doornen, L. J. P., & Boomsma, D. I. (1997). The relation between sensation seeking, alcohol use, and smoking: A multivariate genetic analysis. In J. R. Koopmans (Ed.), *The genetics of health-related behaviors: A study of adolescent twins and their parents* (pp. 71–87). Enschede, the Netherlands: Ipskamp.

Kopnisky, K. L., & Hyman, S. E. (2002). Molecular and cellular biology of addiction. In K. L. Davis, D. Charney, J. T. Coyle, & C. Nemeroff (Eds.), *Neuropsychopharmacology: The fifth generation of progress* (pp. 1367–1379). Philadelphia: Lippincott Williams & Wilkins.

Kopstein, A. N., Crum, R. M., Celentano, D. B., & Martin, S. S. (2001). Sensation seeking needs among 8th and 11th graders: Characteristics associated with cigarette and marijuana use. *Drugs and Alcohol Dependence, 62*, 195–203.

Kraft, M. R., Jr., & Zuckerman, M. (1999). Prenatal behaviors and attitudes of their parents reported by young adults from intact and stepparent families and relationships between perceived parenting and personality. *Personality and Individual Differences, 27*, 453–476.

Krishnan-Saran, S., Rosen, M. I., & O'Malley, S. S. (1999). Naloxone challenge in smokers: Preliminary evidence of an opioid component in nicotine dependence. *Archives of General Psychiatry, 56*, 663–668.

Krueger, R. F., Schmutte, P. S., Caspi, A., Moffitt, T. E., Campbell, K., & Silva, P. A. (1994). Personality traits are linked to crime among men and women: Evidence from a birth cohort. *Journal of Abnormal Psychology, 103*, 328–338.

Kumar, V. K, Pekala, R. J., & Cummings, J. (1993). Sensation seeking, drug use, and reported paranormal beliefs and experiences. *Personality and Individual Differences, 14,* 688–691.

La Grange, L., Jones, T. D., Erb, L., & Reyes, E. (1995). Alcohol consumption: Biochemical and personality correlates in a college student population. *Addictive Behaviors, 20,* 93–103.

Lambert, W., & Levy, L. H. (1972). Sensation seeking and short-term sensory isolation. *Journal of Personality and Social Psychology, 24,* 46–52.

Lando, H. A. (1977). Successful treatment of smokers with a broad spectrum behavioral approach. *Journal of Consulting and Clinical Psychology, 45,* 361–366.

Leckman, J. F., Gershon, E. S., Nichols, A. S., & Murphy, D. L. (1977). Reduced MAO activity in first-degree relatives of individuals with bipolar affective disorders. *Archives of General Psychiatry, 34,* 601–606.

Leigh, B. C., & Stall, R. (1993). Substance use and risky sexual behavior for exposure to HIV: Issues in methodology, interpretation, and prevention. *American Psychologist, 48,* 1035–1045.

Lejuez, C. W., Read, J. P., Kahler, C. W., Richards, J. B., Ramsey, S. E., Stuart, G. L., et al. (2002). Evaluation of a behavioral measure of risk taking: The Balloon Analogue Risk Task (BART). *Journal of Experimental Psychology Applied, 8,* 75–84.

Leonard, K. E., Quigley, B. M., & Collins, L. (2003). Drinking, personality, and bar environment characteristics as predictors of involvement in barroom aggression. *Addictive Behaviors, 28,* 1681–1700.

Lesnik-Oberstein, M., & Cohen, L. (1984). Cognitive style, sensation seeking, and associative mating. *Journal of Personality and Social Psychology, 46,* 112–117.

Levenson, M. R. (1990). Risk-taking and personality. *Journal of Personality and Social Psychology, 58,* 1073–1080.

Leventhal, H., & Cleary, P. D. (1980). The smoking problem: A review of the research and theory in behavioral risk modification. *Psychological Bulletin, 88,* 370–405.

Lidberg, L., Levander, S. E., Schalling, D., & Lidberg, Y. (1978). Urinary catecholamines, stress, and psychopathy: A study of arrested men awaiting trial. *Psychosomatic Medicine, 40,* 116–125.

Lidberg, L., Modin, I., Oreland, L., Tuck, J. R., & Gillner, A. (1985). Platelet monoamine oxidase and psychopathy. *Psychiatry Research, 16,* 339–343.

Lillienfeld, S. O., & Andrews, B. P. (1996). Development and preliminary validation of a self-report measure of psychopathic personality traits in noncriminal populations. *Journal of Personality Assessment, 66,* 488–524.

Limson, R., Goldman, D., Roy, A., Lamparski, D., Ravitz, B., Adinoff, B., & Linnoila, M. (1991). Personality and cerebrospinal monoamine metabolites in alcoholics and normals. *Archives of General Psychiatry, 48,* 437–441.

Linton, D. K., & Wiener, N. I. (2001). Personality and potential conceptions: Mating success in a modern Western male sample. *Personality and Individual Differences, 31*, 675–688.

Litle, P., & Zuckerman, M. (1986). Sensation seeking and music preferences. *Personality and Individual Differences, 7*, 575–577.

Loehlin, J. C. (1992). *Genes and environment in personality development.* Newbury Park, CA: Sage.

Lorch, E. P., Palmgreen, P., Donohew, L., Helm, D., Baer, S. A., & D'Silvia, M. O. (1994). Program context, sensation seeking, and attention to televised anti-drug public service announcements. *Human Communication Research, 20*, 390–412.

Luengo, M. A., Carrillo-de-la-Peña, M. T., Otero, J. M., & Romero, E. (1994). A short-term longitudinal study of impulsivity and antisocial behavior. *Journal of Personality and Social Psychology, 66*, 542–548.

Lukas, J. H., & Siegel, J. (1977, October 7). Cortical mechanisms that augment or reduce evoked potentials in cats. *Science, 196*, 73–75.

Luthar, S. S., Anton, S. F., Merikangas, K. R., & Rounsaville, B. J. (1992). Vulnerability to substance abuse and psychopathology among siblings of opioid abusers. *The Journal of Nervous and Mental Disease, 180*, 153–161.

Luthar, S. S., Merikangas, K. R., & Rounsaville, B. (1993). Parental psychopathology and disorders in offspring. *The Journal of Nervous and Mental Disease, 181*, 351–357.

Lynam, D. R., Caspi, A., Moffitt, T. E., Wikström, P. H., Loeber, R., & Novak, S. (2000). The interaction between impulsivity and neighborhood context of offending: The effects of impulsivity are stronger in poorer neighborhoods. *Journal of Abnormal Psychology, 109*, 563–574.

Lynam, D. R., Milich, R., Zimmerman, R., Novak, S., Logan, T. K., Martin, C., et al. (1999). Project DARE: No effects at 10-year follow-up. *Journal of Consulting and Clinical Psychology, 67*, 590–593.

Lyons, M. J., True, W. R., Eisen, A., Goldberg, J., Meyer, J. M., Faraone, S. V., et al. (1995). Differential heritability of adult and juvenile antisocial traits. *Archives of General Psychiatry, 52*, 906–924.

Maccoby, E. E., & Jacklin, C. N. (1974). *The psychology of sex differences.* Stanford, CA: Stanford University Press.

MacDonald, N. E., Wells, G. A., Fisher, W. A., Warren, W. K., King, M. A., Doherty, J. A., & Bowie, W. R. (1990). High-risk STD/HIV behavior among college students. *Journal of the American Medical Association, 263*, 3155–3159.

Macdonald, S., Mann, R. E., Chipman, M., & Anglin-Bodrug, K. (2004). Collisions and traffic violations of alcohol, cannabis, and cocaine abuse clients before and after treatment. *Accident Analysis and Prevention, 36*, 795–800.

Magnusson, D. (1988). Individual development in an interactional perspective. In D. Magnusson (Ed.), *Paths through life* (Vol. 1, pp. 3–31). Hillsdale, NJ: Erlbaum.

Major, L. F., & Murphy, D. L. (1978). Platelet and plasma amine oxidase activity in alcoholic individuals. *British Journal of Psychiatry, 132,* 548–554.

Marlatt, G. A., Curry, S., & Gordon, J. O. (1988). A longitudinal analysis of unaided smoking cessation. *Journal of Consulting and Clinical Psychology, 56,* 715–720.

Martin, C. A., Kelly, T. H., Rayens, M. K., Brogli, B. R., Brengel, A., Smith, W. J., & Omar, H. A. (2002). Sensation seeking, puberty, and nicotine, alcohol, and marijuana use in adolescence. *Journal of the American Academy of Child and Adolescent Psychiatry, 41,* 1495–1502.

Martin-Soelch, C., Leenders, K. L., Chevalley, A., Missimer, J., Kuenig, G., Magyar, S., et al. (2001). Reward mechanisms in the brain and their role in dependence: Evidence from neurophysiological and neuroimaging studies. *Brain Research Reviews, 36,* 139–149.

Masters, W. H., & Johnson, V. E. (1966). *Human sexual response.* Boston: Little, Brown.

Matthews, G., Tsuda, A., Xin, G., & Ozeki, Y. (1999). Individual differences in driver stress vulnerability in a Japanese sample. *Ergonomics, 42,* 401–413.

Maude-Griffin, P. M., Hohenstein, J. M., Humfleet, G. L., Reilly, P. M., Tusel, D. J., & Hall, S. M. (1998). Superior efficacy of cognitive–behavioral therapy for urban crack cocaine abusers: Main and matching effects. *Journal of Consulting and Clinical Psychology, 66,* 832–837.

McCoul, M. D., & Haslam, N. (2001). Predicting high-risk sexual behaviors in heterosexual and homosexual men: The roles of impulsivity and sensation seeking. *Personality and Individual Differences, 31,* 1303–1310.

McCrae, R. R. (1987). Creativity, divergent thinking, and openness to experience. *Journal of Personality and Social Psychology, 52,* 1258–1261.

McCuller, W. J., Sussman, S., Dent, C. W., & Teran, L. (2001). Concurrent prediction of drug use among high-risk youth. *Addictive Behaviors, 26,* 137–142.

McCutcheon, L. (1981). Running and sensation seeking. *Road Runners Club of America: Footnotes, 9,* 8.

McDaniel, S. R., & Zuckerman, M. (2003). The relationship of impulsive sensation seeking and gender to interest and participation in gambling activities. *Personality and Individual Differences, 35,* 1385–1400.

McGeveran, W. A., Jr. (Ed.). (2006). *The world almanac and book of facts.* New York: World Almanac Education Group.

McGue, M., Pickens, R. W., & Svikis, D. S. (1992). Sex and age effects on the inheritance of alcohol problems: A twin study. *Journal of Abnormal Psychology, 101,* 3–17.

McNeal, R. B., Hansen, W. B., Harrington, N. G., & Giles, S. M. (2004). How All Stars works: An examination of program effects on mediating variables. *Health Education and Behavior, 31,* 165–178.

Mednick, S. A., Gabrielli, W. F., Jr., & Hutchings, B. (1987). Genetic factors in the etiology of criminal behavior. In S. A. Mednick, T. E. Moffitt, & S. A.

Stack (Eds.), *The causes of crime: New biological approaches* (pp. 74–91). New York: Cambridge University Press.

Mednick, S. A., Volavka, J., Gabrielli, W. F., Jr., & Itil, T. M. (1981). EEG as a predictor of antisocial behavior. *Criminology, 19*, 219–229.

Mehrabian, A. (1978). Characteristic individual reactions of preferred and unpreferred environments. *Journal of Personality, 46*, 718–731.

Melis, M. S., & Argiolas, A. (1995). Dopamine and sexual behavior. *Neuroscience and Biobehavioral Reviews, 19*, 19–38.

Mellstrom, M., Jr., Cicala, G. A., & Zuckerman, M. (1976). General versus specific trait anxiety measures in the prediction of fear of snakes, heights, and darkness. *Journal of Consulting and Clinical Psychology, 44*, 83–91.

Merikangaqs, K. R., Stolar, M., Stevens, D. E., Goulet, J., Preisig, M. D., Fenton, B., et al. (1998). Familial transmission of substance use disorders. *Archives of General Psychiatry, 55*, 973–979.

Meszaros, K., Lenzinger, E., Hornik, K., Füreder, T., Willinger, U., Fischer, G., et al. (1999). The Tridimensional Personality Questionnaire as a predictor of relapse in detoxified alcohol dependents. *Alcoholism: Clinical and Experimental Research, 23*, 483–486.

Michel, G., Carton, S., & Jouvent, R. (1997). Sensation seeking and anhedonia in risk taking behaviors: Study in bungee jumpers. *L'Encéphale, 23*, 403–411.

Miles, D. R., van den Bree, M. B. M., Gupman, A. E., Newlin, D. B., Glanz, M. D., & Pickens, R. W. (2001). A twin study of risk-taking behavior and marijuana use. *Drug and Alcohol Dependence, 62*, 57–68.

Miller, J. D., Lynam, D., Zimmerman, R. S., Logan, T. K., Leukefeld, C., & Clayton, R. (2004). The utility of the five factor model in understanding risky sexual behavior. *Personality and Individual Differences, 36*, 1611–1626.

Miller, N. E. (1944). Experimental studies of conflict. In J. M. Hunt (Ed.), *Personality and the behavior disorders* (Vol. 1, pp. 431–465). New York: Ronald.

Moffitt, T. E. (1993). Adolescence-limited and life-course-persistent antisocial behavior: A developmental taxonomy. *Psychological Review, 100*, 674–701.

Moffitt, T. E., Caspi, A., & Rutter. M. (2006). Measured gene-environment interactions in psychopathology: Concepts, research strategies, and implications for research, intervention, and public understanding of genetics. *Perspectives on Psychological Science, 1*, 5–27.

Montag, I., & Birenbaum, M. (1986). Psychopathological factors and sensation seeking. *Journal of Research in Personality, 20*, 338–348

Moss, H. B., Yao, J. K., & Panzak, G. L. (1990). Serotonergic responsivity and behavioral dimensions in antisocial personality disorder with substance abuse. *Biological Psychiatry, 28*, 325–338.

Munafò, M. R., Clark, T. G., Moore, L. R., Payne, E., Walton, R., & Flint, J. (2003). Genetic polymorphisms and personality in healthy adults. *Molecular Psychiatry, 8*, 471–484.

Muramatsu, T., Higuchi, S., & Hayashida, M. (1996). Association between alcoholism and the dopamine D4 receptor gene. *Journal of Medical Genetics, 23,* 113–115.

Murgatroyd, S. (1985). The nature of telic dominance. In M. J. Apter, D. Fontana, & S. Murgatroyd (Eds.), *Reversal theory applications and development* (pp. 20–41). Cardiff, Wales: University College Cardiff Press.

Murgatroyd, S., Rushton, C., Apter, M. J., & Ray, C. (1978). The development of the Telic dominance scale. *Journal of Personality Assessment, 42,* 519–528.

Murphy, D. L., Aulakh, C. S., Garrick, N. A., & Sunderland, T. (1987). Monoamine oxidase inhibitors as antidepressants: Implications for the mechanism of action of antidepressants and the psychology of affective disorders and some related disorders. In H. Y. Meltzer (Ed.), *Psychopharmacology: The third generation of progress* (pp. 545–552). New York: Raven Press.

Murphy, D. L., Belmaker, R. H., Buchsbaum, M. S., Martin, N. F., Ciaranello, K., & Wyatt, R. J. (1977). Biogenic amine related enzymes and personality variations in normals. *Psychological Medicine, 7,* 149–157.

Murphy, D. L., & Weiss, R. (1972). Reduced monoamine oxidase activity in blood platelets from bipolar depressed patients. *American Journal of Psychiatry, 128,* 1351–1357.

Murray, D. M., Perry, C. L., Griffin, G., Harty, K. C., Jacobs, D. R., Jr., Schmid, L., et al. (1992). Results from a statewide approach to adolescent tobacco use prevention. *Preventive Medicine, 21,* 449–472.

Murray, H. W., Patkar, A. A., Manelli, P., De Maria, P., Desai, A. M., & Vergare, M. J. (2003). Relationship of aggression, sensation seeking, and impulsivity with severity of cocaine use. *Addictive Disorders and Their Treatment, 2,* 113–121.

Musolino, R. F., & Hershenson, D. B. (1977). Avocational sensation seeking in high and low risk-taking occupations. *Journal of Vocational Behavior, 10,* 358–365.

Mustanski, B. S., Viken, R. J., Kaprio, J., & Rose, R. J. (2003). Genetic influences on the association between personality and risk factors and alcohol use and abuse. *Journal of Abnormal Psychology, 112,* 282–289.

Naatanen, R., & Summala, H. (1974). A model for the role of motivational factors in drivers' decision making. *Accident Analysis and Prevention, 6,* 243–261.

Neary, R. S. (1975). *The development and validation of a state measure of sensation seeking.* Unpublished doctoral dissertation, University of Delaware, Newark.

Neary, R. S., & Zuckerman, M. (1976). Sensation seeking, trait and state anxiety, and the electrodermal orienting reflex. *Psychophysiology, 13,* 205–211.

Neria, Y., Solomon, Z., Ginzburg, K., & Dekel, R. (2000). Sensation seeking, wartime performance, and long-term adjustment among Israeli war veterans. *Personality and Individual Differences, 29,* 921–932.

Netter, P., Hennig, J., & Roed, I. S. (1996). Serotonin and dopamine as mediators of sensation seeking behavior. *Neuropsychobiology, 34,* 155–165.

Newcomb, M. D., Galaif, E. R., Carmona, J. J., & Vargas, J. (2001). The drug–crime nexus in a community sample of adults. *Psychology of Addictive Behaviors, 15*, 105–193.

Newcomb, M. D., & McGee, L. (1991). Influence of sensation seeking on general deviance and specific problem behaviors from adolescence to young adulthood. *Journal of Personality and Social Psychology, 61*, 614–628.

Noble, E. P. (1998). The D2 dopamine receptor gene: A review of association studies in alcoholism and phenotypes. *Alcohol, 16*, 33–45.

Noble, E. P., Blum, B., Khalsa, M. E., Ritchie, T., Montgomery, A., Wood, R. C., et al. (1993). Allelic association of the D2 dopamine receptor gene with cocaine dependence. *Drug and Alcohol Dependence, 33*, 271–285.

O'Carroll, R. E. (1984). Androgen administration to hypogonadal and eugonadal men: Effects on measures of sensation seeking, personality, and spatial ability. *Personality and Individual Differences, 5*, 595–598.

Ockene, J. K., Hymowitz, N., Sexton, M., & Broste, S. K. (1982). Comparison of patterns of smoking behavior change among smokers in the Multiple Risk Factor Intervention Trial (MRFIT). *Preventive Medicine, 11*, 621–638.

O'Connor, L. E., Berry, J. W., Morrison, A., & Brown, S. (1995). The drug-of-choice phenomena: Psychological differences among drug users who preferred different drugs. *International Journal of the Addictions, 30*, 541–555.

Oetting, E. R., Deffenbacher, J. L., & Donnermeyer, J. F. (1998). Primary socialization theory: Part II. The role played by personality traits in the etiology of drug use and deviance. *Substance Use and Misuse, 33*, 1337–1366.

Olweus, D. (1987). Testosterone and adrenaline: Aggressive antisocial behavior in normal adolescent males. In S. A. Mednick, T. E. Moffitt, & S. A. Stack (Eds.), *The causes of crime: New biological approaches* (pp. 263–282). Cambridge, England: Cambridge University Press.

O'Malley, S. S., Jaffey, A. J., Chang, G., Schottenfeld, R. S., Meyer, R. E., & Rounsaville, B. (1992). Naltrexone and coping skills therapy. *Archives of General Psychiatry, 49*, 881–887.

Ono, A., & Murayama, K. (1980). Stimulation seeking and selective attention in juvenile delinquents. *Memoirs of Osaka Kyoiku University, 35*(1), 33–41.

Oosterlaan, J., Geurts, H. M., Knol, D. L., & Sergeant, J. A. (2005). Low basal salivary cortisol is associated with teacher-reported symptoms of conduct disorder. *Psychiatry Research, 134*, 1–10.

Orlebeke, J. F., & Feij, J. A. (1979). The orienting reflex as a personality correlate. In E. H. van Holst & J. F. Orlebeke (Eds.), *The orienting reflex in humans* (pp. 567–585). Hillsdale, NJ: Erlbaum.

O'Sullivan, D. M., Zuckerman, M., & Kraft, M. (1996). The personality of prostitutes. *Personality and Individual Differences, 21*, 445–448.

O'Sullivan, D. M., Zuckerman, M., & Kraft, M. (1998). Personality characteristics of male and female participants in team sports. *Personality and Individual Differences, 25*, 119–128.

Palmgreen, P., Donohew, L., Lorch, E. P., Hoyle, R. H., & Stephenson, M. T. (2001). Television campaigns and adolescent marijuana use: Tests of sensation seeking targeting. *American Journal of Public Health, 91*, 292–296.

Palmgreen, P., Lorch, E. P., Donohew, L., Harrington, N. G., D'Silva, M., & Helm, D. (1995). Reaching at-risk populations in a mass media drug abuse prevention campaign: Sensation seeking as a targeting variable. *Drugs and Society, 8*, 29–45.

Parsons, J. T., Bimbi, D., & Halkitis, P. N. (2001). Sexual compulsivity among gay/bisexual male escorts who advertise on the Internet. *Sexual Addiction and Compulsivity, 8*, 101–112.

Parsons, J. T., & Halkitis, P. N. (2002). Sexual and drug-using practices of HIV-positive men who frequent public and commercial sex environments. *AIDS Care, 14*, 815–826.

Patkar, A. A., Berrettini, W. H., Hoehe, M., Thornton, C. C., Gottheil, E., Hill, K., & Weinstein, S. P. (2002). Serotonin transporter polymorphisms and measures of impulsivity, aggression, and sensation seeking among African American cocaine dependent individuals. *Psychiatry Research, 110*, 103–115.

Patkar, A. A., Gottheil, E., Berrettini, W. H., Hill, K. P., Thornton, C. C., & Weinstein, S. P. (2003). Relationship between platelet serotonin uptake sites and measures of impulsivity, aggression, and craving among African American cocaine abusers. *American Journal on Addictions, 12*, 432–447.

Patkar, A. A., Murray, H. W., Mannelli, P., Gottheil, E., Weinstein, S. P., & Vergare, M. J. (2004). Pretreatment measures of impulsivity, aggression, and sensation seeking are associated with treatment outcome for African American cocaine dependent patients. *Journal of Addictive Diseases, 23*, 109–122.

Pearson, P. H. (1970). Relationships between global and specific measures of novelty seeking. *Journal of Consulting and Clinical Psychology, 34*, 199–204.

Pederson, W., Clausen, S. E., & Lavik, N. J. (1989). Patterns of drug use and sensation seeking among adolescents in Norway. *Acta Psychiatrica Scandinavica, 79*, 386–390.

Pendery, M. L., Maltzman, I. M., & West, L. J. (1982, July 9). Controlled drinking by alcoholics? New findings and a reevaluation of a major affirmative study. *Science, 217*, 169–175.

Penney, R. K., & Reinehr, R. C. (1966). Development of a stimulus-variation seeking scale for adults. *Psychological Reports, 18*, 631–638.

Pérez, J., Ortet, G., Pla, S., & Simó, S. (1986). A Junior Sensation Seeking Scale. *Personality and Individual Differences, 7*, 915–918.

Pérez, J., & Torrubia, R. (1985). Sensation seeking and antisocial behavior in a student sample. *Personality and Individual Differences, 6*, 401–403.

Perkins, K. A., Gerlach, D., Broge, M., Fonte, C., & Wilson, A. (2001). Reinforcing effects of nicotine as a function of smoking status. *Experimental and Clinical Psychopharmacology, 9*, 243–250.

Petrie, A. (1967). *Individuality in pain and suffering*. Chicago: University of Chicago Press.

Pfaus, J. G., Damsma, G., Wenkstern, D., & Fibiger, H. C. (1995). Sexual activity increases dopamine transmission in the nucleus accumbens and striatum of female rats. *Brain Research, 693*, 21–30.

Pfefferbaum, B., & Wood, P. B. (1994). Self-report study of impulsive and delinquent behavior in college students. *Journal of Adolescent Health, 15*, 295–302.

Pickens, R. W., Svikis, D. S., McGue, M., Lykken, D. T., Heston, L. L., & Clayton, P. J. (1991). Heterogeneity in the inheritance of alcoholism: A study of male and female twins. *Archives of General Psychiatry, 48*, 19–41.

Pierson, A., le Houezec, U., Fossaert, A., Dubal, S., & Jouvent, R. (1999). Frontal reactivity and sensation seeking: An ERP study in skydivers. *Progress in Neuro-Psychopharmacology and Biological Psychiatry, 23*, 447–463.

Pilgrim, C., Luo, Q., Urberg, K. A., & Fang, X. (1999). Influence of peers, parents, and individual characteristics on adolescent drug use in two cultures. *Merrill-Palmer Quarterly, 45*, 85–107.

Platt, J. J., & Labate, C. (1976). *Heroin addiction: Theory, research, and treatment.* New York: Wiley.

Potgieter, J., & Bisschoff, F. (1990). Sensation seeking among medium- and low-risk sports. *Perceptual and Motor Skills, 71*, 1203–1206.

Potts, P., Martinez, I. G., & Dedmon, A. (1995). Childhood risk taking and injury: Self-report and informant measures. *Journal of Pediatric Psychology, 20*, 5–12.

Project MATCH Research Group. (1997). Matching alcoholism treatments to client heterogeneity: Project MATCH posttreatment drinking outcomes. *Journal of Studies on Alcohol, 58*, 7–29.

Prolo, P., & Licinio, J. (2002). DRD4 and novelty seeking. In J. Benjamin, R. P. Ebstein, & R. H. Belmakers (Eds.), *Molecular genetics and the human personality* (pp. 91–107). Washington, DC: American Psychiatric Publishing.

Raine, A. (1996). Autonomic nervous system activity and violence. In D. M. Stoff & R. B. Cairns (Eds.), *Aggression and violence: Genetic, neurobiological, and biosocial perspectives* (pp. 145–168). Mahwah, NJ: Erlbaum.

Raine, A. (1997). Antisocial behavior and psychophysiology: A biosocial perspective and a prefrontal dysfunction hypothesis. In D. M. Stoff, J. Breiling, & J. D. Maser (Eds.), *The handbook of antisocial behavior* (pp. 289–304). New York: Wiley.

Raine, A., Brennan, P., & Mednick, S. A. (1994). Birth complications combined with early maternal rejection at age 1 year predispose to violent crime at age 18 years. *Archives of General Psychiatry, 51*, 948–988.

Raine, A., Buchsbaum, M. S., & LaCasse, L. (1997). Brain abnormalities in murderers indicated by positron emission tomography. *Biological Psychiatry, 42*, 495–508.

Raine, A., & Venables, P. H. (1990). Evoked potential augmenting–reducing in psychopaths and criminals with impaired smooth-pursuit eye-movements. *Psychiatry Research, 31*, 85–98.

Rainey, D. W., Amunategui, F., Agocs, H., & Larick, J. (1992). Sensation seeking and competitive trait anxiety among rodeo athletes. *Journal of Sport Psychology, 15*, 307–317.

Raw, M., Jarvis, M. J., Feyerabend, C., & Russell, M. A. (1980). Comparison of nicotine chewing gum and psychological treatments for dependent smokers. *British Medical Journal, 281*, 481–482.

Raw, M., McNeill, A., & West, R. (1999). Smoking cessation: Evidence-based recommendations for the healthcare system. *British Medical Journal, 318*, 182–185.

Read, J. P., Wood, M. D., Kahler, C. W., Maddock, J. E., & Palfai, T. P. (2003). Examining the role of drinking motives in college student alcohol use and problems. *Psychology of Addictive Behaviors, 17*, 13–23.

Redmond, D. E., Jr., Murphy, D. L., & Baulu, J. (1979). Platelet monoamine oxidase activity correlates with social affiliative and agonistic behavior in normal rhesus monkeys. *Psychosomatic Medicine, 41*, 87–100.

Reiss, S., & McNally, R. J. (1985). The expectancy model of fear. In S. Reiss & R. R. Bootzin (Eds.), *Theoretical issues in behavior therapy* (pp. 107–122). New York: Academic Press.

Reist, C., Haier, R. J., De Met, E., & Cicz-DeMet, A. (1990). Platelet MAO activity in personality disorders and normal controls. *Psychiatry Research, 30*, 221–227.

Resnick, M. D., Bearman, P. S., Blum, R. W., Bauman, K. E., Bearman, P. S., Blum, R. W., et al. (1997). Protecting adolescents from harm: Findings from the National Longitudinal Study on Adolescent Health. *Journal of the American Medical Association, 278*, 823–832.

Reuter, M., Netter, P., Toll, C., & Hennig, J. (2002). Dopamine agonist and antagonist responders as related to types of nicotine craving and facets of extraversion. *Progress in Neuro-Psychopharmacology and Biological Psychiatry, 26*, 845–854.

Reynoso, J., Susabda, A., & Cepeda-Benito, A. (2005). Gender differences in smoking cessation. *Journal of Psychopathology and Behavioral Assessment, 27*, 227–234.

Richardson, D. R., Medvin, N., & Hammock, G. (1988). Love styles, relationship experience and sensation seeking: A test of validity. *Personality and Individual Differences, 9*, 645–651.

Ridgeway, D., & Hare, R. D. (1981). Sensation seeking and psychophysiological responses to auditory stimulation. *Psychophysiology, 18*, 613–618.

Ripa, C. P. L., Hansen, H. S., Mortensen, E. L., Sanders, S. A., & Reinisch, J. M. (2001). A Danish version of the Sensation Seeking Scale and its relation to a broad spectrum of behavioral and psychological characteristics. *Personality and Individual Differences, 30*, 1371–1386.

Rivers, K., Sarvela, P. D., Shannon, D. V., & Gast, J. (1996). Youth and young adult perceptions of drinking and driving prevention programs: A focus group study. *Journal of Alcohol and Drug Education, 41*, 80–91.

Robins, L. N. (1978). Aetiological implications in studies of childhood histories relating to antisocial personality. In R. D. Hare & D. Schalling (Eds.), *Psychopathic behavior: Approaches to research* (pp. 255–272). Chichester, England: Wiley.

Robins, L. N., & Regier, D. A. (Eds.). (1991). *Psychiatric disorders in America: The epidemiologic catchment area study*. New York: Free Press.

Robinson, D. W. (1985). Stress seeking: Selected behavioral characteristics of elite rock climbers. *Journal of Sport Psychology, 7*, 400–404.

Robinson, T. N., Jr., & Zahn, T. P. (1983). Sensation seeking, state anxiety, and cardiac and EDR orienting reactions [Abstract]. *Psychophysiology, 20*, 465.

Rolison, M. R., & Scherman, A. (2003). College student risk-taking from three perspectives. *Adolescence, 38*, 689–699.

Romero, E., Luengo, A., & Sobral, J. (2001). Personality and antisocial behavior: Study of temperamental dimensions. *Personality and Individual Differences, 31*, 329–348.

Rooney, B. L., & Murray, D. M. (1996). A meta-analysis of smoking prevention programs after adjustment for errors in the unit of analysis. *Health Education Quarterly, 23*, 48–64.

Rosenbloom, T. (2003a). Risk evaluation and risky behavior of high and low sensation seekers. *Social Behavior and Personality, 31*, 375–386.

Rosenbloom, T. (2003b). Sensation seeking and risk taking in mortality salience. *Personality and Individual Differences, 35*, 1809–1819.

Rosenbloom, T., & Wolf, Y. (2002a). Sensation seeking and detection of risky road signals: A developmental perspective. *Accident Analysis and Prevention, 34*, 569–580.

Rosenbloom, T., & Wolf, Y. (2002b). Signal detection in conditions of everyday life traffic dilemmas. *Accident Analysis and Prevention, 34*, 763–772.

Ross, M. W., Mattison, A. M., & Franklin, D. R. (2003). Club drugs and sex on drugs are associated with different motivations for gay circuit party attendance in men. *Substance Use and Misuse, 38*, 1173–1182.

Roth, M. (2003). Validation of the Arnett Inventory of Sensation Seeking (AISS): Efficiency to predict the willingness towards occupational chance, and affection by social desirability. *Personality and Individual Differences, 35*, 1307–1314.

Rounsaville, B. J., Anton, S. F., Carroll, K., Budde, D., Prusoff, D., & Gawin, F. (1991). Psychiatric diagnosis of treatment-seeking cocaine abusers. *Archives of General Psychiatry, 48*, 43–51.

Rowland, G. L., Franken, R. E., & Harrison, K. (1986). Sensation seeking and participating in sporting activities. *Journal of Sport Psychology, 8*, 212–220.

Ruchkin, V. V., Koposov, R. A., af Klinteberg, B., Oreland, L., & Grigorenko, E. L. (2005). Platelet MAO-B, personality, and psychopathology. *Journal of Abnormal Psychology, 114*, 477–482.

Russell, G. W. (2003). Sports riots: A social–psychological review. *Aggression and Violent Behavior, 9*, 353–378.

Russell, G. W., & Arms, R. L. (1998). Toward a social psychological profile of would-be rioters. *Aggressive Behavior, 24,* 219–226.

Russell, M. A. H., Stapleton, J. A., Jackson, P. H., Hajek, P., & Belcher, M. (1987). District program to reduce smoking: Effects of clinic-supported brief intervention by general practitioners. *British Medical Journal, 295,* 1240–1244.

Russo, M. F., Stokes, G. S., Lahey, B. B., Christ, M. A. G., McBurnett, K., Loeber, R., et al. (1993). A Sensation Seeking Scale for Children: Further refinement and psychometric development. *Journal of Psychopathology and Behavioral Assessment, 15,* 69–86.

Sannibale, C., & Hall, W. (1998). An evaluation of Cloninger's typology of alcohol abuse. *Addiction, 93,* 1241–1249.

Sannibale, C., & Hall, W. (2001). Gender-related problems and correlates of alcohol dependence among men and women with a lifetime diagnosis of alcohol-use disorders. *Drug and Alcohol Review, 20,* 369–383.

Sarason, I. G., & Spielberger, C. D. (Eds.). (1976). *Stress and anxiety* (Vol. 3). Washington, DC: Hemisphere Publication Services.

Sargent, J. D., Dalton, M. A., Beach, M. L., Mott, L. A., Tickle, J. J., Ahrens, B., & Heatherton, T. F. (2002). Viewing tobacco use in movies: Does it shape attitudes that mediate adolescent smoking? *American Journal of Preventive Medicine, 22,* 137–145.

Satterfield, J. H. (1987). Childhood diagnostic and neurophysiological predictors of teenage arrest rates: An eight-year prospective study. In S. A. Mednick, T. E. Moffitt, & S. A. Stack (Eds.), *The causes of crime: New biological approaches* (pp. 146–167). Cambridge, England: Cambridge University Press.

Saxton, A. J., & Calsyn, D. A. (1992). Alcohol use and high-risk behavior by intravenous drug users in an AIDS education program. *Journal of Studies on Alcohol, 53,* 611–618.

Saxton, P. M., Siegel, J., & Lukas, J. H. (1987). Visual evoked potential augmenting/reducing slopes in cats: Part II. Correlations with behavior. *Personality and Individual Differences, 8,* 511–519.

Schachter, S. (1982). Recidivism and self-cure of smoking and obesity. *American Psychologist, 37,* 436–444.

Schalling, D., Åsberg, M., Edman, G., & Oreland, L. (1987). Markers for vulnerability to psychopathology: Temperament traits associated with platelet MAO activity. *Acta Psychiatrica Scandinavica, 76,* 172–182.

Schinka, J. A., Letsch, E. A., & Crawford, F. C. (2002). DRD4 and novelty seeking: Results of meta-analyses. *American Journal of Medical Genetics, 114,* 643–648.

Schooler, C., Zahn, T. P., Murphy, D. L., & Buchsbaum, M. S. (1978). Psychological correlates of monoamine oxidase in normals. *Journal of Nervous and Mental Disease, 166,* 177–186.

Schroth, M. L. (1995). A comparison of sensation seeking among different groups of athletes and nonathletes. *Personality and Individual Differences, 18,* 219–222.

Schroth, M. L. (1996). Scores on sensation seeking as a predictor of sexual activities among homosexuals. *Perceptual and Motor Skills, 82,* 657–658.

Schuckit, M. A. (1988). A search for biological markers in alcoholism: Application to psychiatric research. In R. M. Rose & J. E. Barrett (Eds.), *Alcoholism: Origins and outcome* (pp. 143–154). New York: Raven Press.

Schuckit, M. A. (1994). Familial alcoholism. In T. A. Widiger, A. J. Francis, H. A. Pincus, M. B. First, R. Ross, & W. Davis (Eds.), *DSM–IV sourcebook* (Vol. 1, pp. 159–167). Washington, DC: American Psychiatric Association.

Schuckit, M. A., & Smith, T. L. (1996). An 8-year follow-up of 450 sons of alcoholic and control subjects. *Archives of General Psychiatry, 53,* 202–210.

Schwing, R. C., & Albers, W. A. (1980). *Societal risk assessment: How safe is safe enough?* New York: Plenum Press.

Segal, B. S., Huba, G., & Singer, J. F. (1980). *Drugs, daydreaming, and personality: Studies of college youth.* Hillsdale, NJ: Erlbaum.

Segal, B. S., & Singer, J. L. (1976). Daydreaming, drug and alcohol use in college students: A factor analytic study. *Addictive Behaviors, 1,* 227–235.

Shekim, W. O., Bylund, D. B., Alexson, J., Glaser, R. D., Jones, S. B., Hodges, K., & Perdue, S. (1986). Platelet MAO and measures of attention and impulsivity in boys with attention disorder deficit and hyperactivity. *Psychiatry Research, 18,* 179–188.

Sher, K. J. (1993). Children of alcoholics and the intergenerational transmission of alcoholism: A biopsychological perspective. In J. S. Baer, A. Marlatt, & R. J. McMahon (Eds.), *Addiction behaviors across the life span* (pp. 3–33). Newbury Park, CA: Sage.

Sher, K. J., Bartholow, B. D., & Wood, M. D. (2000). Personality and substance use disorders. *Journal of Consulting and Clinical Psychology, 68,* 818–829.

Sher, K. J., Bylund, D. B., Walitzer, K. S., Hartmann, J., & Ray-Prenger, C. (1994). Platelet monoamine oxidase (MAO) activity: Personality, substance abuse, and the stress-response-dampening effect of alcohol. *Experimental and Clinical Psychopharmacology, 2,* 53–81.

Shih, J. C., Chen, K., & Ridd, M. J. (1999). Monoamine oxidase: From genes to behavior. *Annual Review of Neuroscience, 22,* 197–217.

Sieber, M., & Angst, J. (1977). *Zur persoenlichkeit von drongen-alcohol-und zigarettenkonsumenten* [Personality in drug, alcohol, and cigarette smoking]. Unpublished manuscript.

Siegel, J., & Driscoll, P. (1996). Recent developments in an animal model of visual evoked potential augmenting/reducing and sensation seeking behavior. *Neuropsychobiology, 34,* 130–135.

Siegel, J., Sisson, D. F., & Driscoll, P. (1993). Augmenting and reducing of visual evoked potentials in Roman high- and low-avoidance rats. *Physiology and Behavior, 54,* 707–711.

Sigvardsson, S., Bohman, M., & Cloninger, C. R. (1996). Replication of the Stockholm adoption study: Confirmatory cross-fostering analysis. *Archives of General Psychiatry, 53,* 681–687.

Silagy, C., Lancaster, T., Stead, L., Mant, D., & Fowler, G. (2005). Nicotine replacement therapy for smoking cessation. *Cochrane Database of Systematic Reviews.* Available from http://www.cochrane.org/reviews/en/ab000146.html.

Simó, S., & Perez, J. (1991). Sensation seeking and antisocial behavior in a junior student sample. *Personality and Individual Differences, 12,* 965–966.

Skolnick, N. J., & Zuckerman, M. (1979). Personality changes in drug abusers: A comparison of therapeutic community and prison groups. *Journal of Consulting and Clinical Psychology, 47,* 768–770.

Slanger, E., & Rudestam, K. E. (1997). Motivation and disinhibition in high-risk sports: Sensation seeking and self-efficacy. *Journal of Research in Personality, 31,* 355–374.

Slater, M. D., Basil, M. D., & Maibach, E. W. (1999). A cluster analysis of alcohol-related attitudes and behaviors in the general population. *Journal of Studies on Alcohol, 60,* 667–674.

Slovic, P. (2000a). Do adolescent smokers know the risks? In P. Slovic (Ed.), *The perception of risk* (pp. 364–371). London: Earthscan.

Slovic, P. (Ed.). (2000b). *The perception of risk.* London: Earthscan.

Slovic, P. (2000c). Perception of risk. In P. Slovic (Ed.), *The perception of risk* (pp. 220–231). London: Earthscan.

Slovic, P., Fischoff, B., & Lichenstein, S. (1979). Rating the risks. *Environment, 21,* 14–20, 36, 39.

Slovic, P., Fischhoff, B., & Lichtenstein, S. (2000a). Facts and fears: Understanding perceived risk. In P. Slovic (Ed.), *The perception of risk* (pp. 137–153). London: Earthscan.

Slovic, P., Fischhoff, B., & Lichtenstein, S. (2000b). Rating the risks. In P. Slovic (Ed.), *The perception of risk* (pp. 104–120). London: Earthscan.

Slutske, W. S. (2005). Alcohol use disorders among U.S. college students and their noncollege attending peers. *Archives of General Psychiatry, 62,* 321–327

Smith, B. D., Davidson, R. A., Smith, D. L., Goldstein, H., & Perlstein, W. (1989). Sensation seeking and arousal: Effects of strong stimulation on electrodermal activation and memory task performance. *Personality and Individual Differences, 10,* 671–679.

Smith, B. D., Perlstein, W. M., Davidson, R. A., & Michael, K. (1986). Sensation seeking: Differential effects of relevant novel stimulation on electrodermal activity. *Personality and Individual Differences, 4,* 445–452.

Smith, D. L., & Heckert, T. M. (1998). Personality characteristics and traffic accidents of college students. *Journal of Safety Research, 29,* 163–169.

Smith, S. S., O'Hara, B. F., Persico, A. M., Gorelick, D. A., Newlin, D. B., Vlahov, D., et al. (1992). Genetic vulnerability to drug abuse. *Archives of General Psychiatry, 49,* 723–727.

Sobell, M. B., & Sobell, L. C. (1976). Second year treatment outcome of alcoholics treated by individualized behavior therapy: Results. *Behavior Research and Therapy, 14*, 195–215.

Solomon, Z., Ginzburg, K., Neria, Y., & Ohry, A. (1995). Coping with war captivity: The role of sensation seeking. *European Journal of Personality, 9*, 57–70.

Soubrié, P. (1986). Reconciling the role of central serotonin neurons in human and animal behavior. *Behavior and Brain Sciences, 9*, 319–364.

Specter, M. (2005, May 23). Higher risk: Crystal meth, the Internet, and dangerous choices about AIDS. *The New Yorker*, pp. 38–45.

Spotts, J. V., & Shontz, F. C. (1986). Drugs and personality: Dependence of findings on method. *American Journal of Drug and Alcohol Abuse, 12*, 355–382.

St. Lawrence, J. S., Brasfeld, T. L., Diaz, Y. E., Jefferson, K. W., Reynolds, M. T., & Leonard, M. C. (1994). Three-year follow-up of intervention that used popular peers. *American Journal of Public Health, 24*, 2027–2028.

St. Lawrence, J. S., Brasfeld, T. L., Jefferson, K. W., Alleyne, E., Shirley, A., & O'Bannon, R. E. (1995). Cognitive–behavioral intervention to reduce African American adolescents' risk for HIV infection. *Journal of Consulting and Clinical Psychology, 63*, 221–237.

St. Lawrence, J. S., Crosby, R. A., Belcher, L., Yazdani, N., & Brasfield, T. L. (1999). Sexual risk reduction and anger management interventions for incarcerated male adolescents: A randomized controlled trial of two interventions. *Journal of Sex Education and Therapy, 24*, 9–17.

St. Lawrence, J. S., Crosby, R. A., Brasfield, T. L., & O'Bannon, R. E. (2002). Reducing STD and HIV risk behavior of substance-dependent adolescents: A randomized controlled trial. *Journal of Consulting and Clinical Psychology, 70*, 1010–1021.

Stacy, A. W. (1997). Memory activation and expectancy as prospective predictors of alcohol and marijuana use. *Journal of Abnormal Psychology, 106*, 61–73.

Stacy, A. W., Newcomb, M. D., & Ames, S. L. (2000). Implicit cognition and HIV risk behavior. *Journal of Behavioral Medicine, 23*, 475–499.

Stacy, A. W., Newcomb, M. D., & Bentler, P. M. (1991). Personality, problem drinking, and drunk driving: Mediating, moderating, and direct-effect models. *Journal of Personality and Social Psychology, 60*, 795–811.

Stalenheim, E. G. (2004). Long-term validity of biological markers of psychopathy and criminal recidivism: Follow-up 6–8 years after forensic psychiatric investigation. *Psychiatry Research, 121*, 281–291.

Stall, R. D., Coates, T. J., & Hoff, C. (1988). Behavioral risk reduction for HIV infection among gay and bisexual men: A review of results from the United States. *American Psychologist, 43*, 878–885.

Stall, R. D., Hays R. B., Waldo, C. R., Ekstrand, M., & McFarland, W. (2000). The Gay 90s: A review of research in the 1990s on sexual behavior and HIV risk among men who have sex with men. *AIDS, 14*(Suppl. 3), 101–114.

Steigerwald, F., & Stone, D. (1999). Cognitive restructuring and the 12-step program of Alcoholics Anonymous. *Journal of Substance Abuse Treatment, 16,* 321–327.

Stein, J. A., Newcomb, M. D., & Bentler, P. M. (1994). Psychosocial correlates and predictors of AIDS risk behaviors, abortion, and drug use among a community sample of young adult women. *Health Psychology, 13,* 308–318.

Stelmack, R. M. (Ed.). (2004). *On the psychobiology of personality: Essays in honor of Marvin Zuckerman.* New York: Elsevier.

Stewart, S. H., Conrod, P. J., Marlatt, A., Comeau, N., Thush, C., & Krank, M. (2005). New developments in prevention and early intervention for alcohol abuse in youths. *Alcoholism: Clinical and Experimental Research, 29,* 278–286.

Stoolmiller, M., & Blechman, E. A. (2005). Substance use is a robust predictor of adolescent recidivism. *Criminal Justice and Behavior, 23,* 302–305.

Straub, W. F. (1982). Sensation seeking among high- and low-risk male athletes. *Journal of Sport Psychology, 4,* 246–253.

Strobel, A., Lesch, K. P., & Brocke, B. (2003, July). *Dopamine D4 receptor gene polymorphism and novelty seeking: Evidence for a modulatory role of additional polymorphisms.* Paper presented at the 11th Biennial Meeting of the International Society for the Study of Individual Differences, Graz, Austria.

Stuettgen, M. C., Hennig, J., Reuter, M., & Netter, P. (2005). Novelty seeking but not BAS is associated with high dopamine as indicated by a neurotransmitter challenge test using mazindol as a challenge substitute. *Personality and Individual Differences, 38,* 1597–1608.

Sullivan, J., Baenziger, J., Wagner, D., Rausher, F., Nurnberger, J., & Holmes, J. (1990). Platelet MAO in subtypes of alcoholism. *Biological Psychiatry, 27,* 911–922.

Sussman, S., Dent, C. W., Burton, D., Stacy, A. W., & Flay, B. F. L. (1995). *Developing school-based tobacco use prevention and cessation.* Thousand Oaks, CA: Sage.

Sussman, S., Simon, T. R., Dent, C. W., Steinberg, J. M., & Stacy, A. W. (1999). One-year prediction of violence perpetration among high-risk youth. *American Journal of Health Behavior, 23,* 332–344.

Svebak, S., & Kerr, J. (1989). The role of impulsivity in preference for sports. *Personality and Individual Differences, 10,* 51–58.

Swett, B., Marcus, R. F., & Reio, T. G. (2005). An introduction to "fight-seeking" and its role in peer-to-peer violence in college campuses. *Personality and Individual Differences, 38,* 953–962.

Syndulko, K. (1978). Electrocortical investigations of sociopathy. In R. D. Hare & D. Schalling (Eds.), *Psychopathic behaviour: Approaches to research* (pp. 145–156). Chichester, England: Wiley.

Tellegen, A. (1985). *Structure of mood and personality and their relevance to assessing anxiety with an emphasis on self-report.* In A. H. Tuma & J. D. Maser (Ed.), Anxiety and the anxiety disorders (pp. 681–706). Hillsdale, NJ: Erlbaum.

Thiffault, P., & Bergeron, J. (2003). Fatigue and individual differences in monotonous simulated driving. *Personality and Individual Differences, 34*, 159–176.

Thomas, M. H. (1999). Abstinence-based programs for prevention of adolescent pregnancies. *Journal of Adolescent Health, 26*, 5–17.

Thorne, G. L. (1971). The Sensation Seeking Scale with deviant populations. *Journal of Consulting and Clinical Psychology, 37*, 106–110.

Thornquist, M. H., & Zuckerman, M. (1995). Psychopathy, passive-avoidance learning, and basic dimensions of personality. *Personality and Individual Differences, 19*, 525–534.

Thornquist, M. H., Zuckerman, M., & Exline, R. V. (1991). Loving, liking, looking, and sensation seeking in unmarried college couples. *Personality and Individual Differences, 12*, 1283–1292.

Thuen, F. (1994). Injury-related behaviours and sensation seeking: An empirical study of a group of 14 year old Norwegian school children. *Health Education Research, 9*, 465–472.

Tillmann, W. A., & Hobbs, G. E. (1949). The accident-prone automobile driver: A study of the psychiatric and social background. *American Journal of Psychiatry, 106*, 321–331.

Tobler, N. S. (1992). Drug prevention programs can work. *Journal of the Addictive Diseases, 11*, 1–28.

Tremblay, R. E., Pihl, R. O., Vitaro, F., & Dobkin, P. L. (1994). Predicting early onset of male antisocial behavior from preschool behavior. *Archives of General Psychiatry, 51*, 732–739.

Trobst, K. K., Herbst, J. H., Masters, H. L., III, & Costa, P. T., Jr. (2002). Personality pathways to unsafe sex: Personality, condom use, and HIV risk behaviors. *Journal of Research in Personality, 36*, 117–133.

True, W. R., Heath, A. C., Scherrer, J. F., Waterman, B., Goldberg, J., Lin, N., et al. (1997). Genetic and environmental contributions to smoking. *Addiction, 92*, 1277–1287.

True, W. R., Xian, H., Scherrer, J. F., Madden, P. A. F., Bucholz, K. K., Heath, A. C., et al. (1999). Common genetic vulnerability for nicotine and alcohol dependence in men. *Archives of General Psychiatry, 56*, 655–661.

Tsuang, M. T., Lyons, M. J., Eisen, S. A., Goldberg, J., True, W., Lin, N., et al. (1996). Genetic influences on *DSM–III–R* drug abuse and dependence: A study of 3,372 twin pairs. *American Journal of Medical Genetics (Neuropsychiatric Genetics), 67*, 473–477.

Tsuang, M. T., Lyons, M. J., Meyer, J. M., Doyle, T., Eisen, M. D., Goldberg, J., et al. (1998). Co-occurrence of abuse of different drugs in men: The role of drug-specific and shared vulnerabilities. *Archives of General Psychiatry, 55*, 967–972.

Ulleberg, P. (2002). Personality subtypes of young drivers: Relationship to risk-taking preferences, accident involvement, and response to a traffic safety campaign. *Transportation Research, Part F: Traffic Psychology and Behavior, 4*, 279–297.

U.S. Department of Health and Human Services. (2000). *National household survey on drug abuse, 1988* (DHHS Publication No. 00-3381). Rockville, MD: Author.

U.S. Public Health Service. (1964). *Smoking and health: Report of the Advisory Committee to the Surgeon General of the Public Health Service* (PHS Publication No. 1103). Rockville, MD: U.S. Department of Health, Education, and Welfare.

Vaillant, G. E. (1983). *The natural history of alcoholism: Causes, patterns, and paths to recovery*. Cambridge, MA: Harvard University Press.

van Beurden, E., Zask, A., Brooks, L., & Dight, R. (2005). Heavy episodic drinking and sensation seeking in adolescents as predictors of harmful driving and celebrating behaviors: Implications for prevention. *Journal of Adolescent Health, 37*, 37–43.

Vando, A. (1974). The development of the R-A scale: A paper-and-pencil measure of pain tolerance. *Personality and Social Psychology Bulletin, 1*, 28–29

Vanwesenbeeck, I., Bekker, M., & van Lenning, A. (1998). Gender attitudes, sexual meanings, and international patterns in heterosexual encounters among college students in the Netherlands. *Journal of Sex Research, 35*, 317–327.

Varma, V. K., Basu, D., Malhotra, A., Sharma, A., & Mattoo, S. K. (1994). Correlates of early- and late-onset alcohol dependence. *Addictive Behaviors, 19*, 609–619.

Venables, P. H. (1987). Nervous system factors in criminal behavior. In S. A. Mednick, T. E. Moffitt, & S. A. Stack (Eds.), *The causes of crime: New biological approaches* (pp. 110–136). Cambridge, England: Cambridge University Press.

Verwey, W. B., & Zaidel, D. M. (2000). Predicting drowsiness accidents from personal attributes, eye blinks, and ongoing driving behavior. *Personality and Individual Differences, 28*, 123–142.

Vicary, J. R., & Karshin, C. M. (2002). College alcohol abuse: A review of the problems, issues, and prevention. *Journal of Primary Prevention, 22*, 299–231.

Virkkunen, M. (1985). Urinary free cortisol secretion in habitually violent offenders. *Acta Psychiatrica Scandinavica, 72*, 40–44.

Virkkunen, M., Nuutila, A., Goodwin, F. K., & Linnoila, M. (1987). Cerebrospinal fluid monoamine metabolites in male arsonists. *Archives of General Psychiatry, 44*, 241–247.

Virkkunen, M., Rawlings, R., Tokola, R., Poland, R. E., Guidotti, A., Nemeroff, C., & Bissette, G. (1994). CSF biochemistries, glucose metabolism, and diurnal activity in alcoholic, violent offenders, fire setters, and healthy volunteers. *Archives of General Psychiatry, 51*, 20–27.

Volavka, J. (1987). Electroencephalograms among criminals. In S. A. Mednick, T. E. Moffitt, & S. A. Stack (Eds.), *The causes of crime; New biological approaches* (pp. 137–145). Cambridge, England: Cambridge University Press.

Volavka, J. (1995). *Neurobiology of violence*. Washington, DC: American Psychiatric Publishing.

Volpicelli, J. R., Krishnan-Sarin, S., & O'Malley, S. S. (2002). Alcoholism pharma-cotherapy. In K. L. Davis, D. Charney, J. T. Coyle, & C. Nemeroff (Eds.), *Neuropsychopharmacology: The fifth generation of progress* (pp. 1445–1459). Philadelphia: Lippincott Williams & Wilkins.

von Knorring, A. L., Bohman, M., von Knorring L., & Oreland, L. (1985). Platelet MAO activity as a marker in subgroups of alcoholism. *Acta Psychiatric Scandinavica, 72,* 51–58.

von Knorring, L., & Johansson, F. (1980). Changes in the augmenter–reducer tendency and in pain measures as a result of treatment with a serotonin reuptake inhibitor, zimelidine. *Neuropsychobiology, 6,* 313–318.

von Knorring, L., & Oreland, L. (1985). Personality traits and platelet monoamine oxidase in tobacco smokers. *Psychological Medicine, 15,* 327–334.

von Knorring, L., Oreland, L., & von Knorring, A. L. (1987). Personality traits and platelet MAO activity in alcohol and drug abusing teenage boys. *Acta Psychiatrica Scandinavica, 75,* 307–314.

von Knorring, L., Oreland, L., & Winblad, B. (1984). Personality traits related to monoamine oxidase activity in platelets. *Psychiatry Research, 12,* 11–26.

von Knorring, L., Palm, U., & Anderson, H. E. (1985). Relationship between treatment outcome and subtype of alcoholism in men. *Journal of Studies on Alcohol, 46,* 388–391.

von Knorring, L., & Perris, C. (1981). Biochemistry of the augmenting–reducing response in visual evoked potentials. *Neuropsychobiology, 7,* 1–8.

Wagner, A. M., & Houlihan, D. D. (1994). Sensation seeking and trait anxiety in hang-glider pilots and golfers. *Personality and Individual Differences, 16,* 975–977.

Wagner, M. K. (2001). Behavioral characteristics related to substance abuse and risk-taking, sensation seeking, anxiety sensitivity, and self-reinforcement. *Addictive Behaviors, 26,* 115–120.

Waters, C. W., Ambler, R., & Waters, L. K. (1976). Novelty and sensation seeking in two academic training situations. *Education and Psychological Measurement, 36,* 453–457.

Watten, R. G. (1996). Coping styles in abstainers from alcohol. *Psychopathology, 29,* 340–346.

Webb, J. A., Baer, P. E., & McKelvey, R. S. (1995). Development of a risk profile for intentions to use alcohol among fifth and sixth graders. *Journal of the American Academy of Child and Adolescent Psychiatry, 34,* 772–778.

Whissel, R. W., & Bigelow, B. J. (2003). The speeding attitude scale and the role of sensation seeking in profiling young drivers at risk. *Risk Analysis, 23,* 811–820.

White, H. R., Bates, M. E., & Buyske, S. (2001). Adolescence-limited versus persistence delinquency: Extending Moffitt's hypothesis into adulthood. *Journal of Abnormal Psychology, 110,* 600–609.

White, W. R., Labouvie, E. W., & Bates, M. E. (1985). The relationship between sensation seeking and delinquency: A longitudinal analysis. *Journal of Research in Crime and Delinquency, 22,* 197–211.

Whiteside, S. F., & Lynam, D. R. (2003). Understanding the role of impulsivity and externalizing psychopathology in alcohol abuse: Application of the UPPS Impulsive Behavior Scale. *Experimental and Clinical Psychopathology, 11,* 210–217.

Whitfield, J. B., Pang, D., Bucholz, K. K., Madden, P. A. F., Heath, A. C., Statham, & Martin, N. G. (2000). Monoamine oxidase: Associations with alcohol dependence, smoking, and other measures of psychopathology. *Psychological Medicine, 30,* 443–454.

Wiederman, M. W., & Hurd, C. (1999). Extradyadic involvement during dating. *Journal of Social and Personal Relationships, 16,* 265–274.

Wiesbeck, G. A., Mauerer, C., Thome, J., Jakob, F., & Boening, J. (1995). Neuroendocrine support for a relationship between "novelty seeking" and dopaminergic function in alcohol dependent men. *Psychoneuroendocrinology, 20,* 755–761.

Wiesbeck, G. A., Wodarz, N., Mauerer, C., Thorne, J., Jakob, F., & Boening, J. (1996). Sensation seeking, alcoholism, and dopamine activity. *European Psychiatry, 11,* 87–92.

Wilde, G. J. S. (1982). The theory of risk homeostasis: Implications for safety and health. *Risk Analysis, 2,* 209–225

Willoughby, T., Chalmers, H., & Busseri, M. A. (2004). Where is the syndrome? Examining co-occurrence among multiple program behaviors in adolescence. *Journal of Consulting and Clinical Psychology, 72,* 1022–1037.

Wills, T. A., Windle, M., & Cleary, S. D. (1998). Temperament and novelty seeking in adolescent substance use: Convergence of dimensions of temperament with constructs from Cloninger's theory. *Journal of Personality and Social Psychology, 74,* 387–406.

Wilson, R. J. (1990). The relationship of seat belt nonuse to personality, lifestyle, and driving record. *Health Education Research, 5,* 175–185.

Windsor, R. A., Cutter, G., Morris, J., Reese, Y., Manzella, B., Bartlett, E. E., et al. (1985). The effectiveness of smoking cessation methods for smokers in public health maternity clinics: A randomized trial. *American Journal of Public Health, 75,* 1389–1392.

Witte, K., & Donohue, W. A. (2000). Preventing vehicle crashes with trains at grade crossings: The risk seeker challenge. *Accident Analysis and Prevention, 32,* 127–139.

Wolitski, R. J., Valdiserri, R. O., Denning, P. H., & Levine, W. C. (2001). Are we headed for a resurgence of the HIV epidemic among men who have sex with men? *American Journal of Public Health, 91,* 883–888.

Wood, P. B., Cochran, J. K., Pfefferbaum, B., & Arneklev, B. J. (1995). Sensation seeking and delinquent substance use: An extension of learning theory. *Journal of Drug Issues, 25,* 173–193.

Woodman, D., Hinton, J., & O'Neill, M. (1977). Abnormality of catecholamine balance relating to social deviance. *Perceptual and Motor Skills, 45,* 593–594.

Wright, J. W. (Ed.). (2002). *The New York Times 2002 Almanac.* New York: Penguin.

Wundt, W. M. (1893). *Grundzuge der physiologischen psychologie* [Basics of physiological psychology]. Leipzig, Germany: Engleman.

Xantidis, L., & McCabe, M. P. (2000). Personality characteristics of male clients of female commercial sex workers in Australia. *Archives of Sexual Behavior, 29,* 165–176.

Xiaoming, L., Stanton, B., Cottrell, L., Burns, J., Pack, R., & Kaljee, L. (2000). Patterns of initiation of sex and drug-related activities among African American adolescents. *Journal of Adolescent Health, 28,* 46–54.

Yagel, D. (2001). Reasoned action and irrational motives: A prediction of driver's intention to violate traffic laws. *Journal of Applied Social Psychology, 31,* 720–740.

Yates, J. F., & Stone, E. R. (1992). The risk construct. In J. F. Yates (Ed.), *Risk-taking behavior* (pp. 1–25). New York: Wiley.

Yu, P., Davis, B., Bowen, R., Wormith, S., Addington, D., & Boulton, A. (1984). Platelet monoamine oxidase activity and plasma trace acid levels in agoraphobic patients and in violent offenders. In K. F. Tipton, P. Dostert, & M. Strolin-Benedetti (Eds.), *Monoamine oxidase and disease* (pp. 643–644). London: Academic Press.

Zaleski, Z. (1984). Sensation seeking and risk-taking behaviour. *Personality and Individual Differences, 5,* 607–608.

Zalsman, G., & Apter, A. (2002). Serotonergic metabolism and violence/aggression. In J. Glicksohn (Ed.), *Neurobiology of criminal behavior* (pp. 231–250). Boston: Kluwer Academic.

Zarevski, P., Marusic, I., Zolotic, S., Bunjevac, T., & Vukosav, Z. (1998). Contribution of Arnett's Inventory of Sensation Seeking and Zuckerman's Sensation Seeking Scale to the differentiation of athletes engaged in high- and low-risk sports. *Personality and Individual Differences, 25,* 763–768.

Zuckerman, M. (1969a). Theoretical formulations. In J. P. Zubek (Ed.), *Sensory deprivation: Fifteen years of research* (pp. 407–432). New York: Appleton-Century-Crofts.

Zuckerman, M. (1969b). Variables affecting deprivation results. In J. P. Zubek (Ed.), *Sensory deprivation: Fifteen years of research* (pp. 47–84). New York: Appleton-Century-Crofts.

Zuckerman, M. (1971). Dimensions of sensation seeking. *Journal of Consulting and Clinical Psychology, 36,* 45–52.

Zuckerman, M. (1976). Sensation seeking and anxiety, traits and states, as determinants of behavior in novel situations. In I. G. Sarason & C. D. Spielberger (Eds.), *Stress and anxiety* (Vol. 3, pp. 141–170). Washington, DC: Hemisphere Publication Services.

Zuckerman, M. (1979a). *Sensation seeking: Beyond the optimal level of arousal.* Hillsdale, NJ: Erlbaum.

Zuckerman, M. (1979b). Sensation seeking and risk taking. In C. E. Izard (Ed.), *Emotions in personality and psychopathology* (pp. 163–197). New York: Plenum Press.

Zuckerman, M. (1983a). Sensation seeking: The initial motive for drug abuse. In E. H. Gotheil, K. A. Druley, & H. M. Waxman (Eds.), *Etiological aspects of alcohol and drug abuse* (pp. 202–220). Springfield, IL: Charles C Thomas.

Zuckerman, M. (1983b). Sensation seeking and sports. *Personality and Individual Differences, 4,* 285–292.

Zuckerman, M. (1984a). Experience and desire: A new format for Sensation Seeking Scales. *Journal of Behavioral Assessment, 6,* 101–114.

Zuckerman, M. (1984b). Sensation seeking: A comparative approach to a human trait. *Behavioral and Brain Sciences, 7,* 413–434.

Zuckerman, M. (1986a). Sensation seeking and augmenting–reducing: Evoked potentials and/or kinesthetic figural aftereffects. *Behavioral and Brain Sciences, 9,* 749–754.

Zuckerman, M. (1986b). Sensation seeking and the endogenous deficit theory of drug abuse. *National Institute of Drug Abuse Research Monographs, 74,* 59–70.

Zuckerman, M. (1987a). Biological connection between sensation seeking and drug abuse. In L. Engel & L. Oreland (Eds.), *Brain reward systems and abuse* (pp. 165–176). New York: Raven Press.

Zuckerman, M. (1987b). Is sensation seeking a predisposing trait for alcoholism? In E. Gotheil, K. A. Druley, S. Pashkey, & S. P. Weinstein (Eds.), *Stress and addiction* (pp. 283–301). New York: Brunner/Mazel.

Zuckerman, M. (1989). Personality in the third dimension: A psychobiological approach. *Personality and Individual Differences, 10,* 391–418.

Zuckerman, M. (1990). The psychophysiology of sensation seeking. *Journal of Personality, 58,* 313–345.

Zuckerman, M. (1991). *Psychobiology of personality.* Cambridge, England: Cambridge University Press.

Zuckerman, M. (1994). *Behavioral expressions and biosocial bases of sensation seeking.* New York: Cambridge University Press.

Zuckerman, M. (1995). Good and bad humors: Biochemical bases of personality and its disorders. *Psychological Science, 6,* 325–332.

Zuckerman, M. (1996a). Item revisions in the Sensation Seeking Scale Form V (SSS–V). *Personality and Individual Difference, 20,* 515.

Zuckerman, M. (1996b). The psychobiological model for impulsive unsocialized sensation seeking: A comparative approach. *Neuropsychobiology, 34,* 125–129.

Zuckerman, M. (1999). *Vulnerability to psychopathology: A biosocial model.* Washington, DC: American Psychological Association.

Zuckerman, M. (2002). Zuckerman–Kuhlman Personality Questionnaire (ZKPQ): An alternative five-factorial model. In B. De Raad & M. Peraigini (Eds.), *Big Five assessment* (pp. 377–396). Seattle, WA: Hogrefe & Huber.

Zuckerman, M. (2003). Biological bases of personality. In T. Millon & M. J. Lerner (Eds.), *Handbook of psychology: Vol. 5. Personality and social psychology* (pp. 85–116). Hoboken, NJ: Wiley.

Zuckerman, M. (2004). The shaping of personality: Genes, environments, and chance encounters. *Journal of Personality Assessment, 82*, 11–22.

Zuckerman, M. (2005). *Psychobiology of personality* (2nd ed., Rev. ed.). New York: Cambridge University Press.

Zuckerman, M. (2006a). Biosocial bases of sensation seeking. In T. Canli (Ed.), *Biology of personality and individual differences* (pp. 37–59). New York: Guilford Press.

Zuckerman, M. (2006b). Sensation seeking in entertainment. In J. Bryant & P. Vorderer (Eds.), *Psychology of entertainment* (pp. 367–387). Mahwah, NJ: Erlbaum.

Zuckerman, M., Ball, S., & Black, J. (1990). Influences of sensation seeking, gender, risk appraisal, and situational motivation on smoking. *Addictive Behaviors, 15*, 209–220.

Zuckerman, M., Bone, R. N., Neary, R, Mangelsdorf, D., & Brustman, B. (1972). What is the sensation seeker? Personality trait and experience correlates of the Sensation Seeking Scales. *Journal of Consulting and Clinical Psychology, 39*, 308–321.

Zuckerman, M., & Cloninger, C. R. (1996). Relationships between Cloninger's, Zuckerman's, and Eysenck's dimensions of personality. *Personality and Individual Differences, 21*, 283–285.

Zuckerman, M., Eysenck, S. B. G., & Eysenck, H. J. (1978). Sensation seeking in England and America: Cross-cultural, age, and sex comparisons. *Journal of Consulting and Clinical Psychology, 46*, 139–149.

Zuckerman, M., Kolin, E. A., Price, L., & Zoob, I. (1964). Development of a sensation seeking scale. *Journal of Consulting Psychology, 28*, 477–482.

Zuckerman, M., & Kuhlman, D. M. (2000). Personality and risk-taking: Common biosocial factors. *Journal of Personality, 68*, 999–1029.

Zuckerman, M., Kuhlman, D. M., & Camac, C. (1988). What lies beyond E and N? Factor analyses of scales believed to measure basic dimensions of personality. *Journal of Personality and Social Psychology, 54*, 96–107.

Zuckerman, M., Kuhlman, D. M., Joireman, J., Teta, P., & Kraft, M. (1993). A comparison of three structural models for personality: The Big Three, the Big Five, and the Alternative Five. *Journal of Personality and Social Psychology, 65*, 757–768.

Zuckerman, M., Kuhlman, D. M., Thornquist, M., & Kiers, H. (1991). Five (or three) robust questionnaire scale factors of personality without culture. *Personality and Individual Differences, 12*, 929–941.

Zuckerman, M., Murtaugh, T. T., & Siegel, J. (1974). Sensation seeking and cortical augmenting–reducing. *Psychophysiology, 11*, 535–542.

Zuckerman, M., & Myers, P. L. (1983). Sensation seeking in homosexual and heterosexual males. *Archives of Sexual Behavior, 12*, 347–356.

Zuckerman, M., Neary, R. S., & Brustman, B. A. (1970). Sensation Seeking Scale correlates in experience (smoking, drugs, alcohol, "hallucinations," and sex) and preference for complexity (designs). *Proceedings of the 78th Annual Convention of the American Psychological Association, 5*, 317–318.

Zuckerman, M., & Neeb, M. (1980). Demographic influences in sensation seeking and expressions of sensation seeking in religion, smoking, and driving habits. *Personality and Individual Differences, 1*, 197–206.

Zuckerman, M., Persky, H., Hopkins, T. R., Murtaugh, T., Basu, G. K., & Schilling, M. (1966). Comparison of stress effects of perceptual and social isolation. *Archives of General Psychiatry, 14*, 356–365.

Zuckerman, M., Persky, H., Link, K. E., & Basu, G. K. (1968). Experimental and subject factors determining responses to sensory deprivation, social isolation, and confinement. *Journal of Abnormal Psychology, 73*, 183–194.

Zuckerman, M., Simons, R. F., & Como, P. G. (1988). Sensation seeking and stimulus intensity as modulators of cortical, cardiovascular, and electrodermal response: A cross-modality study. *Personality and Individual Differences, 9*, 361–372.

Zuckerman, M., Sola, S., Masterson, J., & Angelone, J. V. (1975). MMPI patterns in drug abusers before and after treatment in therapeutic communities. *Journal of Consulting and Clinical Psychology, 43*, 286–296.

Zuckerman, M., Tushup, R., & Finner, S. (1976). Sexual attitudes and experience: Attitude and personality correlations and changes produced by a course in sexuality. *Journal of Consulting and Clinical Psychology, 44*, 7–19.

Zureick, J. L., & Meltzer, H. Y. (1988). Platelet MAO activity in hallucinating and paranoid schizophrenics: A review and meta-analysis. *Biological Psychiatry, 24*, 63–78.

AUTHOR INDEX

Wood, M. D., 117, 126
Wood, P. B., 107, 113, 114, 172
Wood, P. K., 172
Woodman, D., 199
Woodworth, G., 138, 191
Wright, J. W., 118, 123, 124, 170, 208, 231, 233
Wundt, W. M., 4

Xantidis, L., 157
Xiaoming, L., 153
Xin, G., 79

Yao, J. K., 199
Yardley, J. K., 113, 114
Yates, J. F., 51, 52
Yates, W. R., 138, 191
Yazdani, N., 231
Yu, P., 198

Zahn, T. P., 22, 197
Zaidel, D. M., 84
Zaleski, Z., 93, 103

Zalsman, G., 199
Zarevski, P., 91
Zask, A., 222
Zettler-Segal, M., 119
Zimmerman, R. S., 204, 215
Zingaro, M., 100
Zogg, J. B., 83
Zolotic, S., 91
Zoob, I., xiii, 4
Zuckerman, M., xiii, 4, 5, 6, 7, 8, 9, 10, 11, 12, 13, 14, 15, 16, 17, 18, 19, 21, 23, 24, 25, 26, 27, 32, 33, 34, 36, 39, 40, 41, 42, 43, 45, 45n, 47, 48, 49, 52, 56, 57, 58, 60, 61, 62, 63, 64, 67, 68, 69, 74, 76, 77, 79, 81, 82, 83, 88, 93, 97, 101, 108, 109, 114, 115, 116, 118, 119, 125, 126, 131, 133, 135, 136, 146, 147, 148, 149, 150, 150n, 155, 156, 159, 167, 170, 171, 174, 174–175, 175, 177, 178, 185, 186, 187, 190, 192, 193, 195, 196, 197, 199, 200, 225, 233, 234
Zureik, J. L., 23
Zweben, A., 157

SUBJECT INDEX

Arnett's Inventory of Sensation Seeking
(AISS), 39, 45–46, 57, 63, 91,
124, 125, 223
Arousal and arousability, 47, 193–197,
200–201
and fear self-ratings, 67
and heart rate, 78
optimal level of, xiii, 4, 5–6, 74,
117, 193
and parachute jumping, 97
and sensation seeking, 27
Arousal Avoidance subscale, 47
Arousal function, level of, 6
Arousal Seeking Tendency (AST) scale,
47
Arousal theory, and extraverts, 83
Art, and ES subscale, 15
Assortative mating, 36–37
Attention-deficit/hyperactivity disorder
and DRD4 gene, 38
and MAO, 23
Auditory evoked potentials (EPs), 18
Augmenters, 16, 23, 24, 47
Augmenting, 16, 18, 46–47
Aromatization hypothesis, 21
Auto racing, 100
Aversive conditioning
to alcohol, 131, 223
and criminality, 193
against smoking, 120, 213

Balloon Analogue Risk Task (BART),
63–64
Barbiturates, 115, 118
perceived risks and benefits for, 55
See also Drug use
BAS (behavioral approach system), 26
Barron–Welsh Preference for Designs,
9–10
Behavioral inhibition, and serotonin, 27
Beta-endorphin, 133
Big Five personality factors, 3, 47–48,
155
Biochemical studies
on monoamine oxidase (MAO),
22–24
on sex hormones, 21
theory based on, 24–28
Biochemistry, in sensation seeking and
antisocial behavior, 197–198

Biological mechanisms
in alcoholism, 132–134, 135
for heroin and cocaine, 138–140
Biosocial bases of antisocial behavior,
crime and psychopathy, 197–200,
200–201
and arousal or arousability, 193–197,
200–201
biochemistry in, 198–200
Bipolar mood disorder, and MAO, 22, 23
Birth control (contraception), 146, 153–
154, 158
BIS (behavioral inhibition system), 26
Bisexuals, and sexual risk taking, 152
Blacks. See African Americans
Borderline personality disorder
and MAO, 23
and serotonergic response, 199
Boredom
and alcohol use, 129
combat as release from, 75
DA and NE in, 24
and OLA, 5
restlessness as, 8
vs. risky duty, 105–106
in sensory deprivation experiments,
9, 83
Boredom Susceptibility scale. See BS
subscale
Brain
dopamine activity in, 29, 138, 167
and drugs, 138–139
and prenatal testosterone levels, 21
and psychopathy, 194
and smoking, 120
Brief Sensation Seeking Scale (BSSS),
44
Bungee jumping, 98
Buss–Durkee Hostility Inventory (BDHI),
225

Caffeine, perceived risks and benefits
from, 55
California Psychological Inventory, 185
Canoeing, white-water, 100
Catecholamine system activity (CSA),
24–26
Cerebrospinal fluid. See CSF
Change Seeker Index, 46
Chess players, 92

Children's form of Sensation Seeking
 Scale, 39, 113–114, 171
Cigarettes. *See* Smoking (tobacco)
Circuit parties, 166
Clonidine, 30
Cocaine, 26, 29, 135–141
 counteracting results of, 117–118
 dependence percentage for, 205
 and gay sex, 164
 vs. nicotine, 109
 treatment programs for, 222–223,
  225, 228
 and young adults, 115
 See also Drug use
Cognitive–behavioral coping skills
  therapy (CBT–CST), for alcohol
  abuse, 220, 221
Cognitive–behavioral therapy (CBT),
  227
 for alcohol abuse, 224
 for cocaine abuse, 226
 and depression, 226
Cognitive experience seeking, 46
Cognitive impulsivity, 174
Cognitive therapies approach
 for alcoholism, 220
 for cocaine abuse, 226
 for smoking cessation, 208
Comorbidity
 between alcohol, opiates and
  cocaine, 135
 between alcohol disorders and
  other drug disorders, 127
 between tobacco and alcohol, 120
Conditioning, and criminality, 193–
  194
Condom use
 positive and negative associations
  for, 60
 predictors of use of, 230
Congenital influences, 190
Conscientiousness dimension
 and NEO, 48
 and risky sexual behavior, 155
Conscientiousness factor, 186
Conscientiousness scale, 177
Consideration of future consequences
  (CFC) scale, 180
 and aggression, 182, 182–183
Constraint factor, and prediction of
  violence, 179

Construct validity, 4
 research on, 14–15
Content validity, 39
Cortical arousal and arousability, in
  psychopathy, 194–195
Cortical evoked potential (EP), 13, 16–
  21, 28, 46, 194–195
Corticotrophin releasing factor (CRF),
  24, 28, 200
Cortisol, 24, 200
CPI Imp scale, 113
Crime and criminality, xiv
 biosocial bases of, 187–192, 200–201
  and arousal or arousability, 193–
   197, 200–201
  biochemistry in, 198–200
 in "emerging adulthood," 170
 and MAO, 23
 motivation in, 169
 and sensation seeking, 169, 171, 178
  and risk appraisal, 175–176
Crystal methamphetamine, 159
CSA (catecholamine system activity),
  24–26
CSF (cerebrospinal fluid), 28, 29, 29–31
 and augmenters, 23
 cortisol in, 200
 NE in, 200

DA. *See* Dopamine
Danger detection, in driving behavior,
  84–86
Danish adoption study on criminality,
  190
DARE (Project Drug Abuse Resistance
  Education), 207–208
DA receptor genes, and NS, 38
DBH (domapine beta-hydroxylase) 27,
  28
Death anxiety, 91
Death risk, 53–55
Defensive reflex (DR), 10, 15, 197
Delinquency, 170–172
 institutionalized delinquents, 176
 longitudinal studies of, 172–174
 self-reports of, 172
 types of, 172–173
 See also Crime and criminality
Demographic studies, 14
Dependence, 127

Depression
    and CBT for cocaine, 226
    and serotonin activity, 139–140
    and SRIs, 27
Design preferences, 9, 10, 11
    and ES subscale, 15
Developmental type of intervention
    program, 205
Diazepam, 26
Dihydroxyphenylacetic acid (DOPAC),
    29
Dis Experience (Dis-Exp), 41
Disinhibition, and alcohol, 132
Dis Intentions (Dis-Int), 41
Dis (Disinhibition) subscale, 13, 15,
    40
Disulfiram, 223
Divergent thinking, 48
Dominance, 29
Dopamine (DA), 29, 32
    and alcohol, 133
    in animal models, 28
    and approach, 27
    and CSA, 24
    and DA reactivity, 29, 32
    and drugs, 138, 139, 140
    in high P scorers, 32
    and MAOs, 22, 139, 198
    and nicotine, 120, 121, 123
    and novel sensation, 26
    and sensation seeking, 30, 32, 76,
        108, 139, 168
    and sex, 167–168
Dopamine metabolites, 23, 29, 30, 31
Dopaminergic pathways, 38
Dopaminergic reactions, 76
Dopaminergic reactivity, 32
    and MAO, 122
Dopaminergic release, and "ecstasy,"
    143
Dopaminergic system
    and drug use, 136
    and smoking, 121
    and stress, 24
DR (defensive reflex), 10, 15, 197
DRD4 gene, 37, 38, 132, 134, 138, 141
Driving, risky, 73–87
    actual and perceived risk from, 54
    auto racing, 100
    correlations of, 61
    and danger detection, 84–86

    and DWI, 82–83
    following behavior, 80–81
    by police officers, 104
    and seat-belt use, 86
    and traffic violations or accidents,
        81–82
    and vigilance, 83–86
Drug use, 42, 110, 117–118, 135–141,
    234
    in age groups
        high school and middle school,
            110–115
        young adults, 115–117
    correlations of, 61
    and deviance, 170
    and HIV, 156
    and MAO, 23
    polydrug users, 109, 116, 135, 137,
        142, 155, 156, 157, 218
    and postdrug life, 235
    and prenatal environmental risk,
        191
    prevention of, 214–219
    psychedelic drugs, 141–143
    and sensation seeking, 108, 110,
        112, 116, 117–118, 137, 138,
        139, 140, 140–141, 143
        in adolescents, 114, 114–115
        cocaine, 136
        and marijuana or alcohol, 109
        psychedelic drugs, 142
    and sex, 155, 157, 158, 233
        among gay men, 162, 163, 163–
            164, 166, 167
        vulnerability to sexual risk as re-
            sult of, 231
    and stimulant drugs, 26, 117–118
    treatment of, 219–226
    See also Amphetamine; Barbiturates;
        Cocaine; Heroine; Marijuana;
        Morphine; Substance use and
        abuse
DSM. See at Diagnostic and Statistical
    Manual of Mental Disorders

"Ecstasy" (MDMA), 141, 142–143, 166
Educational levels
    and alcohol use, 123–124
    and criminality, 192
Endogenous deficit theory, 133

General Risk Appraisal Scale, 52, 174
Genetics, 3
    and alcohol use, 130–132, 134
    and assortative mating, 36–37
    and changes in environment, 201
    and criminality, 187
        and adoption studies, 190–191,
          192
        and prenatal environmental risk,
          191
        and twin studies, 187–189, 192
    and drug use, 137–138
    molecular, 37–38
    parent–child studies, 35–36
    and risky behavior among
        adolescents, 154
    and sensation seeking, 131, 188, 234
    and smoking, 204
    and tobacco–alcohol comorbidity,
        120, 123
    and twin studies, 32–35
"Getting kicks," 107
Group drug counseling (GDC), 226
Growth hormone (GH), 32

Habituation, 196
    serotonin and MAO in, 25
Hang gliding, 99–100
Harm Avoidance (HA), 43
    and alcoholism types, 128
    and prediction of violence, 179
    and risky sex among adolescents,
        158
    and substance abuse, 117
        alcohol abuse, 124
Hashish, 115
Heart rate (HR), 10, 15, 78, 196–197
Heights, fear of, 71
Heritability
    of alcohol use and dependence, 130,
        134
    of antisocial traits, 188–189
    and sensation seeking, 32
    and smoking, 120, 123
    twin studies on, 35
Heritability–environment interaction
    vs. gene–environment interaction,
        35
Heroin, 26, 135–141
    and DRD4 gene, 38, 138, 141

initial effect of, 108
    perceived risks and benefits for, 55
    See also Drug use
HIV, 146, 156, 158–159, 160, 162, 165,
    166, 167, 228, 232
HIV prevention, 229, 230
HIV-prevention study, 152
Homosexual men
    risky sex among, 157, 158–165, 232,
        233
        in public-service vs. commercial
          environments, 166–167
    and sensation seeking, 229
    treatment and prevention programs
        for, 232–233
Homosexuals, and sexual risk taking, 152
Hopelessness (H) scale, 223
Hormones, 28
    sex, 21
Hospital emergency rooms, 104, 105
HR (heart rate), 10, 15, 196–197
Human genome project, 37
HVA (homovanyllic acid), 28
Hypomania (Ma) subscale of MMPI, 186

Identity, gay, 165
ImpSS *See* Impulsive Sensation Seeking
    Scale of ZKPQ
Imp subscale. *See* Impulsivity subscale
Impulsiveness, and sexual behavior, 156
Impulsiveness, Venturesomeness, and
    Empathy Scale (IVE), 90, 94
Impulsiveness subscale of ImpSS, 186
Impulsive sensation seekers, and sex, 146
Impulsive Sensation Seeking, 26, 27, 155
Impulsive Sensation Seeking (ImpSS)
    scale of ZKPQ, 34, 39, 41–43,
    44, 60, 61, 62
Impulsive Unsocialized Sensation Seeking
    (ImpUSS) factor, 27, 41–42, 81
    vs. aggression, 178
    and psychopathy, 186
    and psychoticism (P), 32, 193
    and Social Deviance, 185
Impulsivity, 26, 185
    and aggression, 182
    cognitive, 174
    and criminality, 171
    and delinquency, 173, 174
    and EP, 195

Impulsivity, *continued*
 and genetic factors in antisocial
  behavior, 188
 perceived risks and benefits for, 55
 and risky behaviors, 65
  sexual, 233–234
 and sensation seeking, 186
 and serotonergic response, 199
 and sex
  among adolescents, 152, 153
  among heterosexuals and homosexuals, 157
 and sports rioting, 184
 and treatment programs, 235 (*see
  also* Treatment and prevention of
  unhealthy risk-taking behaviors)
Impulsivity (Imp) subscale, 90, 94, 95,
 173–174, 178
 and adolescent delinquency, 172
 and incarcerated delinquents, 176
 in treatment program, 225
ImpUSS. *See* Impulsive Unsocialized
 Sensation Seeking factor
Informational social influence program,
 207
Intervention programs
 types of, 205
 See also Treatment and prevention
  of unhealthy risk-taking
  behaviors
Irresponsibility, 185
IVE (Impulsiveness, Venturesomeness,
 and Empathy Scale), 90, 94

"Jingle-jangle" phenomenon, 47
Jogging, perceived risks and benefits for,
 55

Karolinska Scales of Personality, 96, 185
Kayaking, white-water, 91
Kinesthetic Aftereffect (KAE), 16
Kinesthetic Figural Aftereffect (KFA),
 46–47
KSP monotony avoidance scale, 102

Leniency, 84, 85
Life Experiences Questionnaire, 60
Locus of control (LC) traits, 59

Love, styles of, 147–148
LSD, 115, 141–142, 143

MAO. *See* Monoamine oxidase
Marijuana, 109, 115, 214
 and adolescents (middle and high
  school), 112–115
  sensation seeking, 152
  and sexual promiscuity, 153, 154
 dependence percentage for, 205
 and DWI, 83
 and "ecstasy," 142
 and gay sex, 164
 genetic influence on use of, 154
 perceived risks and benefits for, 55
 positive and negative associations
  for, 60
 prevention campaigns against, 216–
  217, 218, 219
 treatment programs for, 222–223
 and young adults, 116
 See also Drug use
MDMA ("ecstasy"), 141, 142–143
Media
 antidrug messages in, 215–217
 SD experiments in, 8
 as smoking influence, 204, 205
MHPG (3-methoxy-4-
 hydroxyphenylglycol), 28, 30, 31,
 199–200
Military and paramilitary vocations,
 102–103
Minnesota Multiphasic Personality
 Inventory (MMPI), 112, 116,
 185
Minnesota separated twin study, 33
Molecular genetics, 37–38
Monoamine oxidase (MAO), 22–24, 25,
 27
 and alcohol use, 133
 and CSA, 25
 and drug use, 139
 reactivity affected by, 28
 and sensation seeking, 22, 122, 198
 and serotonin, 23, 201
 and smoking, 121–122, 123, 139,
  198
Monoamine research
 with animals, 28–29
 with humans, 29–32

Morphine, perceived risks and benefits for, 55
Mortality salience, 78, 79
Motorcycles
    actual and perceived risk from, 54
    perceived risks and benefits for, 55
Motor vehicles
    actual and perceived risk from, 54
    perceived risks and benefits for, 55
    See also Driving, risky
Mountain climbing, 96
    actual and perceived risk from, 54
    perceived risks and benefits for, 55
MSM (men having sex with men). *See* Bisexuals; Homosexual men
Multidimensional Personality Questionnaire (MPQ), 151, 171, 179–180
Musical preferences, 15

NA. *See* Nucleus accumbens
NE (norepinephrine), 30, 199
    and arousal, 27
    and CSA, 24
    and CSF, 31
    and MAOs, 22
    and novel sensation, 26
    and psychopathy, 199, 200
    and stress- or anxiety-producing situations, 200
Need for Change, 46
Negative Emotionality factor, and prediction of violence, 179
NE metabolites, 31
NEO Personality Inventory (NEO-PI), 48
    and conscientiousness dimension, 48
    and sexual risk taking, 151
NEO Personality Inventory, Revised (NEO-PI-R), 48, 155, 177
Neophobia, 18
NEO Revised, 186
NE system, 26
Neuroticism–Anxiety (N-Anx) subscale, 42, 61, 62, 93, 137, 151, 156, 225
Neuroticism (N) scale, 26, 27
New Experience Seeking (NES) scale, 177
Nicotine. *See* Smoking

Nicotine replacement therapy (NRT), xv, 209, 211–212
Nitrate inhalants, 164
Nonsexual Experience Seeking Scale (NSES), 152, 160, 161, 162–163
Nonshared environment, 174, 187
Nonspecific skin conductance fluctuations (NSSFs), and underarousal hypothesis of antisocial behavior, 195
Noradrenergic arousal, 76
Noradrenergic system, 29
Norepinephrine. *See* NE
Normative social influence program, 207
Novelty (novel experiences), 26
    and anxiety, 66
    and drugs, 135
    and reckless driving, 76
    and risk appraisal, 55–56
    and sensation seekers (experiment), 8
        and design preference, 9, 10, 11
    and sensation seeking, 66, 67
Novelty Experiencing Scale, 46
Novelty seeking (NS) scale, 30, 32, 37–38, 43, 46
N scale. *See* Neuroticism scale
NSES (Nonsexual Experience Seeking Scale), 152, 160, 161, 162–163
NS Scale, 39
Nucleus accumbens, 120, 138
    in animals, 28, 29
    dopamine released in, 133, 167

OLA (optimal level of arousal), 4, 5–6, 74, 117, 193
OLS (optimal level of stimulation), 4, 5–6, 9
Openness to Experience (OE) factor, 48
Opiate or opiod use, 109
    and smoking, 121
    See also Heroin
Opioid antagonists, 224
Optimal-level theories, 4–12
    optimal level of arousal (OLA), 4, 5–6, 74, 117, 193
    optimal level of stimulation (OLS), 4, 5–6, 9
Orienting reflexes (ORs), 10–11, 15, 196
    and heart rate, 197
    and sensation seekers, 10–11, 97–98
Outgoingness, 177

P (psychoticism), 26, 27, 32, 41, 96, 97, 103, 176, 186, 193
Panic disorder, and SRIs, 27
Parachutists, 95, 96–97
Paragliding, 99–100
Paranoid schizophrenia, and MAO, 23
Parasailing, 99–100
Parent–child studies, 35–36
PCP, 141
Pearson's Novelty Seeking Scale, 48
Peer behavior or influence
    counteracting of, 234
    and delinquent behavior, 174
    and risky behaviors, 108
Peer programs, 215
Personality Research Form, 46, 110
Personality trait research
    and heritabilities, 32
    and "jingle-jangle" phenomenon, 47
    and nonadditive genetic
        mechanisms, 35
Pharmacological treatment
    for alcoholism, 223–224, 228
    for smoking cessation, 204, 211–212
Phobic situations, 70–71, 72
Physical risk taking, 106
Play, and sports, 87. See also Sports
Police work, 103–104, 106
    actual and perceived risk from, 54
    perceived risks and benefits for, 55
Polydrug users, 109, 116, 135, 137, 142, 155, 156, 157, 218
Postnatal influences, 190
Posttraumatic stress disorder (PTSD)
    after combat or POW experience, 106
    and high- vs. low-sensation seekers, 103
Poverty, and crime, 192
Preference for Complexity scale, 9
Prenatal environmental risk, 191
Prevention studies. See Treatment and
    prevention of unhealthy
    risk-taking behaviors
Primary process thinking, tolerance for, 4
Primary socialization theory, 108, 109
Prosocial occupations, 203. See also
    Vocations, risky
    and risky sports players, 94–95
    sensation seeking, 103–105
Prostitutes, 156–157

Psychedelic drugs, 141–143
    ecstasy, 141, 142–143, 166
Psychopathic Deviate subscale of MMPI, 186
Psychopathic personalities, xiv
    and disinhibition subscale, 13
Psychopathic Personality Inventory, 189
Psychopathy, 184–187. See also
    Antisocial behaviors; antisocial
    personality; antisocial personality
    disorder
    biosocial bases of, 187–192, 200–201
    and arousal or arousability, 193–197, 200–201
    biochemistry in, 198–200
Psychopathy Checklist (PCL), 185–186
Psychophysiological studies
    cortical evoked potential, 16–21, 46
    and orienting and defensive reflexes, 15
Psychosocial factors, and HR risk for
    antisocial behavior, 197
Psychoticism (P), 26, 27, 32, 41, 96, 97, 103, 176, 186, 193
Psychoticism scale, 200
PTSD. See Posttraumatic stress disorder

Race
    and alcohol use, 123
    and BSSS, 44
    and SSS scores, 14
    See also African Americans;
        Ethnicity
Racing, auto, 100
Rape crisis counselors, 105
RAS (reticular activating system), 5, 24
Reactivity to stimuli, 27
Reckless driving, 63
Reducing, 16, 18, 46–47
Reducing–Augmenting (R-A) Scales, 47
Relationship satisfaction, 148–149
Religious belief, among African Americans in cocaine treatment, 226
Reticular activating system (RAS), 5, 24
Reward Dependence, 43
RHA (Roman high-avoidance) strain of
    rats, 19, 24, 28
Rioters, sports, 184
Risk, 51–72
    characteristics of, 52

Sex, *continued*
    reduced fears of, 146
    treatment and prevention of,
      229–234
    in young adolescent populations,
      152–154
    safe sex
      and MSM population, 159
      and sensation seeking, 164
      withholding information on, 230
    and sensation seeking, 145, 146,
      151–152, 158, 228–229, 233–234
      adolescent, 153–154
      biological connections in,
        167–168
      in college populations, 154
      in community populations, 155,
        156, 157–158
      evolutionary significance of, 168
      among gay men, 159–165, 166,
        167
      and relationship satisfaction,
        148–149
      and research volunteers, 149
    and smoking, 121
Sexual Behavior Index, 147
Sex hormones, 21
Sexual Compulsivity (SC) Scale, 152,
    157, 160, 161, 162–163, 166
Sexual excitement (SE) scale, 165
Sexual inhibition, propensity for (SIPC)
    scale, 165
Sexually transmitted diseases (STDs),
    146, 228, 229, 230, 231, 234. *See
    also* HIV
Sexual promiscuity, 153, 154
Sexual Sensation Seeking Scale (SSSS),
    152, 154, 157, 160, 161, 162–
    163, 166
Signal-detection theory, 84
Skiing (downhill), 54, 55, 91, 98
Skin conductance level (SCL), 195–196
Skin conductivity response (SCR), 10–
    11, 193, 196
Skydiving, 97–98
Smoking (tobacco), 118–123, 234
    actual and perceived risk from, 54
    correlations of, 61
    as drug users' first step, 109
    and MAO, 121–122, 123, 139, 198
    in middle and high school, 112–115

    perceived risks and benefits for, 55
    positive and negative associations
      for, 60
    and sensation seeking, 120–121,
      122–123, 204
    treatment and prevention of, 204,
      213–214
      cessation, 208–213, 217
      prevention, 205–208
Snake fear situation, 70–72
Sociability (Sy) scale of ZKPQ, 42, 61,
    62, 119, 125
Social context of drinking scale, 126
Social desirability (SD) response set, 102
Social Deviance, 185
Social norms approach, 205–206
Social reinforcement type of intervention
    program, 206
Socioeconomic (SE) factors
    and adolescents' opportunities, 169
    and criminality, 192
    and HR in risk for antisocial
      behavior, 197
    and personality/self-control as factor
      in crime, 171
    and smoking cessation, 212
    on SSS, 14
Speeding, 76–79
Speeding Attitude subscale (SAS), 77
Sports, 87–102
    comparisons in, 89–92
    interest in, 100–101
    organized competitive athletics,
      92–93
    risky
      vs. antisocial and prosocial
        activities, 94–95
      extreme sports, 15, 59, 88
      vs. nonrisky, 88–89
      specific types of, 96–100
Sports rioters, 184
Sports risk, 65
SR (startle reflex), 10, 15
SSAST (Sensation Seeking and Anxiety
    States Scale), 67–68, 71
SSS (Sensation Seeking Scales), 4, 6–7,
    12–15, 38–48
STDs (sexually transmitted diseases),
    146, 228, 229, 230, 231, 234.
    See also HIV
Stimulus Variation Seeking Scale, 46

ABOUT THE AUTHOR

Marvin Zuckerman, PhD, is professor emeritus, University of Delaware, where he taught and conducted research for 33 years. He received his PhD in clinical psychology in 1954 from New York University. His research and writing have focused on personality, particularly on the trait of sensation seeking, and the psychobiology of personality. Previous books on sensation seeking were published in 1979 and 1994, and books on the psychobiology of personality were published in 1991 and 2005. A book on psychopathology was published in 1999. He is the author or coauthor of well over 200 journal articles and book chapters. He is a fellow of the American Psychological Association and the Association for Psychological Science and a past president of the International Society for the Study of Individual Differences.